MCSE Guide to Microsoft Internet Security and Acceleration (ISA) Server 2000

(Microsoft Certification Exam Objectives #70-227 continues on the last page.)

MCSE Guide to Microsoft Internet Security and Acceleration (ISA) Server 2000

Jeremy Cioara

COURSE
TECHNOLOGY
™
THOMSON LEARNING

Australia • Canada • Mexico • Singapore • Spain • United Kingdom • United States

COURSE TECHNOLOGY

THOMSON LEARNING

MCSE Guide to Microsoft Internet Security and Acceleration (ISA) Server 2000
by Jeremy Cioara

Associate Publisher:
Steve Elliot

Production Editor:
Elena Montillo

Text Designer:
GEX Publishing Services

Senior Editor:
Lisa Egan

Quality Assurance Technical Lead:
Nicole Ashton

Compositor:
GEX Publishing Services

Product Manager:
Amy M. Lyon

Associate Product Manager:
Tim Gleeson

Cover Design:
Joseph Lee, Black Fish Design

Developmental Editor:
Lisa Ruffolo, The Software Resource

Editorial Assistant:
Nick Lombardi

Technical Editor:
Robert Lewis

Marketing Manager:
Toby Shelton

Contents

TABLE OF
Contents

CHAPTER FOUR
Planning to Install Microsoft ISA Server 2000   115

CHAPTER FIVE
Installing ISA Server 2000   147

CHAPTER SIX
Understanding ISA Server 2000 Policies   183

CHAPTER SEVEN
Configuring ISA Server Firewall Components   241

CHAPTER THIRTEEN
Troubleshooting Microsoft ISA Server 2000   **477**

APPENDIX A
Exam Objectives Tracking for MCSE Certification Exam #70-227:   505
Installing, Configuring, and Administering Microsoft Internet Security
and Acceleration (ISA) Server 2000, Enterprise Edition

APPENDIX B
Transport Layer Protocol Numbers and TCP and UDP Well-Known Port   511
Assignments

GLOSSARY   533

INDEX   541

Preface

Welcome to the *MCSE Guide to Microsoft Internet Security and Acceleration (ISA) Server 2000*! This book provides in-depth coverage of the knowledge and skills required to pass Microsoft certification exam 70-227: *Installing, Configuring and Administering Microsoft Internet Security and Acceleration (ISA) Server 2000, Enterprise Edition*. In addition to exam preparation, this book prepares you for building a secure firewall between your internal network and the Internet. Today, you must have a corporate Internet presence to run a successful business. More companies are therefore building Web sites and allowing internal employees to access the Internet. In the rush to provide access to and from the Internet, many of the necessary security precautions have been overlooked. In addition, Internet connections have become quickly overwhelmed with traffic, causing access to slow. Microsoft addresses both of these needs with one integrated product: ISA Server 2000. This book provides the information and exercises necessary to help you master firewalls and Internet acceleration.

THE INTENDED AUDIENCE

This book is intended to serve anyone interested in learning more about Microsoft Internet Security and Acceleration (ISA) Server 2000 Enterprise Edition, particularly those who are interested in obtaining Microsoft certification on this topic. This book guides you through the planning, setup, configuration, and troubleshooting stages of working with ISA Server 2000. When you finish the book, you should be able to deploy ISA Server in a enterprise-scale environment.

CHAPTER DESCRIPTIONS

Chapter 1, "An Introduction to Microsoft Internet Security and Acceleration Server 2000" gives an overview of the environments where you would use ISA Server and the various features offered in the current 2000 release. **Chapter 2**, "Understanding OSI and TCP/IP Fundamentals" lays the foundation material necessary to understand the functionality of the ISA Server firewall features and TCP/IP-based networks. This chapter also introduces a completely new method of TCP/IP subnetting. **Chapter 3**, "Windows 2000 Fundamentals," briefly describes the Windows 2000 features you must be familiar with before configuring ISA Server. During this time, you will learn to deploy Active Directory, and preconfigure Windows 2000 to support ISA Server.

Chapter 4, "Planning Microsoft ISA Server 2000 Implementation," describes the often overlooked, but critical planning portion of ISA Server deployment. During this time, you must diagnose the current state of your network, consider new wide area network alternatives, and select the ISA Server features that would best fit your organization. **Chapter 5**, "Installing ISA Server 2000," covers installing ISA Server. This chapter takes you through the pre-installation requirements of ISA Server, upgrading from Proxy Server 2.0, and performing an unattended ISA Server installation. In addition, this chapter discusses the default configuration of ISA Server following installation, and provides a step-by-step process to allow instant Internet access for internal network users.

Chapter 6, "Working with ISA Server Policies," introduces the primary administrative tool used in configuring ISA Server features: policies. You will learn the function and configuration of array and enterprise policies, policy elements, and rules. The concepts discussed in this chapter are central to the rest of the book.

Chapter 7, "Configuring ISA Server Firewall Components," discusses the firewall-specific policies in ISA Server. It also explains access control through packet filters and IP routing. In addition, you will gain a thorough understanding of the ISA Server application filters which are designed to protect against many common intruder attacks. **Chapter 8**, "Configuring ISA Server Caching Components," focuses on the configuration of ISA Server Web caching features. This chapter also explains the importance of using scheduled content downloads and dynamic caching.

Chapter 9, "Configuring Server Publishing," explains how to make internal servers available to Internet users. Because of the potential security risks this introduces, this chapter also discusses publishing strategies and precautions. In addition, this chapter explores the configuration of H.323 services on the ISA Server to allow for the management of incoming and outgoing Voice over IP traffic.

Chapter 10, "Configuring ISA Server Virtual Private Networking," describes the configuration of the Virtual Private Networking features, and the enhancements provided by ISA Server. **Chapter 11**, "ISA Server Client Configuration," covers the advantages and disadvantages you must consider before choosing which client type(s) to deploy on your internal network. This chapter also discusses the deployment options and process for each client type.

Chapter 12, "Monitoring and Tuning ISA Server 2000," covers the monitoring and modifications you should consider to allow ISA Server to provide optimal service to your network. This chapter also describes how to configure ISA Server to implement intruder detection features. These features are necessary to protect your internal network from outside hacking attempts.

Chapter 13, "Troubleshooting Microsoft ISA Server 2000," steps you through the basic troubleshooting steps to identify and solve many common problems that you may encounter when using ISA Server in a production network.

FEATURES

To ensure a successful learning experience, this book includes the following pedagogical features:

- **Chapter Objectives.** Each chapter in this book begins with a detailed list of the concepts to be mastered within that chapter. This list provides you with a quick reference to the contents of that chapter, as well as a useful study aid.

- **Illustrations and Tables.** Numerous illustrations of server screens and components aid you in the visualization of common setup steps, theories, and concepts. In addition, many tables provide details and comparisons of both practical and theoretical information and can be used for a quick review of topics.

- **End of Chapter Material.** The end of each chapter includes the following features to reinforce the material covered in the chapter:

  - *Summary*–A bulleted list gives a brief but complete summary of the chapter

  - *Review Questions*–A list of review questions tests your knowledge of the most important concepts covered in the chapter

  - *Key Terms List*–A list of all new terms and their definitions

  - *Hands-on Projects*–Hands-on projects help you to apply the knowledge gained in the chapter

  - *Case Study Projects*–Case study projects take you through real world scenarios

- **On the CD-ROM.** On the CD-ROM, you will find **CoursePrep®** exam preparation software, which provides 50 sample MCSE exam questions mirroring the look and feel of the MCSE exams.

TEXT AND GRAPHIC CONVENTIONS

Wherever appropriate, additional information and exercises have been added to this book to help you better understand what is being discussed in the chapter. Icons throughout the text alert you to additional materials. The icons used in this textbook are as follows:

Tips are included from the author's experience and provide extra information on installation.

The Note icon is used to present additional helpful material related to the subject being described.

Each Hands-on Project in this book is preceded by the Hands-On icon and a description of the exercise that follows.

 Case project icons mark the case project. These are more involved, scenario-based assignments. In this extensive case example, you are asked to implement independently what you have learned.

INSTRUCTOR'S MATERIALS

The following supplemental materials are available when this book is used in a classroom setting. All of the supplements available with this book are provided to the instructor on a single CD-ROM.

Electronic Instructor's Manual. The Instructor's Manual that accompanies this textbook includes:

- Additional instructional material to assist in class preparation, including suggestions for classroom activities, discussion topics, and additional projects.
- Solutions to all end-of-chapter materials, including the Review Questions, Hands-on Projects and Case Projects.

ExamView®. This textbook is accompanied by ExamView, a powerful testing software package that allows instructors to create and administer printed, computer (LAN-based), and Internet exams. ExamView includes hundreds of questions that correspond to the topics covered in this text, enabling students to generate detailed study guides that include page references for further review. The computer-based and Internet testing components allow students to take exams at their computers, and also save the instructor time by grading each exam automatically.

PowerPoint presentations. This book comes with Microsoft PowerPoint slides for each chapter. These are included as a teaching aid for classroom presentation, to make available to students on the network for chapter review, or to be printed for classroom distribution. Instructors, please feel at liberty to add your own slides for additional topics you introduce to the class.

ACKNOWLEDGMENTS

There are many individuals I would like to thank that have contributed immeasurably to this project. First and foremost, I would like to thank God who has blessed me with the intelligence and talent this field requires, and continues to provide opportunities for me to do two things I love: teaching and writing. Second, I would like to thank my editor Lisa Ruffolo, who has taken a book that would have given an English professor possible brain damage, and transformed it into a literary masterpiece. I would also like to thank my two technical editors, Jeff Durham and Robert Lewis for always keeping me honest and providing insight and ideas on many of the chapter concepts and exercises. Thanks to my three reviewers, Michelle Plumb, Brian McCann, and Percy Ellis, who read through the material on a tight schedule and provided brutally honest feedback that helped shape the book content. Finally, I would like to thank coffee for playing a significant role in the timely completion of this book.

DEDICATION

I would like to dedicate this book to my father, who never knew what he was getting me into when he brought home that Amiga computer so many years ago. Thanks for always encouraging me to push the limits and do just a little more. I hope I continue to make you proud.

Read This Before You Begin

The hands-on projects in this book have been written to function in a classroom with the minimum required lab equipment and network connections. While it is possible to work through nearly all hands-on projects with the minimum required lab equipment, you (or your students) will have a better experience if you can meet the recommended standards equipment. The minimum requirements allow you to implement all ISA Server features, but do not let you thoroughly test your configuration. If you can meet the recommended classroom requirements, you can modify the projects to allow students to test their configuration on a real Internet connection.

MINIMUM LAB REQUIREMENTS

Hardware:

- Each student requires one server equipped with 128 MB of RAM, a Pentium II or compatible processor running at 300 Mhz or higher, and at least a 2 GB hard disk.

Software:

- You need a copy of Windows 2000 Server or Windows 2000 Advanced Server for each student server. You also need at least Windows 2000 Service Pack 1 and an evaluation copy of ISA Server. You can acquire a 120-day evaluation copy of ISA Server from *www.microsoft.com/isaserver*.

Configuration:

- Each server should be loaded with Windows 2000 Server or Advanced Server. During the installation, choose to create a single partition on the hard disk and format it with the NTFS file system. Following the installation, install the Windows 2000 service pack. Students can emulate either one or both required network cards by using the Microsoft Loopback Adapter (described in Chapter 3). You can create your own IP addressing scheme for the classroom, or use the scheme suggested in the book.

RECOMMENDED LAB REQUIREMENTS

Hardware:

- Each student requires one server equipped with 256 MB of RAM, a Pentium II or compatible processor running at 300 Mhz or higher, at least a 2 GB hard disk, and two network cards. In addition, you should have two switches with enough ports to accommodate one connection for all classroom servers. One switch will accommodate the internal network connections, while the other will accommodate the external network connections. Ideally, the classroom should also have an Internet connection and a shared client PC to connect to the internal network.

Software:

- You need a copy of Windows 2000 Server or Windows 2000 Advanced Server for each student server. You also need at least Windows 2000 Service Pack 1 and an evaluation copy of ISA Server. You can acquire a 120-day evaluation copy of ISA Server from *www.microsoft.com/isaserver*.

Configuration:

- Each server should be loaded with Windows 2000 Server or Advanced Server. During the installation, choose to create a single partition on the hard disk and format it with the NTFS file system. Following the installation, install the Windows 2000 service pack. Students can emulate either one or both required network cards by using the Microsoft Loopback Adapter (described in Chapter 3). You will need to create your own IP addressing scheme for the internal and external classroom based on the IP addressing requirements specific of your network. Figure 1 illustrates the recommended configuration.

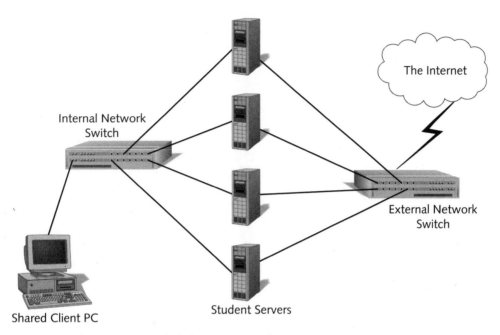

The Internet

Internal Network
Switch

External Network
Switch

Shared Client PC

Student Servers

Figure 1   The recommended classroom configuration

1

INTRODUCTION TO MICROSOFT INTERNET SECURITY AND ACCELERATION SERVER 2000

> **After reading this chapter and completing the exercises, you will be able to:**
>
> ♦ Describe the role of Microsoft ISA Server 2000 in networks
> ♦ Identify differences between ISA Server 2000 Standard and Enterprise editions
> ♦ Understand the major features in ISA Server 2000
> ♦ Identify hardware and software requirements for installing ISA Server 2000

As businesses around the world strive to keep pace with innovations in technology, they rely on Information Technology (IT) experts to design efficient ways to communicate and develop systems to provide products and services. Many of these innovations involve the Internet and the World Wide Web. Web site availability has become the rule, not the exception, for any competitive corporation—yours included. Because of a phenomenon many call the "Internet awakening," your company may have begun to classify Internet connectivity as one of your critical business applications. The more efficient and productive your Internet connection, the more your company can effectively take advantage of what the Internet offers: quick and constant access by customers, suppliers, vendors, and other partners.

Microsoft Internet Security and Acceleration Server 2000 (ISA Server 2000) represents the latest development in network management. ISA Server makes it easier to control network connections to the Internet, and increase network security and performance, while allowing fast and effective troubleshooting. This chapter introduces you to the features of ISA Server 2000 and the advantages it offers corporate networks. Each feature and advantage will be discussed in detail in the subsequent chapters.

WHY USE ISA SERVER?

When Tim Berners–Lee demonstrated the capabilities of his invention that he called the **World Wide Web (WWW)** at a small conference in the early 1990s, conference attendees reacted politely, but mildly. This reaction is understandable considering the Internet was a relatively small network at the time, and was used primarily to transfer government data between government sites and college universities. Even after the adoption of the WWW (also called the Web) as the Internet standard for a systematic linking of electronic pages, use of the Web remained reserved primarily for computer and network experts. It was not until the mid–1990s that universal support made the Internet and the Web the entities that they are today.

Because the Internet and the Web developed so quickly, businesses and other organizations are still trying to fully understand the usefulness, security risks, and the effects on productivity resulting from integrating their networks into the Internet. In businesses where employees have access to the Internet, network administrators devote time and resources in combating the latest e-mail virus, closing the most recent security breach, and protecting the corporate Web site from external tampering. Until recently, network engineers used one set of technologies to maintain network security and another set to improve network performance. ISA Server 2000 integrates these security and performance technologies in a single tool that network administrators can use to prevent security problems *and* to manage their networks effectively.

Microsoft ISA Server is part of the **Microsoft .NET** family of products, a group of applications that allows Windows 2000 to integrate seamlessly into Web-based services. The design of the applications in the .NET package lets you customize the applications to suit your network environment. The .NET suite gives developers flexibility because it treats the Internet as a new operating system. This approach means you can integrate tools and services available anywhere on the Internet into a single, customized application. The goal of Microsoft in developing the .NET package is to make business information accessible from any place, at any time, through any device.

In the .NET system, ISA Server plays the important role of security guard by protecting businesses from Internet attacks, but at the same time, ISA Server keeps the Internet safe and productive for internal business by employees. Figure 1-1 shows a drawing adapted from a page on the Microsoft Web site that describes the complete Microsoft .NET solution.

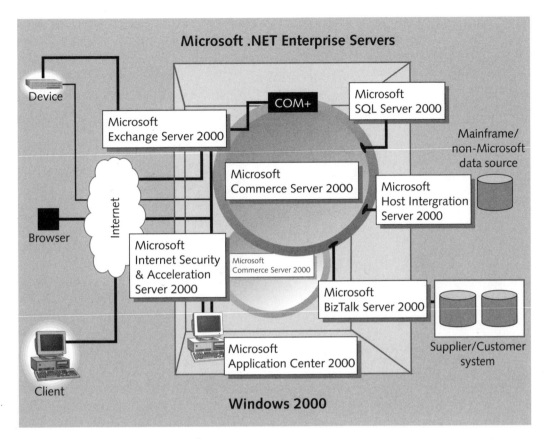

Figure 1-1 The Microsoft .NET product suite

ISA Server is a network firewall and Web-caching server that can handle the demands of a network of any size, from **Small Office/Home Office (SOHO)** environments serving between 10 and 20 users, to enterprise networks serving thousands of users around the world. Briefly defined, a **firewall** is a system of hardware, software, or a combination of the two designed to prevent unauthorized access to or from a private network. A **Web-caching** server reduces network traffic and response time by storing copies of popular content, and then serving the copies instead of repeatedly requesting the content from the original server. ISA Server combines these features into a single interface that integrates with the features and stability of Windows 2000 and your existing network and policy-based security structure.

ISA Server installs in one of three modes: multi-layer firewall, Web-cache, or integrated mode. The multi-layer firewall allows ISA Server to filter packets (pieces of information transmitted from one device to another on a network) based on a variety of requirements, while also providing increased network security. Web caching allows high-performance responses to requests from internal and external clients to access Web server content, and improves overall network performance. Integrated mode provides both multi-layer firewall and Web cache services. Businesses should choose an installation mode depending on the role they want ISA Server to perform. Figure 1-2 shows the logical placement of ISA Server in the network.

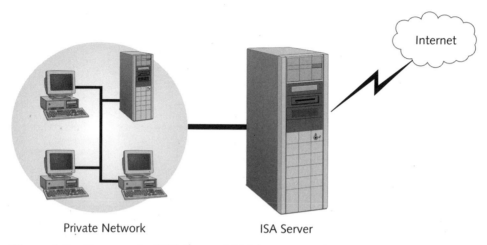

Private Network   ISA Server

Figure 1-2   Placement of ISA Server 2000 in a network

Overall, ISA Server 2000 provides a scalable and secure environment for mission-critical networks—those networks that cannot fail without significantly affecting the overall performance and functioning of a business.

OVERVIEW OF ISA SERVER 2000

Microsoft ISA Server 2000 is one of the focal products of the .NET software series from Microsoft. As you recall, the goal of Microsoft in developing the .NET suite is to make information available from any place, at any time, through any device. Notice that the stated goal does not mention making information available to *anyone*. ISA Server uses its firewall features to make information accessible from anywhere in the world, but to also use those same features to keep information secure. The ISA Server firewall is the first and strongest line of defense against intruders from outside a network. It stops virtually all of the common **Denial of Service (DoS)** attacks (discussed in a later chapter), keeping your internal network safe and running smoothly.

Most businesses require not only high levels of security, but also high performance standards. To address these needs, ISA Server includes Web-caching features. If you analyzed the Internet traffic of a corporation, you would find that most users regularly visit the same sites. For example, at the beginning of the workday, many Internet users visit news and weather Web sites. If the daily news Web site contains 200 kilobytes of graphics and data and, on average, 200 people visit the site every morning, 40 megabytes of the total **wide area network (WAN)** bandwidth of your network would be devoted to serving the news to those 200 users. While you cannot prevent a user from checking the news everyday, you can prevent the loss of network bandwidth. For example, to provide news to the 200 Internet users, 99.5% of the bandwidth required is spent downloading duplicate content. Instead of downloading the same content every time, why not allow users to share the content? This is the idea behind Web caching. As users access Web sites, ISA Server stores the content locally for a specified amount of time. When other users access the same site, ISA Server provides the content from its cache, rather than retrieving it from the original Web site. This greatly improves the efficiency of your business Internet WAN connections.

The firewall and Web-caching features are available in both editions of ISA Server: Standard Edition and Enterprise Edition. Both editions share a similar command set; however, the Standard Edition installs only as a stand-alone server supporting a maximum of four processors. In addition, the security policies of the Standard Edition install only onto the local machine, rather than integrating into the Active Directory structure, which can cause security problems. For example, if you integrate into the Active Directory, you must set security for each server, potentially introducing inconsistency in the network. Installing the Standard Edition onto a local machine avoids this inconsistency. ISA Server Enterprise Edition supports the grouping of multiple ISA Servers into a fault-tolerant, high-performance array of systems and fully integrates with the Active Directory structure of an existing network. This book focuses primarily on the Enterprise Edition software.

Securing Internet Connectivity

When a corporation connects its corporate network to the Internet, it exposes itself to new security and productivity concerns. Most management fears focus on security breaches (informally called hacking attempts) originating from outside the network, such as Internet intruders breaking into the internal network and compromising or destroying sensitive company data. While the number of Internet-based attacks continues to increase (primarily due to the continual growth in e-commerce Web sites), the vast majority of destructive hacking originates from within the internal network. ISA Server protects the borders of your network, allowing you to monitor and control access attempts originating from both the internal users of your network attempting to connect to the Internet, *and* from outside users attempting to connect to your company network. This feature makes ISA Server a secure and reliable firewall.

The technology used by the ISA Server firewall offers multi-layer protection because it includes packet, circuit, and application-level screening (these are discussed in detail in the next section). Screening at all three of these levels provides for secure **Virtual Private Networking (VPN)**, allowing users to connect to the corporate network via the Internet, as shown in Figure 1-3. This also allows you as network administrator to protect internal Web and e-mail servers from outside attacks, and to inspect every frame of incoming or outgoing traffic so that you may restrict traffic based on certain criteria. If an access rule violation occurs, you can configure automatic alert systems so that you and other administrators receive notice of the intrusion and can initiate a rapid response.

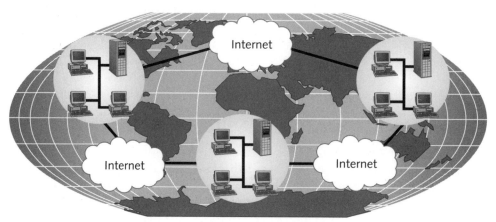

Virtual Private Networking

Figure 1-3 Using the Internet as a backbone to connect worldwide network sites through Virtual Private Networking

 ISA must be installed in integrated mode in order to support VPN.

Providing Fast Web Access

In organizations worldwide, network administrators are concerned about employees accessing the Internet. Not only does Internet access by employees significantly increase security risks, but it can also slow networks, even those with high bandwidth. Expensive WAN connections are soon overwhelmed as users browse, download, and chat on corporate Internet connections. Fortunately, ISA Server allows for an improved Internet access that is fast and cost-effective.

ISA Server speeds Internet access by caching Internet content locally on the network after a network user accesses the content one time. You can also configure active caching, allowing ISA Server to update locally stored information during times of low bandwidth usage. By storing Internet content locally, ISA Server reduces the drain on WAN bandwidth from accessing the same Internet content multiple times. Furthermore, ISA Server performs reverse caching, allowing the content of internal Web servers to be stored on ISA Server. Figure 1-4 shows the difference between forward and reverse caching systems.

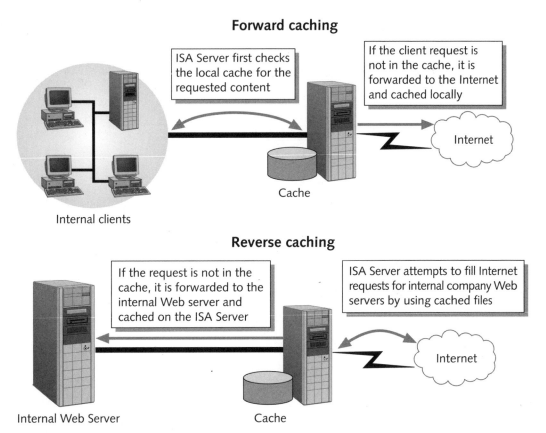

Forward caching

ISA Server first checks the local cache for the requested content

If the client request is not in the cache, it is forwarded to the Internet and cached locally

Internet

Cache

Internal clients

Reverse caching

If the request is not in the cache, it is forwarded to the internal Web server and cached on the ISA Server

ISA Server attempts to fill Internet requests for internal company Web servers by using cached files

Internet

Internal Web Server   Cache

Figure 1-4   Understanding ISA Server caching systems

Unified Management

Because ISA Server combines multi-layer enterprise firewall functionality with Web-caching ability, it reduces network management and minimizes network complexity. Because ISA Server builds on the foundation of Windows 2000 and is a part of the .NET suite of software, administrators who perform Windows 2000 administration tasks will find the ISA Server interface familiar. The majority of ISA Server configuration and administration is performed through the **Microsoft Management Console (MMC)**, as illustrated in Figure 1-5. Windows 2000 establishes security measures by letting you set security policies; ISA Server uses this same approach, allowing restrictions based on user, group membership, application and content types, and schedules. Implementation of these policies occurs at the enterprise level or on a computer-by-computer basis.

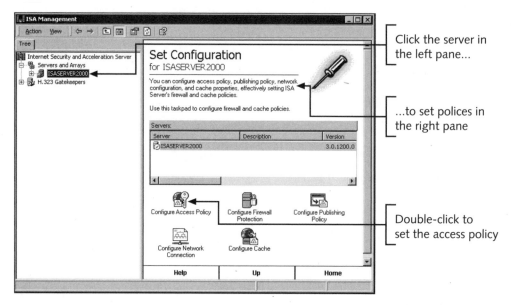

Figure 1-5   ISA Server 2000 management through the Microsoft Management Console

Describing Microsoft .NET Enterprise Servers

Microsoft developed the .NET series of business applications to keep pace with the continued growth of the Internet and its daily integration with the businesses of the world. These products are designed according to today's Web standards, allowing integration with software developed by other vendors under the same Internet standards. The current .NET Enterprise Server package includes the following pieces of software:

- *Internet Security and Acceleration Server 2000*—Improves network performance by integrating Web-caching features and multi-layer firewall functions

- *Microsoft Exchange Server 2000*—Provides messaging and scheduling services, and allows for true Active Directory integration and an improved feature set

- *SQL Server 2000*—Provides an upgrade to one of the industry's most popular database and analysis tools

- *Host Integration Server 2000*—Allows you to integrate host system components

- *Commerce Server 2000*—Allows you to set up and manage online businesses

- *BizTalk Server 2000*—Allows you to effectively manage both internal Web services, and those between your company and other organizations

- *Application Center 2000*—Manages and deploys Web applications built on Windows 2000

ISA Server 2000 Features at a Glance

Microsoft ISA Server 2000 replaces Microsoft Proxy Server 2.0, and is more than an upgrade; it is a completely redesigned Web cache and firewall product that you can use to improve both network performance and security. This section introduces the major features of ISA Server 2000.

Multi-Layer Firewall

A physical firewall is a concrete wall placed between two structures. If one of those structures ignites and burns, the firewall stops the blaze from spreading to other structures. A logical firewall serves a similar purpose. Network firewalls protect the borders of networks. If one network is compromised, the destruction stops at the firewall between the networks, containing it to a specific area. To determine which users and applications should have access beyond the local network segment, network firewalls can filter at different network levels. ISA Server uses three levels of filters to determine what types of information or which users can access a network: packet filtering, circuit-level filtering, and application-level filtering.

Packet Filtering

Packet filtering is one of the simplest and most secure methods of maintaining network security. Packet filtering involves accepting or rejecting incoming or outgoing packets based on service type, source or destination device, or port numbers. When you filter packets, by default the external network interface connecting ISA Server to the public network drops all packets. This creates a secure but inaccessible network. Before users can access the internal or external network, at least one packet filter must be in place.

Packet filters work primarily at the Network and Transport layers of the **Open Systems Interconnection (OSI)** model. The OSI model is a plan that standardizes levels of communication for network computers allowing disparate network systems to effectively communicate. While very few vendors have adopted the OSI communication standards, the OSI model now serves as a teaching model for all other protocols. Figure 1-6 shows packet filtering as it relates to the OSI model. Chapter 2 discusses the OSI model in detail.

Filtering packets at the Transport and Network layers is beneficial because when ISA Server receives incoming or outgoing traffic, it only needs to analyze the data at the bottom four layers of the OSI model, decreasing the processing time of the data. Because of this, packet filtering is the primary security method used in most network firewalls today.

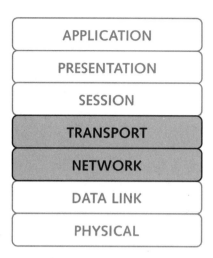

| APPLICATION |
| PRESENTATION |
| SESSION |
| **TRANSPORT** |
| **NETWORK** |
| DATA LINK |
| PHYSICAL |

Figure 1-6   Packet filtering in the OSI model

When filtering is based on the IP address, you can specify which hosts to permit and which hosts to deny. Recall that the default setting for packet filtering is to deny all packets, so to allow for access, you specify which IP addresses to permit. ISA Server allows you to create IP packet filters for both inbound and outbound network traffic. This means you can restrict not only traffic coming into the network from the Internet, but also users attempting to gain access beyond the local network. For example, if an internal user wants to access the Web, you could set the firewall to allow only outbound access on port 80. This means the firewall allows port 80 *out* of the network, but does not mean that port 80 can come *in* to the network. This feature of packet filtering, which works at the Network layer of the OSI model, allows you to specify the particular IP hosts who can access internal and external resources. Figure 1-7 shows typical packet filtering criteria used to secure network access.

As mentioned earlier, packet filters work beyond the Network layer of the OSI model; they also filter at the Transport layer as well. This gives packet filters access to **TCP/IP port numbers**. Port numbers are used in applications based on the **Transmission Control Protocol (TCP)** (reliable and slower transport) and **User Datagram Protocol (UDP)** (unreliable and fast transport). **Request for Comments (RFCs)** define port numbers 0-1024 as well-known port numbers. Many applications, such as Web browsers, e-mail, and FTP clients, use this lower range of port numbers, combined with a source and destination IP address to create a **socket** between communicating devices (these topics are covered in more detail in Chapter 2, "Understanding TCP/IP"). By using packet filters, you can choose to filter incoming and outgoing traffic based on the port number. This allows you to increase network security by filtering out specific TCP- or UDP-based applications, such as allowing Web access while denying FTP.

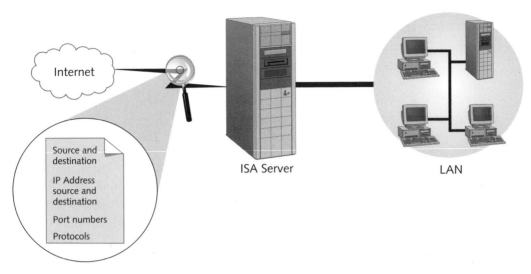

Figure 1-7   Typical packet filtering criteria

By using packet filters at both the Network and Transport layers of the OSI model, you can combine the features of both layers to create tight security. For example, you might need to grant a user access to the Internet so that user can connect to a corporate branch office through a VPN, thus using the Internet as a backbone. Without ISA Server packet filtering, you would be forced to allow all network users to access all of the Internet; however, using the packet filtering features of ISA Server, you can define a **static packet filter** at the Network layer, allowing the individual computer's IP address access through the firewall. Because the user only needs access to the VPN connecting to the branch office, you can also define a Transport layer port filter, allowing the user access only on the specific ports needed for the VPN software to connect.

In addition to static packet filtering, ISA Server 2000 also supports **dynamic packet filtering** (also called stateful filters). Dynamic packet filtering temporarily opens ports in the firewall to allow outside hosts to communicate with internal hosts at the request of the internal host. When implementing static packet filters, you must manually "punch holes" in the ISA Server firewall. For example, if a user on a corporate network wants to access the Web, you must open port 80 (HTTP) on the ISA Server internal interface (to allow the user to send data to the Web) and a port on the external interface (to allow the Web to send data to the user). While static filters allow users to access Web sites with their browsers, it also opens a hole in the firewall, allowing outside users an opening to tunnel into the internal network. However, if you use a dynamic packet filter, you only need to open the HTTP port 80 on the internal network interface. When you attempt to access the Web, ISA Server routes your request to the correct Internet IP address, and then *dynamically* opens a port allowing only that Web site to communicate with the client. Once the transmission of data is complete, the external interface port closes and denies internal network access until another request from an internal client causes it to reopen.

Circuit-Level Filtering

When implementing **circuit-level filtering** (also called protocol filtering), ISA Server monitors a communication session. While packet filters inspect the details of the data, such as the source and destination IP addresses and port numbers, circuit-level filters inspect the session as a whole. As Internet applications increase in complexity, they require more open ports on the server to transmit data. For example, if a computer connects to a destination host using the **File Transfer Protocol (FTP)**, most networks consider allowing access on port 21, the common port number for FTP. However, the FTP protocol uses port 21 only to control messages of the connection, such as synchronization bits, and acknowledgement messages. The actual FTP file data transfer occurs on port 20. When using circuit-level filters, you grant access on an application basis. As in dynamic filtering, ISA Server opens ports only as an application requests them, which increases security. This provides links to applications that require secondary connections to the destination, such as FTP and many streaming media utilities.

Circuit-level filters, or protocol filters, also allow network access to applications that have no built-in firewall or proxy support. ISA Server 2000 includes software for client machines. This client software provides external network access to Windows-based applications lacking firewall/proxy support. When you install the client software, you have, in essence, installed an "application helping hand" onto your client machines. When the Windows-based applications attempt to access the network, the client software intercepts the request and examines it. The client software runs a simple check on the outgoing traffic, determining if its destination is on the local network segment, or if it needs to access an external network, such as the Internet. If the destination is local, the client software sends the data onto the physical wire, unmodified. However, if the destination is remote, the client software redirects the frame to ISA Server. Once ISA Server receives the data, it examines and forwards the data to the external network, if it has access permission. When the external destination attempts to communicate with the internal computer, ISA Server receives the incoming data and routes it to the client software running on the source computer. Because the client software is one of the first components of the computer to receive the data, it strips all references to ISA Server and forwards the data back to the application. The application receiving the data reacts as if nothing has changed.

For clients who either do not support ISA Server client software or do not have it installed, circuit-level filtering occurs with a **Windows Sockets (SOCKS)** filter. The drawback to this access type is that any application accessing the external network must be SOCKS 4.3a compatible. This means the application developer must code the application itself to support SOCKS. If the application does not support SOCKS nor has encoded firewall/proxy support, it cannot access an external network through ISA Server. However, most developers who allow network access through their application do develop a SOCKS support mechanism; applications not having built-in SOCKS support today are the exception and not the rule. An additional advantage of SOCKS is, unlike Winsock (another standard for communications software that provides a TCP/IP socket interface under Windows), it can support any current operating system platform, including Linux, UNIX, and Macintosh.

Application-Level Filtering

Application-level filters provide the most processor intensive and sophisticated level of firewall traffic inspection. These filters allow you to inspect traffic addressed to an individual application and perform application-specific processing such as inspecting, modifying, screening or blocking, and redirecting the data as it enters through the firewall. Application-level filters provide a way of protecting internal application servers such as e-mail, DNS, or Web servers against attacks. One benefit of using application filters is that they support third-party tools that can screen, analyze, and check the content of the incoming data for viruses and other problems. The disadvantage of using application-level filters is that every piece of incoming data must pass up to the Application layer where ISA Server analyzes it. This adds a significant amount to the processing and forwarding time of incoming and outgoing traffic.

Built-in Application Filters

In addition to the standard packet, circuit, and application-level firewall filters, ISA Server provides a sophisticated and expandable group of built-in application filters. Instead of simply examining an IP address or port number, these application filters allow you to redirect, block, analyze, and even modify the incoming or outgoing data stream. Application filters also give individual applications freedom to open secondary ports or connections as needed; this action is accomplished transparently to the user. When these ports are no longer needed, they shut down, barring future access. You can also expand the application filters. Available for download on the Microsoft Web site (*www.microsoft.com*) is the ISA Server Software Development Kit. This kit includes sample filters with the complete source code and step-by-step creation instructions. Out of the box, ISA Server contains the following built-in application filters:

- *HTTP filter*—The HTTP filter works with the ISA Server Web Proxy service to provide transparent caching ability. Clients who do not have their browsers configured to use a proxy can also have content cached, thus saving precious WAN bandwidth. The caching is performed in a manner transparent to the browser application.

- *FTP filter*—The FTP filter redirects SecureNAT clients to the firewall service, and dynamically opens the necessary secondary FTP ports.

- *SMTP filter*—The SMTP filter intercepts e-mail before it reaches the e-mail server, thus protecting it from attacks. This filter can screen e-mail based on size or content and recognize unsafe e-mail content.

- *SOCKS filter*—The SOCKS filter transparently routes SOCKS application traffic that supports the SOCKS 4.3a industry standard.

- *RPC filter*—The RPC filter gives administrative control over Remote Procedure Calls (RPCs), allowing the selection of specific interfaces to respond to RPCs.

- *H.323 filter*—The H.323 filter allows the use of streaming multimedia applications that support the H.323 standard. It also adds the ability to handle incoming calls and to connect to a H.323 gatekeeper computer.

- *Streaming Media filter*—The Streaming Media filter supports most industry-standard streaming media protocols such as RealAudio/RealVideo PNM, RTSP (used by Apple QuickTime), and Microsoft Windows Media. The Streaming Media also supports splitting live media streams that use Microsoft Windows Media technology. This allows multiple users who are requesting the same stream to "share" that stream, thus saving considerable amounts of bandwidth.

- *DNS and POP Intrusion Detection filters*—Two filters that guard against the majority of attacks against Domain Name Service (DNS) and Post Office Protocol (POP) internal network servers

Windows 2000 and Active Directory Integration

Because it is built on the Windows 2000 Server platform, ISA Server uses many features of Windows 2000, or modifies and enhances them as necessary. The following list describes Windows 2000 features either implemented or enhanced in ISA Server 2000.

- *Network Address Translation*—ISA Server modifies the industry-standard Network Address Translation (NAT), which allows virtually any IP-based client a communications path with external networks while conserving public IP addresses. ISA Server 2000 implements SecureNAT, which has all the same functionality of the original NAT, but also allows the application of system firewall policies to NAT clients that do not have any client software installed.

- *Integrated Virtual Private Networking*—ISA Server supports the Windows 2000 Virtual Private Networking (VPN) features, which includes support for the Point-to-Point Tunneling Protocol (PPTP), Layer 2 Tunneling Protocol (L2TP), and Internet Protocol Security (IPSec). This allows outside users to access the internal corporate network securely across a public network, such as the Internet.

- *Authentication*—ISA Server supports all Windows 2000 standard authentication methods, including Basic, NTLM, Kerberos, and certificate-based security.

- *System Hardening*—ISA Server builds upon the Windows 2000 security templates. Because Windows 2000 is the foundation platform for ISA Server, ISA Server never overrides any current Windows 2000 security settings.

- *Active Directory Storage (Enterprise Edition only)*—When using ISA Server Enterprise Edition in a multi-server array (combining separate ISA Servers into a pool which shares a common configuration), all ISA Server policy and configuration information is stored in the central Active Directory database for easy server access and reference. ISA Server also uses the users and groups defined in the Active Directory database to apply access controls.

- *Tiered-Policy Management (Enterprise Edition only)*—Tiered-policy management allows network administrators to apply policies in Active Directory to groups of ISA Server machines. This allows for a scalable model when expanding to multiple groups of ISA Servers.

- *Microsoft Management Console Administration*—ISA Server is a .NET enterprise product, and therefore the management interface follows the standard of MMC snap-in utilities. As a snap-in, an application management utility, ISA Server has many pre-defined Task Pads to graphically simplify administration. Because the MMC is an open source code application, third-party companies can develop products that integrate directly into the ISA 2000 MMC Server snap-in.

- *Quality of Service*—ISA Server allows you to control bandwidth allocations for users connecting beyond their local networks. This integrates with the Windows 2000 Quality of Service (QoS) technology, giving network administrators the ability to prioritize traffic based on the service type (such as always placing queued HTTP traffic ahead of queued FTP traffic, thus giving HTTP preferred treatment).

- *Multiple Processor Support*—ISA Server Standard Edition implements symmetric multiprocessing on up to four processors installed into a stand-alone machine. This essentially allows the processing power of all four processors to combine into one extremely powerful processor. ISA Server Enterprise Edition has no practical limit on the number of usable processors that can be combined.

- *Client-Side Auto-Discover*—When used in conjunction with the Web Proxy Autodiscovery Protocol, Web browser software configures itself to connect to ISA Server without manual configuration.

- *Administration Component Object Model (COM) Object*—Allows a developer to use the COM rules engine and all administrative options.

- *Web Filters*—The ISA Server Web filters, as seen in the previous section, build upon the Internet Server Application Programming Interface (ISAPI) support included in Windows 2000.

- *Alerts*—ISA Server records all system alerts in the Windows 2000 Event Log file.

Remote Management

You use the Microsoft Management Console to manage the features and services of Windows 2000. When adding snap-ins, the MMC typically prompts you to specify whether the snap-in manages the application installed on the local machine or one installed on another computer. Figure 1-8 shows the dialog boxes typically displayed during this process. The ISA Server 2000 MMC snap-in is no different. This allows remote management of ISA Servers that can install the ISA Server 2000 MMC snap-in from anywhere in the network. Furthermore, the ISA Server 2000 MMC snap-ins install on the Windows 2000 Professional platform, allowing remote administration from a client machine. ISA Server management is also possible through Terminal Services in remote administration mode or through command-line scripts that use the **Distributed Component Object Model (DCOM)**.

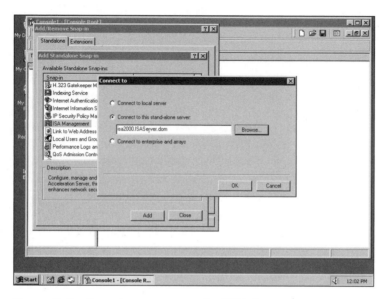

Figure 1-8   Remote management of ISA Server

Network Address Translation

ISA Server 2000 adopts the **Network Address Translation (NAT)** features of Windows 2000. The NAT features of Windows 2000 allow you to circumvent the shortage of Internet-valid TCP/IP addresses. Corporate networks consisting of hundreds or thousands of machines can typically require thousands of Internet-valid IP addresses. NAT allows you to create IP addressing schemes within the walls of a corporate network. These internal addresses are typically created from the InterNIC-designated private address ranges, but can be any address within the first three classes of IP addresses. The NAT server sits on the border of the network and translates private network addressing to addresses valid on the public network, as shown in Figure 1-9. Using this method, you can use one Internet-valid IP address to provide access to thousands of internal network users. A deeper explanation of the NAT functionality and its uses are covered in Chapter 2, "Understanding TCP/IP."

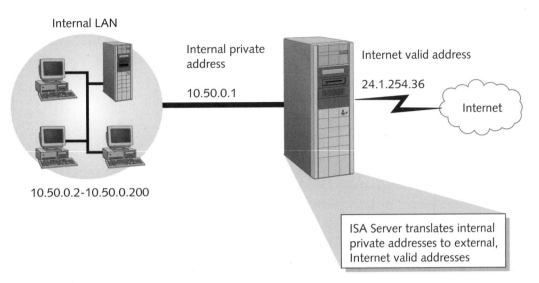

Internal LAN

Internal private
address

10.50.0.1

Internet valid address

24.1.254.36

Internet

10.50.0.2-10.50.0.200

ISA Server translates internal
private addresses to external,
Internet valid addresses

Figure 1-9 Network Address Translation architecture

The ISA Server **Secure Network Address Translation (SecureNAT)** expands Windows 2000 NAT by applying optional policies to incoming and outgoing traffic. The major benefit to using NAT is universal client support. Because the developers of NAT constructed it around RFC standards, it is platform independent. It works with any TCP/IP protocol that the client uses, provided the protocol stack is RFC-compliant. Furthermore, NAT functions without the installation of client-end software. SecureNAT allows you to apply Windows 2000 policies to traffic crossing ISA Server *without the need for the traffic to be Windows 2000 specific.* Because SecureNAT works only at the Network and Transport layers of the OSI model, ISA Server can allow or deny specific IP addresses or port numbers without interacting with the upper layer application data.

Virtual Private Networking

ISA Server 2000 assists you with the setup and maintenance of a VPN. Since the Internet explosion in the early nineties, the usage of VPNs continues to increase, allowing for a relatively inexpensive, secure, and high-speed connection of users and branch offices to corporate networks. A VPN allows the transfer of private, internal network data across public networks, such as the Internet. This process typically entails extremely high security standards, as it involves sending internal data across the Internet. When communicating, ISA Server establishes a private tunnel through the public network, which makes the line seem as if it were a leased connection on a point-to-point private network.

Microsoft simplifies the VPN setup in ISA Server by using wizards to guide you step by step through the process. One wizard guides you through the process of configuring ISA Server to connect to an **Internet Service Provider (ISP)**, which in turn connects ISA Server to the Internet. At this point, VPN clients can connect across the Internet to the internal corporate network. The VPN technology in Windows 2000 supports the use of the Point-to-Point Tunneling Protocol (PPTP) and Layer 2 Tunneling Protocol (L2TP) for clients connecting to ISA Server. Both of these methods are discussed in Chapter 2, "Understanding TCP/IP."

Intruder Detection

When using ISA Server, you can set up automatic alert systems to activate when the server detects an intruder or attack on the network. These alerts can perform a variety of actions when triggered, such as paging or sending an e-mail message to you or other network administrators, writing an event to the event log, stopping network service completely, or running any program or script that you specify. For example, if an Internet hacker attempts to run a port scan on ISA Server to search for any open ports, ISA Server can detect this and e-mail network administrators to notify them of this event. ISA Server can detect intruders at the Packet or Application layers, which allows ISA Server to detect most network attacks. The most frequent attacks in networks are Denial of Service attacks, which aim either to halt a service by disabling the complete system or to make the processor so busy dealing with incoming data that it has no time to handle standard network traffic. Following are descriptions of common attacks that ISA Server 2000 detects.

Packet Filter Intrusions

The following list describes common attacks that occur at the Network layer of the OSI model. Some of these attacks are blatant and others are illegitimate probing of ISA Server to find potential areas to attack.

- *The Ping of Death*—Using the **Internet Control Message Protocol (ICMP)** to send an echo request packet to a target, the hacker attaches a large amount of information to the ping. When the target attempts to respond to the ping packet, it overflows its buffers and crashes.

- *All Ports Scan*—To prevent an all ports scan, you can specify a range of accessible ports. When a user attempts to access a port outside of this range, ISA Server considers it an attack.

- *Enumerated Port Scan*—This is one of the most common types of probing mechanisms. A hacker attempts to see what services are running on a system by sending data to each port and waiting for a response.

- *IP Half Scan*—This is a method used to find open ports and services while avoiding detection. Repeated attempts to connect are sent to each port, but the connection is never established.

- *UDP Bomb*—Modification of UDP packets can result in corrupted data in certain fields, which can cause older operating systems to stop functioning.

- *Land Attack*—Establishment of TCP sessions requires a three-way handshake process. Land attacks send a packet requesting to establish a session where the source and destination IP address and port number are identical. Some TCP implementations continuously loop, attempting to establish a session with a nonexistent computer, and eventually crash.

- *Windows Out of Band Attack*—This method attempts to send an out-of-band, Denial of Service attack series of messages to open computers. The receiving computer typically loses all network connectivity or crashes.

Application Filter Attacks

ISA Server includes two application filters that deny common DNS and POP server attacks. ISA Server allows developers to expand application filters, allowing developers to protect their own software. For example, if your company uses a widget tracking system that logs widget production at branch offices, the software manufacturer could develop an ISA Server application filter that prevents network attacks against the tracking system. The following is a list of common attacks that ISA Server filters by using built-in DNS and POP application filters.

- *POP Buffer Overflow*—In this attack, an intruder attempts to access the root level of a POP server by overflowing the internal buffer.

- *DNS Hostname Overflow*—This attack consists of creating hostnames in the DNS database that exceed a certain fixed length requirement. When some applications query the DNS database, they stop running, giving the hacker an opening on the client computer to execute commands.

- *DNS Length Overflow*—Similar to the DNS Hostname Overflow attack, this attack occurs when IP addresses in the DNS database exceed the fixed length.

- *DNS Zone Transfer from Privileged Ports (1-1024)*—This type of attack occurs when an intruder uses a DNS client machine to attempt a zone transfer from the DNS Server on the well-known ports 1-1024. If successful, the internal IP addressing and hostname database is compromised.

- *DNS Zone Transfer from High Ports (above 1024)*—This is the same attack as above, but uses ports outside of the well-known port range (1025 − 65,536).

Minimal Client Configuration

Because Microsoft ISA Server 2000 uses the SecureNAT system, clients can access ISA Server with little to no configuration. The major benefit of using SecureNAT is that you do not need to install ISA Server client software on user PCs. One of the major drawbacks to Microsoft Proxy Server 2.0 was the need for client installation. All internal network PCs had to have the Proxy Server 2.0 client software installed before they could use many of the Proxy Server features. By requiring a client installation, Microsoft began losing support for the Microsoft Proxy Server series because non-Microsoft clients could not use the majority of the features. Since the release of SecureNAT, all that has changed. SecureNAT builds upon the RFC standard of NAT. Because of this, clients running any

TCP/IP-based operating system can communicate fully with the ISA Server, as shown in Figure 1-10.

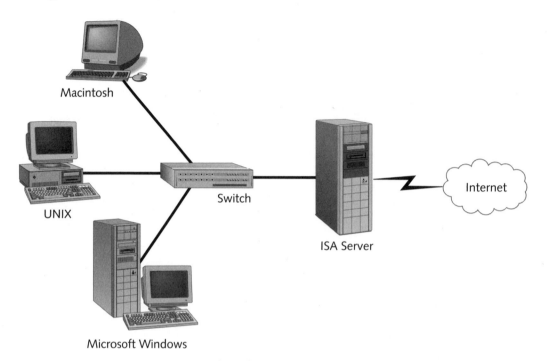

Figure 1-10   Using SecureNAT to broaden client support

SecureNAT is a demonstration of true client transparency. Clients without any Microsoft ISA Server client software can communicate with the ISA Server and connect through it to the Internet. The problem with standard NAT is security: standard RFC-based network address translation does not include security features. SecureNAT, on the other hand, allows you to apply security policies to any client gaining Internet access through ISA Server. These policies can grant or deny access to ISA Server clients based on protocols, ports, IP addresses, and applications. This allows for the application of network security throughout the entire network, not just on certain machines that have client software installed.

Secure Publishing

Today, nearly all major corporations have expanded their influence by publishing news about their current products and releasing public corporate information on the Internet. However, exposing a Web server to the public can put a company's data at risk. Often, these Web servers connect to internal database and e-mail servers. If an intruder compromises the security of the Web server, it also compromises the security of any computers connecting to the Web server. Because of this, internal Web servers have high security requirements. ISA Server meets these requirements through Web publishing, which provides two Web server configuration options. First, ISA Server can be the Web server that external clients access. This method is not typically implemented because many of the Web server components are still exposed to the public network. In the second method, ISA Server continues to function as a firewall and allows you to place Web servers on an internal network. This method significantly increases security as it allows ISA Server to emulate the Web server to external clients, and act as if it were the device servicing their request. Because of this, every request for an internal Web server must first pass through all the security measures implemented on ISA Server.

The applications of secure publishing extend beyond Web publishing. For instance, in addition to having a corporate Web site, a company may have an internal Exchange server. Because companies typically allow internal users to send e-mail to addresses outside of the company, this Exchange server needs to have Internet connectivity. Nevertheless, attaching a direct Internet connection to the Exchange server exposes the server to a variety of attacks from external users. By attaching the Internet connection to ISA Server, you can prevent most e-mail server attacks from reaching the internal server, as illustrated in Figure 1-11. This same logic applies to internal Domain Name Service (DNS) servers, Telnet servers, and VPN Servers.

ISA Server services requests from outside

Internet

ISA Server

Internal Web Servers

Figure 1-11   Using ISA Server to protect internal Internet servers

E-Mail Content Screening

Through the use of the **Simple Mail Transfer Protocol (SMTP)** application filter, ISA Server can protect internal mail servers from direct attacks, and also filter e-mail content to keep potentially damaging e-mails from entering the internal network. You can also configure the SMTP filter to screen out "junk mail" messages before they reach the internal mail server.

When configuring the SMTP filters, you can filter e-mails based on attachments, users and domains, keywords, and SMTP commands. When an incoming e-mail message triggers one of the filters, you can set ISA Server to delete the message, hold the message, or forward the message to a specific e-mail account (usually your own account). The following list describes what each of the filter options provides.

- *Filter based on attachment*—This type of filter allows filtering based on the attachment name, attachment extension (such as .exe, .vbs, .mp3, etc...), and attachment size.

- *Filter based on users and domains*—This type of filter allows filtering based on individual e-mail addresses (such as denying e-mail from hacker@widgets.com), or based on domain names (such as networkdestroyers.org).

- *Filter based on keyword*—This type of filter allows the administrator to specify whether ISA Server should search subject lines or message bodies for specified keywords. This permits content filtering of actual e-mail text.

- *Filter based on SMTP commands*—This type of filter allows filtering of messages that contain potentially dangerous SMTP control commands. The SMTP filter includes a default list of unsafe SMTP control commands that it screens.

Caching Features

One of the most popular ISA Server 2000 features is the ability to cache content. As the demand for the Internet continues to increase, so does the requirement for networks to have Internet connections with considerable bandwidth. ISA Server addresses this need by reducing the amount of network traffic that must actually access the Internet. By storing Internet content locally, or caching, ISA Server gains the resources it needs to satisfy most outgoing requests without forcing the requests to leave the network. ISA Server uses four major forms of caching to store the Internet content in the most efficient method: Web caching, hierarchical and distributed caching, active caching, and scheduled content download.

Web Caching

When a network administrator thinks of caching, **Web caching** (also referred to as **passive caching**) is typically what comes to mind. When a client needs a specific Web document, ISA Server receives the initial request. Before fulfilling the request by forwarding it to the Internet, the server browses through its current Web cache. If it doesn't find the requested document in the cache or if the cache has expired, ISA Server forwards the request to the appropriate Web site. Once ISA Server receives the response, it adds that material to its cache, and then forwards the data on to the client computer. The next time a client requests the same Web site, ISA Server does not need to forward the request to the Internet; it already has the content stored locally.

As ISA Server manages the Web cache, it can store cached content on the server hard drive or in the RAM of the server. ISA Server uses fast RAM caching for the most frequently accessed pages because it allows for a near instantaneous response to client requests. Occasionally, accessed pages are stored on disk. As you might imagine, the more RAM you can install on an ISA Server machine, the more content ISA Server can store in the memory; more content stored in memory means faster response time to client requests.

ISA Server supports caching client requests from the internal network accessing the Internet, or **forward caching**, *and* client requests from the Internet accessing the internal network, or **reverse caching**. In this way, both sending and receiving clients benefit from ISA Server caching features. By using the HTTP Redirector component, ISA Server can cache client requests from both systems that have ISA Server client software installed, and equally from SecureNAT clients without any Web browser reconfiguration.

Distributed and Hierarchical Caching

When you are in a large, enterprise network environment, having one Internet access point may not be enough. Microsoft ISA Server 2000 Enterprise Edition allows you to create **ISA Server arrays**. In short, these arrays combine caching and configuration abilities of many stand-alone ISA Servers into one complete entity. When using either distributed or hierarchical caching, you also gain the advantage of load distribution.

As the name implies, if you are using **hierarchical caching**, you maintain a hierarchy of ISA Server machines that communicates with one another in an upstream system. For example, if a client requests a Web page, the first ISA Server to receive the request is most likely a downstream server (one located physically close to the client). The initial server checks its current Web cache for the content, and fulfills the client request if it locates the correct content. However, if that ISA Server cannot find the content, it forwards the request upstream through the chain of ISA Servers until one locates the requested data, as illustrated in Figure 1-12. Once an ISA Server locates the requested object, it forwards the data back to the client, allowing the data to pass through and cache on each downstream ISA Server the client used when initially accessing the data.

When using **distributed caching**, the caching takes place even closer to the user. You can set up many ISA Servers in the same location using an array structure, as illustrated in Figure 1-13. This ensures that the configuration on all servers remains identical, and cached content distributes evenly across all ISA Server machines. Once the array initializes, ISA Server uses the **Caching Array Routing Protocol (CARP)** to find the most efficient method of caching content, and ensures that the ISA Server cache content does not simply mirror each other. Distributed caching also offers significant fault tolerance for the user because it eliminates a single, physical server point of failure.

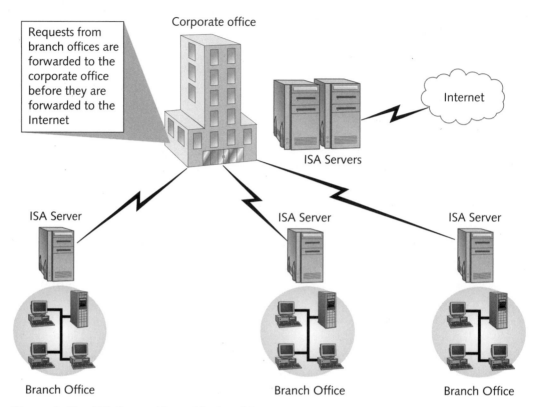

Figure 1-12 ISA Server hierarchical caching

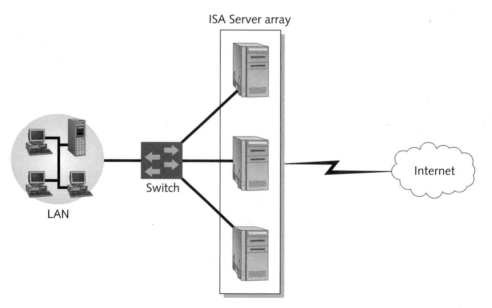

Figure 1-13 ISA Server distributed caching

Active Caching

Active caching puts ISA Server into the proactive caching role. Typically, the cache builds as clients access various content on the Internet. For example, suppose you access *www.microsoft.com* from an ISA Server with Web caching enabled. ISA Server checks its current cache, and cannot locate the requested item, so it forwards the request to the public network interface. Once ISA Server contacts the Web site and obtains the content, it caches it and forwards it on to you. This process repeats for each user accessing the Internet, and the cache continues to grow. ISA Server marks each item in the cache with a specified **time to live (TTL)**. Because Web content is continually changing (such as news headlines and weather reports), this ensures that the content currently located in the cache does not become stale for clients. If the client accesses cached content past its designated TTL, ISA Server checks the content with the current content located on the Web, and verifies that the cached content is indeed the most recent. If it is not, ISA Server downloads and replaces the cached content with the newer Internet content, and serves it to the client.

When you use active caching, you configure ISA Server to update objects before they expire. Furthermore, ISA Server updates these objects typically when network traffic is low, allowing for a quicker update and higher conservation of valuable WAN bandwidth during peak network periods. This allows ISA Server to continually update its cache when there is a high demand for network bandwidth. It would not be efficient for ISA Server to continually update every item contained in the cached content, because clients access some Internet content only once or rarely. Instead, ISA Server only updates those items considered popular on the server. The decision process for choosing the popular content is as follows:

1. A client accesses Internet content for the first time. Following standard Web-caching procedures, ISA Server downloads and caches the information and assigns it a specified TTL.

2. If a client accesses the same cached information before the TTL expires, ISA Server adds the specified content to the active cache list and resets the TTL count.

3. If another client accesses the content before the TTL expires a second time, the content remains on the active caching list and active updating procedures continue.

4. How often the content refreshes depends on how busy ISA Server is. If the server is relatively idle, the cached content updates when it is 50 percent through its TTL. The busier ISA Server becomes, the longer it waits to update the active cached content. The times can range from the 50 percent mark to the entire TTL.

5. If a user does not access the content within the specified active caching period, ISA Server removes the content from the popular list until the content again meets the original active caching standards.

Scheduled Content Download

The **scheduled content download** features of ISA Server give you true control of refreshing cached content. These features allow you to track the time of day and addresses of Web sites accessed by network clients. After a period of recording and analyzing, certain trends may emerge in accessing Web sites. For example, you could monitor ISA Server Web usage for a week and find that every morning 23 percent of network users access the local news via the same local news site, and 15 percent of users access a common stock quote site to check the recent market data. Using scheduled content downloads, you can set ISA Server to download these popular sites 10-15 minutes before most company employees arrive at the office. When the morning Internet access rush begins, approximately 38 percent of the Internet traffic is stored on the local network, minimizing WAN Internet access during a notoriously high-traffic time of day.

When you schedule content download, you specify exactly what content you would like to download. You can specify a single URL, multiple URLs, or an entire Web site. This allows you to not only download the title page of the local news site, but to choose to follow and cache every link from that title page without user intervention. This means you can cache the initial pages accessed by users and the links they might access. For example, ISA Server could cache all daily news, current weather, and current theater movie times in addition to the default Web page. However, exercise caution when using scheduled content downloads. Configuring ISA Server to follow too many links on a Web site could send many megabytes of content to ISA Server.

HARDWARE AND SOFTWARE REQUIREMENTS FOR ISA SERVER 2000

As the capabilities of Internet firewall software increase, so do the demands on computer hardware requirements. If you used Microsoft Proxy Server 2.0, you will notice a significant increase in the requirements to run ISA Server 2000. Much of this comes from the increasing requirements of the base operating system, Windows 2000.

Hardware Requirements

To use Microsoft ISA Server 2000, you need the following equipment:

- 300 MHz or faster Pentium II or compatible processor
- 256 MB of RAM
- Minimum of 20 MB available hard disk space
- Windows 2000-compatible network card for communicating with the internal network; additional network card or modem connection is strongly recommended for external network communication, but not required
- To implement an array, you need at least one additional ISA Server computer.

Software Requirements

The software requirements to install Microsoft ISA Server are as follows:

- One of the following operating systems:

  Windows 2000 Server with Service Pack 1 or later installed

  Windows 2000 Advanced Server with Service Pack 1 or later installed

  Windows 2000 Datacenter Server

- One local, hard disk partition formatted with the NTFS file system

- To implement an ISA Server array or advanced policies, you must have Windows 2000 Active Directory installed and available.

CHAPTER SUMMARY

- ISA Server 2000 is part of the Microsoft .NET product suite. This product provides firewall, caching, and redundancy features to companies connected to the Internet.

- ISA Server provides a multi-layer firewall. This means it can filter incoming and outgoing data at multiple layers of the OSI model, giving you complete control over the precise types of data to block.

- Through the use of packet and application filters, the ISA firewall can block most of the common DOS attacks.

- ISA Server provides two categories of packet filters: stateful filters, causing you to statically open holes in the firewall, and dynamic filters, allowing ISA Server to open and close ports as needed.

- Application filters allow ISA Server to perform content filtering and virus checking for incoming and outgoing data on a per application basis.

- You can configure ISA Server to cache frequently accessed content. Forward caching stores Internet content locally on ISA Server, while reverse caching stores internal Web content on ISA Server. Forward and reverse caching can be configured to cache passively or actively. Passive caching allows you to determine cached content through accessing a variety of Internet content. Active caching allows you to determine cached content along with the times ISA Server should update the content.

- You can use distributed and hierarchical caching to balance loads among ISA Servers, minimize WAN traffic, and eliminate a single point of failure.

- Network redundancy and load balancing can be attained through the use of ISA Server arrays. This allows multiple ISA Server machines to act as one administrative unit.

KEY TERMS

active caching — Allows the ISA Server to update cached content before the time to live expires.

application-level filters — Developed on a per application basis. Allows for detailed content filtering since the filter can access the incoming or outgoing data stream. ISA Server supports third-party development of application filters.

Caching Array Routing Protocol (CARP) — Protocol used by ISA Servers in an array to ensure each server maintains its own unique cache, but does not have duplicate items cached on other ISA Servers.

circuit-level filtering — Instead of filtering per port number, filtering applies on a per session basis. This allows applications to open needed ports to communicate without administrators manually opening up needed firewall ports.

Denial-of-Service attacks — An attack on a network designed to render the network services inoperable by flooding it with useless traffic.

distributed caching — Allows ISA Servers combined in an array to share cached content. Provides both server redundancy and load balancing. Uses the CARP protocol to ensure duplicate items do not cache on multiple servers.

Distributed Computer Object Model (DCOM) — A protocol that enables software components to communicate directly over a Windows network, and is designed for use across multiple network transports, including Internet protocols such as HTTP.

dynamic packet filter — Also called a stateful filter. Opens ports dynamically on the public network interface on a user request to allow public traffic from the requested object to enter the private network. Once session ends, the public port closes.

File Transfer Protocol (FTP) — A protocol used typically on the Internet to send and receive files.

firewall — A system designed to prevent unauthorized access to or from a private internal network.

forward caching — Occurs when users on the internal network access the external network and the requested objects are cached.

hierarchical caching — Also called *chained caching*. Occurs when ISA Servers use one another in a hierarchical method to cache data. Directs forwarded requests from lower-level cache servers to higher-level cache servers which, if the content is not found, then direct the request to the Internet.

Internet Control Message Protocol (ICMP) — A Network-layer Internet protocol that provides error correction and other information relevant to IP packet processing.

Internet Service Provider (ISP) — A company that provides access to the Internet.

ISA Server arrays — Formed when combining two or more ISA Servers into a collection of machines sharing configuration and cache information.

Microsoft .NET — Family of Microsoft products, created as a group of applications that allows Windows 2000 to seamlessly integrate into mission-critical Web-based services.

Microsoft Management Console (MMC) — Used primarily in Windows 2000 as a tool which houses snap-ins to perform application-specific administrative tasks.

Network Address Translation (NAT) — Allows internal networks to use one set of IP Addresses, while another set of IP addresses is used on the external network. NAT then translates between them and hides the internal addresses from ever being seen or used on the external network.

Open Systems Interconnection (OSI) model — A model designed by the International Standards Organization (ISO) describing how devices communicate across a network. It divides networking architecture into seven layers: Application, Presentation, Session, Transport, Network, Data Link, and Physical.

packet filter — Applied at network firewalls, this filters incoming and outgoing traffic by analyzing IP addresses and port numbers.

Request for Comments (RFC) — A series of notes about the Internet started in 1969. Anyone can submit an RFC, and, if it gains enough interest, it may become an Internet standard.

reverse caching — Occurs when users on the external network access the internal network and the requested objects are cached.

scheduled content download — A manual configuration allowing administrators to configure the ISA Server to download specific Web contents on certain time-of-day intervals.

Secure Network Address Translation (Secure NAT) — A Microsoft modification to NAT which allows for application of ISA Server Policies to incoming and outgoing NAT traffic.

Simple Mail Transfer Protocol (SMTP) — This is an industry standard e-mail transmission protocol.

Small Office/Home Office (SOHO) — A computing environment typically for 2–20 users who work at home or in small offices.

socket — Formed by two communicating applications, consisting of an IP address combined with a port number.

static packet filter — Packet filter configured manually by an administrator, combined with a permit or deny statement to allow or stop incoming or outgoing traffic on specific IP addresses or port numbers.

TCP/IP port numbers — Used by TCP and UDP to pass information to the correct upper-layer application.

Time to Live (TTL) — The amount of idle time content remains in the cache before deleted.

Transmission Control Protocol (TCP) — Enables two hosts to establish a connection where data transfer and delivery is reliable.

User Datagram Protocol (UDP) — Provides a fast, "best-effort" delivery system for IP-based packets. Typically used for broadcasts.

Virtual Private Network (VPN) — Allows private internal network communication across a public network backbone.

Web caching — Also referred to as passive caching. This is the typical form of caching supported on most proxy servers. As a user accesses Web content, the ISA Server retrieves the requested data for the user and caches it, allowing the next user accessing the data within the TTL to retrieve the content locally.

Wide Area Network (WAN) — This is typically two or more Local Area Networks (LANs) connected across a relatively large geographic area.

Windows Sockets (SOCKS) — A platform independent protocol for handling TCP traffic through a proxy server. Individual application design must support the SOCKS protocol to use it when communicating.

REVIEW QUESTIONS

1. If an application used the SOCKS protocol to communicate, that application could be running on:

   a. Windows 2000

   b. Macintosh OS

   c. UNIX

   d. Linux

   e. all of the above

2. At which layers of the OSI model do standard packet filters typically operate?

   a. Application and Presentation

   b. Presentation and Session

   c. Session and Transport

   d. Network and Transport

3. When referring to ISA Server, the content TTL represents:

   a. the length of time until a session resets

   b. how many routers a packet can go through before being discarded

   c. how long a cached item exists before being deleted

   d. how long an ISA Server is running

4. Flooding packets to a certain TCP or UDP port on a given device is called?

   a. virus attack

   b. Smurf attack

   c. Ping of Death attack

   d. Denial of Service attack

5. If you continually receive malicious e-mail causing Visual Basic virus scripts (.vbs extension) to run, you might implement an ISA Server:

    a. application filter

    b. e-mail filter

    c. packet filter

    d. circuit filter

6. ISA Server's SecureNAT protocol requires that client software be installed on hosts accessing the Internet because SecureNAT is not an RFC standard. True or False?

7. As corporate network clients access the Internet using dynamic filters, internal ports open to allow Internet access on port 80, and then close once the session completes. True or False?

8. Caching internal Web server content to serve to external clients is called:

    a. active caching

    b. dynamic caching

    c. forward caching

    d. reverse caching

9. Microsoft's Caching Array Routing Protocol allows multiple ISA Servers to do what?

    a. compress cached content, saving up to 80 percent of space on the hard disk

    b. communicate directly with clients accessing the cached content without TCP usage

    c. ensure that duplicate cache on multiple servers does not occur

    d. connect together to form an array

10. Which of the following is *not* a requirement to install ISA Server 2000?

    a. Internet Information Server 5.0

    b. Service Pack 1

    c. Windows 2000 Server platform

    d. 20 MB of space on the hard-disk

11. ISA Server 2000 can filter e-mail content using the new circuit-filtering feature. True or False?

12. What two application filters are included in ISA Server 2000 with the source code?

    a. Web and e-mail server

    b. DNS and WINS Server

    c. SQL and Oracle Server

    d. Word and Excel

13. TCP port numbers 1–1024 are considered:

    a. application ports

    b. well-known ports

    c. dynamic ports

    d. common firewall ports

14. Which type of caching allows ISA Server to update popular content?

    a. scheduled download caching

    b. passive caching

    c. active caching

    d. dynamic caching

15. ISA Server secures your internal network from the majority of attacks occurring in today's industry. True or False?

16. What is the feature that allows multiple ISA Servers to be combined into a single entity?

    a. server farming

    b. multiple processor support

    c. symmetric multiprocessing

    d. server arrays

17. ISA Server can be configured with only an internal network interface card installed. True or False?

18. The SMTP application filter allows you to filter e-mail based on the user who sent it. True or False?

19. ISA Server 2000 provides the ability to run both ISA Server and Internet Information Server (IIS) 5.0 on the same machine. This provides the same security benefits as running the IIS machine from the internal network. True or False?

20. Which form of caching provides redundancy and load balancing?

    a. active caching

    b. hierarchical or chained caching

    c. passive caching

    d. distributed caching

HANDS-ON PROJECTS

Project 1-1

Rather than continuing to upgrade the Proxy Server line of products, Microsoft has redesigned their firewall and caching line with ISA Server 2000. Using the Microsoft Web site as a resource, write one to two pages describing the major differences between the Proxy Server line of products and ISA Server.

Project 1-2

Using the Web or appropriate trade magazines, research the .NET suite of software products from Microsoft. Write one to two pages describing the major components of the suite and what business needs they address, how ISA Server fits into the .NET picture, and the future outlook of the .NET suite of products.

Project 1-3

Using the Web, research the networking and security features of ISA Server 2000. For example, visit *www.isaserver.org* and *www.microsoft.com* to find descriptions of ISA Server 2000. Create a list of the networking and security features, and describe each one.

Project 1-4

Using the Web or appropriate trade magazines, find two to three recent reviews of ISA Server 2000. Based on these reviews, write one to two pages explaining the strengths and weaknesses of ISA Server 2000.

CASE PROJECTS

Case Project 1-1

Jeremiah Danielson is the owner of a new dotcom startup company developing a cost-efficient, Internet-based training method for corporations. This "e-training" system requires redundancy, security, and load balancing to deliver reliable training to clients on time. The company is currently located at a single location in Mexico, Missouri. You are designing Mr. Danielson's network structure using ISA Server 2000 as the primary server for Internet access. What features of ISA Server would you recommend? How would you provide for the redundancy and load balancing requirements?

Case Project 1-2

Susan Fulmer is the network administrator at ACME enterprises—a large, worldwide book publisher. ACME has Internet connectivity at each of the 50 corporate sites. Recently, e-mail viruses have become the plague of the company. Susan typically finds herself rebuilding the company's e-mail servers at least once every four months. Furthermore, network monitoring has revealed that ACME employees are visiting inappropriate Web sites and using unapproved Internet software on their machines. Susan has heard that ISA Server can help resolve these issues. What specific features of ISA Server should she implement? How should those features be used? Could Susan manage all fifty ISA Servers from one location? Why or why not?

2

UNDERSTANDING OSI AND TCP/IP FUNDAMENTALS

After reading this chapter and completing the exercises, you will be able to:

♦ Demonstrate an understanding of the OSI model by fully explaining network communication

♦ Explain the functions and design of the TCP/IP protocol suite

♦ Describe the purpose of router and firewall equipment in today's networks

♦ Demonstrate conceptual understanding of Network Address Translation and Virtual Private Networking

♦ Break classful network addresses into required subnets

In this chapter, you examine the basic network infrastructure that must be in place for ISA Server to function. Before you build a network, you must understand the **Open Systems Interconnection (OSI) model**. This model describes the essence of network communication. You use the OSI model to understand and develop computer-to-computer communications. An understanding of the fundamental functions of the OSI model is necessary not only to use Microsoft ISA Server 2000, but also to comprehend network concepts in general and in environments composed of other platforms and networking systems.

This chapter also focuses on the TCP/IP protocol suite and common TCP/IP functions. TCP/IP has become the fundamental protocol suite in nearly all corporate networks. Before you can install and configure ISA Server, you must understand TCP/IP fundamentals, such as logical addressing and subnetting, and the protocols included in the TCP/IP protocol suite. For those experienced with TCP/IP, this chapter provides a review of the TCP/IP concepts necessary to understand ISA Server configuration.

DEFINING NETWORK COMPONENTS

The last two decades have brought about major changes in the networking environment. One significant change has been the transition from the terminal-mainframe network arrangements to client-server configurations. In a terminal-mainframe arrangement, a terminal consisting of a monitor and keyboard, but no internal microprocessor, connects to a mainframe computer. Users share the mainframe to perform their computer tasks; they cannot do anything except type at their terminals. In contrast, in a client-server configuration, the client is a complete, stand-alone personal computer (not a "dumb" terminal), and it offers the user its full range of power and features for running applications. Clients are connected to a server, a computer that manages data, lets clients share information, and provides sophisticated network administration and security features. A client-server computer network established in one location, such as an office or building, is called a **local area network (LAN)**. However, networks that use ISA Server 2000 usually have expanded to allow their networks to connect two or more LANs in separate locations into a **wide area network (WAN)**, a network connecting geographically distant locations, such as those in different branch offices for an organization.

Many people confuse intranets and the Internet with local and wide area networks, and while they are related, they are not the same. The **Internet** is a collection of local area networks that forms one large, loosely tied, worldwide network of millions of users. **Intranets** are private networks that allow users to access internal information within a company or organization. Many intranets tie closely into the Internet, allowing private internal information to be accessed from a public network. The security requirements for this type of undertaking are very high. Exposing an intranet to the Internet requires extensive planning to avoid security problems. Many company and network managers determine that the risk of exposing an intranet to external users outweighs the rewards of allowing access from the Internet, and choose to use another method (such as dial-up connections) to allow private access. Although you should have high security on your intranet/Internet border, most hacking attempts originate from the internal network, emphasizing the additional importance of internal network security.

EXPLORING THE OSI MODEL

As a network administrator, one challenge you will probably face is dealing with malfunctioning computers. Users often label trouble they have performing regular tasks as problems with the entire system, reporting that the computer is no longer working. Your first task is to identify the problem by narrowing its definition, and trying to focus on the component causing trouble. Your troubleshooting checklist probably includes the following questions: Is the hardware malfunctioning? Does the core operating system code have an error? Did the user cause the computer to malfunction in some way? Did the application itself cause a system crash? Once you identify the faulty component, you can begin to solve the problem. If you look at the computer as a whole, you tax yourself with troubleshooting the entire computer every time a problem occurs.

2

Networks are no different from stand-alone computers in this respect. It is more effective to view a network as a collection of components rather than a single entity. For example, the statement, "The network is down," does not provide enough information to identify and solve the problem to get the network running again, whereas a statement such as "the switch does not seem to have a physical connection" isolates the potential problem quickly. Fortunately, the International Standards Organization (ISO) developed the Open Systems Interconnection (OSI) model in 1980 to describe communication between two devices on a network. The OSI model separates network communication into seven layers: Application, Presentation, Session, Transport, Network, Data Link, and Physical.

Why is this advantageous? First, troubleshooting techniques are greatly improved. Network administrators can troubleshoot any network scenario, layer by layer. Second, it helps network administrators build a network infrastructure that permits dissimilar components to operate with each other. Nearly all protocols designed for use in today's networks meet the standards of the OSI model. This means that common standards reach across platform boundaries. Networks would be impossible to use if only Apple computers could communicate with Apple computers and IBM computers could only communicate with IBM computers. The Internet in particular would not be possible. Finally, the OSI model helps vendors design layer-specific equipment. This means that vendors can design components to work at one or more layers, but not necessarily all seven layers. The result is specialized and more effective network equipment. The OSI model divides network communication into seven separate layers, which are shown in Figure 2-1.

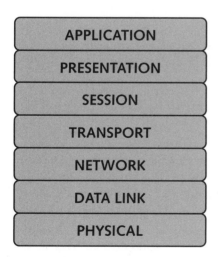

Figure 2-1   The seven layer OSI model

Table 2-1 explains the purpose of each layer in the OSI model.

Table 2-1 OSI Layer Functionality

OSI Layer	Functionality
Application	Provides the user interface
Presentation	Converts application-specific data to a generic format (ASCII, BMP, GIF, etc...), compression of data, data encryption
Session	Begins, maintains, and ends network sessions between two devices. Handles the sequencing of packets. Keeps data streams separate between multiple applications running on PCs.
Transport	Handles the reliability of the network communication
Network	Works with logical addressing of network devices
Data Link	Works with the physical addressing of network devices
Physical	Encompasses physical network cable types and connections, electrical signaling, the sending of bits

Application Layer

Most users are familiar with the Application layer because it provides the applications they work with regularly, such as Internet Explorer or Outlook. The Application layer represents the user interface of the application. It allows users to work with a program without interacting with the complexity of the network system. The programs that use the Application layer are known as **application processes**. Developers may code the program to work directly with the next layer in the OSI model, the Presentation layer, or they may rely on application-specific elements. **Application-specific elements** are modules, usually written into the base operating system, that perform many common network tasks for communicating between applications. By using these modules, application developers can avoid rewriting large amounts of code and increase application stability.

Presentation Layer

The purpose of the Presentation layer is to format data passed between computers into a common language (syntax) that all communicating machines can understand. This syntax formatting can occur even though the applications used during communication may be completely different. A good example of this is accessing a Web site on the Internet. The two applications connecting are completely different: one is a Web server, the other is a Web browser. However, they can negotiate and decide on a common syntax to use, such as HTML or BMP, which is also considered a data type. Once the applications negotiate a common syntax, that data type is used to communicate until a change in syntax is needed. For example, the browser may initially access the Web page using HTML, but change the data syntax to GIF when it needs to transmit a Web page graphic.

The Presentation layer can also compress data. This reduces the amount of data transmitted and can save precious WAN bandwidth. To allow for increased security, the

Presentation layer can also encrypt data. Because of the design of the OSI model, both compression and encryption can be application independent. This means that application developers do not need to create their own encryption methods and standards. Banks and other financial services companies employ this technology extensively to secure electronic fund transfers.

Session Layer

The Session layer starts up, maintains, and shuts down a communication session. The Session layer also keeps individual application data isolated from other applications. For example, a user may have three instances of Internet Explorer open, each connected to a different Web site. If the computer has only one modem and all three browsers are downloading at the same time, the Session layer identifies which browser window to send the requested data to by assigning a unique port number to each browser session. Because all incoming data is tagged with a unique port number, the user's computer directs the Web data to the correct browser window based on that port number.

The TCP/IP protocol suite groups the top three layers of the OSI model (the Application, Presentation, and Session layers) into one functional Application layer because the application and its operating system usually handle the tasks those layers perform. ISA Server 2000 works primarily with the bottom four layers of the OSI model. These layers—Transport, Network, Data Link, and Physical—are most often manipulated when a packet of data travels across the network.

Transport Layer

Once the application has assigned a port number and added the Session layer data, it moves down to the Transport layer. Data passing through this layer is called a **segment**. The primary function of this layer is to handle reliability. Depending on the design of the protocol suite, it may allow different reliability levels. For example, if an application uses the TCP/IP protocol suite, it can choose two reliability levels: Transmission Control Protocol (TCP), which is slow but reliable, or User Datagram Protocol (UDP), which is fast but unreliable.

If an application chooses to use TCP, it ensures delivery of data by requiring acknowledgements from the receiving computer. This slows communication, but increases reliability. If high speeds are necessary, the application developer can use UDP communication. This Transport layer protocol calls for a "best-effort delivery," meaning that UDP can send data much faster, but some of that data may be lost or corrupted in transit. An example of an application that uses this type of transmission is video streaming. When sending data, the application tries to deliver it as fast as possible, resulting in a smooth video feed. If a few packets are lost, the video image may jump, but overall the video runs more smoothly than a TCP connection. When using UDP, the application design must be able to handle missing or corrupted data.

Network Layer

When data leaves the communicating device, all of the OSI layers add data referring to reliability and application functions until it reaches the Network layer. Data that passes through the Network layer is called a **packet** or a **datagram**. This layer provides the necessary information to route packets to the correct destination computer. To ensure that the router can send a packet to the correct destination, it must rely on the network address located in the header of the packet. Once the protocol has tagged the data with the correct source and destination network address, it forwards it down to the Data Link layer.

Data Link Layer

After adding data at the Network layer, the protocol stack passes it down to the Data Link layer. Data Link layer functionality is composed of two sub-layers: **Logical Link Control (LLC)** and **Media Access Control (MAC)**. When the Network layer packet passes through the Data Link layer, both a header and trailer are attached to the packet. Because of this, data referenced at the Data Link layer is called a **frame**. Because the frame is the first logical information the receiving computer analyzes, both the header and trailer have very specific and critical functions.

When communicating, devices use the network address to identify the specific network segment on which a destination device resides. Once the correct network segment has been determined, the final routing device must then identify the individual network card to which the data is to be sent. The routing device uses a MAC address to find the physical destination. Every network address (or logical address, such as IP or IPX) maps to an individual MAC address, typically burned into the network card. The **Address Resolution Protocol (ARP)** translates logical addresses to physical (MAC) addresses.

In today's modern network environments, it is common to have many different protocol suites running on the same network segment. Deciphering these protocol suites is the responsibility of the Logical Link Control (LLC). When a computer receives a frame, it determines to which MAC address the frame is destined. If the MAC address matches the computer's network card, it then determines to which Network layer protocol the data should be sent. At this point, the LLC acts simply as a pointer and directs the data to the correct Network layer protocol (such as IP or IPX).

The trailer portion of the frame contains the **Cyclical Redundancy Check (CRC)**, which ensures the application running at layer seven does not receive corrupted data. When the Network layer passes data down to the Data Link layer, the sending device passes the data through a mathematical formula. The result of that mathematical formula becomes the CRC appended to the packet. The computer receiving the data puts the data through the same mathematical formula and checks to make sure the answer it obtains is the same as the answer located in the CRC. If so, the frame continues up to the Network layer; if not, the receiving computer assumes data corruption, and discards the frame.

Physical Layer

The final stage the data reaches before transmission across the network is the Physical layer. This layer addresses the physical components of the network and deals with topics such as signaling standards, connection types, and electrical signals. The transmitting device adds no additional data at this layer. Data transmitted at the Physical layer comes in **bits**. Most network administrators concern themselves only with the basics of the Physical layer, and leave the electrical signaling to qualified technicians. The most common knowledge gained from the Physical layer is the maximum length of the various cable types you can use before signal attenuation occurs.

Communicating Between Layers

Once you have a thorough understanding of the OSI model, you can describe network communication between devices. As data passes from one device on a network segment to another, the sending and receiving protocols completely assemble and disassemble the data. A network segment is a part of a network where all devices can communicate without passing through a router or a modem. As the device sends the data, each layer adds its own control information, or header and trailer (the Data Link layer's CRC is the primary example of a trailer). The control information and user data is called a **Protocol Data Unit (PDU)**. Because the PDU contains different information as it moves up and down the OSI model, it is given a more specific name depending on the data it contains. A PDU containing the control information from the Transport layer is called a segment; from the Network layer it is called a packet; from the Data Link layer it is called a frame; and from the Physical layer it is referred to as bits.

The process of devices attaching control information to a PDU is called encapsulation. When a specific layer of the OSI model receives data, it attaches its own control information and passes it to the lower layers. This process continues until the data reaches the Physical layer and transmission occurs. On the flip side, the receiving device reads the initial frame control information to determine if the MAC address the frame contains matches the MAC address assigned to the device's network card. If the MAC addresses match, the device strips the control information and passes the packet up to the Network layer. This control information stripping process continues until the data reaches the receiving application. This process is called de-encapsulation.

LEARNING TCP/IP HISTORY

What is now known as the Internet began as a project funded by the U.S. Department of Defense (DOD) in the late 1960s. Before then, the small amount of communication between network devices occurred across the **Public Switched Telephone Network (PSTN)**, which was not the most reliable or speedy way to send data. In December 1968, the **Advanced Research Projects Agency (ARPA)** contracted Bolt Beranek and Newman (BBN), an Internetwork research company, to design and deploy a packet-switching network. The first network node was installed at UCLA in September of 1969, and by 1973, the newly termed **ARPANET** spanned the continental U.S. and included connections to Europe.

The ARPANET gave birth to many new network protocols, one of the most memorable being **X.25**, the original Data Link layer packet-switching protocol. The first client-to-client protocol introduced was the **Network Control Protocol (NCP)**. This protocol allowed end clients to communicate effectively, but soon proved to be excessively slow as data transmission rates increased. This prompted the development and deployment of the **Transmission Control Protocol (TCP)** and **Internet Protocol (IP)**. The developing team originally designed TCP and IP as a single protocol for end-to-end client communication. This is now known as TCP/IP, which describes the collection of applications and protocols called the **TCP/IP protocol suite**.

UNDERSTANDING THE **TCP/IP** PROTOCOL SUITE

As TCP/IP development continued to expand and the demand for more functionality increased, the TCP/IP protocols evolved into a protocol suite. Similar to the seven-layer OSI model, the TCP/IP protocol uses a five-layer design. These five layers describe communication between any TCP/IP-based network devices. Figure 2-2 shows a comparison of the OSI and TCP/IP models.

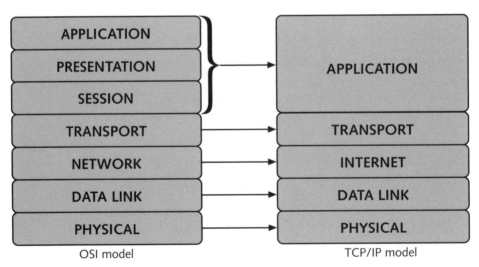

Figure 2-2 Comparing the architecture of the TCP/IP model to the OSI model

Application Layer

Whereas the OSI model uses three top layers—the Application, Presentation, and Session layers—the TCP/IP model uses only one: the Application layer. This is because the group designing the architecture of TCP/IP realized the end-user application or network operating system typically handles the functions of the upper three layers of the OSI model. Most network administrators naturally consider the end-user interface as characteristic of the TCP/IP Application layer; however, this is not entirely accurate. While the Application layer does provide the user interface for applications, the application itself uses sub-application protocols to achieve client-to-client network communication. The TCP/IP protocol suite uses **port numbers** assigned at the Transport layer to determine which incoming and outgoing data belongs to which applications. Some of the common TCP/IP Application layer protocols are shown in Table 2-2.

Table 2-2   Common TCP/IP Application Layer Protocols

Protocol Acronym	Protocol Name	Description
Telnet	Telecommunication Network	Allows clients to communicate through the use of a virtual terminal protocol
FTP	File Transfer Protocol	Allows clients to transfer files between hosts
SMTP	Simple Mail Transfer Protocol	Standard for transmitting electronic mail over the Internet
HTTP	Hypertext Transfer Protocol	The basis for the exchange of information across the World Wide Web (WWW)
Finger	None	Determines the status of users or hosts on the network
POP	Post Office Protocol	Used for mail transfer between end-user client software and e-mail servers
DNS	Domain Name System	Associates user-friendly names with IP addresses
SNMP	Simple Network Management Protocol	Used in conjunction with Management Information Bases (MIB) to monitor TCP/IP-based networks and equipment
PING	Packet Internet Groper	Determines status of connection and latency information between two TCP/IP hosts

Transport Layer

Just as the OSI model design dictates, the communicating application must choose between a reliable or unreliable connection at the Transport layer. In the TCP/IP protocol suite, the choice is between TCP and UDP. Strictly speaking, an application is not TCP/IP based when it does not use TCP as the Transport layer protocol. If the application chooses to use TCP as the Transport layer protocol, the communicating devices establish a session for communication. This session is a three-step process called the **TCP three-way handshake**. Once the application establishes a session, all data transmitted between the two computers will require **acknowledgements**. This ensures that every bit of data sent arrives at the destination intact and provides a reliable connection. Common TCP applications consist of Web browsers and FTP client utilities. Recall that applications that use UDP attempt a "best-effort delivery." This means that the applications do not establish a session, and do not send acknowledgements for the data. In essence, the application sends the data and hopes it gets there, but if it happens to become corrupted or lost along the way, the application does not correct it. By choosing this method of transmission, the application elects a faster, more unreliable transmission. Common UDP **(User Datagram Protocol)** applications include Voice over IP, video streaming, and online games.

While TCP and UDP are the primary protocols used by applications, other Transport layer protocols are commonly used in the industry. One such protocol is the **Internet Control Message Protocol (ICMP)**. This protocol is so integral to IP communication, it often resides in many network diagrams at the TCP/IP Internet (or OSI model Network) layer. However, because applications access ICMP using an Internet layer protocol number, it is technically considered a Transport layer protocol. This protocol is responsible for delivering different types of messages to communicating end devices. The commonly deployed messages are as follows:

- *Destination Unreachable*—Notifies the source communicating device that the packets are undeliverable

- *Echo and Echo Reply*—These are used to identify connectivity between two network devices; one device signals with an Echo, the other responds with an Echo Reply, which is the basis for the Ping application

- *Parameter Problem*—Indicates that the host or transition router identified an error in the packet header

- *Redirect*—Notifies the host that the packets should be directed to another network IP address

- *Source Quench*—Used by communicating devices to inform the source device to slow transmission rate when packets arrive too quickly

- *TTL Exceeded*—When a packet reaches a router and the TTL expires, the last router to decrement the TTL issues an ICMP message to the sender, notifying the source device that the packet TTL expired

The Transport layer also assigns application port numbers. Because most network devices only have one incoming stream of data via a modem or network card, port numbers give the operating system a method to separate and direct data to the correct sending or receiving application. TCP and UDP have a distinct and separate range of 65,535 ports that applications can use to uniquely identify themselves. Ports 1-1023 are considered **well-known port numbers**, since common applications use them. (See Appendix B for a list of well-known ports.) Any port numbered 1024 and above fits into the **dynamic port number** range, as applications typically assign these ports dynamically for network communication. For a network application to communicate, TCP and UDP both require a source and destination port number. For example, if a user opens Internet Explorer to contact a Web site, the application tags the outgoing request with a TCP destination port of 80, the well-known port number for HTTP. This tells the destination computer to give the incoming data to the Web server. However, in addition to the well-known HTTP destination port number, the application dynamically generates a source port number as a number above 1023. This gives the Web server a destination port with which to communicate to the client, and also allows the client to have *multiple* Web browsers open and going to *different* Web sites because each instance of Internet Explorer *dynamically generates a unique and distinct source port number*. In Figure 2-3, two devices are establishing a TCP-based communication. The Internet Explorer client is connecting to the Web server by using destination port 80 (the TCP port assigned to HTTP). In addition, the client has dynamically opened port 1028 and assigned it to the active Internet Explorer window. When the Web server attempts to communicate back to the client, it uses destination port 1028 and source port 80.

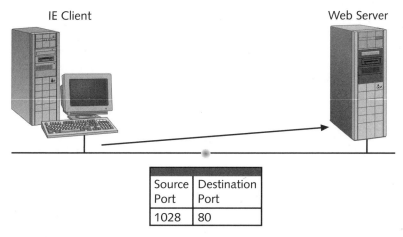

IE Client	Web Server

Source Port	Destination Port
1028	80

Figure 2-3   Port numbers keep application sessions separate and unique

Internet Layer

Despite the complexity of TCP/IP communication at all layers of the TCP/IP model, most network administrators think of the Internet layer as the point where all the action happens. This is because this layer usually requires the majority of administrative configuration on a network. The Internet layer is where all network devices receive a logically configured IP address used for network communication. Setting up IP addressing schemes is one of the most important duties of a network administrator. It involves planning for future network expansion, assigning proper gateway and client addresses, and configuring common IP services such as DHCP, DNS, and WINS in efficient and fault-tolerant locations. This is discussed later in this chapter.

The IP packet or datagram header contains much key communication information; however, the primary goal of the header is to present the source and destination IP addresses and the upper Transport layer protocol number to use. The source and destination IP addresses are just that, the source IP address of the computer originating the packet, and the destination IP address of the computer receiving the packet. The **protocol number** identifies the upper Transport layer protocol that should receive the incoming data. For example, if an application uses TCP as the Transport layer protocol, it assigns a protocol number of six. For UDP, applications use a protocol number of 17. Appendix B provides a reference of commonly used transport protocol numbers.

 Do not confuse the protocol number with the port number! Remember, the protocol number identifies the Transport layer protocol used in network communication, whereas the port number identifies the upper layer application, the final destination of transmitted data.

Once the communicating device identifies the destination IP address with which to communicate, the device must identify the Data Link layer MAC address to reach the bottom layers of communication. The TCP/IP protocol suite includes the Internet layer utility ARP to resolve IP addresses to MAC addresses. To attain the correct MAC address, the communicating device first looks at the IP address to determine if the location of the destination host is on the same local network segment. If the IP address turns out to be local, the source device issues a **broadcast** ARP request for the corresponding MAC address. At that point, provided the destination computer is running, it responds with a **unicast**, or directed message, stating its network card's MAC address. If the client finds that the destination IP address is on a remote network segment, it sends an ARP request for the MAC address of the local network segment's default gateway (the router allowing you to leave the local network segment).

Data Link/Physical Layer

Some TCP/IP architecture diagrams group the Data Link and Physical layers together as a single, combined Physical layer because the majority of functions in both layers fall outside the scope of the TCP/IP suite. The TCP/IP Data Link layer allows for different encapsulation methods or frame-types for WAN communication. The commonly used encapsulation types are the **Point-to-Point Protocol (PPP)**, or PPP's predecessor, the **Serial Line Internet Protocol (SLIP)**. These protocols are discussed in more detail later in this chapter. The functionality of these two layers mirror the OSI model Data Link and Physical layer functionality. Refer to the previous discussion of the OSI model for further detail.

BUILDING THE **TCP/IP** NETWORK ENVIRONMENT

In the TCP/IP network environment, many different types of equipment communicate across the network. Network technology has reached a stage where anything can have an IP address assignment, including computers, cars, kitchen appliances, and family pets. Regardless of the type of network device, it is called a **TCP/IP client**.

TCP/IP Clients

The term TCP/IP client refers to any network device that has a valid TCP/IP address. This enables the device to communicate with other TCP/IP hosts on the network. A network administrator can configure an IP address on a network device in two ways: using a static assignment or dynamic assignment. Although it once was the most common way to assign IP addresses, static assignment is not used as often as dynamic assignment. Static assignment requires the network administrator to manually configure each network device with, at minimum, the IP address and subnet mask, and usually the default gateway as well. Today, only devices with addresses that cannot change use static addressing. These devices typically include Web servers, DNS and/or WINS servers, default gateways (or routers), network printers, and file/print servers. Because configuring every device manually requires an overwhelming amount of administrative overhead and troubleshooting, administrators typically rely on dynamic address assignment. Dynamic assignment allows the administrator to configure a machine to acquire an IP address from a **Bootstrap Protocol (BOOTP)** compliant server (for more information regarding the BOOTP protocol, see RFC 1542 at *http://www.ietf.org/rfc/rfc1542.txt*). The most common implementation of the BOOTP protocol is the **Dynamic Host Configuration Protocol (DHCP)**. DHCP allows you to configure a pool of IP addresses on a designated DHCP server. When a TCP/IP client that is configured to use DHCP boots up, it sends out a broadcast DHCP request message. When the DHCP server receives the request, it responds and assigns the requesting client, at a minimum, an IP address and subnet mask.

TCP/IP Routers

TCP/IP routers give IP-based networks the ability to expand to enterprise-sized networks. Without TCP/IP routers, the Internet could not exist. On a hub or switch-based network, the quality of TCP/IP broadcasts increases significantly as the number of devices on a network segment increases. This places restrictions on the number of computers a network segment can have. The number of broadcasts on a network segment affects not only the amount of network traffic, but also the amount of load on the processors of the attached devices. You can significantly degrade a computer's performance by simply plugging in a network cable. A measurable processor load can be seen on devices attached to networks with as few as 20 broadcasts per second. Table 2-3 provides general guidelines for network size restrictions based on protocols in use.

Table 2-3   Maximum Suggested Clients Residing on a Flat Network Segment

Protocol	Maximum Number of Workstations
IP	500
IPX	300
AppleTalk	200
NetBIOS	200
Mixed	200

While routers do serve a variety of other functions, the main purpose of a router is to split up **broadcast domains**. A broadcast domain is defined by how far a broadcast can travel on a network before it ends. Most broadcasts in networks are Data Link layer broadcasts or MAC broadcasts. Because routers work at the OSI model Network layer, layer-two (Presentation) level broadcasts do not propagate past the router. Imagine the network chaos if one broadcast could traverse the entire Internet! When designing TCP/IP networks, deciding where to place routers determines network traffic levels on all network segments, and limits broadcast-based network services such as DHCP and service advertisements. Figure 2-4 demonstrates a network divided into two broadcast domains.

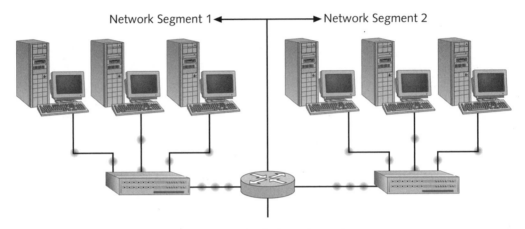

Network Segment 1 ◄━━━━━━►Network Segment 2

Figure 2-4   Splitting a network into multiple broadcast domains

In addition to splitting up broadcast domains, routers also provide remote access to private networks. This allows network users to dial into the network using a modem, or allows connections to the network through a public network, usually the Internet, by using **Virtual Private Networks (VPNs)**, as shown in Figure 2-5. The router and internal network treats these users as if they were directly connected to the LAN segment until the user terminates the connection.

Because routers work at the Network layer, they naturally deal with IP and IPX logical addressing. By viewing the incoming network address, routers can determine the next network point to which the packet should be forwarded. Routers can also view the packet and identify a variety of attributes located in the IP or IPX header. By using these attributes, routers can make intelligent forwarding decisions. Administrators can also use these attributes to place restrictions as to what traffic can enter and leave the network through the router. Once these Network layer restrictions are in place, this router can be called a network firewall.

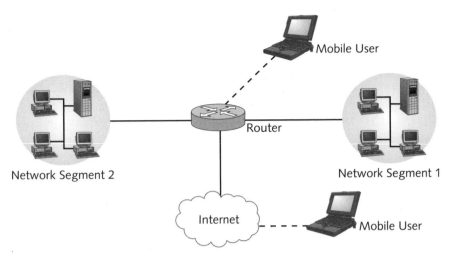

Figure 2-5   Providing internal LAN access to remote access clients

Network Firewalls

A **network firewall** is a system designed to prevent unauthorized access to or from a private network. There are many different implementations of network firewalls through different vendor platforms. These implementations may be either hardware or software based. Firewalls typically protect internal, private networks as well as intranets from unauthorized access by Internet users. The network firewall determines what internal network services, if any, are accessible from the external network. The firewall inspects all data passing through to ensure illicit traffic does not enter or leave the network.

The simplicity of using network firewalls is its major benefit. Many people believe that to increase network security, administrators need to implement complex security schemes throughout the enterprise network. However, as the security methods increase in complexity, in the end, they become easier to break through. Increased complexity means more programming code, and more programming code leaves more room for error. All that hackers need in order to break a security scheme is one poorly written line of code to manipulate to their advantage. Network firewalls use a basic security implementation, which examines the packet and segment headers, looking at who is sending the data and what they are attempting to access. This allows hackers much less application code to manipulate.

Network firewalls usually work at the Network and Transport layers of the OSI model, allowing them to view source and destination IP addresses and port numbers. In recent implementations (such as ISA Server 2000), the firewalls have advanced to nearly all layers of the OSI model, breaking apart code at the Application layers, allowing true content screening for various applications.

Another way to increase security with network firewalls is to use a **Demilitarized Zone (DMZ)**. The DMZ is the portion of your LAN placed between two firewalls: an external firewall and an internal firewall. See Figure 2-6 for an illustration of a DMZ. The DMZ typically contains devices accessible from the Internet such as Web servers, FTP servers, and e-mail servers. The security on the external firewall is not as high as the security on the internal firewall. This allows external clients to access public servers, such as your Web server, without compromising the security of internal clients. DMZ configuration strategies are further discussed in chapter seven.

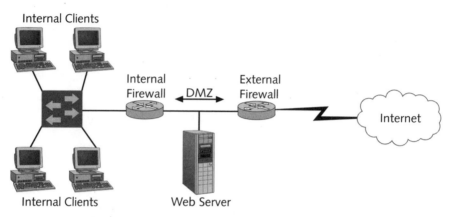

Figure 2-6   The Demilitarized Zone

 Demilitarized Zones are also known as perimeter networks.

Deploying TCP/IP Address and Hostname Management

Through time, the TCP/IP suite of protocols was developed to include more utilities and conventions to make it easier for network administrators to configure devices for TCP/IP and assign user-friendly names to devices instead of just four-octet decimal numbers. As development of TCP/IP continued, different conventions emerged for address assignment and host naming; however, three standards became prominent in the industry: the DHCP, which automatically configures IP addressing information on client systems, the **Domain Name System (DNS)**, which maps device hostnames to IP addresses, and the **Windows Internet Name Service (WINS)**, which maps NetBIOS names to IP addresses.

DHCP Overview

DHCP is an extension of the older BOOTP standard for allocating IP addresses. However, DHCP is compatible with older BOOTP clients and routers, making it much easier for administrators to upgrade their networks gradually. DHCP adds enhancements to the prior BOOTP protocol making it the preferred protocol in major networks. For example, DHCP supports the concept of a lease which assigns a specific amount of time that a client can have an assigned IP address before it must renew the assigned address. If the client does not renew, the DHCP server reclaims the address. This feature is primarily implemented by Internet service providers who assign short lease times to IP addresses, thus preventing the public Internet address pool from running out of addresses.

The address assignment process involves broadcasts, which emphasizes the importance of planning router placement. As a DHCP device attaches to the network for the first time, it broadcasts a DHCPDISCOVER packet in an attempt to find a DHCP server on the local segment. If a DHCP server resides on the segment, it replies with a DHCPOFFER packet, which contains IP configuration information, including the IP address assignment. If there is no DHCP server on the local network segment, the network administrator must configure the routers either to forward BOOTP broadcasts to all attached segments, or to implement an **IP Helper-Address**, allowing the router to send a directed message to a DHCP server on the network segment. Once the client receives and accepts the assigned IP address, it issues a DHCPREQUEST packet to the DHCP server that sent the offer, confirming the decision to keep the IP address. To finish the process, the DHCP server issues a DHCPACK, acknowledging and finalizing the IP assignment.

DNS Overview

DNS is an Internet service that translates host and domain names into IP addresses. The sole purpose behind DNS is to make names easier to remember. The Internet, however, bases all communication on IP addresses. Therefore, every time a user types in a domain name, such as *www.microsoft.com*, a DNS server somewhere must translate the name into the corresponding IP address, such as 207.46.230.219.

The DNS system is a network itself, using a hierarchical structure to resolve hostnames. Since the Internet has grown to an enormous size, the idea of having the entire DNS name-mapping database on every Internet DNS server is nearly impossible. Because of this, the Internet DNS servers have specific groups of names they are responsible for, which are called their **zone of authority**. When a user types a domain name into an Internet browser, DNS resolves the name from right to left. For example, in the hostname *www.microsoft.com*, the .com extension resolves first, followed by Microsoft, then www. The upper-level DNS servers maintain the data for the top-layer zones such as .com, .edu, and .org, among many others. These servers then redirect name resolution requests down to the servers containing the more specific data. Figure 2-7 shows a basic example of a DNS namespace hierarchy. At the top of the scheme is the root domain, represented by a dot (.). These servers look for the extension of the DNS name (such as .com, .edu, or .org) and redirect the resolution to a domain-level DNS server. The next level down resolves the domain name (such as Microsoft, Yahoo, or Ebay) of the DNS request and forwards the request down to the second-level DNS domain server. These

DNS servers are typically located on the individual company's internal network and usually resolve the hostname (such as www or sales) of the internal server, but can also resolve sub-domains, such as training, as shown in Figure 2-7.

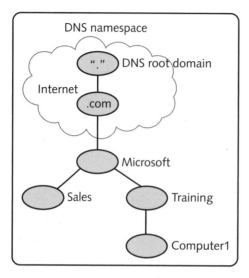

Figure 2-7   Example of a DNS namespace hierarchy

Because DNS servers hold the key to Internet and internal network hostname resolution, they are susceptible to a variety of attacks from hackers. Therefore, DNS servers typically reside behind multiple firewalls, having a high degree of security protection.

UNDERSTANDING NETWORK ADDRESS TRANSLATION

Network Address Translation (NAT) allows businesses to work around the shortage of public Internet addresses and provides Internet access to hundreds, if not thousands, of internal users. NAT serves two primary purposes: first, to provide a type of firewall, hiding internal addresses from the Internet; second, to allow companies to use private internal addressing schemes without conflicting with public addresses. The popularity of NAT in corporate networks continues to increase daily.

Administrators can configure NAT in one of two primary modes: **static NAT** or **dynamic NAT**. Network administrators using static NAT usually concern themselves more with the security features of NAT than the address conservation benefits. Static NAT involves a one-to-one mapping of public IP addresses to private IP addresses. For example, a network administrator might map the internal IP address 10.30.5.26 to the public IP address 24.1.254.63. From this point on, whenever the host 10.30.5.26 attempts to access the Internet, it always uses 24.1.254.63. Without security configuration, this process also happens in the reverse: anyone from the Internet accessing

24.1.254.63 is translated to 10.30.5.26. Because nearly every NAT router also has firewall capabilities, this process is controllable. Devices using static NAT usually need to be accessible to the public, which is why the one-to-one IP translation is necessary. These devices can include, but are not limited to Web and FTP servers, VPN Servers, and telnet servers. In Figure 2-8, three internal clients using private addressing are statically mapped to three public IP addresses (i.e. 192.168.0.2 is seen on the Internet as 131.107.1.10).

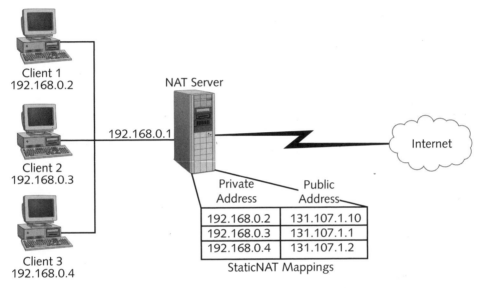

Figure 2-8   Mapping private IP addresses to public IP addresses one-to-one

Dynamic NAT provides a measure of security, but also allows many private internal addresses to share one public, Internet address. This can allow you to purchase one or two public Internet addresses to grant access to thousands of internal users. Dynamic NAT implementations can vary in the method used to translate private to public addresses, but most of these implementations work through the use of dynamically assigned port numbers. For example, suppose a user on the internal LAN whose computer has the IP address 10.20.5.1, attempts to access *www.microsoft.com* through a Web browser. The NAT server receives the request and sees that it must forward the request to the Internet. The NAT server creates an address translation table and dynamically assigns the client a port number, typically above 8000. For this example, suppose the NAT server assigns the client port 8050. At this point, the NAT server replaces the private, internal network address with the public, Internet valid address. It then forwards the request to *www.microsoft.com* using the public address with the destination port of 80 (default port number for HTTP) and a source port of 8050. The Web server at *www.microsoft.com* receives the request on port 80, and sends the requested data to the public address of the NAT server with a destination port of 8050. Once the NAT server receives the requested data from *www.microsoft.com*, it compares the destination port number with the memory-resident address translation table and locates the entry that shows port 8050 has been assigned to the internal address 10.20.5.1. Once the NAT server locates the mapping, it forwards the data from the Web site to the internal client, as illustrated in Figure 2-9. Using this method of access allows the NAT server to translate for many internal users accessing the Web at the same time simply by assigning them different dynamic port numbers. The only limitation is the number of available, unused port numbers that the configuration of the NAT server allows it to use.

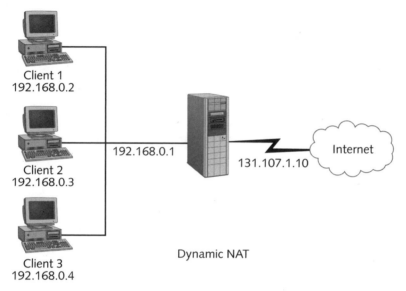

Figure 2-9   Mapping private IP addresses to public IP addresses using a one-to-many relationship

UNDERSTANDING TUNNELING

Because of the high cost of dedicated WAN connections between remote offices, many businesses have turned to the Internet to lower expenses. When leasing a connection from a service provider, it is much less expensive to purchase a connection to the Internet than to buy a dedicated connection between two remote sites. Once you connect two locations to the Internet, you can use virtual private networking to create a tunnel through the Internet connecting the remote sites. However, when using a public network, such as the Internet, to connect your WAN sites, you take security risks. To keep the VPN secure, Microsoft allows two choices of secure tunneling protocols included with ISA Server: the Point-to-Point Tunneling and Layer Two Tunneling protocols.

Understanding the Point-to-Point Tunneling Protocol

The Point-to-Point Tunneling Protocol (PPTP) is a relatively new technology used in creating virtual private networks. PPTP, as the name implies, creates a virtual tunnel across the Internet or other public network, allowing home offices, mobile users, and branch offices to tie into their corporate network through a low-cost connection. It accomplishes this by encapsulating multiple protocols (IP, IPX, and NetBEUI) inside IP packets and transmitting them across the public network. While transmitting, PPTP uses Point-to-Point (PPP) encryption to ensure the data sent across the public network remains secure. In addition, PPTP supports the commonly used authentication protocols such as **Password Authentication Protocol (PAP)** and the **Microsoft Challenge Handshake Authentication Protocol (MS-CHAP)**, which will be discussed in detail in later chapters.

The designers of PPTP include Microsoft Corporation, U.S. Robotics, and several other remote-access companies. The PPTP is currently waiting for Internet standardization and is currently available only on networks using Windows NT, Windows 2000, or Linux servers.

Understanding the Layer Two Tunneling Protocol

Layer Two Tunneling Protocol (L2TP) has become the next step in the evolution of PPTP in providing for VPN access through public networks. Designers consider L2TP to be a type of hybrid protocol, combining the best features of Microsoft's PPTP and Cisco's Layer Two Forwarding (L2F). The improvements of L2TP threaten to push PPTP technology to the sidelines. Some of the key differences between PPTP and L2TP are as follows:

- L2TP uses the industry standard **Internet Protocol Security (IPSec)** for encryption, while PPTP uses PPP encryption. Although the PPTP can use IPSec encryption in addition to PPP encryption, the performance degradation of a dual-encryption technique typically outweighs any security benefit.

- L2TP supports header compression, whereas PPTP does not. This causes significant performance gains over WAN connections.

- L2TP has the ability to tunnel authentication, while PPTP does not.

- L2TP can function over any packet-oriented network providing point-to-point connectivity. This can include IP, Frame Relay Permanent Virtual Circuits (PVCs), X.25 VCs, or Asynchronous Transfer Mode (ATM) VCs. PPTP requires the network be IP based.

CONFIGURING IP ADDRESSES

Before installing any firewall system or ISA Servers, the complete IP addressing scheme for the internal corporate network must be in place.

A thorough understanding of IP addressing is necessary for the Microsoft ISA Server 2000 Certification exam.

Every device connected to a TCP/IP network requires a unique IP address. Because the current industry standard is TCP/IP version four, IP addresses consist of four separate octets, as shown in Figure 2-10. Due to the limitations of a 32-bit addressing scheme, digits in each octet can range only from zero up to 255. Before discussing IP addressing and subnetting strategies, you must understand binary conversion tactics, discussed in the following section.

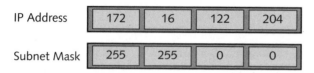

| IP Address | 172 | 16 | 122 | 204 |
| Subnet Mask | 255 | 255 | 0 | 0 |

Figure 2-10   Standard Class B IP address

Binary Conversion

Suppose that Mark Fellmer, scientist extraordinaire, recently stumbled across a formula allowing him to create unbreakable bricks. After patenting his discovery, he opened a brick shop, calling it *Unbreak-o-brick*, to sell his invention. Word of the *Unbreak-o-brick* caught on, and soon many customers began to visit Mark's business. Unfortunately, Mark was science minded and did not have much sense for business management. To start the company, he had manufactured 25,000 bricks and placed them in a large pile in the back of the shop. For every customer who bought bricks, Mark would run to the back, manually count out the order, and bring it to the customer's vehicle, brick by brick. Soon, lines began to build, and customers became impatient, many of them leaving without their orders being satisfied. Late one evening, Mark attempted to think of a system allowing him to serve customers speedily. Suddenly it hit him! He could palletize all the bricks, allowing him to quickly fulfill customer's orders. With that, Mark sorted the pile of 25,000 bricks into even pallets of the following sizes, as shown in Table 2-4.

Table 2-4   Brick Pallet Sizes

Pallet Size:	128 Bricks	64 Bricks	32 Bricks	16 Bricks	8 Bricks	4 Bricks	2 Bricks	1 Brick

Because Mark had no experience operating a forklift, he hired an experienced forklift operator to move pallets to each customer's vehicle. Now, when a customer places an order, Mark will fill out the paperwork, and then send a document to a printer located next to the forklift operator, showing which size pallets to move. When the first business day of the week arrived, the initial customer through the door requested 96 bricks. It was time to put the system to the test. Mark filled out the necessary paperwork, and printed a document to the forklift operator that looked like the order in Table 2-5.

Table 2-5   Unbreak-o-Brick Order #452

Pallet Size:	128	64	32	16	8	4	2	1
Quantity Required:	0	1	1	0	0	0	0	0

The forklift driver quickly moved the flagged pallets to the customer's vehicle while Mark continued helping customers in the lobby. The next customer ordered 220 bricks, typically a daunting task for the old system. Instead, a sheet similar to Table 2-6 printed on the forklift operator's printer.

Table 2-6   Unbreak-o-Brick Order #453

Pallet Size:	128	64	32	16	8	4	2	1
Quantity Required:	1	1	0	1	1	1	0	0

Sure enough, Mark's system was a success. Customer's satisfaction ratings went through the roof, and Mark lived happily ever after. So, what is the moral of this short story? Binary conversion is as simple as palletizing bricks.

Binary conversion follows nearly an identical scheme to Mark's palletizing system. When people deal with IP addresses, they typically think in decimal numbers, such as 50.32.201.25, or 10.64.70.130. When a network device works with IP addresses, it works with binary numbers. IP addresses define two critical pieces of information used to locate network devices: the network and the host portion of the IP address (this is discussed in the following sections). To find which portion of the IP address defines the network and which portion defines the host, you must convert the IP address and **subnet mask** to binary. Because a standard TCP/IP address is 32 bits long, each of the four octets receives eight bits. This eight-bit limitation is the reason each octet can only reach a value of 255. Each of these eight bits represents a specific decimal number, which happens to be the same numbers Mark used when palletizing bricks. Many math-minded individuals may recognize these numbers as two raised to incremental exponential powers, as shown in Table 2-7.

Table 2-7   Incremental Powers of Two

Exponential Power	7	6	5	4	3	2	1	0
Resulting Value	128	64	32	16	8	4	2	1

The process for converting a complete IP address to binary requires us to move one octet at a time. Take the IP address 50.32.201.25, octet by octet, as shown in Tables 2-8 through 2-12.

Table 2-8   Octet One, Decimal Value 50

128	64	32	16	8	4	2	1
0	0	1	1	0	0	1	0

Table 2-9   Octet Two, Decimal Value 32

128	64	32	16	8	4	2	1
0	0	1	0	0	0	0	0

Table 2-10   Octet Three, Decimal Value 201

128	64	32	16	8	4	2	1
1	1	0	0	1	0	0	1

Table 2-11   Octet Four, Decimal Value 25

128	64	32	16	8	4	2	1
0	0	0	1	1	0	0	1

Table 2-12   Complete IP Address Binary Conversion

Decimal	50	32	201	25
Binary	00110010	00100000	11001001	00011001

Subnet Mask

The subnet mask is the only other configuration field required for TCP/IP to operate successfully on a local network segment. The subnet mask allows the source network device to determine whether the destination device is on the local network segment, or a remote network segment. The telephone company makes this same decision every time you make a phone call. When you dial a number, the telephone company central office (CO) determines if the number is local to the area. If it is, it switches the signal to the correct local telephone set. However, if you dial out of the area, the CO must then route the call to another CO that handles the specific area you dialed. In the same way, by processing the configured subnet mask, the source device knows if it has to send the frame on the local network segment, or if it needs to send the frame to a **router** that can determine the correct network segment to send it to.

Every IP address has two components: a network identifier and a host identifier. The subnet mask simply identifies the two pieces. Because of this, the subnet mask is complementary to the IP address, that is, it never stands on its own. Take, for instance, the following IP address and subnet mask pair:

IP address: 172.16.32.55
Subnet mask: 255.255.0.0

Before you can determine the network and host portions of the IP address, you must convert both the IP address and subnet mask to binary form using "Mark's palletizing method."

> IP address: 10101100.00010000.00100000.00110111
> Subnet Mask: 11111111.11111111.00000000.00000000

When you look at a subnet mask in binary form, all bits of the IP address that match the ones represent the network identifier, and all bits of the IP address that match the zeros represent the host identifier. In this example, 172.16 represents the network, and 32.55 represents the host. The communicating device consistently uses this critical information to determine whether a given device is local or remote. If the IP address begins with anything other than 172.16, it considers it a remote device and sends all frames to the local segment's router to determine the correct path to the remote segment. Otherwise, the source device attempts to communicate with the destination device on the local network segment. When working with subnet masks, try not to get into the habit of looking at the decimal form of the subnet mask and dividing the network and host portions. When using the standard class A, B, and C subnet masks (discussed in the following section), this may be fairly simple; however, once you work with more complex subnet examples, binary conversion becomes a necessity.

Binary conversion is also helpful in determining the number of host addresses available on a network segment. By using the formula $(2^n) - 2$, where n equals the number of bits used for host addressing, you can find how many usable host addresses you can assign. For example, if you use the subnet mask 255.255.0.0 (binary = 11111111.11111111.00000000.00000000), 16 are bits used for host addressing. Using the formula, you find that $(2^{16}) - 2$, provides 65,536 possible host addresses on the network segment.

When working with IP addressing, you must be aware of certain restrictions on host addresses. No device or interface on a network can have a setting of all zeros or ones. Subtract two in the host calculation formula $(2^n) - 2$ to account for these unusable addresses. Host addresses set to all zeros (i.e., 172.16.0.0) serve as an identifier for the network itself. When referring to the 172.16.0.0 IP address, you refer to the entire range of IP addresses from 172.16.0.0 to 172.16.255.255, assuming a subnet mask of 255.255.0.0. Routers also use this type of identification in locating the network to receive routed packets. Likewise, host address bits set to all ones (i.e., 172.16.255.255) represent a broadcast address for the network segment. If a network device wanted to send data to all devices on the 172.16.0.0 network, it would set the destination address of the packet to be 172.16.255.255, assuming a 255.255.0.0 subnet mask.

Classes of Addresses

In the initial development stages of TCP/IP, no classes of addresses were defined. Eventually, to make IP addressing simpler, ARPA developed five major classes of IP addresses for administrators to work with:

- *Class A*—Class A addresses use the first eight bits of the IP address to represent the Network ID, leaving the last 24 bits to represent the Host ID. Class A addressing provides for the following:

  Range of network numbers: 1.0.0.0 to 127.0.0.0
  Default subnet mask: 255.0.0.0
  Number of possible networks: 127
  Number of possible hosts per network: 16,777,214

- *Class B*—Class B addresses use the first 16 bits of the IP address to represent the Network ID, leaving the last 16 bits to represent the Host ID. Class B addressing provides for the following:

  Range of network numbers: 128.0.0.0 to 191.255.0.0
  Default subnet mask: 255.255.0.0
  Number of possible networks: 16,384
  Number of possible hosts per network: 65,534

- *Class C*—Class C addresses use the first 24 bits of the IP address to represent the Network ID, leaving the last eight bits to represent the Host ID. Class C addressing provides for the following:

  Range of network numbers: 192.0.0.0 to 223.255.255.0
  Default subnet mask: 255.255.255.0
  Number of possible networks: 2,097,152
  Number of possible hosts per network: 254

- *Class D*—Class D addresses are reserved for **multicasting** purposes; that is, sending a stream of IP addressed data to a group of computers. Multicast addresses reside in the network ranges 224.0.0.0 to 239.255.255.255.

- *Class E*—Class E addresses are reserved for experimental purposes and are not used in production environments. This address range encompasses the addresses after 240.0.0.0.

In addition to the five classes of IP addresses, TCP/IP developers identified three ranges of IP addresses called **private networking ranges**. One range of private addresses resides in each of the first three address classes. They are as follows:

- *Class A*—10.0.0.0 to 10.255.255.255

- *Class B*—172.16.0.0 to 172.31.255.255

- *Class C*—192.168.0.0 to 192.168.255.255

These ranges were developed to address the issue of conflicting Internet address usage on internal LANs. As unique Internet addresses became increasingly scarce, network administrators began to run TCP/IP as their internal LAN protocol by selecting arbitrary IP addresses and assigning them to client machines. This works fine for internal communication, but can cause major problems if the internal network connects to the Internet. Because no two host addresses can be identical, once the exposure of the internal LAN to the Internet occurs, all network communication ceases. The private addresses in the ranges listed above prevent this from happening because they do not forward data after they reach Internet routers. All data coming from these address ranges is discarded by the first Internet router reached, which eliminates the potential for disruption of network communication.

When developing a network addressing scheme, these private classes of addresses not only allow specialized uses of IP addressing, but also permit a great amount of network address flexibility based on network sizes. If you are working with an enterprise-size network, you might choose to use a Class A or B addressing scheme, allowing for much expandability. For Small Office/Home Office (SOHO)-size networks, you might choose to use a Class C addressing scheme. As you might imagine, no physical network topology currently can support the Class A or Class B host addressing ability of addressing, respectively, 16,777,214 or 65,534 hosts per network segment. Because of this, you must modify the subnet mask to allow more realistic host address numbers without wasting large amounts of IP addresses. This introduces the practice of custom subnetting.

IMPLEMENTING CUSTOM SUBNETTING

In the past five to ten years, TCP/IP has moved from the protocol used in connecting computers to the Internet to the standard LAN and WAN protocol used throughout the industry. Likewise, five to ten years ago, custom subnetting was a concept primarily left to ISPs and specialized TCP/IP experts. Today, however, understanding custom subnetting is critical to your success in *any* TCP/IP-based network environment. This next section discusses TCP/IP custom subnetting in depth.

The Purpose of Subnetting

To work around the set boundaries of the standard Class A, B, and C subnet masks, administrators can develop their own custom subnetting schemes. Using custom subnetting allows you to work around the "one network, many hosts" system of standard **classful** IP addressing. The term classful IP addressing describes any network situation where a network administrator uses only standard Class A, B, and C subnet masks to build their network. This can be very limiting since you have only the option to have one network of approximately 16 million, 65 thousand, or 254 hosts. For example, if you use the network 10.0.0.0 in its classful state, you would have one network with over 16 million host addresses available. Today, large networks with large amounts of bandwidth can handle somewhere between two to three thousand hosts on a network segment. Imagine using the classful 10.0.0.0 address in this situation. This provides enough addresses for the segment, but once you use the 10.0.0.0 network range, you cannot reuse it anywhere else on the network. This wastes millions of potentially unusable IP addresses.

Custom subnetting lets you look at a network design scenario from a **classless** point of view where you are able to apply subnet masks other than the default configuration. When you lift the classful restriction, instead of having one network with many hosts, you can have many networks with fewer hosts. The concept behind subnetting is simple. IP subnetting takes bits from the host side and adds them to the network side of the subnet mask. These subnet mask modifications are done on a bit-by-bit basis, allowing for complete control over how many bits can change roles from representing either the network or the host portion. Because of this, it is essential to understand and be comfortable working with binary IP addressing.

Subnet Addressing

Modifying the subnet mask of a large network extends the network bits to allow for more reasonably sized sub-networks. It becomes your responsibility as a network administrator to decide the size of these subnets (this is discussed later in this chapter). A network device uses the subnet mask in determining what portions of the IP address represent the network, the subnet, and the host addresses, as illustrated in Figure 2-11.

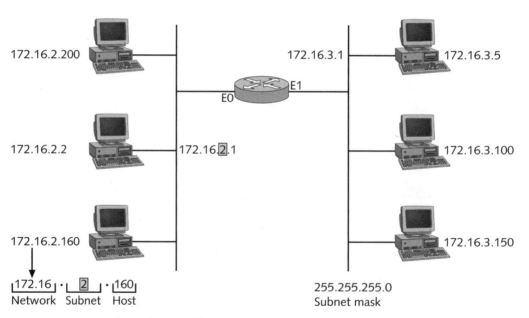

Figure 2-11 Breaking the IP address into three portions: the network, sub-network, and host addresses

This information is critical to the communicating device because by observing the subnet mask it can determine if the host it is attempting to communicate with is located on the local network segment or on a remote network segment. If it finds that the destination IP address is on the local segment, it sends an ARP broadcast request, attempting to resolve the local host's MAC address. If it finds the destination IP address to be on a remote segment, it sends an ARP broadcast message to resolve the MAC address of the default gateway, or router, that can communicate with segments other than the local one.

Planning and Defining a Subnet Mask

Before you apply any subnet masks to network segments and assign any IP addresses to host devices, be sure to complete a planning phase where you plan and define the IP addressing scheme you will use. This planning phase of IP addressing includes data that you as a network administrator gather from the current network and any assumptions and projections you can make based on future plans. The biggest mistake that administrators can make is to not plan for the future of the corporate network. When designing an IP addressing scheme for a company, talk with management. Have them present their plans for the company's future. Find out which divisions could see the most growth, and what the growth potential in the best and worst-case scenario could be. This could mean a complete network reconstruction within a few months to a few years, depending on the pace of company growth. Make sure that you choose an IP addressing scheme that does not closely limit the number of hosts you can add on a network segment. For example, management might want you to set up an IP addressing scheme to accommodate five groups of 55 people. It would not be prudent to choose a subnetting scheme that allows a maximum of 62 people on a network segment. Unless the company does not plan to grow at all, this subnetting scheme becomes unusable once the company adds seven more users on one network segment. Do not use a subnet mask that gives networks a "tight fit." While it may look great on paper, this type of subnetting scheme does not allow for flexibility in segment growth and will need an overhaul within a short period of time. Before any subnetting occurs, ensure that you have three critical pieces of information written down:

1. *Class of address to subnet*—By identifying the IP address as being Class A, B, or C, you identify the default subnet mask to work with.

2. *Number of sub-networks needed*—You are breaking one large network range of IP addresses into smaller sub-networks. Identify how many smaller networks you will need.

3. *Number of hosts per sub-network*—When subnetting, you are essentially stealing bits from the host portion of the IP address and giving them to the network portion. Ensure that you identify the number of hosts needed on each network segment, and allow room for expandability.

Defining Subnet Bits

After you plan the company growth patterns and identify the three key pieces of information for subnetting, you can begin working with the subnet mask. By moving the boundary of the standard subnet mask, you begin to create the bits used in the sub-networks. For example, if you decide to use the Class B subnet range 172.16.0.0 for your network, you would have a standard subnet mask of 255.255.0.0, designating the first two octets as your network identification bits and the last two octets as your host identification bits. If you "stole" eight bits from the host portion by appending the subnet mask 255.255.255.0 to your network address, you would then have the first two octets (16 bits) of the IP address still representing the network identification, the third octet (eight bits) representing the sub-network identification, and the fourth octet (eight bits) representing the host identification. By using the formula $(2^n) - 2$, you find that you can have a maximum of 254 sub-networks with a maximum of 254 hosts located on each.

In this subnetting example, you dedicated an entire octet to the sub-networks (in essence, you appended a Class C subnet mask to a Class B address). By doing this, you moved from having 65,534 available host addresses on one network down to 254 available host addresses on many networks. This is quite a jump! To accommodate all the network sizes of today, you need to get into the binary of the subnet mask to work in host numbers that are more reasonable.

USING THE A-F SUBNETTING PROCESS

You can use a variety of methods to find subnet masks. If you have already been introduced to the concept of subnetting and are comfortable with your current method, feel free to continue using it. The following is a compilation of many methods into one systematic process. This process allows network administrators to develop a network-wide subnet mask to fit the corporate needs. You can divide this process up into six general steps, A–F:

1. **A**cquire the number of subnets

2. **B**inary equivalent

3. **C**onvert to the "high-order"

4. **D**ecimal translation

5. **E**valuate the increment

6. **F**ormula for subnets and hosts

Step 1: Acquire the Number of Subnets

The first step in the six-step process involves identifying the number of sub-networks your company needs. This number can come from a variety of sources. Many network

administrators base the number of subnets on geographical location or wide area network connections (i.e., one subnet allocated for Tokyo, one for California, one for
England, and so on). If you choose to use this method, ensure that you also plan around
the size of the locations. For instance, if California houses the corporate headquarters of
the company, it may have double or triple the users compared to the rest of the sites.
This may require using two different subnet masks in the company, one in California
and one for the rest of the sites. This strategy is called **Variable Length Subnet
Masking (VLSM)**. You can also find the number of subnets you need from the organizational structure of the company or the existing network infrastructure. Once you
identify the number of subnets needed, write the resulting number down.

These steps use the ACME Corporation as an example scenario.

Acme Corporation Scenario

In Step 1, you collect information from ACME. They have decided to use the Internet-
valid IP address range 163.45.0.0. However, instead of having one network with 65,534
hosts, you must break it down to 26 sub-networks for each of the geographic locations
around the world. It is good strategy to write down the given information before continuing to Step 2. Figure 2-12 shows the customer, ACME Corporation, and the given
subnetting information.

Subnetting Scenario

• Customer purchased a Class B
  IP address range (163.45.0.0)

• Subnet the range into 26 segments

Figure 2-12   Step 1: Gathering required information

Step 2: Binary Equivalent

After you identify the number of subnets you need, you must convert this number to binary.
This allows you to identify the number of bits needed for the subnet mask. Figure 2-13
shows this process and the current recorded information.

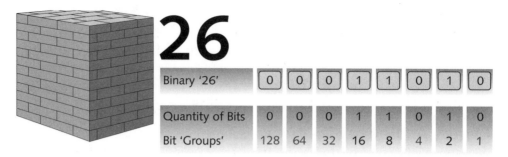

Acme Corporation scenario:
Network range: 163.45.0.0
Subnets required: 26
Binary conversion: 00011010

Figure 2-13   Step 2: Finding the binary equivalent

Step 3: Convert to High-Order

After identifying the binary equivalent of the number of subnets needed, convert this binary number to the high-order. This process involves identifying the number of bits needed to represent the number of subnets. For example, in the ACME Corp. scenario, to represent the number 26, you need five bits. You cannot represent the number 26 with any less than five bits. If the scenario required 38 subnets, you would need six bits. Once you identify the number of bits required, you change those bits to one value, and move them to the left of the octet. Because the binary equivalent of 26 is 00011010 and you need five bits for the ACME network, change those five bits to ones and move them to the left of the octet. The result becomes the binary equivalent 11111000. Figure 2-14 shows this high-order conversion process and the current recorded information.

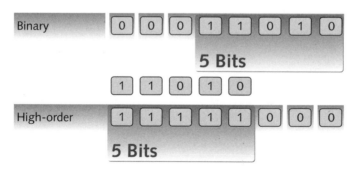

Network range: 163.45.0.0
Subnets required: 26
Binary conversion: 00011010

High-order conversion: 11111000

Figure 2-14   Step 3: Change to the high-order

Step 4: Decimal Translation

After you have converted the binary subnet representation into the high-order, convert the high-order back to decimal. Reversing the "brick palletizing" binary conversion method does this. By taking the decimal equivalent of the places in the high-order binary number 11111000 that equal one, you end up with 128, 64, 32, 16, and 8. Adding these five numbers together provides the decimal equivalent of the high-order conversion, which in this case is 248. By appending this number to the default subnet mask, you now have the subnet mask used in the enterprise wide network. Because you began with the default Class B subnet mask of 255.255.0.0, the new subnet mask becomes 255.255.248.0. This subnet mask provides a sufficient number of subnets to meet the needs of the ACME Corp. Figure 2-15 shows the decimal conversion process and the current recorded information.

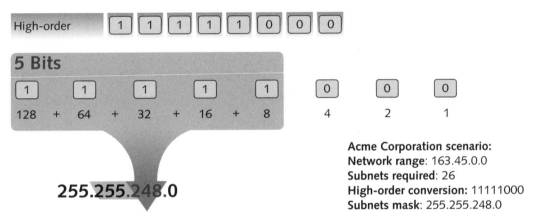

Figure 2-15   Step 4: Decimal translation

Step 5: Examine Network Ranges

In Step 4, you found the subnet mask to use throughout the corporate network; however, knowing this information is not helpful until you know the proper network ranges. After finding the network subnet mask, you must now find the valid sub-network IP address ranges to assign to your network segments. To do this, you once again refer to the high-order conversion from Step 3. By using the decimal equivalent of the lowest value, high-order bit as a type of incremental counter, you can identify the valid network ranges. For example, the ACME Corp high-order conversion is 11111000. The lowest valued, high-order bit is in the place value of the decimal number eight. With that knowledge, you can use eight as your incremental counter, as shown in Figure 2-16.

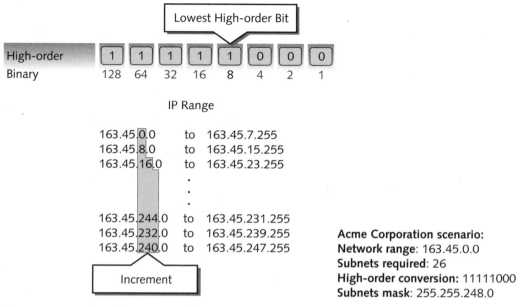

Figure 2-16   Identifying network ranges

You must also remember that the first and last number of each range is unusable. The first number acts as the network identifier, the last number acts as the broadcast IP for the entire subnet, as shown in Figure 2-17.

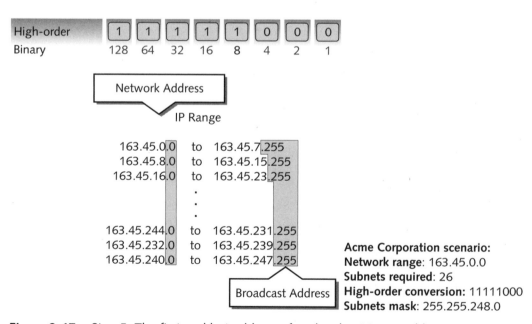

Figure 2-17   Step 5: The first and last address of each subnet is unusable

Step 6: Formula for Subnets and Hosts

At this point in the process, you have identified the number of subnets required, the proper subnet mask, and the network ranges to use for the individual network segments. There is one piece of the puzzle remaining: finding how many total sub-networks and how many hosts per subnet the given subnet mask provides. To find this information, you first need to convert the entire subnet mask to binary. 255.255.248.0 in binary becomes 11111111.11111111.11111000.00000000. The first two octets can be ignored, as these represent your original Class B subnet mask; in this case, you need to focus on the last two octets. The five ones in the third octet represent the sub-network bits used to identify the subnet. The 11 zeros following the five ones represent the host bits. To find the number of sub-networks and hosts available, refer again to the formula discussed earlier. By entering the number of dedicated subnet bits into the $(2^n) - 2$ formula, you have $(2^5) - 2 = 30$ available sub-network ranges to use. Note that you still need to subtract two from the final result. This is because the subnet bits cannot be all zeros or all ones; these are invalid subnet representations. Using the same formula for the host bits, $(2^{11}) - 2 = 2046$ hosts' addresses available in each sub-network range. Figure 2-18 demonstrates this process and the current recorded information.

$$(2^5 - 2) = 30 \text{ Subnets}$$

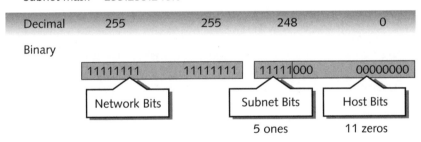

$$(2^{11} - 2) = 2046 \text{ Hosts per subnets}$$

Acme Corporation scenario:
Network range: 163.45.0.0
Subnets required: 26
High-order conversion: 11111000
Subnets mask: 255.255.248.0
Number of available sub-networks: 30
Number of available host address per sub-network 2046

Figure 2-18   Step 6: Counting subnets and hosts

Exception

Every rule has an exception. The six-step process works for any subnet number, with the exception of subnet numbers that change all-low order binary bits to one in Step 2. In Step 2, you convert the number of subnets required to binary. For example, when you convert 31 to binary, you get the binary number 00011111. Note that all the low-order bits are ones. This rule applies to all the numbers listed in Figure 2-19. The simple fix for this is to always add one to your required sub-network number. For example, if you need 31 sub-networks, work through the process as if you needed 32. By always adding one to the network number, you avoid this exception rule.

Number of Subnets	Binary Equivalent	Modified High-Order
3	00000011	11100000
7	00000111	11110000
15	00001111	11111000
31	00011111	11111100
63	00111111	11111110
127	01111111	11111111

Figure 2-19   Exception rule

Why the Six-Step Process Works

Remembering this six-step process can usually get you through any certification exam subnetting situation; however, in the real world, network environment, you need to know the mechanics behind it. By working through this formula, you are finding the number of subnet bits to reserve, then calculating the number of host bits left over. In Steps 1 and 2, you found how many sub-networks the company needed and converted it to binary. This revealed the number of bits you need to set aside to represent the sub-networks. You then changed the number of bits to one and moved them to the left of the octet, causing them to identify the sub-network and not the host. Any bits left over (the zero bits) then became the host bits.

Understanding the mechanics behind this six-step process can allow you to solve any subnetting problem. Minor modifications to the process allow easy solutions to many different scenarios. For example, so far you have seen examples of scenarios where clients needed a certain amount of sub-networks designed for their company. However, what if a client requests a certain amount of hosts per sub-network rather than a certain number of sub-networks? By understanding the binary behind the six-step process, you would see that this request requires only a minor modification from Step 2 to Step 3. It now entails converting the number of *hosts* requested to binary, identifying the number of bits required to represent the host decimal number, changing them to *zero*, and moving them to the *right* of the octet.

Once you get into the habit of working with the binary system, creating sub-networks of any size becomes an easy task. The importance of gaining a thorough understanding of TCP/IP continues to grow as it permeates the entire networking industry.

2

PRACTICING SUBNETTING EXAMPLES

Following are three examples of subnetting using Class A, B, and C address ranges.

Class A Subnetting Sample

Joe Brungs, an aspiring network administrator, has recently sold everything he owns, and purchased the last remaining Class A (30.0.0.0) address from the InterNIC (the government body created to manage the assignment of public, Internet-valid IP addresses). He plans on splitting it into 60 different sub-networks and selling them to private corporations. You need to find:

- The subnet mask to use

- Sub-network ranges of IP addresses

- The number of total hosts per sub-network

- The total number of sub-networks provided

Given: Class A address, 30.0.0.0; Require a minimum of 60 subnetworks

1. Identify the number of sub-networks needed:

   Number of subnets = 60

2. Convert the number of subnets needed to a binary number:

   60 = 00111100

3. Convert the binary number to the high-order (take the # of bits you used to get 60 subnets, which is six, move them to the left-most six bits, and turn them all into ones):

   00111100 becomes 11111100

4. Convert this new binary number to decimal; this becomes your new subnet mask:

   11111100 = 252 therefore Subnet = 255.252.0.0

5. To identify sub-network ranges, take the decimal equivalent of the lowest value, high-order bit, and use it as your increment:

11111100 lowest bit = 4 (this is now your increment). Subnet ranges:
30.0.0.0 – 30.3.255.255 (this is subnet 0, and is not used)
30.4.0.0 – 30.7.255.255 (this is subnet 1)
30.8.0.0 – 30.11.255.255 (this is subnet 2)
...
30.248.0.0 – 30.251.255.255 (final subnet)

Remember the first IP address from the range is your network address, and the final IP address will be your broadcast address for the given subnet.

6. To find the total number of hosts per subnet or the total number of subnets, the formula is the same:

$(2^n - 2)$ where n is the number of bits:
No. of subnets = 6 subnet bits = $(2^6 - 2)$ = 62 subnets
No. of hosts per subnet = 2 host bits (2nd octet) + 8 bits (3rd octet) + 8 bits (4th octet) = $(2^{18} - 2)$ = 262,142 total hosts per subnet

Class B Subnetting Sample Question

You are the network administrator for a large accounting firm. You will be using a private range of Class B addresses for your internal network combined with Network Address Translation (NAT) to provide Internet access for your clients. You decide to use the reserved IP range 172.16.0.0. You want to split this off into 45 separate sub-networks.

Given: IP Network Range 172.16.0.0, need 45 subnets

1. Determine the number of sub-networks needed (45).

2. Convert the number of subnets to binary (00101101).

3. Convert the binary digits to the high-order (11111100).

4. Convert the high-order bits to a decimal number (252) and use this number as your subnet mask (255.255.252.0).

5. To identify network ranges, use the lowest high-order bit as your increment:

11111100 lowest bit = 4, thus network ranges are as follows:
172.16.0.0 – 172.16.3.255 (subnet 0, not used)
172.16.4.0 – 172.16.7.255 (subnet 1)
172.16.8.0 – 172.16.11.255 (subnet 2)
172.16.12.0 – 172.16.15.255 (subnet 3)
...
172.16.244.0 – 172.16.247.255
172.16.248.0 – 172.16.251.255 (final subnet)

Remember the reservations for the first and last IP address for the network and broadcast addresses, respectively.

6. To find the number of sub-networks, use the $(2^n - 2)$ formula, n being the number of bits:

sub-networks $= (2^6 - 2) = 62$ subnets
hosts per subnet $= 2$ bits (3rd octet) $+ 8$ bits (4th octet) $= 10$ bits;
$(2^{10} - 2) = 1022$ hosts per subnet

Class C Subnet Sample Question

You are planning the network schematics for a company that has a Class C Internet-valid IP range reserved (210.40.20.0). This company has a few, small distribution points around the USA, and needs its one class C range split into 12 sub-networks.

Given: Class C address 210.40.20.0; need 12 subnets.

1. Determine the number of subnets the network needs

2. Convert the number of required subnets to binary (00001100)

3. Move the binary digits to the high-order (11110000)

4. Convert the high-order bits to a decimal (240)

5. This becomes your subnet mask (255.255.255.240)

6. Use the lowest high-order bit as your increment; lowest bit of 11110000 is 16. This gets a little tricky, as you now have to make sure you note your network and broadcast domains.

210.40.20.0-15 (subnet 0, not used Network IP = 210.40.20.0, Broadcast = 210.40.20.15)
210.40.20.16-31 (subnet 1, Network IP = 210.40.20.16, Broadcast IP = 210.40.20.31)
210.40.20.32-47 (subnet 2, Network IP = 210.40.20.32, Broadcast IP = 210.40.20.47)
...
210.40.20.224-239 (final subnet, Network IP = 210.40.20.224, Broadcast IP = 210.40.20.239)

7. Total number of subnets & hosts:

subnets $= (2^4 - 2) = 14$ sub-networks
hosts per subnet $= (2^4 - 2) = 14$ hosts per subnet

CHAPTER SUMMARY

❑ The OSI model describes communication between two network devices, and eases the process of network troubleshooting.

❑ Each layer of the OSI model has its own assigned function and process for adding information to the application data.

- The TCP/IP protocol suite was originally comprised of two primary protocols: TCP (describing reliable, session-based communication) and IP (allowing for user-configurable, logical addresses).

- DNS allows for the mapping of user-friendly hostnames to IP addresses.

- Dynamic NAT gives network administrators a method of working around the shortage of Internet-valid IP addresses by allowing many internal, private addresses to share one public IP address. Static NAT gives internal servers an additional layer of security because their IP address is no longer directly exposed to the Internet.

- PPTP and L2TP allow the establishment of VPNs through the Internet. This permits remote users to access the internal LAN without long distance telecommunication costs.

- Classful subnets restrict you to using the standard Class A, B, or C subnet masks.

- Classless subnets allow you to customize your subnet mask to fit your network environment.

- VLSM gives you the ability to use different subnet masks in each area of your network.

KEY TERMS

acknowledgement — Packets sent, typically with TCP-based communication, to acknowledge receipt of data.

Address Resolution Protocol (ARP) — A broadcast-based process used at the Network layer to attain a device's MAC address.

Advanced Research Projects Agency (ARPA) — An agency in the U.S. Department of Defense that created a large area network (LAN) in the 1960s for the free exchange of information between universities and research organizations.

application processes — The programs that use the Application layer in the OSI model.

application-specific elements — Modules, usually written into the base operating system, that perform many common network tasks for communicating between applications. By using these modules, application developers can avoid rewriting large amounts of code, and thus increase application stability.

ARPANET — The precurser to the Internet. The large, wide area network created in the 1960s by the Advanced Research Projects Agency.

bits — Data transmitted at the Physical layer.

Bootstrap Protocol (BOOTP) — A method of allowing a diskless workstation to discover its IP address and boot from a network server.

broadcast — Data addressed to all hosts on a given network segment.

broadcast domain — Describes the scope of devices a given broadcast frame can reach on a network segment. All reachable devices are in the same broadcast domain.

2

classful IP addressing — A network structure where a network administrator uses only standard Class A, B, and C subnet masks to build a network.

classless IP addressing — A network structure where a network administrator applies custom subnet masks to network addresses.

Cyclical Redundancy Check (CRC) — Also called Frame Check Sequence (FCS). A mathematical check at the Data Link layer that allows the receiving device to determine if transmitted data is corrupt.

datagrams — Data passing through the Network layer.

Demilitarized Zone (DMZ) — The LAN segment between the external and internal firewall, allowing more lenient security standards for external hosts to access internal Web, SMTP, and FTP servers.

Domain Name System (DNS) — A TCP/IP service that translates user-friendly hostnames to IP addresses.

Dynamic Host Configuration Protocol (DHCP) — A modern implementation of BOOTP allowing for the dynamic allocation of IP addresses.

dynamic network address translation (dynamic NAT) — Allows a one-to-many translation from private IP address ranges to public IP addresses. Dynamic NAT gives network administrators a method of working around the shortage of Internet-valid IP addresses by allowing many internal, private addresses to share one public IP address.

dynamic port number — The port numbers above 1024 that are available for network application usage.

frame — Data referenced at the Data Link layer between a header and a footer. The frame is the first logical information a receiving computer analyzes.

Internet — A collection of local area networks that forms one large, loosely tied, worldwide network of millions of users.

Internet Control Message Protocol (ICMP) — A TCP/IP sub-protocol that handles connection error control and informational messages. Used most commonly with the PING utility.

Internet Protocol (IP) — The method of Network layer logical addressing implemented by the TCP/IP protocol suite.

Internet Protocol Security (IPSec) — A set of protocols currently being developed by the Internet Engineering Task Force (IETF) to allow for secure encryption at the Network layer.

intranet — Private networks that allow users to access internal information within a company or organization. Many intranets tie closely into the Internet, allowing private internal information to be accessed from a public network.

IP Helper-Address — An address that allows routers to propagate certain broadcast frames, such as a DHCP client request, to different network segments.

local area network (LAN) — A client-server computer network established in one location, such as an office or building.

Logical Link Control (LLC) — The sub-layer of the Data Link layer that acts as a pointer to an upper Network layer protocol such as IP or IPX.

Media Access Control (MAC) — The sub-layer of the Data Link layer that handles the physical addressing of frames.

Microsoft Challenge Handshake Authentication Protocol (MS-CHAP) — A Microsoft proprietary implementation of CHAP, a secure user authentication protocol.

Multicast — A bandwidth-saving method of addressing data to groups of users instead of sending multiple unicast messages.

Network Control Protocol (NCP) — The first client-to-client protocol developed for the ARPANET.

network firewall — A network system designed to prevent access to or from a network.

Open Systems Interconnection (OSI) model — A model designed by the International Standards Organization (ISO) describing how devices communicate across a network. It divides networking architecture into seven layers: Application, Presentation, Session, Transport, Network, Data Link, and Physical.

packet/datagram — The Protocol Data Unit (PDU) found at the Network layer.

Password Authentication Protocol (PAP) — A basic user authentication protocol where transmission of the username and password occurs in clear text.

Point-to-Point Protocol (PPP) — A Data Link layer method of connecting a computer to the Internet or Virtual Private Network (VPN). The current successor to SLIP.

port numbers — Used by the Transport layer to tag each data segment with the correct application for which it belongs.

private networking ranges — Describes the group of IP address ranges used on internal LANs; addresses within such ranges are dropped by Internet routers.

Protocol Data Unit (PDU) — Terminology used to describe data as it reaches the various layers of the OSI model. A PDU containing the control information from the Transport layer is called a segment; from the Network layer it is called a packet; from the Data Link layer it is called a frame; and from the Physical layer it is called bits.

protocol number — Used by the Network layer to direct data to the correct Transport layer protocol.

Public Switched Telephone Network (PSTN) — The network of telephone lines that services most homes around the world.

router — A network device with multiple ports that connects LANs and WANs. Routers are commonly used for remote access.

segment — The PDU found at the Transport layer.

Serial Line Internet Protocol (SLIP) — An older data-link method of connecting a computer to the Internet that does not support username/password encryption or DHCP.

static network address translation (static NAT) — Maps external, public IP addresses to private, internal LAN addresses on a one-to-one basis.

subnet mask — Used in conjunction with an IP address to determine what portion of the address represents the source and network destinations.

2

TCP three-way handshake — The process TCP-based clients use to exchange sequence and acknowledgement numbers before establishing a reliable session.

TCP/IP client — Any network device that has a valid TCP/IP address.

TCP/IP protocol suite — A suite of protocols allowing for network connectivity. Most commonly used when connecting to the Internet.

Transmission Control Protocol (TCP) — A reliable, Transport layer protocol allowing two clients to exchange streams of data with guaranteed delivery.

unicast — A data frame addressed to one individual network device.

User Datagram Protocol (UDP) — The connectionless and unreliable, but faster, alternative to the Transport layer TCP protocol.

Variable Length Subnet Masking (VLSM) — A strategy that uses two different subnet masks in an organization, such as one in California and one for the rest of the sites.

Virtual Private Network (VPN) — A private network that uses a public network, such as the Internet, as a backbone to connect devices.

well-known port numbers — The port numbers below 1024 that are reserved for specific network applications.

wide area network (WAN) — A network connecting geographically distinct locations, such as those in different countries or in different branch offices for an organization.

Windows Internet Name Service (WINS) — A system that maps NetBIOS names to IP addresses.

X.25 — The first packet-switching network technology developed. Predecessor to frame-relay.

zone of authority — The scope of hostnames assigned to a given DNS server to manage.

REVIEW QUESTIONS

1. The OSI model describes:

   a. the tunneling process used to communicate across a Virtual Private Network (VPN)

   b. the process used by clients to communicate outside of their own local network segment

   c. the method used by applications to process data

   d. how devices communicate in a network

2. Packets are a concept associated with which OSI model layer?

   a. Physical layer

   b. Data Link layer

   c. Network layer

   d. Transport layer

3. Which of the following is typical of a Presentation layer process?

   a. compressing data

   b. converting data into binary

   c. adding a Protocol Data Unit (PDU) header and trailer

   d. username and password verification

4. As data is sent down the OSI model, it becomes _____ at each layer.

   a. a Protocol Data Unit

   b. de-encapsulated

   c. encapsulated

   d. encrypted

5. Port numbers are used to distinguish between:

   a. network segments

   b. layer-four protocols

   c. individual NICs

   d. applications

6. Which of the following TCP/IP protocol suite components would typically be used in applications such as video streaming and network games?

   a. TCP

   b. ICMP

   c. UDP

   d. SMTP

7. If a network device sent out an ARP message, it would be looking for:

   a. a MAC address

   b. an individual network segment

   c. an IP/IPX address

   d. availability of network services

8. Which of the following is supported in SLIP?

   a. dynamic IP address assignments

   b. Encrypted passwords

   c. clear text authentication

   d. all of the above

9. BOOTP was commonly used for:

   a. dynamically assigning pools of addresses to workstations

   b. allowing diskless workstations to boot from network servers

2

c. disconnecting a user after a certain amount of time

d. allowing fast power-on features for Windows 2000-based computers

10. A router that has three different interfaces connected to three different segments has what?

    a. three broadcast domains

    b. decreased collision domains

    c. more available bandwidth

    d. a multi-card adapter interface installed

11. In what scenario would you expect to see a source quench message?

    a. A network card is sending above nine broadcast messages per second.

    b. A network card is sending data too quickly.

    c. as a termination message at the end of a session

    d. used in multicasting to stop transmission to one group member

12. If an application used port number 1022, it would be using:

    a. a well-known port number

    b. a dynamic port number

    c. a secondary port number

    d. an unsupported port number

13. Which of the following is the correct binary representation of the number 210?

    a. 11001010

    b. 11010010

    c. 11001010

    d. 10110110

14. Which of the following is not a valid IP address?

    a. 1.1.1.1

    b. 50.0.0.1

    c. 192.255.255.63

    d. 186.256.202.1

15. What protocol from the TCP/IP protocol suite provides addressing and routing functions?

    a. SMTP

    b. FTP

    c. TCP

    d. IP

16. Which of the following is an Internet valid address?

    a. 10.53.16.90

    b. 248.16.2.3

    c. 172.21.5.1

    d. 172.5.21.32

17. An IP address of 192.255.0.1 is valid with a Class C subnet mask applied. True or false?

18. If a computer can communicate with local hosts but not remote hosts, what is most likely the problem?

    a. The IP address is not in a valid range.

    b. The DNS configuration for the computer is incorrect.

    c. The default gateway setting is invalid.

    d. The DHCP server is not running correctly.

19. DNS servers resolve NetBIOS names to IP addresses. True or false?

20. What is the protocol number used for in the TCP/IP protocol stack?

    a. to determine which upper Transport layer protocol to use (i.e. TCP, UDP)

    b. to determine the correct Application layer program to pass the data

    c. to find the correct Network layer protocol to use (i.e. IP, IPX)

    d. to find the correct route to a given network segment

HANDS-ON PROJECTS

Project 2-1

Your company has recently converted from IPX/SPX to TCP/IP as the protocol for your network. A new addressing scheme must be designed to allow for connectivity. The corporation has 14,000 network users spread across 20 separate locations. The largest of these locations is in California, which has 1,500 users. You have been asked to develop an addressing scheme that not only supports 20 sub-networks, but in the future would also accommodate the greatest number of users per sub-network. The company plans on using the reserved private address range 10.0.0.0 and does not want to use Variable Length Subnet Masking. Find the network-wide subnet mask, five of the network address ranges assigned at corporate sites, and the maximum number of sub-networks and hosts per sub-network this solution will give you.

Subnet mask: _____

Network range one: _____

Network range two: _____

Network range three: _____

Network range four: _____

Network range five: _____

Maximum number of sub-networks: _____

Maximum number of hosts per subnet: _____

Project 2-2

You run a business that sells power pinwheels—small devices that attach to the roof of a house to generate electricity from the wind. Your company has 30 small, sales offices throughout the United States. Each office has three computers. The Internet is the primary retail sales medium for the power pinwheels, and for this reason, each of the 90 sales office computers must have Internet access. Because your company is small, you purchase the Class C address range 195.16.32.0. Find the network-wide subnet mask, five of the network address ranges assigned at corporate sites, and the maximum number of sub-networks and hosts per sub-network this solution will give you.

Subnet mask: _____

Network range one: _____

Network range two: _____

Network range three: _____

Network range four: _____

Network range five: _____

Maximum number of sub-networks: _____

Maximum number of hosts per subnet: _____

Project 2-3

You are a network administrator working on contract for several local companies. You are beginning to work at a local ISP that has an increasing number of employees and clients. The ISP recently purchased the Class B address 152.16.0.0 to allocate to DSL clients. To make the address pool more manageable, you are asked to break up the address pool into 80 pieces via the subnet mask. Find the proper subnet mask, five of the ISPs assignable network address ranges, and the maximum number of sub-networks and hosts per sub-network provided.

Subnet mask: _____

Network range one: _____

Network range two: _____

Network range three: _____

Network range four: _____

Network range five: _____

Maximum number of sub-networks: _____

Maximum number of hosts per subnet: _____

Project 2-4

Using ISA Server documentation (located at *www.microsoft.com/isaserver*), write a one to two page research paper detailing how ISA Server functions at each of the OSI model layers. Give specific examples of firewall and packet filter features. You can group the tasks of the top three layers of the OSI model (the Application, Presentation, and Session layers) into one, functional Application layer.

Project 2-5

Network address translation (NAT) and virtual private networking (VPN) are functions that are included in the Windows 2000 networking features. In one to two paragraphs, describe in detail how ISA Server improves upon the base functionality of these networking features. You may use this book or any Web resources necessary.

CASE PROJECT

Raising Waters is a water purification company that has eight offices located around the country, each staffed with 50 onsite personnel. In addition, they have over 800 traveling sales people who visit potential customers nationwide. The traveling employees are each equipped with a laptop that they use to dial into one of the eight office locations every evening to submit their daily orders and check company e-mail. Recently, Raising Waters migrated from a Novell Netware 3.11 environment to Windows 2000. You have been hired to assist in the movement from IPX/SPX to TCP/IP. Construct a subnetting scheme that provides enough IP addresses for each of the eight offices to expand to 75 employees. The offices should use a private addressing scheme, but management would also like to allow users to have Web access. Finally, management of Rising Waters would like you to devise a method to reduce the amount of long distance charges used in directly connecting the remote employees to the office.

3

WINDOWS 2000
FUNDAMENTALS

> **After reading this chapter and completing the exercises, you will be able to:**
>
> ♦ Understand the basic differences between the four versions of Windows 2000
>
> ♦ Configure network cards and the TCP/IP protocol for network connectivity in Windows 2000
>
> ♦ Work with the Microsoft Management Console
>
> ♦ Understand the fundamental concepts of Microsoft Active Directory Service

Because ISA Server 2000 uses Windows 2000 as its base operating system, you need to understand the fundamentals of Windows 2000. This chapter highlights many of the Windows 2000 essentials you must understand before working with ISA Server and taking the ISA Server certification exam. Instead of asking direct questions about Windows 2000, the exam integrates Windows 2000 concepts into ISA Server questions. Thus, the test measures your skills in both areas at once.

If you already understand Windows 2000 and Active Directory operation, you can use this chapter to review the concepts. If you're new to Microsoft technology, this chapter introduces you to Windows 2000 and Active Directory.

Understanding Windows 2000 Platforms

Instead of creating a single platform for Windows 2000, Microsoft developed four versions to address separate demands for network infrastructure. These four versions are not completely different from one another, but build on each other to become successively more powerful platforms. The versions range from Windows 2000 Professional, a reliable and secure end-user workstation, to Windows 2000 Datacenter, which is designed to handle demands for high-performance data warehousing. Overall, these platforms provide small businesses with low-cost server software and large businesses with fault tolerance and high performance.

Windows 2000 Professional

Windows 2000 Professional replaces all prior Microsoft Windows operating systems with one common platform. Before Windows 2000 Professional was developed, users who needed their computers for business applications chose Windows NT Workstation, which promised stability and efficient use of resources. Those who bought computers for home use and leisure typically chose the Windows 9x platform, which provided features such as Plug and Play for hardware devices and backward compatibility with older applications and games.

Windows 2000 Professional combines the stability of Windows NT and the ease of use of Windows 9x. Windows 2000 is designed to replace Windows NT Workstation, and offers features such as Plug and Play for hardware devices along with stronger encryption and authentication methods. You can also use Windows 2000 Professional as a file and print server in a peer-to-peer network environment, though it can only handle limited clients and offers few network services.

Windows 2000 Server

Windows 2000 Server is the first of three server platforms offered by Microsoft. It contains all the features in Windows 2000 Professional, but expands support in many areas. This platform supports a maximum of four processors and up to four gigabytes of physical memory. Beyond the hardware support, Windows 2000 Server is the first platform to support Active Directory. Active Directory is a database that allows you to link multiple domain controllers into a single, consistent network for performing common administrative tasks, such as adding users and groups and managing printers. Active Directory is discussed in depth later in this chapter.

Windows 2000 Server also adds support for Group Policy, which controls user access to specific workstations, applications, and data. ISA Server 2000 has adopted Group Policy, giving administrators complete control over network access, content filtering, and Web site availability. These policies are administered through Active Directory, allowing centralized management of network resources and ISA Server policies.

3

Windows 2000 Advanced Server

Windows 2000 Advanced Server doubles the hardware support available in Windows 2000 Server. Advanced Server supports up to eight gigabytes of memory and supports **symmetric multiprocessing** for up to eight processors. This allows Windows 2000 to assign up to eight processors for one task. In addition, Advanced Server adds support for server clustering, which lets you link multiple servers so they act as one machine. Clustering provides not only the benefit of load balancing, but also provides built-in redundancy. Clustering ensures that if one server fails, another carries the additional workload. ISA Server 2000, when combined with the clustering features of Windows 2000 Advanced Server, provides virtually fault-tolerant operation. ISA Server 2000 Enterprise Edition also implements server arrays, allowing you to store unique cached content among multiple servers.

Windows 2000 Datacenter

Windows 2000 Datacenter is designed for large-scale Internet service providers or data warehouses. Any business that needs long periods of processor time and dedicated memory will find these features and capabilities in this platform.

Windows 2000 Datacenter has all the features of Windows 2000 Server and Advanced Server, plus offers additional hardware support. Windows 2000 Datacenter can handle up to 32 processors running in a symmetrical multiprocessing system. The memory support has been upgraded to 64 gigabytes, which is eight times the expansion capability of the Advanced Server platform.

CONFIGURING NETWORK CONNECTIVITY

Before you can install ISA Server, you need to configure Windows 2000 to have network connectivity. This requires at least two network cards: one should connect to the external or public network (typically the Internet), and the other to an internal or private network. If you are configuring a test machine in a lab environment and two network cards are not available, you can use the Microsoft loopback adapter to create a virtual, configurable network card. After configuring the internal and external network cards, you must configure the TCP/IP protocol on each active interface.

Configuring Network Cards

ISA Server installation requires at least one installed network card, and most ISA Server features require two. Fortunately, installing and configuring network cards is easy in Windows 2000. If you are using a Plug and Play card, exit Windows, install the hardware, reboot, and follow the wizard installation instructions. If the card is not Plug and Play, use the Add/Remove Hardware feature in the Control Panel to work through the installation process.

Once your network adapters are in place, identify their icons with descriptive names. You can then easily recognize which networks are attached to the interfaces.

To rename network adapters:

1. On the Windows 2000 desktop, right-click the **My Network Places** icon, and then click **Properties** on the shortcut menu. The Network and Dial-up Connections window opens, as shown in Figure 3-1.

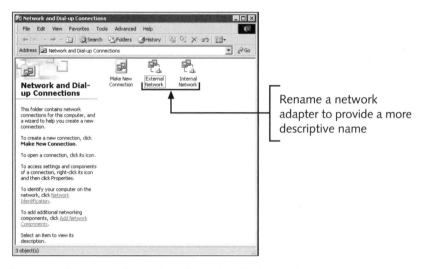

Figure 3-1   Renaming network cards with logical names

2. Right-click the appropriate connection icon, and then click **Rename** on the shortcut menu.

3. Type a descriptive name for each card. Use names that are meaningful to you, as you use these names often when configuring ISA Server.

Installing the Microsoft Loopback Adapter

If you are learning about ISA Server to pass a certification exam or to configure a test environment, setting up the **Microsoft loopback adapter** is a simple, cost-effective way to emulate a network card in Windows 2000. The loopback adapter allows you to work around the ISA Server requirement of using two network cards by installing a nonexistent interface. Windows treats these "virtual adapter cards" as standard **network interface cards (NICs)** installed on the server. You can configure security, protocols, and services to use the interface just like a physical adapter, except that you do not connect to a network.

To configure a Microsoft loopback adapter card:

1. Click **Start** on the Windows 2000 taskbar, point to **Settings**, click **Control Panel**, double-click **Add/Remove Hardware,** and then click **Next** on the Welcome page.

2. Click **Add/Troubleshoot a device**, if necessary, and then click **Next**.

3. Click **Add a new device**, and then click **Next**.

4. Click **No, I want to select the hardware from a list**, and then click **Next**.

5. Click **Network adapters**, and then click **Next**.

6. In the Manufacturers list, click **Microsoft**.

7. In the Network Adapter list, click **Microsoft Loopback Adapter**, as shown in Figure 3-2.

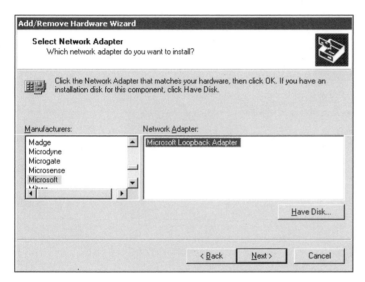

Figure 3-2   Installing the loopback adapter

8. Click **Next**.

9. Click **Next** on the Start Hardware Installation page, and then click **Finish** to install the loopback adapter.

After you install the loopback adapter, Windows identifies it as a LAN connection. To make sure you have installed the loopback adapter correctly, open the Network and Dial-up Connections window in Control Panel, right-click the connection using the loopback adapter, and then click Properties on the shortcut menu. You see a Properties dialog box similar to the one in Figure 3-3. Use this dialog box to configure all options as you would on a standard network interface card.

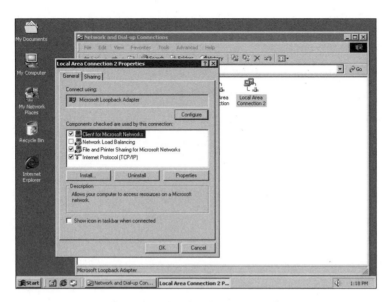

Figure 3-3   Verifying loopback adapter installation

The drawback to using loopback adapters is that you cannot test implemented ISA Server features. If you filter out HTTP traffic on port 80, for example, you must trust that the ISA Server configuration is working correctly because no network traffic is generated on loopback interfaces.

Configuring TCP/IP

After you have installed and configured the NICs, you must configure TCP/IP. Most Windows 2000 machines already have this protocol installed, but if TCP/IP is not listed as a network component, you must manually install it. The predecessor of ISA Server, Proxy Server 2.0, supported protocol translations between IPX/SPX and TCP/IP, allowing administrators to run IPX on their internal LANs and still connect to the Internet through the proxy server. However, because of its diminishing network use, ISA Server 2000 does not support IPX/SPX protocol translation. Therefore, configuring TCP/IP on both the internal and external network card is mandatory.

For each NIC, the only required parameters in configuring TCP/IP are the IP address and subnet mask. Usually, you also need the default gateway and DNS server address on the external (Internet) network interface. While ISA Server 2000 does not require static IP address assignments, it is highly recommended that the server use static assignments instead of dynamic assignments to eliminate potential network difficulties. You assign the IP address and subnet mask in the Internet Protocol (TCP/IP) dialog box, as shown in Figure 3-4.

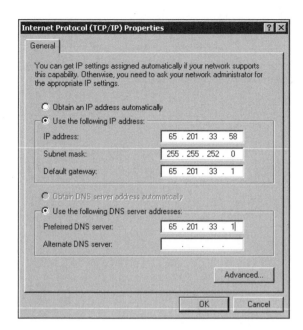

Figure 3-4   TCP/IP configuration

 Do not configure the default gateway of the internal network interface to point to the external interface IP address. Windows 2000 and ISA Server handle routing between the two interfaces on their own.

Ensure that the NIC and TCP/IP configuration is complete and working before installing ISA Server. You can do this by using the IPConfig.exe and Ping.exe command line utilities. If any network configuration problems exist, installing ISA Server further complicates the problems.

USING THE MICROSOFT MANAGEMENT CONSOLE

In Windows 2000, Microsoft standardized on one management system for all network administrative tasks: the Microsoft Management Console (MMC). Although the MMC has been used since Windows NT 4.0 for applications such as Internet Information Server, SQL Server, and Exchange, it has never become truly standardized until Windows 2000. Now, you use the MMC for nearly all Windows server administration tasks, and ISA Server 2000 is no exception. To understand ISA Server, you must first learn to work with the MMC.

Microsoft Management Console Fundamentals

The primary function of the MMC is to provide a common environment for snap-ins from Microsoft and third-party software vendors. By itself, the MMC provides no functionality. When you open it for the first time, you see a blank, Windows Explorer-style window, as in Figure 3-5. The MMC simply provides a standardized user interface; snap-ins give the console its functionality.

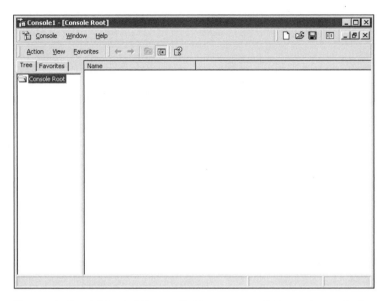

Figure 3-5   A blank Microsoft Management Console ready for customization

The MMC snap-ins are tools you add to the MMC to manage your OS and network, and are comparable to video game consoles. To play a new game, you insert a game cartridge, CD-ROM, or DVD. When you turn on the console, the game loads. Snap-ins work in a similar way—as you add them to your management console, they load, and then provide separate administrative functions. Administrative consoles can have one snap-in installed, with a dedicated console managing one specific component, or they can have multiple snap-ins installed, allowing many facets of network administration to occur from one place.

Single-point administration makes the MMC beneficial to network administrators. Windows NT 4.0 had separate tools and interfaces for every administrative task. If you wanted to manage users and groups, you needed the User Manager for Domains. To examine CPU utilization, memory usage, or network statistics, you used the Performance Manager. Each tool had a different look, feel, and method.

With the Windows 2000 MMC, all snap-ins have a common working environment. Once you are familiar with the MMC, you know how to interact with every snap-in you add. The MMC also allows third-party development of snap-ins; any vendor can design its utilities to work with the other Windows 2000 administration tools.

The MMC can also save administrative consoles for later use. For example, if you create a console and add the Active Directory Sites and Services snap-in, the Active Directory Users and Computers snap-in, and Internet Information Server snap-in, you can save the console as a file with an .msc file extension. You can then open the console with all its snap-ins later. You can also e-mail the .msc file to other administrators and create custom administrative consoles across the enterprise network, provided that all computers have the same snap-in capabilities. The MMC also lets you save customized consoles in a user mode, which keeps other administrators from changing settings.

The following steps help you create a customized MMC:

1. To open the Microsoft Management Console, click **Start** on the Windows 2000 taskbar, and then click **Run**. Type **mmc** in the Run dialog box, and then click **OK**.

2. To add and configure the required snap-ins, click **Console** on the menu bar, and then click **Add/Remove Snap-in**.

3. To configure the MMC console mode, click **Console** on the menu bar, and then click **Options**. Select one of the following two general modes:

   - *Author mode*—This mode allows other administrators to change the console to fit their responsibilities. Author mode gives others complete control over adding and removing snap-ins, and customizing the look and feel of the console itself.

   - *User mode*—This mode limits the ability of other administrators to modify the console. The three levels of User mode are full access, limited access-multiple window, and limited access, single window. Each is successively more restrictive in terms of administrator rights. In User mode, you can also prevent users from saving changes to the console by selecting the "Do not save changes to this console" check box in the Options dialog box.

4. To configure the MMC console view, click **View** on the menu bar, and then click an option. By doing so, you can remove and add the toolbars and console trees, thus controlling which parts of the console the user can access.

5. To save the MMC console, click **Console** on the menu bar, click **Save As,** and then enter the name and location of the .msc file. Click **Save** to save the console.

Whether you save the MMC in Author or User mode, you can still reopen it in Author mode by right-clicking the saved .msc console file and then clicking Author. The only way to prevent changes to customized consoles is to remove the NTFS Write permission from the .msc file.

Once you create the customized MMC console, you can distribute it as you would any other file. Because .msc files do not contain the actual snap-ins used for administration, the file sizes are typically small. Thus, administrators can send the custom console via e-mail or place it on a network server or floppy disk. However, the administrator who accesses the .msc file must at least have Read permission for it, and all referenced snap-ins must be installed on the computer where the administrator uses the console.

Configuring Taskpads

Taskpads are user-friendly customizations of the MMC console. They simplify the console by hiding the details of the snap-ins. Taskpads can help novice administrators or users who only occasionally perform minor network functions, such as password changes.

Using a taskpad is similar to using a series of shortcuts. For example, you might work with a Windows server and commonly need to change the host file in Winnt\system32\ drivers\etc. Rather than finding the path every time you need to change a hostname to IP mapping, you can add a shortcut to an easily accessible place like the desktop. Taskpads work in a similar way. To perform administrative tasks that consist of many small steps, administrators can use taskpads to group the steps into one mouse click. The ISA Server interface has many taskpads designed by Microsoft to simplify server administration, as shown in Figure 3-6.

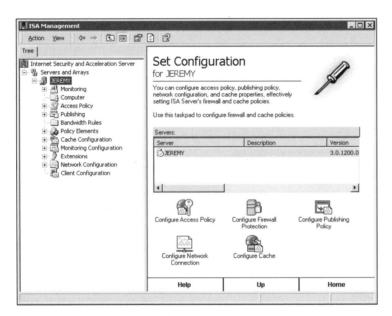

Figure 3-6   ISA Server 2000 taskpad interface

You can create custom taskpads for other administrators or yourself.

To create a taskpad:

1. Create an MMC console (as described in the "To create a customized MMC" steps in the previous section) and add any required snap-ins.

2. Open the Taskpad Creation wizard by right-clicking the item to which the task applies, and then clicking **New Taskpad View** on the shortcut menu. The Taskpad View Creation wizard opens and helps you define the taskpad name, description, function, and appearance.

3. Configure the task by following the steps in the wizard.

4. To simplify the interface, remove the console tree by clicking **View** on the menu bar, clicking **Customize**, and then deselecting the **Console Tree** check box.

5. Finally, save the console in User mode.

MICROSOFT ACTIVE DIRECTORY SERVICE FUNDAMENTALS

Active Directory, the matrix that oversees a Windows 2000 network, is essentially a database that stores information about network resources. Windows 2000 makes this database available to network users, and allows network administrators to organize, manage, and control access to resources from a central location.

Active Directory is standards-based; it derives its structure from the standards of the Domain Name Service (DNS). In addition, Active Directory works with the **Lightweight Directory Access Protocol (LDAP)**, which allows directory access from non-Microsoft clients such as Web browsers, Novell Netware, and Linux. LDAP even allows Active Directory to synchronize with other tree structures such as the Novell Directory Service (NDS), permitting a synchronized, user database between platforms. Because ISA Server 2000 integrates with and uses the **Active Directory Service (ADS)**, understanding it is critical to your success.

Active Directory is a network directory service loosely based on the industry **X.500** standards. X.500 is a global directory structure designed by the International Organization for Standardization and International Telecommunication Union (ITU), which organizes network resources in a hierarchical format. The fundamental Active Directory design is the structure of an upside-down tree. The top of the tree is the root level. Because the ADS structure follows the DNS system, the root level of an ADS tree is typically the DNS name of an organization, such as Microsoft.com or ACME.org. As you move down the tree, the DNS name expands to include domains and resources, such as Printer.Atlanta.ACME.org or Server.Arizona.ACME.org.

Active Directory Structure

Because Active Directory is a database of network resources, and the amount of resources on an enterprise-scale network can be overwhelming, Microsoft developed a system to organize them. The ADS database has four major divisions to keep network resources manageable:

- Forests
- Trees
- Domains
- Organizational Units

Forests

A forest is a group of trees that do not share the same DNS namespace, such as Microsoft.com and ACME.org. However, the trees in a forest do share a common **schema** (types of ADS objects you create, and their properties) and **global catalog** (the master database that contains all ADS objects and their properties). An administrator might create a forest for two partner or merging organizations, allowing them to share resources and administrative functions. Forests must contain two or more trees.

Trees

Trees are groups of Windows 2000 domains that use a common DNS namespace. As you add domains to an ADS tree, the new domains become children of the parent domains and build an upside-down tree structure. For example, an administrator might manage the ACME Corporation and create an ADS tree for the network. The first domain in the tree would be the **root domain** and would most likely use the name ACME.com. From there, the administrator would create sub-domains of ACME.com representing the geographical locations of ACME. These domains become the **child domains** of ACME.com, inheriting the parent's DNS namespace. Potential child domains might be Arizona.ACME.com, Florida.ACME.com, and Colorado.ACME.com. A further division by company function might result in domains such as Sales.Arizona.ACME.com and Marketing.Colorado.ACME.com. All domains share a common namespace from a centrally administered Active Directory tree.

Domains

Domains are the building blocks that keep the Active Directory structure together. All **domain controllers** (the servers designated to maintain copies of the Active Directory database for the local domain) within a domain contain identical Active Directory information. As a result, many administrators divide their Windows 2000 network into many domains. By doing so, administrators accomplish two things: they control Active Directory replication, and they create a security boundary.

Because all Active Directory data within a domain remains identical and synchronized between domain controllers, domains serve as a boundary of replication for the ADS servers. When data changes in the Active Directory database, all domain controllers within the domain must synchronize their databases. These changes can be as simple as user password changes, address changes, or even logging on. Because of this, administrators commonly create domains based on the geographical locations of their corporate network. By doing so, they keep normal ADS replication traffic confined to the LAN, and free the WAN connections for other types of traffic.

Administrators also create domains to establish Active Directory security boundaries. A domain administrator has permissions and rights to perform administrative tasks within that domain only, unless other domain administrators explicitly grant permission to do so in their domains.

The tie that binds multiple domains in the Active Directory tree is a **trust relationship**. Trust relationships allow administrators to grant users and groups access to resources across domain boundaries. In Windows NT 4.0, all trust relationships were manually created for each domain. Windows 2000 automates the process—as you add domains to an Active Directory tree, Windows 2000 automatically creates two-way transitive trust relationships between them. If you have transitive trust relationships, you don't have to create manual trust relationships for each domain. For example, if Domain A trusts Domain B, and Domain B trusts Domain C, then, because of transitive trusts, Domain A automatically trusts Domain C.

Organizational Units

Administrators use Organizational Units (OU) as containers to organize objects within a domain. In Windows NT 4.0, the user database had a flat structure; that is, as the administrator created users, Windows added and alphabetized them in a general pool of user accounts. As the network grew larger, the pool of accounts became enormous and difficult to manage. Windows 2000, by contrast, uses OUs to organize network resources into different containers. These containers can divide resources based on departments, geographical boundaries, or administrative responsibilities, such as sales, marketing, and management. Once you create the OU and move users and network resources into the correct container, Windows 2000 allows you to delegate OU control to other administrators. For example, you could create a Marketing OU and give the marketing manager administrative control of the users and resources in that OU. Figure 3-7 shows OUs in Active Directory.

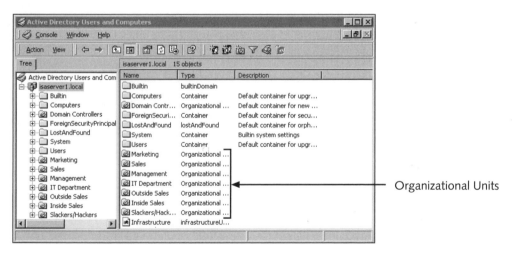

Figure 3-7   Active Directory organizational units

Because each domain in Active Directory can contain millions of objects, many corporations are moving their domain structure to a single domain model with OUs. Administrators then can have a single, consistent, synchronized database within one domain to represent the enterprise network. OUs allow the Active Directory database to remain manageable, even with thousands of users.

Installing Active Directory

Before you can install ISA Server into an array, you must install Active Directory. You can install Active Directory either during or after the installation of Windows 2000. Most network administrators install Active Directory after Windows 2000 because of the planning and complexity involved. Enterprise-sized networks often spend months planning an Active Directory network rollout. Before you install Active Directory, you should draw the complete structure on paper or diagram it in CAD presentation software, such as Microsoft Visio. The planning phase of Active Directory should take much longer than the actual implementation. This course does not focus on ADS planning, as many other books are dedicated to the topic.

Because the structure of Active Directory comes from the DNS structure, you must install the DNS service before installing ADS. The DNS server does not have to be a Windows 2000 machine, but it must support the service location (SRV) resource records and should support dynamic DNS updates, as described in RFC 2136. Microsoft highly recommends that you run the primary DNS service used for Active Directory on a Windows 2000-based machine. You can install the DNS service during Windows 2000 installation or in the Networking Services dialog box, as shown in Figure 3-8. To open the Networking Services dialog box, double-click the Add/Remove Programs icon in the Control Panel, click the Add/Remove Windows Components button to start the Windows Components wizard, and then double-click Networking Services in the Components list.

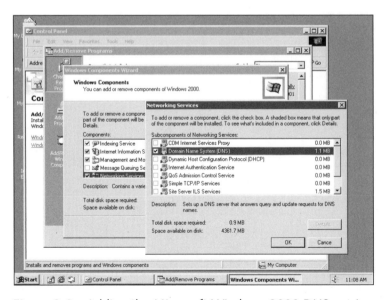

Figure 3-8   Adding the Microsoft Windows 2000 DNS service

Once you have structured the DNS database, you can install Active Directory. Click Start on a stand-alone Windows 2000 server, click Run, and then type dcpromo. This starts the Active Directory wizard shown in Figure 3-9, which you use to promote the machine from a stand-alone server to an Active Directory domain controller.

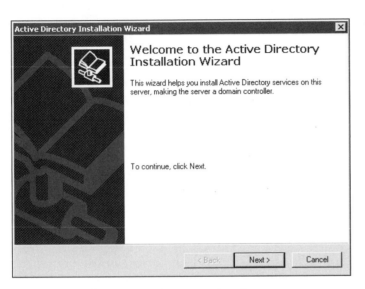

Figure 3-9   The Active Directory wizard

The wizard helps you create a new Windows 2000 domain, tree, or forest. At a minimum, you need to have the full DNS name of your organization documented before working through the wizard. After you enter the necessary data in the wizard, Windows 2000 installs Active Directory and the necessary administrative tools.

Managing Active Directory Rights and Permissions

Once you organize the logical structure of Active Directory, you must secure your network by assigning rights. Windows 2000 maintains a **discretionary access control list (DACL)** for every object in the Active Directory. This list allows administrators to define which users and groups can access individual Active Directory objects and what actions they can perform on each object. Most user rights are assigned using the Active Directory Users and Computers tool. Each class of Active Directory objects can have different assignable permissions, but most objects in the tree have the following standard permissions:

- *Full Control*—Gives the user full control of the specified object
- *Read*—Allows users to view objects and their attributes
- *Write*—Allows users to change object attributes
- *Create All Child Objects*—Allows creation of child objects to an OU
- *Delete All Child Objects*—Allows removal of child objects from an OU

When assigning these rights, administrators have three options: Allow, Deny, or neutral, as shown in Figure 3-10. By checking the Allow box, you permit the user to perform a specific action, such as reading or writing to an object. When you check the Deny box, you revoke a user's right to perform the selected action. If you do not check either the Allow or Deny box, you leave the permission at its default neutral setting, and deny the user the right to perform the action, although the user can gain the rights elsewhere, such as from a group assignment.

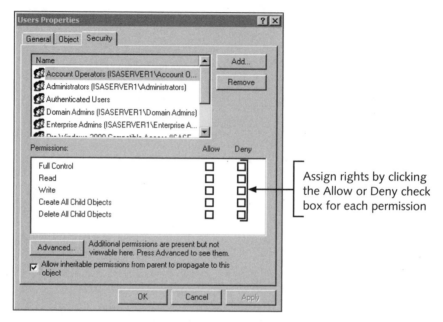

Assign rights by clicking the Allow or Deny check box for each permission

Figure 3-10   Assigning rights through the Active Directory Users and Computers

A user can be a member of multiple groups, and can have multiple permission assignments for one Active Directory object. The user's effective rights to a given object are the combination of all rights assignments. For example, if an administrator granted read access to an Active Directory printer object and a user belonged to a group that had write access to the same object, the user's effective rights would include both read and write.

Multiple assignments open the door to conflicting permissions. For example, an administrator might grant one salesman read access to a printer object while denying access to the sales group. All you need to remember in these situations is that *Deny always takes precedence.* Therefore, you should use the Deny permission only when you must deny a specific user who belongs to a group with the Allow permission.

When granting permissions to container objects, such as OUs, in the Active Directory structure, you can apply permissions to all child objects of that container. By selecting this option, you invoke permission inheritance; that is, child objects inherit all permission assignments from the parent container. Using permission inheritance greatly increases the efficiency of assigning rights, but also allows administrators to potentially overwrite many custom rights assignments. Use permission inheritance with care.

 The NTFS permission logic has not changed since NT 4.0. By default, all users still have Full Control permission to all files and folders on all hard disks.

CHAPTER SUMMARY

- ❏ There are four versions of Windows 2000: Professional, Server, Advanced Server, and Datacenter. Windows 2000 Professional fits the niche that Windows NT Workstation once filled. Windows 2000 Server, Advanced Server, and Datacenter are essentially the same server platform with added hardware and clustering support.

- ❏ Before installing ISA Server, you must install and configure TCP/IP, and bind it to at least one network adapter card (two are highly recommended).

- ❏ You can use the Microsoft loopback adapter to emulate physical network cards, although doing so means you cannot generate any network traffic for testing purposes.

- ❏ Rename the network interface cards to represent the networks they support (for example, External Network or DMZ) as you begin to install and configure ISA Server.

- ❏ All Windows 2000 and ISA Server management occurs through the Microsoft Management Console, using snap-ins to administer individual components.

- ❏ You can use taskpads to create user-friendly buttons to simplify administrative tasks. By default, ISA Server uses taskpads for most major functions.

- ❏ ISA Server integrates with the Microsoft Active Directory Service. This allows deployment in an enterprise-scale network.

- ❏ You can assign rights and permissions in Active Directory to users and groups by using DACLs.

KEY TERMS

Active Directory Service (ADS) — The Windows 2000 implementation of the X.500 database standard. *See* X.500.

child domains — Domains below the root domain.

discretionary access control list (DACL) — A list of users and groups assigned permissions to an object in the ADS database.

domain controllers — Designated computers in each Windows 2000 domain that manage the ADS database for that domain.

global catalog — The master database that contains all ADS objects and their properties.

Lightweight Directory Access Protocol (LDAP) — A universal protocol used to access information from X.500-based directory services.

Microsoft loopback adapter — A virtual interface designed to emulate a physical network interface card.

network interface card (NIC) — The device that enables a workstation to connect to the network and communicate with other computers.

root domain — The first domain created in an ADS tree, typically named after a company Internet domain name.

schema — A list of objects and their properties which can be created in the Active Directory.

symmetric multiprocessing — A computer architecture that provides fast performance by making multiple processors work together on a single task. Multithreaded applications take the most advantage of multiprocessing since individual tasks in the application can be assigned to different processors.

trust relationships — Logical links that tie together Windows 2000 domains and allow rights assignments between domains.

X.500 — The ISO standard for the structure of global network directories.

REVIEW QUESTIONS

1. Michael Fulton manages a start-up tax consulting company. He has four employees, and would like to allow them access to common client files on his computer. What is the minimum operating system required for this task?

    a. Windows 2000 Professional

   b. Windows 2000 Server

   c. Windows 2000 Advanced Server

   d. Windows 2000 Datacenter

2. Michael's tax consulting business has recently expanded to three locations. Michael would like to implement Active Directory across the network. What is the minimum operating system that allows a two-server cluster in Arizona?

   a. Windows 2000 Professional

   b. Windows 2000 Server

   c. Windows 2000 Advanced Server

   d. Windows 2000 Datacenter

3. What is the minimum number of network cards needed to install ISA Server?

    a. one

    b. two

    c. three

    d. none

4. What is the Microsoft loopback adapter?

    a. a device at address 127.0.0.1

    b. a 10-Mbps NIC manufactured by Microsoft

    c. a virtual network card

    d. two network cards connected with a crossover cable

5. Which of the following is required by Windows 2000 to allow for TCP/IP communication beyond the local subnet?

    a. IP address and subnet mask

    b. IP address, subnet mask, and default gateway

    c. just the IP address

    d. IP address, subnet mask, default gateway, and DNS servers

6. When configuring a Windows 2000 router, the default gateway of the internal network card must be set to the IP address of the external network card and vice versa. True or false?

7. The Microsoft Management Console is all you need to administer a Windows 2000 Server. True or false?

8. _____ are tools added to the MMC that allow for administration tasks.

    a. Add-ins

    b. Mix-ins

    c. Administrative tools

    d. Snap-ins

9. What is a taskpad?

    a. a series of icons that simplify administrative tasks

    b. a tool in Windows 2000 that allows scheduling of administrative tasks

    c. an application similar to Notepad

    d. a tool added to the MMC to allow for full administrative management

10. On what international standard is ADS based?

    a. X.509

    b. NDS

    c. DNS

    d. X.500

11. _____ is a platform-independent utility used to access standards-based directory services.

   a. NetBIOS

   b. LDAP

   c. Windows Explorer

   d. HTTP

12. If you install Windows 2000 Server, Advanced Server, or Datacenter, then Active Directory is installed by default. True or false?

13. Which of the following is used to segment replication traffic?

   a. forest

   b. tree

   c. domain

   d. Organizational Unit

14. On Monday morning, Rayford Clipp noticed that when he created users, he could now specify their favorite colors in the User Properties dialog box. This is because the _____ changed over the weekend.

   a. Active Directory User Profiles

   b. Network schema

   c. ADS database

   d. X.500 standards

15. Permissions can be granted to OUs, thus granting access to all users in the OU. True or false?

16. Which rights assignment always takes precedence?

   a. Full control

   b. Deny

   c. Read-only

   d. Permit

17. What is the default NTFS permission logic for Windows 2000?

   a. Allow all users access to everything, and the administrator restricts permissions as necessary.

   b. Deny all users access to everything, and the administrator allows permissions as necessary.

   c. Give users rights to the default shares (C$, D$, etc.), but not to newly created shares.

   d. Default rights assignments depend on which version of Windows 2000 is installed.

18. By default, Active Directory creates two-way transitive trust relationships to all Windows 2000 domains added to an ADS tree. This allows administrators in each domain to grant rights within a given domain to any user from the tree. True or false?

19. The machine that holds a master copy of the domain database in a Windows 2000 domain is a(n) _____.

    a. Primary Domain Controller (PDC)

    b. Backup Domain Controller (BDC)

    c. Domain Controller (DC)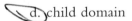

    d. the PDC Emulator

20. The domain Marketing.Arizona.Widgets.com is a(n) _____ of the Widgets.com ADS tree.

    a. root domain

    b. management domain

    c. DNS domain

    d. child domain

HANDS-ON PROJECTS

Before installing ISA Server 2000, you must configure at least one network card in Windows 2000. Most projects in this book require you to have two network cards installed. These hands-on projects help you configure a Microsoft loopback adapter (if necessary), assign each NIC a logical name, and install the TCP/IP protocol suite. To perform these configurations, you must have the original Windows 2000 CD.

Project 3-1

To install the Microsoft Loopback Adapter:

1. Open the Control Panel, and then double-click the **Add/Remove Hardware** icon. The Add/Remove Hardware wizard appears.

2. Click **Next**. Ensure that **Add/Troubleshoot a device** is selected, and then click **Next**.

3. Windows 2000 now attempts to detect any new Plug and Play devices. The Choose Hardware Device window opens, as shown in Figure 3-11. Click **Add a new device**, and then click **Next**.

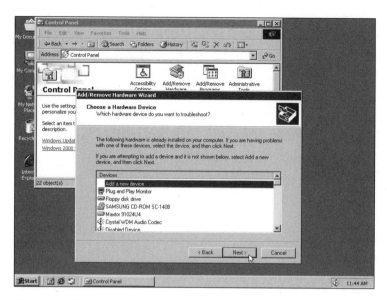

Figure 3-11

4. Click the **No, I want to select the hardware from a list** option button, and then click **Next**.

5. Click **Network Adapters** in the list of devices, and then click **Next**.

6. In the Manufacturers list, click **Microsoft**, click **Microsoft Loopback Adapter** in the Network Adapter list, and then click **Next**.

7. Click **Next** to begin copying files.

8. Click **Finish** to complete the installation.

Project 3-2

To configure logical NIC names:

1. Open the Control Panel, and then double-click the **Network and Dial-up Connections** icon. The Network and Dial-up Connections window opens, as shown in Figure 3-12.

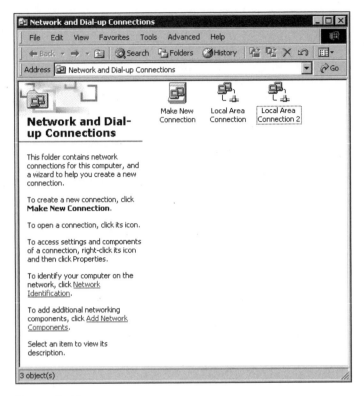

Figure 3-12

2. Click the first network card, click **File** on the menu bar, and then click **Rename**.

3. Assign the NIC a logical name such as Internal or External network, and then repeat the process for the remaining network cards, as illustrated in Figure 3-13.

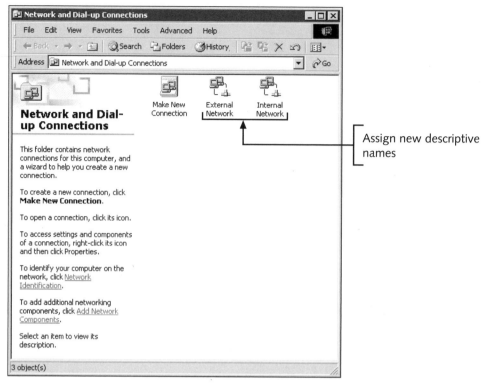

Assign new descriptive names

Figure 3-13

Project 3-3

To configure the necessary TCP/IP address information:

1. Open the Control Panel, and then double-click the **Network and Dial-up Connections** icon. The Network and Dial-up Connections window opens.

2. Click the **External Network** card or its equivalent, click **File** on the menu bar, and then click **Properties**. The Network Properties dialog box appears.

3. Make sure the TCP/IP protocol appears in the list. If it is not listed, you must first install it using the **Install** button. After you have installed TCP/IP, continue with Step 4.

4. Click **Internet Protocol (TCP/IP)**, and then click the **Properties** button. The TCP/IP Properties dialog box appears.

5. Click the **Use the following IP address** option button. You may need to obtain your IP address, subnet mask, default gateway, and DNS settings from your instructor. Otherwise, use the IP address **192.168.0.200** with a subnet mask of **255.255.255.0**, and then configure the DNS server IP address as **192.168.0.200**, as shown in Figure 3-14.

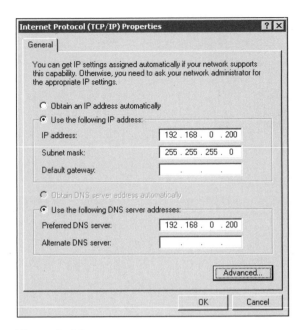

Figure 3-14

6. After configuring all necessary IP address information, click **OK** to close the TCP/IP Properties dialog box, and then click **OK** to close the Network Properties dialog box.

7. Repeat Steps 1 through 6 for the **Internal Network** card. Again, you may need to obtain all IP addressing information from the instructor. Otherwise, use the IP address **10.50.1.1** with a subnet mask of **255.255.255.0**. Leave the default gateway and DNS settings blank, as shown in Figure 3-15.

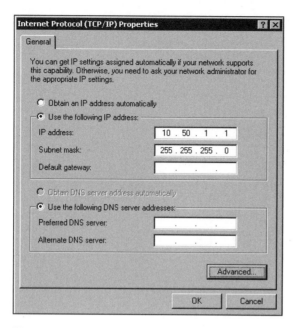

Figure 3-15

8. Click **OK** to close any network dialog boxes, and then close the Network and Dial-up Connections window.

9. Ensure that the IP address is properly configured by opening a command prompt and using the **ping** *IP_Address* command to ping both the internal and external network addresses. (Substitute the IP address you entered for *IP_Address*.)

Project 3-4

To take full advantage of ISA Server, you must set up DNS and Active Directory on your network.

To configure DNS for Active Directory on your Windows 2000 server:

1. Open the Control Panel, and then double-click the **System** icon. The System Properties dialog box opens. Click the **Network Identification** tab.

2. Click the **Properties** button. In the **Computer Name** text box, type **ISAServerX** (where X is your student number). Click the **More** button.

3. In the **Primary DNS suffix of this computer** text box, type **SecureX.local** (where *X* is your student number), and then click **OK**. Your configuration should look like the one in Figure 3-16.

3

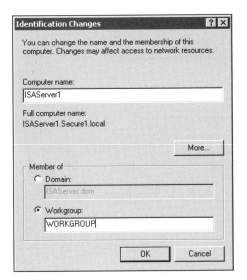

Figure 3-16

4. Click **OK** to close the Identification Changes dialog box. When Windows 2000 prompts you to reboot, click **OK** to close the System Properties dialog box. Click **Yes** to restart your computer.

5. Log on using the administrator account once the server has started again.

6. Open the Control Panel, double-click the **Add/Remove Programs** icon, and then click **Add/Remove Windows Components**.

7. Click **Networking Services**, and then click **Details**. Click the check box next to the **Domain Name System (DNS)**, and then click **OK**. Click **Next** on the Windows Components wizard page. Windows might prompt you for the Windows 2000 CD. Click **Finish**.

8. Close all open windows, click **Start**, point to **Programs**, point to **Administrative Tools**, and then click **DNS**.

9. Right-click your server name in the console tree, and then click **Configure the server**, as shown in Figure 3-17.

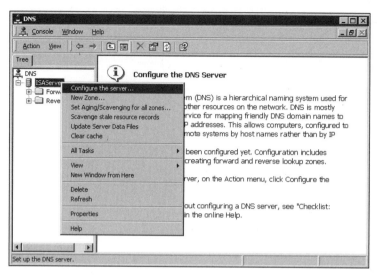

Figure 3-17

10. Click **Next** on the Configure DNS Server wizard dialog box.

11. Ensure that the **Yes, create a forward lookup zone** option button is selected, and then click **Next**.

12. On the Zone Type page, ensure that **Standard primary** is selected, and then click **Next**.

13. On the Zone Name page, enter **SecureX.local** (where *X* is your student number) in the **Name** box, and then click **Next**. Accept the defaults on the Zone File page, and then click **Next**.

14. On the Reverse Lookup Zone page, choose **Yes, create a reverse lookup zone**, if necessary, and then click **Next**.

15. On the Zone Type page, ensure that **Standard primary** is selected, and then click **Next**.

16. On the Reverse Lookup Zone page, ensure that **Network ID** is selected, type the first three octets of your server's external IP address, then click **Next,** as shown in Figure 3-18.

17. Accept the default settings by clicking **Next** on the Zone File page, then click **Finish**.

18. In the DNS tree, expand the Forward Lookup Zones, right-click the new **ServerX.local** zone, and then click **Properties** to open the properties dialog box for your new **ServerX.local** zone.

19. Select **Yes** in the Allow dynamic updates selection list, and then click **OK**. You have successfully set up a DNS server for the SecureX.local domain. Next, you set up Active Directory. Close the DNS window.

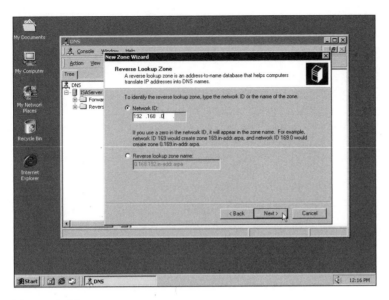

Figure 3-18

Project 3-5

To configure Active Directory on your Windows 2000 server:

1. Click **Start**, click **Run**, type **dcpromo** in the Run dialog box, and then click **OK**. The Active Directory Installation wizard opens. (*Note:* Windows 2000 requires that at least one hard drive partition be formatted with the NTFS file system for Active Directory storage. You may need to enter **convert** *drive_letter:* **/fs:NTFS** from a command prompt to convert a drive before Active Directory can install.)

2. Click **Next** on the Welcome screen. Ensure that **Domain controller for a new domain** is selected, and then click **Next**.

3. Ensure that **Create a new domain tree** is selected, and then click **Next**.

4. Verify that **Create a new forest of domain trees** is selected, and then click **Next**.

5. Enter **SecureX.local** (where **X** is your student number) as the full DNS name of the new domain, and then click **Next**.

6. Accept **SECUREX** as the default Domain NetBIOS name, and then click **Next**.

7. Accept the default locations for the database and log files by clicking **Next**.

8. Accept the default location to be shared as the system volume, and then click **Next**. (*Note:* If the default location is not an NTFS partition, you may need to convert it to NTFS or redirect the default location to an NTFS-formatted partition.)

9. Ensure that **Permissions compatible with pre–Windows 2000 servers** is selected, and then click **Next**.

10. Type **password** for the Directory Services Restore Mode Administrator Password, and then click **Next**. Click **Next** on the Active Directory summary screen. The Active Directory installation begins. This may take between five and 15 minutes.

11. Click **Finish** on the final screen, and then click **Restart Now** when prompted.

Project 3-6

Read Case Project 3-3 later in this chapter and then complete the Case Project. After you finish, perform the steps you outlined to configure Windows 2000 to run in a single domain with two Windows 2000 domain controllers.

Project 3-7

Read Case Project 3-3 later in this chapter and then complete the Case Project. After you finish, perform the steps you outlined to configure ISA Server to run in the environment described in Case 3-3.

CASE PROJECTS

Case Project 3-1

The Rady Corporation is a worldwide network with corporate sites in Seattle, Taiwan, Mexico, and Australia. Until now, the company has allowed each location to keep its local area networks separate from the rest of the company. Each location has sales, marketing, human resource, and management departments. With the release of Windows 2000, the Rady Co. decides to centralize its network administration into a single, enterprise-wide Active Directory domain. The company also decides to create a corporate Internet presence at RadyCo.com. Draw a rough Active Directory tree structure for the Rady Corporation global network. Identify the location of trust relationships, domains, and Organizational Units.

Case Project 3-2

Terminal Processing Systems (TPS) is a worldwide IT consulting firm with more than 500 network consultants. TPS has corporate sites in Arizona and Missouri. Management has divided the network consultants in each location into three groups based on skill sets: Microsoft, Cisco, and Novell. TPS has just moved from a Novell-based network to Windows 2000, and needs an Active Directory tree design. Because security is an important concern, each group requires a secure domain boundary. Design an Active Directory tree structure for TPS. Identify the location of trust relationships, domains, and Organizational Units.

Case Project 3-3

D&T Enterprises is a new company based in San Jose, CA. They are building their Windows 2000 network from the ground up. They are planning to deploy a single domain with two Windows 2000 domain controllers and an ISA Server array of two servers. This structure should support the 200 employees the company currently has on staff. Outline the steps the company should take when deploying Windows 2000 and ISA Server.

Case Project 3-4

MCS International is a company that develops and markets Voice over IP (VoIP) hardware and software. Their network is currently managed by Novell 4.11, but they are planning to move to a Windows 2000 environment. They would like to provide clustering capabilities for fault tolerance and run Active Directory. Because they are a relatively new company, cost is a factor. What Windows 2000 platform(s) would you recommend for MCS International? Justify your answer.

4

PLANNING TO INSTALL MICROSOFT ISA SERVER 2000

> **After reading this chapter and completing the exercises, you will be able to:**
>
> ♦ Understand the need for planning
>
> ♦ Characterize a network environment
>
> ♦ Choose the necessary features to use with ISA Server
>
> ♦ Explain the benefits of ISA Server arrays
>
> ♦ Choose an ISA Server installation mode
>
> ♦ Address Internet connectivity considerations, including selecting the best WAN topology for Internet access and choosing an Internet service provider
>
> ♦ Make final preparations, including recording corporate security policies, placing ISA Server in the network, determining the need for backup connections, and provisioning server hardware

Before you install ISA Server 2000, you must dedicate time and resources to planning for the installation. As network applications become more sophisticated and networks quickly grow from single sites to worldwide, enterprise WANs, thorough planning will help you avoid significant network problems. Start by creating a complete design document that describes the state of the network before and after ISA Server installation. For example, before you install ISA Server, you should document the current applications and protocols used on the network and sketch the network structure. Also plan for tasks you will perform after you install ISA Server, such as recording corporate security policies. The design document should also describe the installation process itself, providing details about which features you install.

UNDERSTANDING THE NEED FOR PLANNING

Many network administrators begin their careers by managing a small network with 20 to 30 users. In such a setting, you learn new skills, but can also develop bad habits. For example, because you can upgrade a small network quickly, you don't need to plan extensively for the upgrade. You can probably solve any installation or performance problems you encounter as you upgrade, or shortly afterwards.

For a large network in the enterprise environment, however, improper planning of a major upgrade can cause significant problems. For organizations that rely on networks to connect offices, branches, vendors, and customers that are located around the world, an enterprise-wide network failure that interrupts services for days or even hours could cause a business to collapse. Therefore, extensive planning and testing is necessary to identify and solve potential problems, avoid service interruptions, and generally ensure a smooth transition through any network upgrade.

Although ISA Server can benefit networks connecting to the Internet, improper installation or configuration can disable network communication on every client computer. For example, you usually install the ISA Server firewall client software on large groups of PCs using an automated process, and one of the required configuration components of the software is the **Local Address Table (LAT)**. Clients use the LAT to determine which hosts reside on their local network segment and which hosts are located on the Internet. If the LAT configuration is incorrect, communication can be interrupted between internal clients and the Internet, and between clients on the same network segment. This means that a corporation could not communicate via its network at all.

Installing ISA Server can affect every device in a network environment; this single fact underscores the need for a detailed installation plan. Time and resources devoted to formal analysis before you install ISA Server can save you hours, days, or weeks of troubleshooting later, and can prevent a significant interruption of network service that impairs business operations.

CHARACTERIZING THE NETWORK ENVIRONMENT

Before you can upgrade a network, you must first examine the existing network and address any failures. If the network has structural problems or is not performing as it should, installing ISA Server only complicates matters and can introduce destructive network failures. Before installing ISA Server, you should address and repair any current network problems.

Many independent consultants create network checklists when they are introduced to a network. These checklists provide a systematic format so that consultants can thoroughly examine network characteristics and identify potential problems. Create your own checklist to address each of the following areas and to analyze the state of the network.

Documenting the Customer's Applications

When documenting a network, you should first list the applications it uses. Many administrators only categorize applications that access the network because they do not think locally installed applications affect the network. However, understanding the current applications on the network can help identify patterns of network traffic, security flaws, and port numbers that you may need to open at the firewall. You should therefore document the name of each application installed on the network, the number of users that access each application, and the number of hosts or servers that provide the application.

4

Classifying the Customer's Protocols

Once you have documented network applications, record which protocols the network uses. Most large networks use more than one protocol. Rather than recording the name of the protocol suite (such as TCP/IP), you should record which sub-protocols are used, such as SNMP, FTP, and SMTP. Next, identify the number of people, hosts, and servers that use the protocols. This information helps you gauge traffic generated on the network. Because each protocol generates different types of network traffic, you cannot use a single formula to calculate traffic levels. You must use a different formula to calculate traffic levels on each network. Table 4-1 shows an example of a TCP/IP protocol analysis. (You can also find this analysis on *http://www.microsoft.com/technet/win2000/win2ksrv/w2kstart.asp*.)

Table 4-1   TCP/IP Protocol Analysis

Frame	Source	Destination	Protocol	Description
1	Client	Server	SMB	DNS 0x3:Std Qry for _kerberos._tcp.Default-First-Site-Name._sites.dc._msdcs.DCCLAB.LOCAL. of type Srv Loc on class INET
2	Server	Client	SMB	DNS 0x3:Std Qry Resp. for _kerberos._tcp.Default-First-Site-Name_sites.dc._msdcs.DCCLAB.LOCAL. of type Srv Loc on class
3	Client	Server	LDAP	LDAP ProtocolOp: SearchRequest (3)
4	Server	Server	LDAP	LDAP ProtocolOp: SearchResponse (4)
5	Client	Server	Kerberos	Kerberos KRB_AS_REQ **(request for TGT)**
6	Server	Client	Kerberos	Kerberos KRB_AS_REP
7	Client	Server	Kerberos	Kerberos KRB_TGS_REQ **(request for DC$)**
8	Server	Client	Kerberos	Kerberos KRB_TGS_REP
9	Client	Server	R_LOGON	Kerberos KRB_TGS_REQ **(request for Kerberos Service)**
10	Server	Client	R_LOGON	Kerberos KRB_TGS_REP

This packet exchange produces approximately 8 kilobytes (KB) of network traffic

The information in a protocol analysis helps you accurately estimate the amount of network traffic generated prior to making a network connection to a host.

Documenting the Network Structure

Because upgrading network software and hardware often means redesigning the network structure, you must first document the current network structure before you change it. Some administrators sketch the network layout on paper, while others use a CAD design program such as Microsoft Visio 2000, shown in Figure 4-1.

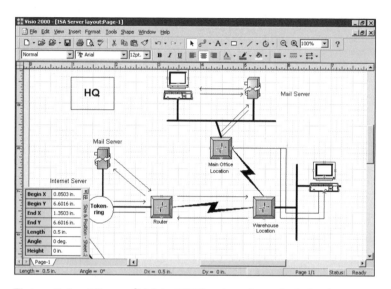

Figure 4-1   Microsoft Visio 2000 network analysis tools

A network diagram should specify the location of network segments and major groups of servers and clients. It should also label every network segment or WAN connection with the type and speed of the line. When using ISA Server, you should also document the network-addressing scheme and the names and functions of the major networking devices, such as Web servers, FTP servers, and mail servers. If you are new to an organization or are performing contract network services, check to see if someone has already created a drawing of the network design. Figure 4-2 shows a sample design diagram for an organization.

If your network already uses TCP/IP (and most do), you can use the **Simple Network Management Protocol (SNMP)** to chart remote network devices. Many design programs allow you to diagram your network using SNMP; you can diagram your entire LAN/WAN structure without leaving your desktop.

4

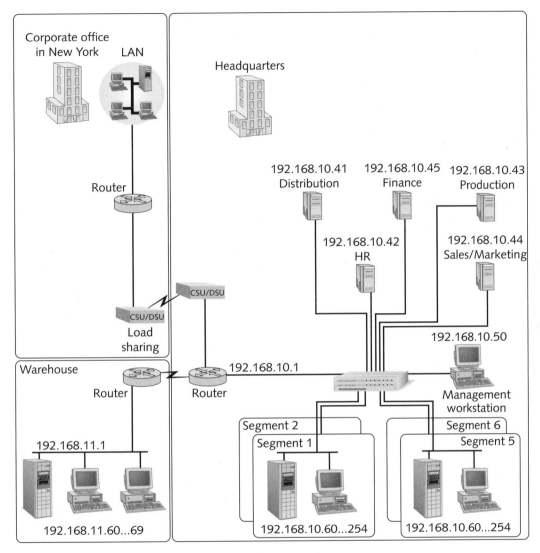

Figure 4-2 Sample network diagram

Identifying Potential Network Bottlenecks

Before you introduce ISA Server into a network, identify any potential bottlenecks in the current environment. Small to medium-sized companies typically have a single exit point on the network to access the Internet. This could mean that hundreds or even thousands of machines spread across different network segments are attempting to squeeze through one WAN connection. When identifying network bottlenecks, the first step is to categorize traffic patterns. To do so, monitor the network using a protocol analyzer. Divide the network traffic into two major categories: local traffic accessing the local network segment, and local traffic accessing a remote network segment.

Years ago, administrators used the 80/20 rule as a guideline, which stated that 80% of network traffic should access the local network segment resources and 20% should access remote resources. Figure 4-3 illustrates the 80/20 rule.

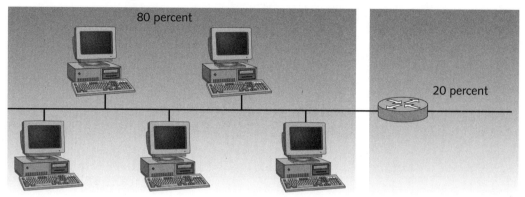

Figure 4-3   The 80/20 rule

Today, with the explosion of the Internet, the 80/20 rule has been reversed, now stating that 80% of network traffic should access remote resources, and 20% should access local network resources. In either case, the best way to minimize excessive WAN network traffic is to place network resources close to the users who access them. For example, if a department accesses a large SQL inventory database file throughout the day, you should place a server that can handle the SQL requests on the same network segment as the computers that need access. This approach keeps local users from crossing the WAN link to access frequently used data.

Other potential bottlenecks include processor use, network interfaces, and the amount of memory on the network router. These three components work together. As users begin to access resources on remote segments, the amount of routed traffic increases. As the amount of routed traffic between network segments increases, demands on the processor increase. If the traffic between segments continues to increase, the network eventually reaches a point where the processor can no longer handle its traffic.

When a network reaches its capacity, the router uses memory buffers to temporarily store packets while the processor handles as much traffic as it can. If the processor in your router is too slow, the incoming stream of traffic slows down and collects at the processor, causing the memory buffers to fill quickly. If these buffers are limited, they soon fill and the router begins to drop packets. The sending computer then must resend the data, doubling the initial amount of network traffic, processor time, and memory usage of the router. Network performance becomes exponentially worse as the router becomes increasingly overwhelmed.

Microsoft therefore recommends using a router that can handle your current and future network demands. Figure 4-4 compares network performance and overall network use on an Ethernet segment. Notice that after the traffic reaches a saturation point, network performance degrades exponentially.

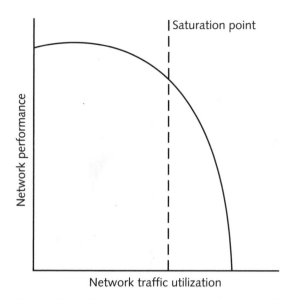

Figure 4-4   Network use versus network performance on Ethernet

Considering Business Policies and Constraints

You must work with company management to determine which business policies and constraints need to be considered. First, identify which business processes and data are key to the company and ensure that those processes are fault tolerant. For servers, use RAID technology to guarantee that data and applications are always available, even in the case of hard-disk failure. On central servers, consider using multiple NICs to prevent physical media and NIC failures from stopping server connections. For WAN connections, consider having a low-bandwidth, cost-efficient leased line or ISDN connection if the primary WAN connection fails.

Next, the management of your organization should provide company policies on approved vendors and protocols. Many companies have partner or reseller relationships with network equipment vendors, and receive discounted prices if they commit to purchase a certain number of products. Such arrangements could require you to use certain types of equipment on the network.

Likewise, you might not be able to use certain protocols on a network because they are proprietary. For example, your network may run Cisco equipment, but the company might not want to use EIGRP (a Cisco proprietary routing protocol) because it requires them to use only Cisco routers. Also, a company might have Windows 2000 servers running Active Directory, but not want to switch the ADS tree to native mode because it prevents them from using any Windows NT 4.0 domain controllers to support the network.

Finally, you need to understand the technical expertise of your client or employer. Whether you are an independent consultant or a staff network administrator, you need to explain what you are doing to their network. Not everyone understands the architecture behind

TCP/IP communication or the fundamentals of network address translation. Therefore, you should be able to explain basic concepts to people who have little computer training, and be ready to discuss the detailed, technical considerations of network design to those with advanced skills.

If you are an independent network consultant, your client's technical expertise might also dictate how often you return to the company. For example, if you configure ISA Server for the client's network, and the staff network administrator knows little about the product, you will probably be contacted first when a problem occurs. To prevent unnecessary visits, you should train the local network administrator to maintain and troubleshoot the product.

Recording Network Availability

To record current network availability, track the cost of network outages. Begin by finding the hourly cost to a specific department or division if its portion of the network were to fail. Once you determine costs to individual departments, find the hourly cost for the entire organization if the corporate network were to fail. Record this data based on a theoretical system; do not crash the customer's network and record the results. Be sure to include all losses to the company, including lost employee wages, lost production time, and lost customer service.

In addition to recording potential failure costs, record the failure rate for the current network. Ask when the last failure occurred, what caused it, and how long afterward the network was down.

Finding this data benefits you in three important ways.

- Identifying critical network components and finding ways to make them fault tolerant is important to the survival of any business. For example, if you find that a failure in the sales SQL server could cost the company thousands of dollars per hour, you might want to create a server cluster for the SQL server. This creates a back-up system that takes over in case the server fails.

- Finding the cost per hour of network outages supplies you with facts to take to management. Management is more likely to stretch the budget for fault tolerance when faced with glaring figures of potential losses.

- Finding data on network failures illuminates problem areas to keep under surveillance. For example, while recording past network problems, you might discover that a hard disk in the RAID array fails every few months. This not only alerts you to keep a back-up supply of hard disks, but also to research the company's hardware vendor that supplies that make and model of hard disk.

Calculating the Current Network Performance

Before you change the current network, you should first record a network baseline. A **network baseline** is a chart of the current levels of network traffic and client performance. Without a baseline, you cannot tell if performance has improved after an upgrade.

The baseline should measure current network use on a per-minute basis. Figure 4-5 shows an example of comparing a baseline of network utilization to daily network use.

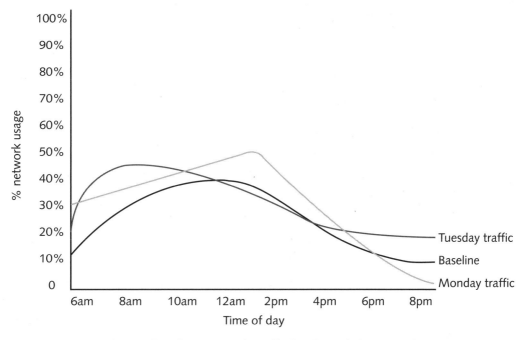

Figure 4-5   Comparing baseline network traffic levels to daily network usage

Measuring traffic levels per protocol allows you to identify characteristics of your network traffic, thus helping you to optimize network performance. For example, while monitoring traffic levels on a network segment, you might find an excessive amount of NetBIOS name resolution broadcasts. After performing a brief network analysis, you might find that the client IP configuration does not include a WINS or DNS server. Instead, clients are using broadcasts to resolve all hostname to IP address mappings. In this case, a minor reconfiguration of the network can save a significant amount of name resolution traffic.

 When monitoring the network, account for any traffic the network analysis software creates. Some monitor software generates a small amount of network traffic while monitoring, which can give you inaccurate results.

After you complete the network upgrade, run the network analysis software again to create a new baseline for the upgraded network. Compare the new baseline to the old one to find the increase or decrease in network traffic after the upgrade. The new baseline also acts as a point of reference for network performance in future readings.

INSTALLING CONSTRUCTIVE FEATURES

From packet filters to server arrays to Web page caching, ISA Server is designed to meet every concern a network administrator may have when connecting an internal LAN to the Internet. This surplus of features also presents a problem. Many network administrators install ISA Server with all its features, regardless of whether a feature is required. When you install unnecessary features, you add extra overhead, cycles, and memory consumption; meanwhile, features that your users need on a daily basis do not perform well.

Install only the features that your company needs. For example, if a business wants to use ISA Server only for its Web-caching features and is not concerned with security, you should install the server in cache-only mode. If instead you install ISA Server in integrated mode, the Web-cache features will still function, but not at an optimal level. The reason being even though the packet filters would not actively be used on ISA Server, the service would still verify the security restrictions for every frame passing through the server.

CONSIDERING ARRAY FUNCTIONALITY

If you are installing more than one ISA Server on the network, you may want to consider an array configuration. Array architecture requires all ISA Server machines to share a common Active Directory domain and site. Table 4-2 lists the primary considerations when choosing to install an array or a stand-alone ISA Server.

Table 4-2   Considerations for Array Functionality

Consideration	Array	Stand-alone Server
Scalability and fault tolerance	Can have one or more member servers	Limited to only one member
Active Directory requirement	Yes. Must be installed only in Windows 2000 domains with Active Directory installed. However, the local network can include Windows NT 4.0 domains.	No. Can be installed in Windows NT 4.0 domains. Configuration information is stored in the registry.
Enterprise policy	Yes. A single policy can be applied to all arrays in the enterprise.	No. Only a local array policy can be applied.

An array allows a group of ISA Server computers to be treated as a single machine. In an array, all management options performed on one server apply to all servers. This makes configuring global changes in your network much easier than managing ISA Servers individually. In addition to the management benefits, an array configuration provides scalability, fault tolerance, and load balancing.

Array Scalability

When using a single ISA Server in a medium to large network environment, you eventually reach a scalability limit—the maximum number of users your Internet connections can support. As the number of hosts on the network continues to grow, network traffic naturally increases. Because ISA Server is primarily a manager for incoming and outgoing network traffic, its load increases until ISA Server itself becomes a network bottleneck, even if you are using Web caching. Creating an ISA Server array increases the number of users your Internet connections can support. This number depends on the hardware configuration and the type and amount of traffic your network users are sending and receiving. Some networks can support over 1,000 Internet users with one ISA Server if users access the Internet on a limited basis, but other networks using streaming audio and video applications may require more hardware resources.

Array Fault Tolerance

Using a single ISA Server creates a potential single point of failure on the network. If that server fails, the network becomes isolated from the outside world. Many companies today rely on the Internet, and the loss of network connectivity could seriously damage their business. Therefore, you may want to use ISA Server arrays to guarantee fault tolerance. If one ISA Server machine fails, the second machine takes over. You can even attach separate WAN connections to each ISA Server, creating a fault-tolerant WAN in addition to fault-tolerant servers. For example, using two ISA Servers in an array with separate WAN connections gives you a completely redundant server and WAN connection if one should fail, as shown in Figure 4-6. If you had Web caching on the network, the back-up ISA Server would begin to rebuild the cached content contained on the faulty ISA Server. Furthermore, ISA Server arrays can contain many ISA Server machines, which allows for additional fault tolerance in a network environment.

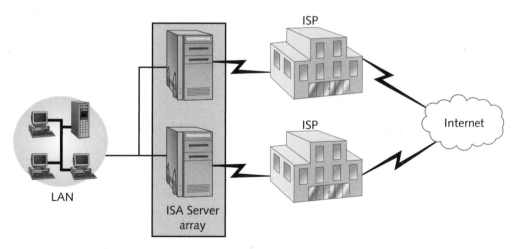

Figure 4-6   A fully redundant ISA Server configuration

Array Load Balancing

ISA Server arrays provide load balancing, which is related to their ability to grow. When using more than one ISA Server in an array, you can configure your network clients to balance the load evenly across machines. This prevents one server from handling most of the load and becoming a bottleneck. In addition, if you are using Web caching, the machines in the ISA Server array communicate to ensure they are not storing duplicate cached content. For example, if five network users access *www.microsoft.com* from an array of three ISA Server machines, only one machine will cache the content. If each ISA Server has 5 GB of hard-disk space dedicated to Web caching, the array configuration gives you a true 15 GB of storage space, rather than duplicating cached content across multiple machines.

CHOOSING AN ISA SERVER INSTALLATION MODE

Before you install ISA Server, document the server mode you plan to use. ISA Server allows for three modes of configuration: firewall mode, cache-only mode, and integrated mode. Firewall mode focuses on the security features of ISA Server, while cache-only mode increases the speed of outgoing and incoming requests by storing the requested Internet content locally. Integrated mode combines both features. Document all the requirements for your network environment, and choose the installation type that best fits your needs. Table 4-3 shows the major features provided by each installation method. Note that integrated mode contains all listed features.

Table 4-3   Choosing an ISA Server Installation Method

Feature	Firewall mode	Cache mode
Access policy	Yes	Yes (HTTP and HTTPS protocol only)
Application filters	Yes	No
Cache configuration	No	Yes
Enterprise policy	Yes	Yes
Firewall and SecureNAT client support	Yes	No
Packet filtering	Yes	No
Real-time monitoring	Yes	Yes
Reports	Yes	Yes
Server publishing	Yes	No
Virtual private networking	Yes	No
Web filters	Yes	Yes
Web publishing	Yes	Yes
Web proxy client support	Yes	Yes

ADDRESSING INTERNET CONNECTIVITY CONSIDERATIONS

Before you can connect a corporate network to the Internet, you must consider which type of WAN connection you want to use and which Internet Service Provider (ISP) to choose. You also need to review corporate security policies for Internet use. Administrators often overlook these areas until final implementation, leading to uninformed decisions and greater expenses to the company. You should document each of these areas before installing ISA Server.

Planning Necessary WAN Topology

Ensuring the proper bandwidth for your Internet service is critical when installing a WAN connection. Too little bandwidth results in excessively slow response times, but too much bandwidth is expensive. Because the WAN connection significantly affects network performance, your decision requires extensive planning and consideration. Various WAN topologies provide different levels of speed and bandwidth.

Most WAN connections are available in dedicated or nondedicated systems. A dedicated connection guarantees permanent and exclusive access to the Internet, but comes at a price. Nondedicated systems put you in competition with other customers of the WAN service provider for your Internet connection. Because nondedicated systems do not guarantee a connection, they cost much less than dedicated connections. Typical corporate networks require a dedicated service for a WAN connection; you should only consider a nondedicated service if your company cannot afford a dedicated connection.

WAN connection types are divided into three major categories: leased lines, packet switching, and circuit-switching networks.

- *Leased lines*—A leased line is also known as a point-to-point connection. This provides a single WAN connection path from the customer's network to a remote network through a service provider. The service provider reserves the WAN connection for the client's exclusive use. When data is sent between locations, all packets take the same path. This type of connection eliminates many problems associated with shared bandwidth topologies (discussed next), but can be costly. The bandwidth of these lines typically ranges from 56 Kbps to 45 Mbps (T3 speeds).

- *Packet switching*—Packet switching is a WAN topology in which network devices share a common pool of network bandwidth. The service provider uses **virtual circuits (VCs)** to provide end-to-end connectivity through the carrier's network. Packet switching is similar to leased lines, but because the devices in a packet-switched network share bandwidth, the cost is generally lower. The networks also can allow packets to take the fastest path among multiple paths to a destination. Packets can arrive out of order at the destination, so the protocol stack must be able to handle them. Packet-switching networks commonly provide bandwidth speeds from 56 Kbps up to T3, but some recent technologies such as **Asynchronous Transfer Mode (ATM)** have attained speeds of more than 40 Gbps.

- *Circuit switching*—Circuit switching is a WAN connection method in which a dedicated circuit path must exist between a sender and receiver for the duration of the call. As soon as the call ends, the connection between the sending and receiving devices is terminated. This method is most commonly used in technologies such as ISDN and dial-up modem connections, and in environments that only require a sporadic WAN connection. Connection speeds range from 2,400 bps to 1.544 Mbps (T1 speed).

Each major category of WAN connection includes a variety of options; all offer different advantages and disadvantages to network administrators. The key to selecting the proper WAN connection type is balancing functionality against cost. You should consider each of the following connection types during this phase of planning.

Plain Old Telephone Service

The Plain Old Telephone Service (POTS) is still the most common type of WAN connection on the market. This circuit-switched technology offers a reliable connection at a reasonable cost, but is often rejected because it is not dedicated. Businesses may use a POTS connection as a backup to another, more reliable type of WAN connection. Today, POTS is primarily used to connect mobile and home-based users into a corporate network.

Integrated Services Digital Network

The Integrated Services Digital Network (ISDN) is a circuit-switched technology that provides users with more bandwidth than standard POTS connections. Service providers divide ISDN connections into channeled interfaces, making traffic easier to manage. Each ISDN connection is composed of multiple B channels and one D channel. The B channels only carry data, and have a bandwidth of 64 Kbps each. The D channel carries 16 Kbps of bandwidth, performs call signaling and setup, and remains connected to the service provider at all times, which allows extremely fast call setup. While a POTS connection may take between 30 and 45 seconds to become active, ISDN service makes all the necessary connections in less than a second.

In the United States, ISDN is available in two forms: the Basic Rate Interface (BRI) and the Primary Rate Interface (PRI). BRI connections are made up of two B channels for data transfer and one D channel for call management, also known as 2B+D. When using both B channels, you obtain a speed of 128 Kbps. PRI connections use 24 B channels and one D channel (24B+D). If all 24 B channels are in use, you can reach speeds of 1.544 Mbps (equal to T1 speeds). BRI connections usually serve as the primary link for smaller businesses with 10 to 20 users, and as a back-up link for small to medium-sized companies. PRI connections can usually service a network with hundreds of users without becoming a bottleneck.

56-Kbps Leased Lines

56-Kbps leased lines are the entry-level connection in the leased line category. Unlike a 56-Kbps dial-up connection, a leased line is a direct link between two points (a point-to-point connection) that bypasses the central office of the telephone company. The connection is dedicated between the two networks, which requires both ends of the link to provide a **Channel Service Unit/Data Service Unit (CSU/DSU)**. The CSU provides protective and diagnostic functions on the line, while the DSU connects the end terminal device to a digital network. You can think of the CSU/DSU as a high-powered and expensive modem.

56-Kbps lines are a cost-effective connection type and, because of their low bandwidth, are typically used as a back-up connection to a faster primary line. Some areas do not support 56-Kbps leased lines because most subscribers prefer to purchase an ISDN connection.

T1 and Fractional T1 Leased Lines

T1 lines have long been the standard connection type for medium-sized businesses. They provide a dedicated bandwidth of 1.544 Mbps in a point-to-point connection. Like 56-Kbps leased lines, T1 lines directly connect two networks and require a CSU/DSU at the endpoints of each connection, but the additional dedicated bandwidth makes them more expensive. Because a T1 line is a combination of 24 individual 64-Kbps channels, service providers have begun to sell smaller portions of T1 lines to companies who may not need the entire 1.544 Mbps of bandwidth. These partial T1 lines are called fractional T1 connections, and cost significantly less.

T3 Leased Lines

While T1 lines can support hundreds of network users, large corporations with thousands of users at each location may require more bandwidth. T3 connections provide 44.736 Mbps of dedicated bandwidth, the equivalent of 28 T1 lines. Larger networks use T3 as the backbone of their network, but only large organizations can afford it. The cost of installation, equipment, and setup is about $11,000, and the monthly service fee is $30,000 to $40,000.

Cable Modems

Cable modems provide shared bandwidth by using the existing cable system as a backbone for high-speed Internet access. Cable modems are currently designed to service only Small Office/Home Office (SOHO) environments; the cable television network is not intended to handle commercial network traffic. Although cable modems are WAN connections, the network structure acts and performs like a LAN network segment. As each cable modem service area becomes saturated with subscribers, the available bandwidth for each network connection decreases. Nonetheless, many cable modems can provide up to 2 Mbps of network bandwidth, provided other users who share the same service areas do not overload the network segment with traffic.

Digital Subscriber Lines

Digital Subscriber Lines (DSL) are the telephone company's version of cable modems. Instead of using the structure of the cable television network, DSL relies on the structure of the telephone network. Because DSL is a general term for a variety of services, it is often called xDSL. Asymmetric DSL (ADSL), Symmetric DSL (SDSL), and Very High-Speed DSL (VDSL) are three common types offered to subscribers. Like cable modems, DSL is found primarily in SOHO environments, mainly because of current distance limitations. The further you are from the telephone company's central office, the less bandwidth you can receive. Subscribers within a few thousand feet of the central office are rewarded with VDSL download speeds of up to 55 Mbps, while those who are further away only attain speeds of 600 Kbps to 3 Mbps.

A major benefit of using DSL is that the bandwidth is dedicated, unlike cable modems. For example, if you subscribe to a 640-Kbps connection, you may get more than 640 Kbps if extra bandwidth is available, but you never drop below 640 Kbps.

Frame Relay

Frame relay is a packet-switching technology that offers high-bandwidth solutions at a relatively low cost. It establishes connections between sites through the use of permanent virtual circuits (PVCs) and switched virtual circuits (SVCs). PVCs and SVCs are established through a frame relay cloud, which is a pool of service provider bandwidth shared by companies that link sites through permanent and temporary point-to-point connections. The service providers use **data-link connection identifiers (DLCIs)** to identify each connection to the frame relay cloud. DLCIs work on the WAN the same way MAC addresses work on the LAN. For example, the service provider could assign a New Mexico site a DLCI of 53. If any other connection to the frame relay cloud wanted to send data to the New Mexico site, it would address the data to DLCI 53.

When purchasing frame relay from a service provider, two required specifications are your **Committed Information Rate (CIR)** and the **local access rate**. The CIR is the bandwidth level *guaranteed* by the service provider; the higher the CIR you specify, the more you pay for the connection. The local access rate is the physical port speed of the connection to the service provider; you cannot exceed this rate. When using a frame relay network, you are typically allocated more bandwidth than your CIR. However, if you transmit above your CIR during a busy time of day, your data may be lost. For example, if you signed up for a 128-Kbps CIR and a 1.544-Mbps local access rate, you could potentially attain T1 speeds, but any data transmitted beyond the first 128 Kbps would not be guaranteed. Figure 4-7 shows a typical frame relay DLCI and CIR configuration. Frame relay can currently support up to T3 levels of bandwidth.

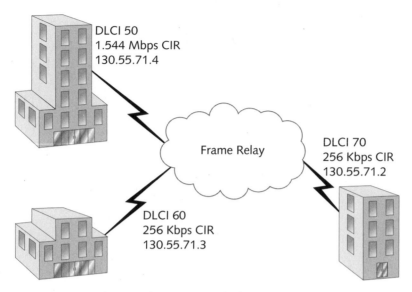

Figure 4-7   A frame relay WAN with three connected sites

Asynchronous Transfer Mode

Asynchronous Transfer Mode technology is a high-bandwidth, packet-switching network designed to transfer packets of a fixed size (called *cells*) between locations. The fixed cells are relatively small, so audio, video, and data packets can share the same bandwidth. Because ATM offers speeds between 155 Mbps and 2.4 Gbps, it is expensive, although not as costly as purchasing a comparable leased line between site locations.

Because of the high bandwidth of ATM, the WAN connection can often be used like a LAN connection, allowing broadcasts and routing updates to cross the ATM network. **LAN Emulation (LANE)** is the built-in technology that allows such broadcasts and updating in WANs. With ATM bandwidth now reaching speeds of gigabits per second, many users find the WAN connection faster than the LAN. To achieve these speeds, ATM networks often use fiber-optic, **Synchronous Optical Network (SONET)** technology.

Switched Multimegabit Data Services

Switched Multimegabit Data Services (SMDS) is a transport method similar to frame relay. It is a shared-bandwidth, packet-switching network, which keeps the cost below that of leased lines. Unlike frame relay, SMDS offers bandwidth of up to 44.736 Mbps (T3 speeds), allowing it to service enterprise-scale networks. SMDS is often based on SONET physical layer architecture.

Choosing an Internet Service Provider

Choosing a WAN network topology allows you to connect to the Internet from your local network, provided you have an Internet Service Provider. When choosing an ISP, network administrators typically pick one with the lowest cost or a recognizable name, but beware: choosing the wrong ISP can waste money, lead to cumbersome network troubleshooting, and cause hours of Internet downtime. Although you can change ISPs, doing so can be a difficult and frustrating process. Before you decide on an ISP, take time to research ISPs using the criteria in the following sections.

Technical Support

If you have questions or problems with Internet connectivity, your ISP should be able to help. When you contact an ISP for help, you should be able to reach a support technician quickly. The support technicians also should know the basics of networking technology. Before subscribing to an Internet service, find out how many technicians are on staff, and inquire about their troubleshooting history, experience level, certifications, and other education. In addition, ask about the ISP's business hours. If your organization operates 24 hours a day, seven days a week, you probably also need round-the-clock ISP support.

Some larger ISPs might charge for technical support. Find out whether the ISP provides free technical support, on a paid basis only, or starts charging after so many hours of access. Most ISPs provide basic connectivity troubleshooting for free, but charge a fee once you go beyond this basic troubleshooting. Also, ask about areas for which the ISP claims no responsibility, even if you have a problem. Document how far the ISP will go to resolve your network problems.

Web Services

Once you establish a connection through your ISP, you can usually connect to every service on the Internet, and other users can connect to every service offered at your location. However, some ISPs have begun to filter access to "high-risk" areas of the Internet and prevent outside Internet users from accessing your location. This often prevents you from being able to host Web services, such as a corporate Web site. While many ISPs allow you to host Web sites from their locations, the amount of Web storage space allocated on the ISP's hard disk is usually too limited to hold the entire site. While the ISP may offer additional storage space if requested, it usually attaches a monthly charge for the extra service. Before deciding on an ISP, be sure you understand its filtering and Web hosting policies.

Virtual Private Networking

If you have users connecting to the corporate LAN remotely, virtual private networks (VPNs) are a cost-effective way of providing remote access. VPN allows users to connect to the LAN using the Internet as a backbone. This saves on any long distance charges because users can dial a local ISP, connect to the Internet, and then connect to your corporate LAN.

If you plan to use VPN services, ensure that the ISP you select allows for and can handle the network load associated with VPNs.

Downtime

No ISP can guarantee 100% reliability, but keeping downtime at a minimum should be at the top of your priority list. Check with the service provider on its downtime history. Find out why failures have occurred, what the ISP has done to fix them, and how it plans to prevent future failures. Also inquire about the redundant systems the ISP uses and whether it provides refunds or discounts for lapses in the connection.

Business History

Many ISPs have come and gone, so it is unwise to use one that has been in business for less than one or two years. Find a seasoned ISP that has already worked most problems out of its system. You might also research the business history of the ISPs you are considering. Ask the Better Business Bureau if any complaints have been filed against the ISPs. In addition, find out what future plans the ISP has. If your ISP plans to merge with another ISP or if a larger ISP acquires it, the transition could be difficult for your company and the ISP.

Bandwidth Options

Before choosing an ISP, verify that it can support the bandwidth requirements of your company. If you plan to have a T3 connection to the Internet, ensure that the ISP can support it. In addition, make sure the ISP can accommodate future bandwidth expansions by your company. If your company foresees significant growth in the next five years or plans to offer many new Web-based services, make sure the ISP can support them.

You should also ask about the ISP's peak traffic times. ISPs have many other customers, so knowing the peak times allows you to plan your own network services and caching system accordingly. For example, if the peak bandwidth of your ISP is at 8 a.m., you can schedule your company's daily database upload for 9 a.m.

RECORDING CORPORATE SECURITY POLICIES

When connecting a company to the Internet, your network becomes vulnerable to many new security risks. While most managers believe that an Internet connection exposes the company to attacks from external hackers, most of the danger is internal—from employees. Before the corporate network connects to the outside world, be sure to document the company policy for the following:

- *E-mail*—E-mail can contain some of the most dangerous data on the Internet. Virus attachments disguised as innocent jokes or pictures can bring down the entire network. Some companies are so wary of attacks that they restrict e-mail to internal use only. You may need to filter for common destructive attachments such as .vbs or .exe files. You may also need to limit file attachment sizes; otherwise, you may find your e-mail server quickly running out of storage space.

- *Web site access*—Before you grant employees access to the entire World Wide Web, learn the corporate policies regarding Web access. The Web is the most diverse source of information in the world, and while it has many business applications, it can also be a playground full of needless material. Filtering out unnecessary Web sites can improve employee productivity and prevent inappropriate Web content from entering your company's network.

- *Other Internet-based applications*—You must also know the company's policy on other Internet-based applications, including chat programs, FTP clients, online games, and other file sharing utilities. Using ISA Server's firewall, you can block any TCP/IP-based application. Remember, the more openings the firewall has for incoming application data, the more exposed your internal network is to outside attacks.

Some companies impose time restrictions for Internet usage to keep network traffic at a minimum and employees focused on work during business hours. For example, your company may restrict Internet usage to e-mail traffic from 9 a.m. to 4 p.m. Consider all corporate policies *before* providing Internet access to employees. It is much easier to deny employees access from the beginning than to provide Internet access for a month and then take it away. When installing ISA Server security, do not use your own judgment to decide what Internet data should be filtered or allowed. Rely on a company policy so that managers and employees alike know what to expect from the network.

PLACING ISA SERVER IN THE NETWORK

Designing your network correctly is critical for efficient use of Internet bandwidth and the caching and firewall features of ISA Server. Network designs can vary among companies, but they all follow a basic layout. This layout includes an internal LAN connected to the Internet with ISA Server acting as the mediator between the private and public networks. Figure 4-8 illustrates the basic ISA Server network configuration.

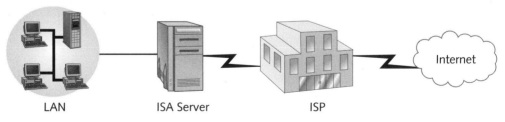

LAN   ISA Server   ISP

Figure 4-8   The basic ISA Server layout

The basic layout works well for small to medium-sized companies, but when you upgrade to a larger network configuration, issues such as WAN redundancy, ISA Server fault tolerance, and load balancing become important. ISA Server arrays are a solution to all three concerns. Figure 4-9 shows a sample configuration of an ISA Server array.

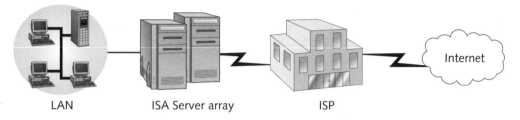

LAN   ISA Server array   ISP

Figure 4-9   Sample ISA Server array layout

As you can see from Figure 4-9, each of the ISA Servers are balancing loads, and are fully redundant. A client computer can be serviced from any one of the three machines. However, there is still a single point of failure in the design. Because the individual ISA Servers at the top of the design are the only ones with a WAN connection to the Internet, the connection breaks if the WAN, ISP, or the individual ISA Server machine fails. The ISA Server array could potentially handle repeat client requests for Web pages from the cached content until the content reaches the TTL. New client requests would not receive Internet service.

To provide full redundancy, you must have multiple WAN connections attached to multiple ISA Server machines, as shown in Figure 4-10. Only the largest corporations can afford this type of connectivity. Mid-sized companies typically use a high-speed primary link through a service provider, and a slower back-up connection through the same service provider, but often run through a different central office.

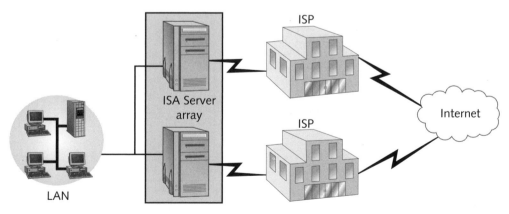

Figure 4-10   ISA Server array with multiple WAN connections

ISA Server chaining, also called hierarchical caching, is an alternative to ISA Server arrays, and provides a cost-effective method of load balancing. ISA Server chaining allows each server to handle requests in a hierarchical system. A client request first passes through the initial ISA Server machine, which services most requests from the cache. If the request is not found in the cache, the request is forwarded to the next ISA Server in the chain. This process continues until the request reaches the final server in the chain and is forwarded, if necessary, to the Internet, as shown in Figure 4-11.

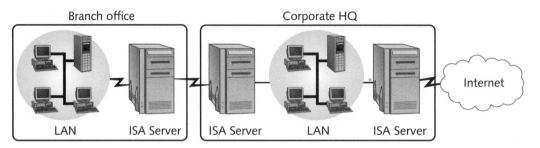

Figure 4-11   ISA Server chaining

At first glance, ISA Server chaining may seem like a poor design, but it actually improves performance because of the load distribution. Think of the first ISA Server in the chain as a helpful algebra instructor. When you ask the instructor a math-related question, she usually knows the answer. However, if your question is outside the scope of her knowledge, she might need to ask another instructor, perhaps a calculus teacher, to get the information for you. The algebra instructor thus finds the answer to your question and simultaneously learns the answer herself.

This is exactly how ISA Server chaining works. The client sends the request to the first server in the chain, which attempts to answer the request. If that ISA Server does not have the answer cached, it forwards the request to a higher-level server in the chain. This continues until the ultimate source, the Internet, is referenced. Once ISA Server locates the content, it is passed back to the client who requested it and is cached at every server in the chain.

ISA Server chaining improves performance, but lacks fault tolerance, because a single break in the chain causes a loss of service. To resolve this issue, large organizations combine the performance of chaining with the fault tolerance of ISA Server arrays to attain the ideal solution, as shown in Figure 4-12.

As you can see, several network designs are possible for ISA Server. Your network may mirror one of these designs exactly or look completely different. The key to a successful design is that all traffic leaving the private LAN must exit through ISA Server. If your LAN has another exit point, or users have dial-up access to the Internet, you have essentially eliminated the security, performance features, and usefulness of ISA Server on the network. To ensure security, you must seal all possible holes in the LAN that could allow alternative access to outside networks.

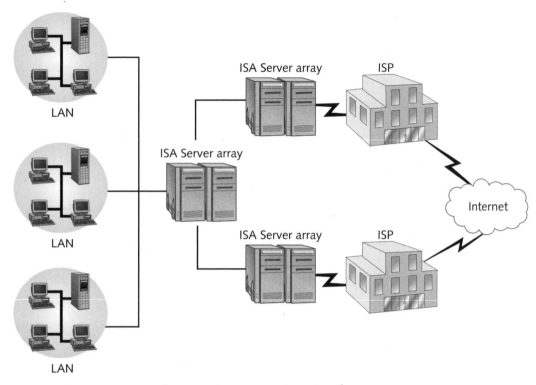

Figure 4-12   ISA Server chains and arrays combined

DETERMINING THE NEED FOR BACK-UP CONNECTIONS

As reliable as WAN service providers have become, you still need back-up connections. Minutes of network downtime can equal thousands of dollars in lost revenue, so you should include a back-up link in your plan. Even if the company can only afford a 56-Kbps dial-up connection, it is better than nothing. 56 Kbps is sufficient bandwidth to send work orders to off-site contractors or to receive the end-of-day report from a sales branch office. The key to successful network administration is to always have back-up resources for everything, regardless of how insignificant the backup may seem.

When choosing a back-up connection, try to find the budget for a connection that uses at least a quarter of the primary line's bandwidth. For example, if the primary connection is a 256-Kbps fractional T1 line, try to have at least a 64-Kbps back-up connection to ensure acceptable levels of connectivity. Although the connection may be four times slower than what the company prefers, the access speed is still bearable through typically short intervals of downtime.

Furthermore, if you have a dedicated back-up connection rather than dial-up service, you can use load balancing between the lines and combine the bandwidth of the primary and back-up lines for a faster connection. In the previous example, you could combine the bandwidth of the 256-Kbps primary line and the 64-Kbps back-up connection to attain a 320-Kbps WAN pipeline.

PROVISIONING SERVER HARDWARE

The type of hardware you use in the ISA Server machine can greatly affect the quality of service your network users receive. There are no strict hardware rules to follow when it comes to ISA Server; because the type and amount of network data vary significantly between network environments, no single hardware configuration works best for all situations. For example, 10 users who stream video and audio from the Internet to their PCs consume many more resources than 10 users surfing the Web. The following table lists Microsoft's hardware recommendations for ISA Server, based on the number of users. Use Table 4-4 as a general design guideline, not as an absolute rule.

Table 4-4   Server Hardware Considerations

# Users	ISA Server Computer Minimum Configuration	RAM (MB)	Disk Space Allocated for Caching
Up to 500	Single ISA Server computer with Pentium II, 300-MHz processor	256	2-4 GB
500–1,000	Single ISA Server computer with two Pentium III, 550-MHz processors	256	10 GB
More than 1,000	Two ISA Server computers, each with Pentium III, 550-MHz processors	256 for each server	10 GB for each server

Many network administrators believe upgrading the server's processor best improves performance; however, memory is the primary hardware resource that affects performance. The more memory you can add to the server, the better your network runs. While the hard disk stores most of the cached content, the server stores the most commonly accessed Internet content in RAM. Users who access the Web site content stored in the memory of the ISA Server machine receive an almost instantaneous response to their requests. This response requires minimal processor time and virtually no hard-disk access time, leaving ISA Server to focus on other tasks. When upgrading ISA Server, maximize memory first.

CHAPTER SUMMARY

❏ You must thoroughly plan an ISA Server installation before installing the software.

❏ Before you can redesign a network, you must examine and characterize the customer's existing network. This extensive process analyzes current protocols and applications running on the network. This analysis helps identify the requirements and performance demands for ISA Server before it is installed.

❏ Install only the ISA Server features that benefit your company. This approach improves the performance of commonly used features and does not waste resources on rarely used features.

❏ ISA Server arrays can provide for fault tolerance, load balancing, and easier administration.

❏ You must determine which mode of ISA Server installation you plan to use: firewall mode, cache-only mode, or integrated mode.

❏ You must determine company bandwidth requirements before choosing a WAN connection. The three categories of WAN connections—packet switching, circuit switching, and leased lines—provide a variety of bandwidth levels for different business requirements.

❏ Before connecting a company to the Internet, document corporate policies regarding security risks, such as e-mail.

❏ Back-up connections provide WAN redundancy and should have at least a quarter of the primary line's bandwidth capacity. Load balancing can be performed on dedicated back-up links to create a larger bandwidth pipeline for peak network hours.

❏ When provisioning hardware for the ISA Server machine, memory is the most important resource you can add. Hardware requirements also depend on the quantity and type of traffic on the corporate network.

KEY TERMS

Asynchronous Transfer Mode (ATM) — An extremely fast, packet-switched WAN solution that transfers data using fixed packet sizes called cells.

Channel Service Unit/Data Service Unit (CSU/DSU) — A network device, similar to a modem, required to interface with a service provider for T1 and T3 connections. The CSU performs diagnostic functions, and the DSU provides the physical interface.

Committed Information Rate (CIR) — A specified amount of guaranteed bandwidth on a frame relay service.

data-link connection identifiers (DLCIs) — Unique identifiers for virtual circuits in a frame relay WAN. Similar to the MAC address on LANs.

LAN Emulation (LANE) — ATM technology that allows the Ethernet or Token Ring LAN to treat the ATM network as another LAN subnet.

local access rate — The maximum speed allowable from the physical, frame relay connection.

Local Address Table (LAT) — The ISA Server table that identifies an internal network by IP address ranges.

network baseline — The average network usage under normal circumstances. Used when measuring the effect of adding or removing network resources.

Simple Network Management Protocol (SNMP) — A communications protocol used to manage devices on a TCP/IP network.

Synchronous Optical Network (SONET) — A defined standard for connecting fiber optic transmission systems at the physical layer.

virtual circuits (VCs) — Paths defined through the frame relay cloud that act like a physical connection between two end devices.

REVIEW QUESTIONS

1. ISA Server can translate between TCP/IP on the public network and _____ on the private network.

   a. IPX/SPX

   b. IPX/SPX and TCP/IP

   c. TCP/IP

   d. NetBEUI and TCP/IP

2. The 80/20 rule describes what?

   a. the ideal amount of local versus remote traffic in a network design

   b. the ideal amount of remote versus local traffic in a network design

   c. the total amount of traffic on a given network segment

   d. the unicast versus broadcast traffic levels on an ideal Ethernet segment

3. What is an example of a business constraint?

   a. WAN bandwidth should remain below 70 percent over a five-minute interval.

   b. The users local group is given read-only access to a public folder.

   c. All ISA Servers must have NAT running.

   d. All client machines must run Microsoft operating systems only.

4. Which of the following allows a reduction in NetBIOS name resolution broadcasts?

   a. WINS Server

   b. ISA Server

   c. routers

   d. Windows 2000

5. Which of the following is required for ISA Server to be installed in an array configuration?

    a. WINS Server

    b. 512 MB of RAM

    c. Active Directory

    d. Pentium 3,500-MHz processor

6. Frame relay qualifies as what category of WAN technology?

    a. circuit switching

    b. packet switching

    c. leased lines

    d. dial-up

7. Circuit-switching networks are typically _____ connections.

    a. PVC

    b. dedicated

    c. IPX/SPX

    d. nondedicated

8. You are guaranteed to get at least your CIR in a frame relay connection. True or false?

9. What technology allows users to connect to the private LAN using the Internet as a backbone?

    a. Telnet

    b. VPN

    c. network address translation

    d. authentication

10. The network baseline allows you to _____.

    a. analyze network security standards

    b. identify future network bottlenecks

    c. compare current network performance to its previous performance

    d. grant users access only to certain Web sites

11. ISA Server chains provide a redundant WAN. True or false?

12. ISA Server arrays provide what three things?

    a. easier administration, fault tolerance, and tighter security

    b. tighter security, load balancing, and fault tolerance

    c. tighter security, load balancing, and easier administration

    d. load balancing, easier administration, and fault tolerance

13. Which e-mail extensions most commonly contain virus attacks?

    a. .doc and .exe

    b. .bas and .txt

    c. .vbs and .exe

    d. .bas and .exe

14. Back-up connections should ideally provide at least _____ of the primary line's bandwidth.

    a. 25%

    b. 50%

    c. 75%

    d. 100%

15. What is the function of the LAT?

    a. to define ranges of usable Internet IP addresses

    b. to differentiate between public and private addresses

    c. to perform port translation for Internet applications

    d. to block Web sites that have inappropriate content

16. ISA Server stand-alone servers can be used in a Windows NT 4.0 domain. True or false?

17. In what three modes can you install ISA Server?

    a. firewall filtering, cache array, and isolated

    b. inclusive, caching only, and firewall

    c. public, private, and DMZ network

    d. firewall, cache-only, and integrated

18. How much bandwidth does a PRI ISDN connection provide?

    a. 128 Kbps

    b. 64 Kbps

    c. 1.544 Mbps

    d. 28.8 Kbps

19. What is an ISDN D channel used for?

    a. data transfer

    b. data error correction

    c. data filtering

    d. call setup

20. In what layer of the OSI model would SONET be categorized?

a. Physical

b. Data-link

c. Network

d. Transport

HANDS-ON PROJECTS

Project 4-1

Use the Web to research the current implementation of the following WAN connections: Frame Relay, DSL, ATM, and cable modems. In a one to two page paper, describe the current minimum and maximum speeds, areas of availability, and usage scenarios. Also describe the benefits and drawbacks to each WAN topology.

Project 4-2

Research at least two Internet Service Providers and ask the following questions:

1. How many support technicians are on staff?

2. How many years of experience do support technicians have working with networks? Troubleshooting Internet connection problems? What kinds of certification and education do they have?

3. What are the business hours of the ISP?

4. What are the filtering and Web hosting policies of the ISP?

5. Does the ISP allow for, and can they handle, the network load associated with VPNs?

6. What is the downtime history of the ISP? Why have failures occurred? What has the ISP done to fix them, and how will it prevent future failures?

7. What types of redundant systems does the ISP use? Does the ISP provide refunds or discounts for lapses in the connection?

8. How long has the ISP been in business? What are its future business plans? How does it plan to manage growth? Will it merge with another ISP?

9. If you have a T3 connection to the Internet, can the ISP support it?

10. What are its peak traffic times?

Project 4-3

SNMP is one of the primary protocols used to monitor the performance of local and wide area networks. Using RFC 1157 (*http://www.cis.ohio-state.edu/cgi-bin/rfc/rfc1157.html*), describe the architecture and functionality of SNMP in a one to two page paper.

Project 4-4

Widgets LLC is a company attempting to enter the e-commerce field by advertising and selling their products through a Web site. Widgets LLC currently has four locations in the United States. They run their Web site from offices located in southern Nevada. Their site receives approximately 5,000 visitors between the hours of 6 a.m. and 12 p.m. who download, on average, 200 kilobytes of data. The Nevada location must also connect to the Phoenix and Detroit sites to update the record database when a user orders a product. The Nevada site sends an average of 500 updates, each about 5 KB. Describe the WAN topologies and speeds that would meet the needs of Widgets LLC. Create a network diagram showing the configuration of the WAN connections and the placement of ISA Server.

Project 4-5

Blue Ocean, Inc., is a company that sells model navy ships at hundreds of retail outlets worldwide. They need an intranet Web site containing recently produced model ships, ship descriptions, and suggested retail prices. This Web site should not be accessible by the public. Suggest a WAN topology that connects all the Blue Ocean retail outlets, and allows them to access the intranet Web site. Create a network diagram showing the configuration of the WAN connections and the placement of ISA Server.

Project 4-6

You have been hired as a network consultant for Fig-Tek LLC, a small startup company with a single location and 50 employees that use the Internet connection to check competitor product pricing. They plan to deploy ISA Server to provide caching and firewall services for the company. In addition, they plan to provide access to the internal Web servers and redundancy for the ISA Server. Draw a proposed network diagram for Fig-Tek that includes the placement of ISA Servers, internal Web servers, and the type of WAN connection you suggest.

Project 4-7

You are the network administrator at Elite Industries, a nationwide company with a corporate office in New York and branch offices in Arizona, Missouri, Michigan, and California. Each branch office has a leased T1 connection to the corporate office, and the corporate office has a OC-192 connection to the Internet. Elite Industries wants to deploy ISA Server at all locations using arrays for redundancy, and a chained configuration. Draw a proposed network diagram for Elite Industries showing the WAN connections and ISA Server placement.

CASE PROJECTS

Case Project 4-1

The Rady Corporation has decided to install Microsoft ISA Server on its network, and you have been hired to plan the network rollout. Rady has sites in Taiwan, Mexico, Australia, and Seattle, each supporting 700 to 800 network users. Each network location has a T1 primary line and a 128-Kbps ISDN back-up connection. The Rady corporate Web site is supported by a three-server array in Seattle, and has links to smaller Web servers at each location. Create a planning worksheet that includes questions for management, documents hardware requirements, the network analysis required, and a network layout diagram.

Case Project 4-2

Terminal Processing Systems has decided to build a Web site to allow its 500 remote network consultants to submit work orders to the company through the Internet. The company also plans to use ISA Server for security and caching at its sites in Arizona and Missouri. The firewall should allow access to the internal Web servers and support VPN access. The company plans to use a new WAN topology with the rollout of ISA Server. (It currently uses multiple 56-Kbps dial-up connections for remote access and to link corporate sites.) You have been contracted to install ISA Server at both corporate sites. Create a planning worksheet that includes questions for management, documents hardware requirements, the network analysis required, and a network layout diagram.

Case Project 4-3

TD, Inc. is planning to deploy ISA Server to improve the current Internet access speed by adding caching capabilities. This deployment should support the current 900 employees on staff, but also be able to expand to 1200 employees within the next five months. The ISA Server should be able to handle redundant DSL connections in case the primary T1 connection fails. Create a planning worksheet that documents questions for management, hardware requirements, network analysis required, and a network layout diagram.

Case Project 4-4

Elite Enterprises is a nationwide company with headquarters in Washington, D.C. and over 100 branch offices nationwide. The company wants to deploy ISA Server in a hierarchical system. Each of the branch offices will have 128 Kbps WAN connections to the main office. Sketch the WAN topology that would best fit the company.

CHAPTER 5

INSTALLING ISA SERVER 2000

After reading this chapter and completing the exercises, you will be able to:
◆ Verify that your system meets the ISA Server 2000 hardware and software requirements
◆ Review the product licensing program for ISA Server
◆ Complete the pre-installation checklist
◆ Use the ISA Server Enterprise Initialization tool to modify the Active Directory schema
◆ Install ISA Server 2000
◆ Understand the default installation settings
◆ Test the configuration by allowing outbound Web requests
◆ Repair or remove ISA Server

This chapter guides you through the steps of installing ISA Server 2000. In the previous chapters, you learned how to sketch the current network design, analyze network requirements, install network interfaces and Active Directory, and configure and bind the TCP/IP protocol. After you perform those tasks, you should prepare for installation by verifying that your system meets the ISA Server hardware and software requirements, reviewing your ISA Server licensing agreement, and completing a pre-installation checklist. If you are installing ISA Server Enterprise Edition, you must also run the ISA Server Enterprise Initialization tool to modify the schema of Active Directory. This chapter guides you through these steps to prepare for installation.

When you are ready to install ISA Server 2000, you will use a wizard to guide you through the steps. Although using a wizard simplifies the installation, you must understand what you are configuring and how your decisions affect your network. In addition to providing step-by-step instructions for installing ISA Server 2000, this chapter also explains the background material you need to configure ISA Server to meet the needs of your network.

In addition to installing ISA Server 2000, this chapter explains how to add ISA Server management tools to the MMC so you can administer the server remotely. It also provides instructions for upgrading Microsoft Proxy Server 2.0 to ISA Server 2000, and for performing an unattended installation of ISA Server. To make sure you have set up ISA Server correctly, this chapter explains how to test your configuration. Finally, this chapter describes how to repair or remove ISA Server, if necessary, to resolve a failed or problematic installation.

VERIFYING THAT YOUR SYSTEM MEETS HARDWARE AND SOFTWARE REQUIREMENTS

Before installing ISA Server, make sure that your server meets the minimum hardware and software requirements that Microsoft outlines in the documentation for ISA Server. Your server must meet the following minimum requirements:

- A 300-MHz or faster Pentium 2 or compatible processor
- 256 MB of RAM
- 20 MB of available hard-disk space
- The server should have a Windows 2000-compatible network card for communicating with the internal network. An additional network card or modem connection is highly recommended for external network communication, but is not required.
- If you plan to use an array or advanced policies, you must have Windows 2000 Active Directory installed and available, and have at least one additional ISA Server computer.
- One local hard-disk partition formatted with the NTFS file system

To install ISA Server 2000, you must use one of the following operating systems:

- Windows 2000 Server with Service Pack 1 or later
- Windows 2000 Advanced Server with Service Pack 1 or later
- Windows 2000 Datacenter Server

These are the minimum requirements for ISA Server in a production environment. In a lab or classroom, where few or no clients access the Internet through ISA Server, you may be able to run with less than the minimum requirements.

REVIEWING ISA SERVER LICENSING

Microsoft provides a licensing program so that organizations can purchase site licenses that allow them to install and use ISA Server 2000. Microsoft based its Proxy Server 2.0 licensing on **Client Access Licenses (CALs)**, in which administrators could purchase a site license for the whole company or on a per-client basis. ISA Server uses a simplified "per-processor" licensing system. You purchase one license for each system on which you install ISA Server. This license allows unlimited client access from within or outside of your network. If you are upgrading from Proxy Server 2.0, the site licensing fee is typically half that of the full release price. The standard and enterprise versions of ISA Server each have their own pricing structures. For details concerning an ISA Server processor license, visit *www.microsoft.com/ISASERVER/productinfo/pricing.htm*.

5

COMPLETING THE PRE-INSTALLATION CHECKLIST

Before you install ISA Server 2000, verify that the following items are properly installed and configured:

- *Service Pack installation*—Install the latest version of the Windows 2000 service pack before installing ISA Server.

- *Network adapter configuration*—Ensure that all internal and external network adapters are installed and configured. Verify the connectivity and functionality of both network cards. If you are configuring ISA Server in an isolated environment, you can use a laptop computer equipped with a network card and crossover cable to test and troubleshoot ISA Server. If you are connecting the external network adapter to a service provider's ISDN, T1, T3, xDSL, or cable modem, make certain that any connection and addressing problems have been resolved. In addition, confirm that both network cards are properly labeled in the Network and Dial-up Connections window. Finally, ensure that the correct network cable is connected to the correct network card. Misconnections are a common error among network administrators of every experience level. Some administrators label network cables with colored masking tape for quick identification.

- *TCP/IP settings*—Check all IP addresses assigned to ISA Server. At the very least, you should be using static IP addressing for the internal interface of the server. Ensure that the default gateway of the internal interface does not point to the IP address of the external interface. Verify valid internal and external IP addressing by using the Ping utility to test connectivity.

- *Adequate hard-disk space*—Ensure that you have adequate hard-disk space not only to install the ISA Server program files, but also for cached Internet files.

- *Routing table*—Before you begin installation, list the internal network ranges used on the LAN. This list assists you in building the Local Address Table (LAT), which defines the local and remote network addresses. If you have a routing table correctly set up on the Windows 2000 server, ISA Server can build the LAT automatically. At a command prompt, type "route print" (without quotation marks) to view the current routing table.

- *Server backup*—If you are using a production server for ISA Server installation, back up the current configuration. This step is critical if the server is currently running Proxy Server 2.0. A recent backup allows you to restore the server should anything go wrong during the installation.

- *Internet Information Server (IIS)*—If you plan to run IIS on the ISA Server machine, you need to stop IIS from listening on ports 80 and 8080 by assigning different dynamic ports for IIS. ISA Server will reroute incoming requests on ports 80 and 8080 to the ports you assign.

USING THE ISA SERVER ENTERPRISE INITIALIZATION TOOL

If you plan to use the Enterprise version of ISA Server to set up an array configuration or enterprise-wide policies, ISA Server must modify the schema of Active Directory. ISA Server modifies the schema to create the necessary objects and properties in the ADS tree. To modify the Active Directory schema, you must be a member of the Enterprise Admins and Schema Admins groups.

 Installing the ISA Server Active Directory schema extensions is an irreversible process. You cannot uninstall the schema modifications. Ensure that you back up a current version of Active Directory before you proceed.

To install the ISA Server schema:

1. Insert the ISA Server Enterprise Edition CD in the CD drive, or double-click the **ISAAutorun.exe** file in the ISA Server Enterprise CD directory. The Microsoft ISA Server Setup window appears, as shown in Figure 5-1.

2. Click the **Run ISA Server Enterprise Initialization** icon. A message warns that the schema modifications are irreversible. Click **Yes** to continue.

3. The ISA Enterprise Initialization dialog box appears, as shown in Figure 5-2.

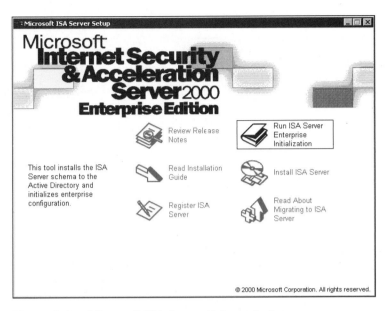

Figure 5-1   Microsoft ISA Server Setup window

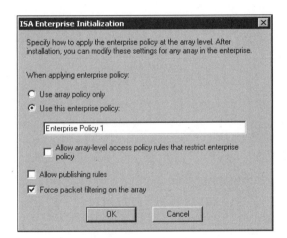

Figure 5-2   ISA Enterprise Initialization dialog box

Choose one of the settings listed below and click **OK**. You have the following options:

- *Use array policy only*—This option restricts the use of enterprise-wide policies and allows the application of ISA Server policies on an array-by-array basis.

- *Use this enterprise policy*—This option creates a default enterprise policy with the name you specify in the field. The default enterprise policy defines rules that affect all ISA Servers in the Active Directory tree.

- *Allow array-level access policy rules that restrict enterprise policy*—This check box allows administrators to define lower-level array policies for individual network segments that further restrict the enterprise-level policy.

- *Allow publishing rules*—This option allows you to create Web server publishing rules on a per-array basis rather than only allowing enterprise-wide publishing rules.

- *Force packet filtering on the array*—This option forces all ISA Server arrays to use packet filtering configured through the firewall service.

See Chapter 6 for a complete discussion of these options.

4. ISA Server installs the necessary classes, objects, and properties into the Active Directory schema. See Figure 5-3. Once the installation is finished, a success message is displayed. Click **OK** to complete the enterprise initialization.

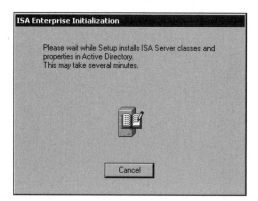

Figure 5-3 Modifiying the Active Directory schema

INSTALLING ISA SERVER 2000

After installing Windows 2000 Service Pack 1 and the ISA Server Active Directory schema, you can begin to install ISA Server. This chapter focuses on installing the Enterprise Edition of ISA Server. Installing the Standard version is similar, except that you don't set up ISA Server arrays.

Disconnect the ISA Server machine from the Internet during installation to ensure that no security breaches can occur. Also note that Web services running on the server are unavailable during installation.

To install ISA Server Enterprise Edition:

1. Insert the ISA Server Enterprise Edition CD in the CD drive, or double-click the **ISAAutorun.exe** file in the ISA Server Enterprise CD directory.

2. When the Setup window appears, click the **Install ISA Server** option.

3. On the Welcome window, click the **Continue** button.

4. The CD Key window opens. Enter the CD Key number from the ISA Server CD or use the 120-day demo CD Key **880–2897414**, then click **OK**. The next window displays your product ID number. Record this number in case you need to contact Microsoft technical support. Click **OK**.

5. The Setup Wizard looks for installed components, then displays the End User License Agreement dialog box. Click the **I Agree** button to continue.

6. The installation selection window appears, as shown in Figure 5-4.

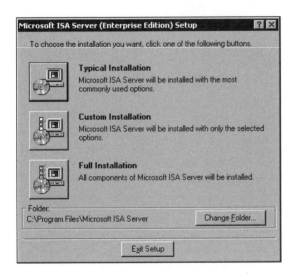

Figure 5-4   ISA Server Setup dialog box

Click one of the following buttons to choose an installation option:

- *Typical*—installs the most commonly used components
- *Custom*—allows you to select necessary installation components
- *Full*—installs all components

By default, the Setup Wizard installs the ISA Server program files on the windows partition in the \Program Files\Microsoft ISA Server folder. To change this location, click the **Change Folder** button, then navigate to the folder you want to use for the program files.

7. If you choose the Custom Installation option, select the components you want to install. See Figure 5-5. For example, you can install only the administration tools; this allows you to set up a remote administration console on any Windows 2000 machine. Select the components you want, then click **Continue**.

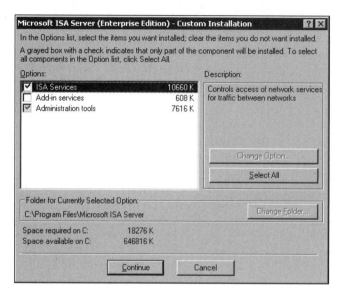

Figure 5-5   ISA Server Custom Installation dialog box

8. The Setup Wizard searches Active Directory for the ISA Server schema. If the wizard cannot find the schema, you must install the ISA Server machine as a stand-alone server or as an array member. If you want ISA Server to be an array member, click **Yes** in the dialog box. If you want to install ISA Server as a stand-alone server, click **No**.

9. If you click **Yes**, the Setup Wizard searches for existing ISA Server arrays. If it finds an array, you can select it to make ISA Server a member of that array. If the Setup Wizard cannot find an array, a dialog box appears that allows you to create an ISA Server array. To do so, enter the default enterprise policy settings of the array, as shown in Figure 5-6. Select the policy settings, then click **Continue**.

10. After you create an array or join an existing one, click **OK**.

11. In the next Microsoft ISA Server Setup dialog box, shown in Figure 5-7, select the mode you want to use for this server.

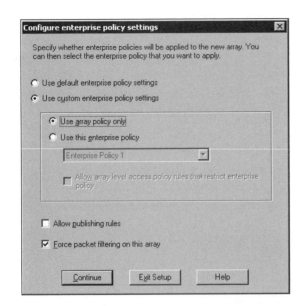

Figure 5-6   Enterprise policy settings for a new ISA Server array

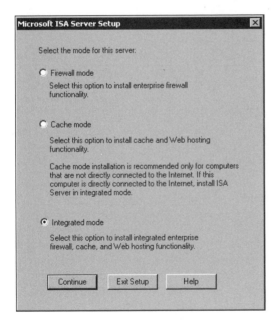

Figure 5-7   ISA Server installation modes

Click one of the following option buttons, then click **Continue**.

- *Firewall mode*—Choose Firewall mode to install only the security and packet filtering features of ISA Server.

- *Cache mode*—Choose Cache mode to install only the Web-caching features of ISA Server. This mode is only suggested for ISA Servers that have another form of firewall protection or an ISA Server that is part of an array, and is downstream from the other servers.

- *Integrated mode*—Choose Integrated mode to allow the use of all ISA Server features. This is the most common installation mode.

12. The next Microsoft ISA Server Setup dialog box informs you that the IIS publishing service (w3scv) has been stopped, and that you must reassign IIS ports 80 and 8080 after the installation. Click **OK**.

13. If you chose to install ISA Server in Cache or Integrated mode, use the dialog box, as shown in Figure 5-8, to select where to store cached files.

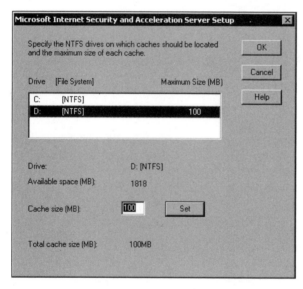

Figure 5-8   Selecting cache storage space

In the Drive list, click a drive that uses the NTFS file system. (You can only store cached files on a drive formatted with the NTFS file system.) In the Cache size text box, type the amount of space (in megabytes) you want to dedicate to cache storage, if necessary, and then click the **Set** button. If necessary, ISA Server distributes the cache across several hard disks, thus improving performance and fault tolerance. Click **OK** to continue.

14. In the next Setup dialog box, shown in Figure 5-9, you construct the Local Address Table.

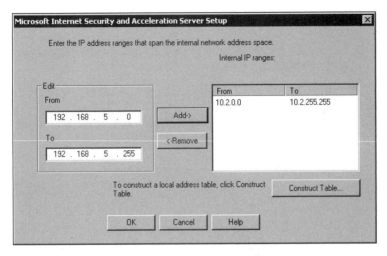

Figure 5-9   Building the Local Address Table

The LAT defines the internal IP addressing scheme of your network. You should have recorded these addresses during your planning phase. You must construct the LAT accurately. ISA Server uses the LAT to determine which requests should be sent to the Internet and which requests should remain on the local network. If you construct the table inaccurately, internal requests could be sent to the Internet and Internet requests could remain on the LAN.

Because most companies use the reserved ranges of private addresses described in RFC 1918 (*www.ietf.org/rfc/rfc1918.txt*), you can construct a LAT based on these ranges. To do so, click the **Construct Table** button. The Local Address Table dialog box appears, as shown in Figure 5-10, which you use to generate your LAT based on areas you select.

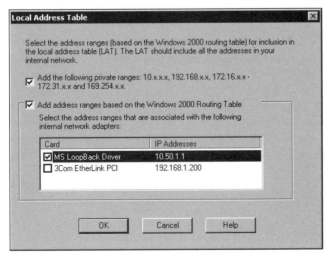

Figure 5-10   Auto-generating the Local Address Table entries

15. To include the addresses from the reserved private IP addressing space, click the first check box, if necessary, to select it. To add the ranges in the current Windows 2000 routing table, click the second check box, if necessary, to select it.

    Before ISA Server can add the ranges in the routing table, you must select the network adapter that connects to the internal LAN. *Do not* check the external NIC or include any ranges in the LAT that encompass the external NIC IP address. This can cause unpredictable results, including a possible loss of Internet connectivity through ISA Server. Click the appropriate card, then click **OK**. The ranges you specified are added to the Internal IP ranges box in the dialog box, as shown in Figure 5-9.

16. After you construct and verify your complete LAT, click **OK**.

    ISA Server stops the necessary services, checks for available hard-disk space, and copies program files. Next, the Launch ISA Management Tool dialog box appears, giving you the option to start the Getting Started Wizard once the installation is complete. This wizard allows you to set up the primary and default configuration parameters for ISA Server, and is discussed in the following section.

17. Click the **Getting Started Wizard** check box, if necessary, to run the wizard, and then click **OK**.

18. When notified that the ISA Server setup is complete, click **OK** to exit the Setup Wizard. You have successfully installed ISA Server.

Using the Getting Started Wizard

If you chose to run the Getting Started Wizard at the end of the installation, the ISA Management MMC snap-in opens after the Setup Wizard closes, showing the contents of the Getting Started Wizard in the right pane. See Figure 5-11.

Use the Getting Started Wizard to configure the primary features of ISA Server. For first-time users of ISA Server, the wizard also helps explain the purpose and configuration of many major components.

 The Getting Started Wizard is a great way to get ISA Server running because it guides you through the steps of defining the rules and policies that allow Internet access. If you do not define this set of rules and policies allowing Internet access, ISA Server does not function, because it denies all incoming and outgoing traffic by default.

The following sections explain how to use the Getting Started Wizard.

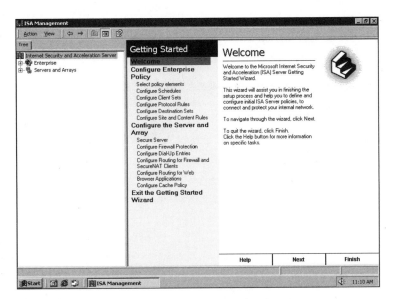

Figure 5-11   The Getting Started Wizard for ISA Server

Starting the Wizard

When the ISA Management console opens, you should see the Getting Started Welcome pane, as displayed in Figure 5-11. If you closed the console or elected not to open it when you finished the Setup Wizard, you can open it on your own.

To open the Getting Started Welcome pane in the ISA Management console:

1. Click **Start** on the taskbar, point to **Programs**, point to **Microsoft ISA Server**, then click **ISA Management**. Once the console opens, the Getting Started Wizard should run automatically. If it does not, click the **Getting Started Wizard** icon in the right panel of the screen.

2. Click **Next** to begin configuring the enterprise policy.

Configuring the Enterprise Policy

From the Configure Enterprise Policy window, you can configure the default policy ISA Server uses to grant or deny access when handling incoming requests.

To configure the enterprise policy:

1. Click the **Configure Enterprise Policy Default Settings** icon in the right panel of the MMC. If you do not see the Configure Enterprise Policy Default Settings icon, you are managing the individual server, not the array. To connect to an array, ensure that your server is selected, click **Action** on the menu bar, and then click **Connect to**. In the Connect to dialog box, select the **Array or Enterprise** option button, and then click **OK**. The Set

defaults window opens, as shown in Figure 5-12. This window also appeared during the ISA Server installation, and now allows you to select the level of policy for ISA Server arrays that use default enterprise policy settings.

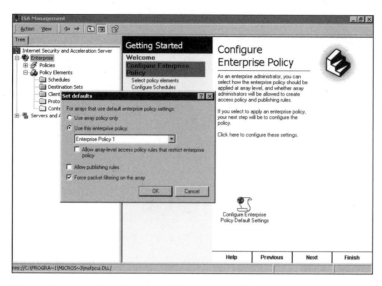

Figure 5-12   Configuring ISA Server default policy settings

2. In the Set defaults dialog box, select options according to the following descriptions:

- *Use array policy only*—Click this option button to allow each ISA Server array to have its own policies managed by individual network administrators. By default, ISA Server creates an enterprise policy named Enterprise Policy 1.

- *Use this enterprise policy*—Click this option button, and then click the list arrow and select an enterprise policy to use array-level policies that augment the current enterprise policy. This is extremely useful, because you can define an enterprise policy that applies company restrictions to Internet access to all ISA Servers, and then use array policies to become more restrictive. For example, suppose upper management at your company wants to stop all employees from using the ICQ protocol (commonly used for online chat applications) during work hours. The manager of the Marketing Department wants to further restrict her employees from accessing the World Wide Web. Using ISA Server, you could create an enterprise policy denying use of the ICQ protocol on any ISA Server in the corporate network. You could then create an array policy for the marketing manager and deny the use of HTTP from any machine accessing the Internet through the marketing ISA Server array.

- *Allow array-level access policy rules that restrict enterprise policy*—Click this check box if you want to be able to create array-level policies.

3. Once you configure the default policy settings, click **OK**, then click **Next** twice to move to the select policy elements page.

Selecting Policy Elements

After configuring the default policy for ISA Server arrays, you must select the policy elements you want to filter.

To select policy elements:

1. In the ISA Management console, click the **Select policy elements** icon in the right pane to display the Select Policy Elements dialog box, as shown in Figure 5-13.

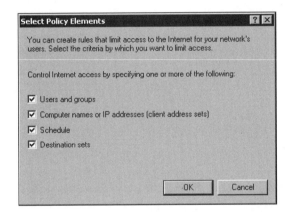

Figure 5-13 ISA Server Select Policy Elements dialog box

2. Click to select one or more of the options you want to use in filtering Internet access:

- *Users and groups*—Select this check box to grant or deny access based on users and groups in the Local Security Database (LSA) for stand-alone ISA Servers, or in the Active Directory database for ISA Server array members.

- *Computer names or IP addresses (client address sets)*—Select this check box to grant or deny access based on computer names or client address sets (described in the following section).

- *Schedule*—Select this check box to grant or deny access based on the time or day of the week.

- *Destination sets*—Select this check box to grant or deny access based on the destination hostname or IP address the client is attempting to access.

3. Click **OK**.

After you complete the Select Policy Elements window, continue through the rest of the Getting Started Wizard, first configuring each policy for the enterprise, then focusing on the array and individual server configurations. For an explanation of these configuration items, see the following chapter.

Installing ISA Server Management Tools

Because of concern for the physical security of network servers, many network administrators keep the company servers behind closed doors and manage all administrative tasks remotely. Because ISA Server integrates into the MMC, you can administer it remotely from any Windows 2000-based platform (including Windows 2000 Professional). Before you can do this, you must install the ISA Server management tools on your workstation.

To install the management tools:

1. Insert the ISA Server Enterprise Edition CD in the CD drive of your server, or double-click the **ISAAutorun.exe** file in the ISA Server Enterprise CD directory. When the Setup window opens, click the **Install ISA Server** option button.

2. The Welcome window opens. Click the **Continue** button. Enter your assigned CD key in the following dialog box, and then click **OK**.

3. The installation options dialog box appears. Click the **Custom Installation** button.

4. In the Custom Installation dialog box, deselect the **ISA Services** and **Add-in services** check boxes, select the Administration tools, and then click the **Change Option** button.

5. The Administration tools option list appears, as shown in Figure 5-14. Use this dialog box to select the management tools you want to install.

   Ensure that the **ISA Management** box is checked. If you are managing H.323 services, also check the **H.323 Gatekeeper Administration Tool** box, if necessary. (H.323 services are discussed in a later chapter.) Click **OK** to return to the Custom Installation dialog box, and then click **Continue**.

6. The Setup Wizard copies the necessary files, prompts you to run the Getting Started Wizard, and then closes.

Once you have installed the ISA Server management tools, you need to connect to the server you want to manage. Open the ISA Management console, click the Connect to icon, type the computer name of the ISA Server you want to manage, and then click OK. Provided the server is accessible, the ISA Management console should connect and be able to perform any administrative function remotely.

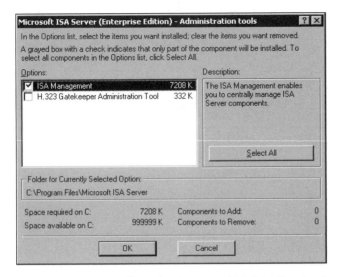

Figure 5-14   Installing ISA Server administration tools

Upgrading Microsoft Proxy Server 2.0 to ISA Server 2000

If you are running Microsoft Proxy Server 2.0 in a Windows NT environment and are planning an upgrade to ISA Server 2000, consider the following points:

- ISA Server does not support a direct upgrade from Proxy Server 1.0, BackOffice Server 4.0, or Small Business Server 4.0.

- Once you upgrade from Proxy Server 2.0 to ISA Server 2000, you cannot use an automated process to return to Proxy Server 2.0.

- Proxy Server 2.0 supports translation between the IPX and IP protocols; ISA Server does not support the IPX protocol.

- Before you can upgrade an array of Proxy Server 2.0 computers, you must remove all of the members. This should not cause any problems because all array configurations are copied to each stand-alone Proxy Server machine.

Before you can upgrade Proxy Server 2.0 to ISA Server 2000, you must first upgrade the operating system from Windows NT 4.0 to a Windows 2000 server platform. Upgrading to Windows 2000 while Proxy Server 2.0 services are running can cause problems; before beginning the upgrade, stop each Proxy Server 2.0 service by typing "net stop service_name" at a command prompt. The following table lists the Proxy Server services you should stop.

Table 5-1 Proxy Server Services

Proxy Server Service	Service Name
Microsoft Winsock Proxy service	wspsrv
Microsoft Proxy Server Administration	mspadmin
Proxy Alert Notification service	mailalrt
World Wide Web Publishing service	w3svc

Once you stop these services, you can upgrade to Windows 2000, and then begin the ISA Server setup. During the upgrade, you may receive a message stating that Proxy Server 2.0 does not work on Windows 2000. You can ignore this message.

When you upgrade a Proxy Server machine to ISA Server, all of your current configurations are maintained. For example, if the Proxy Server has rules that allow all Web traffic and filtered FTP and SMTP traffic, these rules migrate to ISA Server during the upgrade. In addition to the packet and content filter rules, the LAT, automatic dial settings, alerts, log settings, and client configurations are also maintained during the upgrade. While the migration process is fairly straightforward and simple, you need to know which Proxy Server rules migrate into which ISA Server categories. The following table lists the Proxy Server 2.0 categories and the resulting ISA Server 2000 categories.

Table 5-2 Proxy Server 2.0 to ISA Server 2000 Rule Migration

Proxy Server 2.0	ISA Server 2000
Domain filters	Site and content rules
Winsock permission settings	Protocol rules
Publishing properties	Web publishing rules
Static packet filters	Open or blocked IP packet filters
Web Proxy routing rules	Routing rules

If the company budget does not allow for a full migration from Proxy Server 2.0, ISA Server supports having both platforms active on the network. For example, you can use a chained configuration with a downstream ISA Server handling the bulk of the client requests and routing them to an upstream Proxy Server connected to the Internet. However, since ISA Server supports many features that Proxy Server does not, ISA Server does not support mixed platform arrays (Proxy Servers and ISA Servers sharing the same array).

Performing an Unattended Installation of ISA Server

ISA Server supports using an unattended server installation script. If you are installing more than one ISA Server machine and they all share a similar configuration, you may want to consider this fast and efficient option. You can start the ISA Server installation and literally walk away; a script answers all prompts in the Setup utility, filling in the needed information. Before you can use the unattended installation, you must create a file called msisaund.ini and place it in the root directory of the first hard disk (typically the C: drive) of your server. The following table lists the file entries that answer the Setup prompts. If one of these fields is missing or is filled out incorrectly, the Setup utility stops. Microsoft has built an example msisaund.ini file and placed it in the ISA directory on the ISA Server CD.

Table 5-3   msisaund.ini Script Contents

Section	Entry	Description
[ISA Setup Install]	Install Dir	Specifies the installation directory for ISA Server. If it is not specified, ISA Server is installed on the first hard disk with enough storage space.
[ISA Setup Install]	Override Existing Configuration	If there has been a prior installation of ISA Server, you can either allow or stop the Setup script from overwriting the existing configuration. By default, the existing configuration is not overwritten.
[Array Membership]	Join Existing Array	Allows you to join an existing ISA Server array on the network. Ensure that the ISA Server schema has been installed in Active Directory if this option is selected.
[Array Membership]	Create New Array and Join	Allows you to create and join a new array. Ensure that the ISA Server schema has been installed in Active Directory if this option is selected.
[Features]	Installation Option	Specifies the mode (cache, firewall, or integrated) in which ISA Server will be installed. The default is integrated.
[Firewall LAT Config]	Include Ranges From All Cards	If set to 1, creates the LAT from the IP ranges assigned to all network cards and assumes that the dial-up connection connects to the Internet.
[Firewall LAT Config]	Include Private Ranges	If set to 1, includes all private IP address ranges described in RFC 1918 in the LAT.
[Firewall LAT Config]	Range1, Range2...	Allows you to specify ranges for the LAT in x.x.x.x, y.y.y.y format. For example, Range1=10.1.0.0 10.1.255.255, Range2=192.168.1.0 192.168.1.255.

5

Table 5-3   msisaund.ini Script Contents (continued)

Section	Entry	Description
[Cache Config]	Drive=drive size_min size_max	Allows you to set the drive letter along with minimum and maximum cache sizes. For example, Drive=C 100 200 sets the C drive to cache with a minimum size of 100 MB and a maximum of 200 MB. If the maximum size exceeds the amount of available hard-disk space, Setup will use all available remaining space. If the minimum size exceeds the available hard-disk space, Setup fails. Ensure that all caching drives have an NTFS format.
[Cache Config]	Enable Cache	If set to 1, enables caching. If set to 0, disables caching. If not specified, default is 1.

Once you have created the msisaund.ini file and placed it in the root directory of the first hard disk on the server, you can run the ISA Server unattended setup. To begin, type the following from a command line:

Path**Isa****Setup /qt /k "your CD Key number"**

For easier and quicker installation on multiple machines, you could create a batch (.bat) file with this line, copy it to a floppy disk or network location, and access it at each server.

UNDERSTANDING THE DEFAULT SETTINGS

After you install ISA Server, you need to understand its default configuration settings. These settings are discussed in detail in the next chapter. Until any changes are made, the following configuration is in place:

- *Access control*—ISA Server grants all access requests by default. However, until you create an initial protocol rule (allowing some type of protocol to pass through the ISA Server), all traffic is denied.

- *Alerts*—All alerts are active except the following: all-port scan attack, dropped packets, protocol violation, and UDP bomb attack.

- *Caching*—The cache size is set to the size you specified during setup. HTTP and FTP caching are enabled when active caching is disabled.

- *Enterprise policy settings*—New arrays adopt the default enterprise policy.

- *Local Address Table*—The LAT contains the entries you specified during setup.

- *Packet filtering*—If you installed ISA Server in Firewall or Integrated mode, packet filtering is enabled by default. In Cache mode, it is disabled.

- *Publishing*—Publishing is disabled by default, keeping all internal Internet services inaccessible from outside clients.

- *Routing*—ISA Server retrieves all Web client requests directly from the Internet.

- *User permissions*—If using a stand-alone server, only members of the Administrators group can configure policies. If using an array, members of the Domain Admins and Enterprise Admins groups can configure policies.

TESTING THE CONFIGURATION: ALLOWING OUTGOING WEB REQUESTS

Now that ISA Server is installed, you can test your configuration by allowing ISA Server to retrieve data from the Web for a client. Since the default settings of ISA Server deny all incoming and outgoing requests, you must make some minor configuration changes using the Getting Started Wizard.

To test the ISA Server configuration:

1. In the Getting Started Wizard, click **Configure Protocol Rules**, and then click **Create a Protocol Rule**. Using the wizard, create a rule allowing the use of all protocols by all clients at all times.

2. In the Getting Started Wizard, click **Configure Site and Content Rules**, then click **Create a Site and Content Rule**. Using the wizard, create a rule allowing access to all content at all destinations by all clients.

3. In the console pane of the ISA Management MMC, double-click the **Servers and Arrays** section, double-click your array name, double-click **Network Configuration**, and then click **Routing**. Verify that a routing rule named **Default rule** is configured to **Retrieve the request directly** under the Action heading. See Figure 5-15.

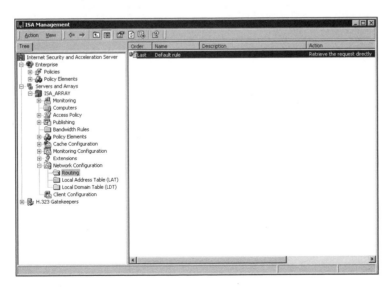

Figure 5-15   Verifying routing rules

4. Using Internet Explorer on a client machine, click **Tools** on the menu bar, and then click **Internet Options**. Click the **Connections** tab, then click the **LAN Settings** button. In the Local Area Network (LAN) Settings dialog box, check the **Use a proxy server** box, and then assign the IP address and port number of the ISA Server. See Figure 5-16. The default port number is 8080.

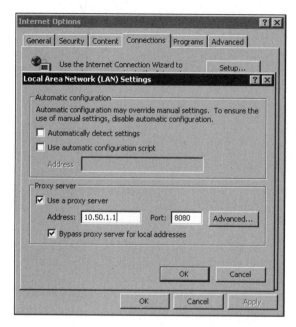

Figure 5-16   Client browser configuration

5. On the client machine, attempt to connect to an Internet Web site. If ISA Server is working correctly, the client machine should connect.

REPAIRING OR REMOVING ISA SERVER

By running the ISA Server installation program a second time, you can change your installation options, repair your previous installation, or remove ISA Server from your system completely. When you run the Setup utility a second time from the ISA Server CD, you have the options shown in Figure 5-17.

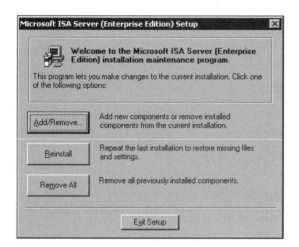

Figure 5-17   ISA Server repair or removal

Choose an option according to the following descriptions:

- *Add/Remove*—Allows you to customize your installation of ISA Server by adding or removing any component

- *Reinstall*—Allows you to run the installation again to restore missing program files or repair a corrupted installation

- *Remove All*—Removes ISA Server completely from your system

CHAPTER SUMMARY

- Before you install ISA Server, you should have a machine with at least a Pentium 2, 300-MHz processor; 256 MB of RAM; and 20 MB of free, hard-disk space.

- ISA Server is licensed on a per-processor basis; that is, you only need to purchase one license per ISA Server, regardless of how many clients access the Internet through that ISA Server.

- Before installing ISA Server, you should reassign ports 80 and 8080 in IIS because ISA Server takes control of those ports.

- Before installing an ISA Server array, you must update the Active Directory schema using the ISA Server Enterprise Initialization tool.

- Enterprise policies should only be as restrictive as the strictest company policy. Use array policies to further restrict network access.

- You can install ISA Server in one of three modes: Firewall mode (for security), Cache mode (for Internet access acceleration), or Integrated mode (installs both Firewall and Cache features).

- The Local Address Table (LAT) is a list of all internal LAN IP addresses. It allows ISA Server to determine which IP addresses should route to the Internet and which should remain on the local network.

- The Getting Started Wizard helps you configure all the major ISA Server rules, policies, and schedules.

- ISA Server is capable of unattended installation. All configuration items are stored in a file named MsISAund.ini in the root directory of the first server's hard disk (typically the C: drive).

- You can repair or reinstall ISA Server by running the installation utility a second time.

KEY TERMS

Client Access Licenses (CALs) — A license typically required when accessing a Microsoft server across the network.

REVIEW QUESTIONS

1. It is best to have IIS and ISA Server operating on the same computer. True or false?

2. During installation, one of your server's hard disks is grayed out when selecting your cache storage space. What is the problem?

   a. The hard disk does not have enough available storage space.

   b. The hard disk is not formatted with the FAT32 file system.

   c. The hard disk is corrupt.

   d. The hard disk is formatted with the FAT32 file system.

3. ISA Server 2000 and Proxy Server 2.0 can work together in a chained, hierarchical configuration. True or false?

4. What file is used for an unattended installation of ISA Server?

   a. Msunatten.ini

   b. MsunaISA.ini

   c. MsftISAu.ini

   d. MsISAund.ini

5. Which of the following is not a valid ISA Server installation mode?

   a. integrated

   b. firewall

   c. incorporated

   d. cache

6. When ISA Server is removed from the system, the schema is uninstalled from Active Directory. True or *False*

7. What is the minimum hard-disk space required for a full installation of ISA Server?

a. 20 MB

b. 2 GB

c. 200 MB

d. 2 MB

8. Which of the following should the LAT contain?

a. all IP addresses local to the network

b. all restricted IP addresses

c. any IP address allowed to access ISA Server

d. all IP addresses that are external to the network

9. A(n) _____ policy contains all corporate restrictions.

a. array

b. enterprise

c. restrictive

d. local

10. You are working with the ISA Management console and it reports that the ISSfltr.dll file is corrupt or could not be found. What should you do?

a. Run the Setup utility, and reinstall ISA Server.

b. Use FDISK.exe or *Delpart.com* to correct the problem.

c. Attempt to locate the file on the support Web site for ISA Server.

d. Call for Level Two technical support from Microsoft.

11. Which of the following platforms can manage ISA Server?

a. Windows 2000 Professional

b. Windows Millennium

c. Windows NT Server, Enterprise Edition

d. Windows NT Workstation

12. Which of the following is turned off by default in an ISA Server Integrated installation?

a. packet filtering

b. Web publishing

c. caching

d. alerts

13. You are installing the ISA Server Enterprise Edition and you are not prompted to join an ISA Server array. How can you resolve this problem?

    a. Install the ISA Server schema.

    b. Run the installation program with the /JoinArray *array_name* switch.

    c. Select the Custom Installation process.

    d. Upgrade the system from Windows NT Server to Windows 2000 Server.

14. The default gateway of the ISA Server Internal LAN NIC should be assigned to the IP address of the External LAN NIC. True or false?

15. When installing only the ISA Server management tools, which type of installation should you choose?

    a. typical

    b. full

    c. custom

    d. MMC snap-in only

16. The MsISAund.ini file should be placed in the same directory as the ISA Server installation files. True or false?

17. If you are using an unattended installation script to install ISA Server and the amount of free space does not meet the number entered for the [Cache Config] size_max switch, what occurs?

    a. Installation proceeds, provided the hard disk has at least the minimum size.

    b. The unattended script stops and waits for you to enter a valid number.

    c. Installation stops with an error message.

    d. Windows 2000 generates an event in the Event Viewer log file.

18. During installation, the ISA Server should be connected to the Internet to allow DNS name resolution to occur. True or false?

19. Before installing ISA Server, you must have which of the following?

    a. Internet Information Services

    b. ISA Server schema installed

    c. Active Directory configured

    d. Windows 2000 Service Pack 1

20. If you upgrade your configuration from Microsoft Proxy Server 2.0, domain filters are migrated to which ISA Server rule set?

    a. site and content rules

    b. routing rules

    c. protocol rules

    d. This upgrade is not possible.

HANDS-ON PROJECTS

Project 5-1

To ensure a smooth installation of ISA Server, verify the following items:

1. Open the System Properties dialog box by opening the Control Panel and double-clicking the **System** icon. Ensure that at least Windows 2000 Service Pack 1 is installed, and the machine is equipped with at least 128 MB of RAM. See Figure 5-18.

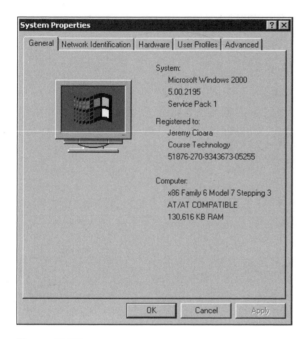

Figure 5-18

2. Close the System Properties dialog box, and then double-click the **My Computer** icon on the desktop. Right-click the **C: drive**, then click **Properties**. Verify that the file system is NTFS, and the hard disk has at least 50 MB of free space.

3. Close all open windows, then open a command prompt by clicking **Start**, clicking **Run**, and then typing **cmd**. Once the command prompt is open, type **ipconfig**, and document the IP address of both the internal and external NICs.

4. Your computer is now ready to install ISA Server 2000.

Project 5-2

To install the ISA Server schema into Active Directory:

1. Insert the ISA Server Enterprise Edition CD in the CD drive, or double-click the **ISAAutorun.exe** file in the ISA Server directory. The Microsoft ISA Server Setup window appears.

2. Click **Run ISA Server Enterprise Initialization**. Click **Yes** when prompted to continue. The ISA Enterprise Initialization dialog box appears.

3. Click **Use this enterprise policy**, as shown in Figure 5-19, and then click **OK**.

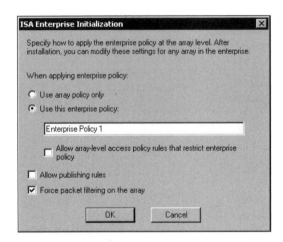

Figure 5-19

4. ISA Server installs all necessary files into the Active Directory schema. Once the success message is displayed, click **OK**. You have successfully installed the ISA Server schema into Active Directory.

Project 5-3

To install ISA Server 2000:

1. Insert the ISA Server Enterprise Edition CD in the CD drive, or double-click the **ISAAutorun.exe** file in the ISA Server directory. The Microsoft ISA Server Setup dialog box appears.

2. Click **Install ISA Server**. The Welcome window opens.

3. Click **Continue** in the Welcome window. The CD Key dialog box appears.

4. Enter **880–2897414** as the CD Key, and then click **OK**. Click **OK** in the Product ID dialog box that follows. The End User License Agreement appears.

5. Click **I Agree**. The installation selection dialog box appears.

6. Click **Custom Installation**. The Custom Installation dialog box appears.

7. Click **Select All** in the Custom Installation dialog box. All three check boxes should be selected. Click **Continue**. See Figure 5-20.

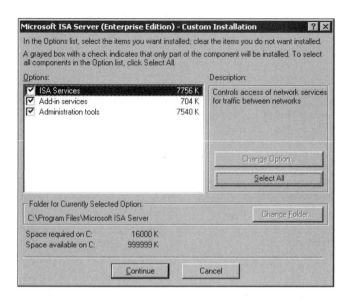

Figure 5-20

8. When prompted to install the server as an array member, click **Yes**. Type
   ISAArrayX (where *X* is a unique number assigned by your instructor) in the
   Array name box, and click **OK**. The Configure enterprise policy settings dialog
   box appears, as shown in Figure 5-21.

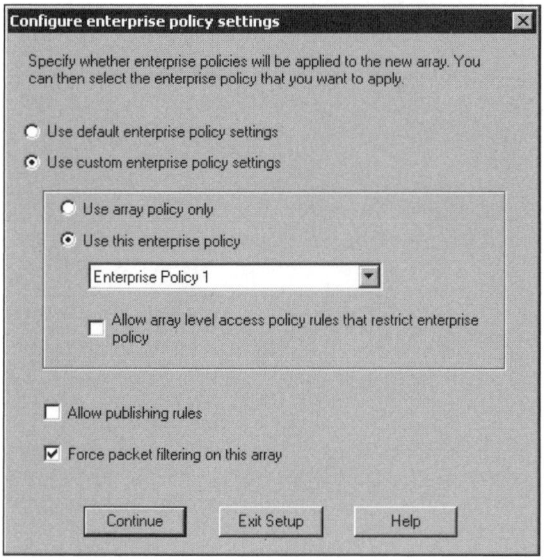

Figure 5-21

9. Click **Use custom enterprise policy settings**, click **Use this enterprise policy**, and then click **Continue**. The Mode Selection dialog box appears.

10. Ensure that **Integrated mode** is selected, and then click **Continue**. When an informational dialog box appears, click **OK**. The cache selection window appears.

11. Ensure that the drive where ISA Server is installed is selected, change the cache size to **10** MB, and then click **Set**. The Maximum Size column next to the C: drive should change to 10 MB. Click **OK**. The Local Address Table (LAT) dialog box appears.

12. Click **Construct Table**. In the LAT window, deselect the **Add the following private ranges** check box, and then click **Add address ranges based on the Windows 2000 Routing Table**, if necessary. Select the network card that corresponds to your internal LAN, and then click **OK**. See Figure 5-22. A message notifies you that the LAT has been constructed. Click **OK**, then click **OK** in the original LAT window. Setup stops all necessary services, then copies the program files to your server. The Launch ISA Management Tool dialog box appears.

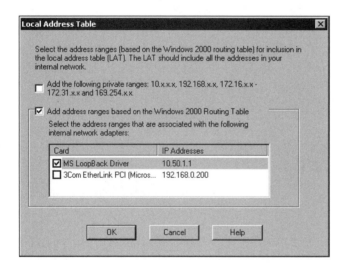

Figure 5-22

13. Ensure that the **Start ISA Server Getting Started Wizard** check box is selected, and then click **OK**. Click **OK** in the completion window. ISA Server has been successfully installed.

Project 5-4

To permit all outgoing Web requests:

1. If it is not already open, start the Getting Started Wizard in the ISA Management console by clicking **Start**, pointing to **Programs**, pointing to **Microsoft ISA Server**, clicking **ISA Management**, and then clicking the **Getting Started Wizard** icon.

2. In the Getting Started column, click **Configure Protocol Rules**. The Configure Protocol Rules for Enterprise Policy 1 window appears, as shown in Figure 5-23.

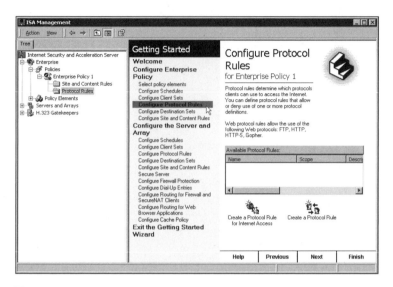

Figure 5-23

3. Click **Create a Protocol Rule**. The Protocol Rule Wizard appears and prompts you to enter the name of the protocol rule. Type **Protocol Freedom** for the protocol rule name, and then click **Next**. The Rule Action dialog box appears.

4. Choose **Allow** for the client response, if necessary, and then click **Next**. Select to apply this rule to **All IP traffic** in the Protocols window, and then click **Next**. The Schedule window appears.

5. Choose to **Always** use this schedule, if necessary, and then click **Next**. In the Client Type window, choose to apply this rule to **Any request**, if necessary, and then click **Next**. Click **Finish** in the protocol rule summary window. You should see Protocol Freedom under the Available Protocol Rules table.

6. In the Getting Started column of the ISA Management console, click **Configure Site and Content Rules**, and then click **Create a Site and Content Rule** in the right pane. The Site and Content Rule Wizard appears and prompts you to enter the name of the site and content rule. Type **Site Freedom** for the rule name, and then click **Next**. The Rule Action window appears.

7. Choose to **Allow** client requests for access, and then click **Next**, as shown in Figure 5-24. Select to apply this rule to **All destinations** in the Destination Sets window, and then click **Next**. The Schedule dialog box appears.

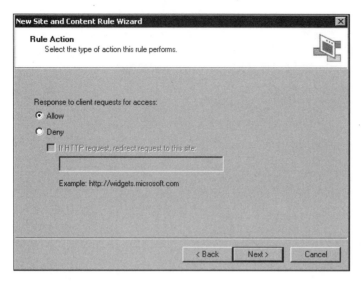

Figure 5-24

8. Choose to **Always** use this schedule, and then click **Next**. In the Client Type dialog box, choose to apply this rule to **Any request**, and then click **Next**. Click **Finish** in the site and content rule summary window. You should see Site Freedom under the Available Site and Content Rules table.

9. Double-click the **Servers and Arrays** node, and then double-click your array. Double-click **Network Configuration**, then click **Routing**. Verify that a rule named **Default rule** is configured to **Retrieve the request directly** under the Action heading. See Figure 5-25.

10. On a client machine (or on the ISA Server itself), open Internet Explorer, click **Tools** on the menu bar, and then click **Internet Options**. The Internet Options dialog box appears.

11. Click the **Connections** tab, and then click the **LAN Settings** button. Deselect **Automatically detect settings**, and then click **Use a proxy server**. Enter the *internal* IP address of the ISA Server computer, then enter **8080** as the Port. See Figure 5-26. Click **OK** twice to close both windows.

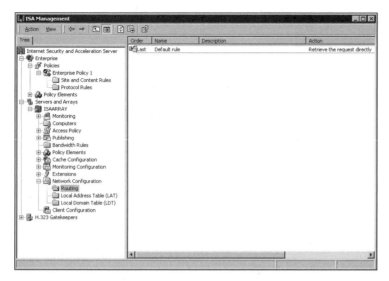

Figure 5-25

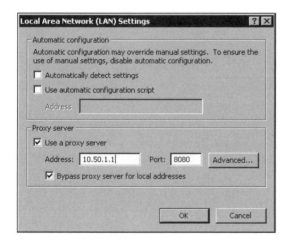

Figure 5-26

12. If you have a valid Internet connection, attempt to connect to *www.microsoft.com* using Internet Explorer on the client (or the ISA Server itself). Provided the server is configured correctly, you should connect to the Web site.

Project 5-5

You successfully installed ISA Server and allowed outgoing requests for the external network. However, the internal network has grown to include two more subnets: 172.16.5.0/24 and 172.16.6.0/24. To accommodate this growth, you must modify the current LAT to include the new subnets.

To add entries to the current LAT:

1. In the ISA Management console, expand the **Servers and Arrays** node, expand your array, and then expand the **Network Configuration** node.

2. Right-click the **Local Address Table (LAT)** node, point to **New**, and then click **LAT Entry**. The New LAT Entry dialog box appears.

3. In the **From** text box, enter **172.16.5.0**. In the **To** text box, enter **172.16.6.255**. This covers all the IP addresses in the 172.16.5.0/24 and 172.16.6.0/24 subnet ranges.

4. Once you have entered the IP address ranges, click **OK**. The new entry appears in the local address table.

Project 5-6

You have just finished installing ISA Server 2000, but your clients cannot access the network. You created a Site and Content rule allowing outbound access to content types and external destinations. You created a protocol rule allowing the internal network users to work with any TCP/IP-based protocol. You reviewed the LAT table, and found it lists the IP addresses of the ISA Server network interface cards and all internal network IP addresses. The client is configured to access ISA Server for all outbound requests. You can successfully ping the internal interface of ISA Server. What is the most likely cause of the problem?

CASE PROJECTS

Case Project 5-1

The Rady Corporation has decided to install ISA Server on its company network. The Rady Corp. uses an array of five Microsoft Proxy 2.0 machines to connect to the Internet, and would like to keep the current configuration on the proxy servers if possible. You have been contracted as a consultant to oversee the upgrade process. What pre-installation checks should you perform? Will there be any problems maintaining the current Proxy Server 2.0 configuration? Create a step-by-step list that details the upgrade process.

Case Project 5-2

Terminal Processing Systems (TPS) wants to install ISA Server 2000 at its network sites in Arizona and Missouri. Each site uses a direct dial-up connection to the Internet. The dial-up connections will both be replaced with fractional T1 lines before ISA Server is installed. While security is a concern, TPS is interested in ISA Server primarily for its caching and reverse-publishing features. What installation mode would you suggest for TPS? Describe the network preparation and installation processes in detail.

Case Project 5-3

Elite Systems Inc. has just installed two ISA Servers that they would like to administer as an array. They are using Windows 2000 Server as the base operating system. The installation went smoothly on both ISA Servers, but afterwards, they were unable to administer the servers as an array. The ISA Management console treated both servers as stand-alone servers and did not allow for the creation of any enterprise policies. What is the most likely cause of this problem? How can you fix the problem?

Case Project 5-4

You have finished installing ISA Server on a Windows 2000 test server and applied all the necessary policies to allow for full Internet access. The internal network interface is connected to a small hub with one client attached, and the external network interface is attached to a DSL connection. Before you installed ISA Server 2000, you could successfully connect to both the Internet and the internal client from ISA Server, but now you cannot. What is the most likely cause of the problem? How would you solve the problem?

5

6

UNDERSTANDING ISA SERVER 2000 POLICIES

After reading this chapter and completing the exercises, you will be able to:

♦ Compare enterprise, array, and server policies

♦ Work with the ISA Server MMC

♦ Configure enterprise policies, including the default enterprise policy and its behavior

♦ Define and configure policy elements

♦ Configure enterprise and array policy rules to allow or restrict network access

As you learned in Chapter 5, the default installation of ISA Server denies all incoming requests and restricts all traffic from entering or leaving the internal network. Before internal users can access external resources, you must configure ISA Server access policies. Policies allow you to filter users based on their network address, the applications they use, or the content they access. You can configure these policies to affect only the local server, an array of servers, or all servers in the entire enterprise. This chapter explains how to set enterprise, array, and server policies.

You work with ISA Server policies to configure nearly every feature in ISA Server 2000. Microsoft implemented this policy-based administration to closely reflect the group policy style of Windows 2000. Setting ISA Server policies involves establishing rules to maintain network security. In addition to security, you also set ISA Server policies to configure caching, alerts, VPNs, and many other features. ISA Server provides a number of wizards to guide you through the process of configuring policies. However, you must understand the functionality and effects of implementing each ISA Server policy before you can effectively complete the policy configuration wizards. This chapter explains the concepts and implications of creating and configuring ISA Server policies.

COMPARING ENTERPRISE, ARRAY, AND SERVER POLICIES

For ISA Server 2000, you can set enterprise, array, and server policies. An **enterprise policy**, by default, applies to all ISA Servers in the corporate network. Use enterprise policies to establish and enforce rules that apply to all network users. For example, an enterprise policy would restrict FTP access if FTP is not permitted on the corporate network. An **array policy** applies to the single ISA Server arrays throughout the network. These policies typically contain restrictions set for each department within the organization. You can use array-level policies to further restrict the guidelines configured in the enterprise policy. Unlike enterprise policies, array policies apply to specific groups of network users. For example, the ISA Server enterprise policy might restrict FTP access, but an array policy also might restrict HTTP access for users not requiring access to the World Wide Web. Figure 6-1 shows a sample configuration using both enterprise and array-level policies. Notice the enterprise policy which restricts access to *Novell.com* applies to all users. Additional restrictions are then applied on an array-by-array basis.

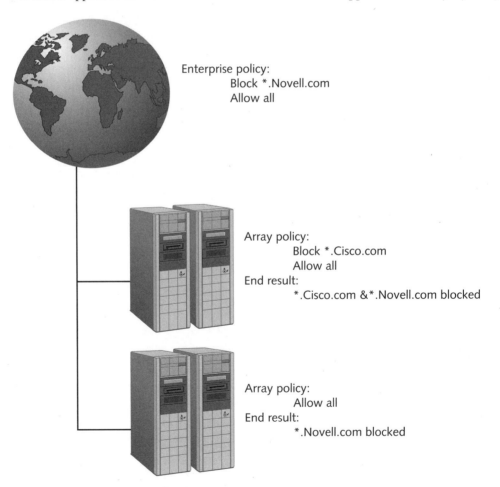

Enterprise policy:
    Block *.Novell.com
    Allow all

Array policy:
    Block *.Cisco.com
    Allow all
End result:
    .Cisco.com &.Novell.com blocked

Array policy:
    Allow all
End result:
    *.Novell.com blocked

Figure 6-1   ISA Server policy logic

While you can set many enterprise policies and select the arrays to which they apply, the best approach is to keep the enterprise policy restrictions as broad as possible and use array policies to become more restrictive.

 An array policy can *never* overrule the enterprise policy to grant more access. It can only make a policy more restrictive. For example, if the enterprise policy denies HTTP and FTP traffic, the array policy can only restrict more protocols *in addition to* HTTP and FTP. The array policy could not grant access to the HTTP or FTP protocols. Because of this, the enterprise policy should only be as restrictive as the strictest corporate rule.

A **server policy** is only implemented on stand-alone ISA Server installations. Enterprise and array policies do not affect stand-alone ISA Servers, and likewise, stand-alone ISA Servers do not affect the enterprise or array policies. If the ISA Server configuration is not integrated into Active Directory, server policies are the only ones you can create. Stand-alone ISA Servers are typically used in small companies that have yet to deploy Active Directory, or in independent departments that do not want the enterprise or array policies to affect them, such as the IT department.

How you deploy ISA Server policies influences the effectiveness of the server. Therefore, you should carefully plan the policies before configuring them. You need to review each of the restrictions and other elements that build each policy (discussed in the following sections) and define the company stance for each restriction.

WORKING WITH THE ISA SERVER MMC

Before you begin configuring ISA Server policies, you should become familiar with the **ISA Management console**. This tool is a collection of well-organized taskpads designed to manage every aspect of your server. To open the ISA Management console, click Start, point to Programs, point to Microsoft ISA Server, and then click ISA Management. The ISA Management window opens and looks similar to Figure 6-2.

Figure 6-2   The ISA Management Welcome window

 You can also add the ISA Management console to the MMC as a tool. To do so, select the Add/Remove snap-in option from the MMC Console menu.

The left pane of the console arranges enterprise policies, array policies, and H.323 Gatekeeper configuration options into a hierarchical tree. As in Windows 2000, you click a plus (+) sign to expand a list of options, and click a minus (–) sign to collapse the list. When you select an option, ISA Server shows a new set of corresponding taskpads in the right pane. You use these taskpads to configure the option you selected.

Some administrators prefer not to use the taskpad-based interface and choose to use the Advanced view instead. The Advanced view provides an interface similar to most Windows 2000 administration tools. Rather than configuring through taskpads, you use a menu-driven system to administer ISA Server. To switch to Advanced view, right-click the Internet Security and Acceleration Server icon in the left pane, point to View on the shortcut menu, and then click Advanced, as shown in Figure 6-3.

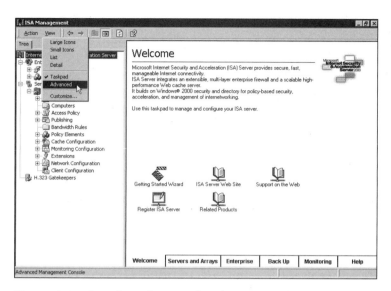

Figure 6-3 Switching from Taskpad view to Advanced view

The ISA Management window switches to Advanced view.

 In this book, use Advanced view as you work with ISA Server policies.

CONFIGURING ISA SERVER ENTERPRISE POLICIES

If you have installed the ISA Server schema into the Active Directory as described in Chapter 5, you can configure enterprise-level policies. Recall that enterprise policies affect every ISA Server array in your network. Because these policies affect every network user, carefully consider any changes to an enterprise policy.

Setting Default Enterprise Policy Behavior

When you initially set up ISA Server, you had the option to set the policy behavior for newly installed arrays by using default enterprise policy settings. The **enterprise policy behavior** settings determine how ISA Server applies enterprise and array policies for the entire network. The following steps show how to modify the enterprise policy behavior settings you selected during installation.

To change a default enterprise policy behavior:

1. In the left pane of the ISA Management window, right-click the **Enterprise** icon, and then click **Set Defaults** on the shortcut menu. The Set defaults dialog box opens, as shown in Figure 6-4.

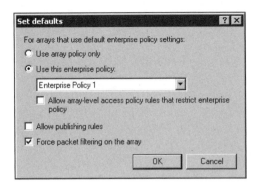

Figure 6-4   Configuring default policy settings

2. Choose an option in the Set defaults dialog box according to the following descriptions:

- *Use array policy only*—Click this option button to restrict the use of enterprise-wide policies and allow the application of ISA Server policies on an array-by-array basis.

- *Use this enterprise policy*—Click this option button, and then click the list arrow to select which enterprise policy you want to use by default. The default enterprise policy defines rules that affect all ISA Servers in the Active Directory tree.

- *Allow array-level access policy rules that restrict enterprise policy*—Check this box to define lower-level array policies that further restrict the enterprise-level policy for individual network segments.

- *Allow publishing rules*—Check this box to create Web server publishing rules on a per-array basis rather than by only allowing enterprise-wide publishing rules.

- *Force packet filtering on the array*—Check this box to have all ISA Server arrays use packet filtering configured through the firewall service.

As you select an option in the Set defaults dialog box, consider the effects of the settings you choose. For example, if you deselect the check box to allow array-level access policies, you turn off all lower-level access rules configured for each array. This could open security holes in your network.

3. Click **OK**. The Set defaults dialog box closes, and the settings take effect immediately.

Setting the Default Enterprise Policy

By default, when you install ISA Server, you create a single enterprise policy (called Enterprise Policy 1) that restricts all traffic entering or leaving ISA Server. If you installed ISA Server into a corporate environment, this is typically the first policy you configure. The enterprise policy should enforce all corporate guidelines as defined by the management of your organization. In the last chapter, you modified Enterprise Policy 1 to permit all traffic to route through the server, primarily to test the configuration. This "allow everything" configuration is common for many corporations that have lax Internet security. They use this configuration to instantly allow full access to the Internet for the company LAN, and then apply restrictions as necessary.

The default enterprise policy affects all ISA Server arrays and all machines that comprise the arrays. It is the furthest reaching policy in ISA Server. Because of this, you should only enforce the rules management has provided you. Do not apply any department-specific policies at this level unless they are verified by management. You can apply more restrictive policies at the array or server levels without affecting the entire company.

Each enterprise policy is made up of site, content, and protocol rules that define which network users can access a given Internet or intranet destination (**site rules**), what types of content they can access (**content rules**), and what protocol they can use to access the destination (**protocol rules**). The following sections explain how to set the properties and other configuration options for these rules.

Adding Enterprise Policies

Microsoft designed ISA Server to handle networks of any size, from small home networks to those linking sites around the world. When planning policies for larger organizations, you may not be able to find a corporate standard for security policies. For example, you might be working with a company that has 50 offices in the United States and 30 offices in Europe. The 50 offices in the U.S. might have strict Internet access standards that do not apply to the 30 offices in Europe. Because of this, you could not design one enterprise policy to apply to all ISA Server arrays. Fortunately, ISA Server allows you to change the default enterprise policy and create multiple enterprise policies. You can also choose which ISA Server arrays each enterprise policy affects.

To create additional enterprise policies:

1. In the left pane of the ISA Management console, expand the Enterprise group, right-click **Policies**, point to **New**, and then click **Policy**, as shown in Figure 6-5.

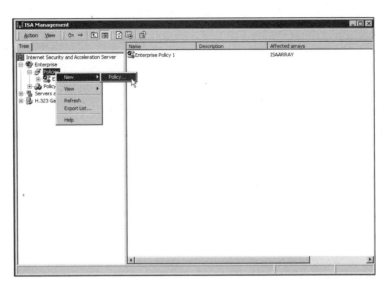

Figure 6-5   Creating a new enterprise policy

   2. The New Enterprise Policy Wizard starts. Type the name of the new enter-
      prise policy, such as **Enterprise Policy 2**, and then click **Next**. The last dia-
      log box in the wizard appears.

   3. Click the **Finish** button. The new policy appears in the left pane of the win-
      dow, under the Policies node. See Figure 6-6.

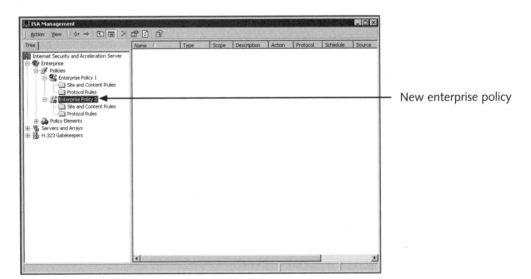

Figure 6-6   Multiple enterprise policies

When you create an enterprise policy, ISA Server creates a unique set of site, content, and protocol rules for the new enterprise policy. The configurations of these rules are not related to other enterprise policies. Although ISA Server allows you to create an unlimited number of enterprise policies, Microsoft recommends that you create the minimum amount necessary to deploy the company policies.

Once you create multiple enterprise policies, you may need to select which policy ISA Server applies to which arrays. If you do not make any configuration changes, the enterprise policy created first (typically Enterprise Policy 1, created during the installation process) is used as the default enterprise policy.

To change the default enterprise policy:

1. In the ISA Management console, right-click the enterprise policy you want to set as the default, and then click **Set as Default Policy** on the shortcut menu. The current default policy is marked in the ISA Management console with a dark circle containing a white checkmark, as shown in Figure 6-7.

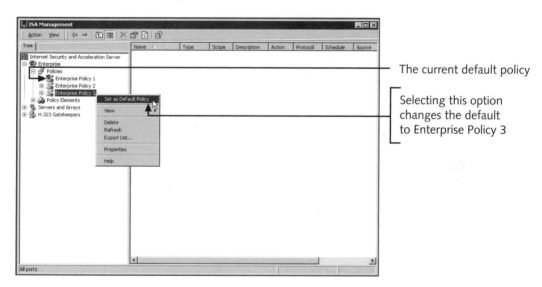

Figure 6-7   Setting the default enterprise policy

Selecting the Affected Arrays

If you create multiple enterprise policies, you must select the ISA Server arrays they affect. ISA Server enterprise policies are comparable to Active Directory group objects, and ISA Server arrays are comparable to Active Directory user objects. When a user is a member of a group, all rights and restriction assignments apply to that user. ISA Server policies use this same logic. Any ISA Server array that is a member of an enterprise policy group is affected by all rules and regulations assigned to that policy. An ISA Server array *cannot* be a member of more than one policy group—in other words, an array cannot be affected by more than one enterprise policy. By default, all arrays are members of the default enterprise policy.

To select the scope of arrays the enterprise policies affect:

1. In the left pane of the ISA Management console, expand the Enterprise group, and then expand the Policies group, if necessary. Right-click the policy you want to modify, and then click **Properties**. The Properties dialog box for the policy you selected appears.

2. Click the **Arrays** tab. The arrays affected by this policy are checked, while unaffected arrays are unchecked. See Figure 6-8. The currently applied policy is listed in the Policy column.

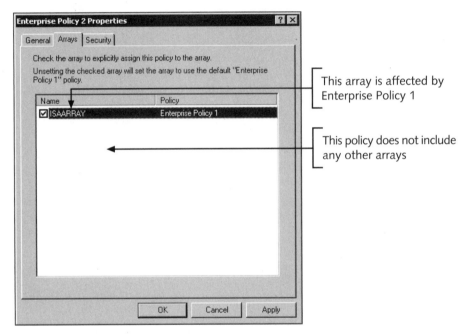

Figure 6-8　Applying enterprise policies to ISA Server arrays

3. Click to insert checks in boxes for the arrays you would like this enterprise policy to affect, and then click **OK**. If another enterprise policy is currently applied to the array you select, ISA Server automatically removes the association and replaces it with the enterprise policy you configure.

Remember that array policies can never be less restrictive than the enterprise policies applied to them; they can only restrict access *in addition* to what the enterprise policy has allowed. If you choose to apply an enterprise policy to an array that has more restrictive rules than the array policy, ISA Server will remove the conflicting array policy rules.

DEFINING AND CONFIGURING POLICY ELEMENTS

Before you can begin to configure rules allowing inbound and outbound network access, you must understand the policy elements in the rules. **Policy elements** define the criteria used when deciding to allow or deny a client inbound or outbound access to the LAN or Internet. Both enterprise and array policies include standard policy elements, shown in Figure 6-9.

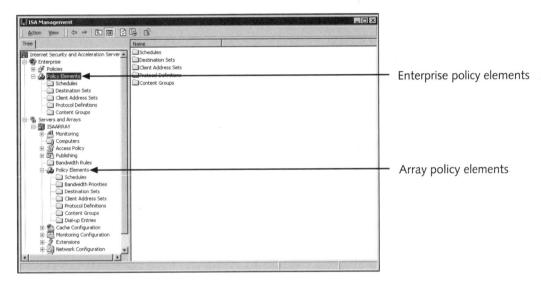

Figure 6-9   Enterprise and array policy elements

Each policy element folder contains the elements used to build enterprise or array-level rules. For example, the Destination Sets folder can contain hostnames or IP addresses that you allow or deny access by following certain rules. The standard policy elements are independent of each other. For example, a schedule created as an enterprise policy element does not appear in the array policy elements. Policy elements are always used with rules and have no functionality on their own. For example, you might construct a rule to deny access to a group of sports Web sites during business hours. The rule you create performs the action of denying the user access; however, in this case, the rule is based on two policy elements: destination sets (the sports Web sites) and schedules (work hours).

To create effective rules in ISA Server, you must understand the configuration and purpose of the policy elements. The following sections define all policy elements used in configuring ISA Server rules and provide steps to configure each of them.

The policy elements discussed in the following section are configured at the array policy level. Enterprise policies contain all but two of the array-level policy elements. This is because the two array policy elements not included in the enterprise policy elements (Bandwidth Priorities and Dial-up Entries) tend to be specific to a given array.

Using Schedule Policy Elements

When configuring ISA Server rules, use **schedule** policy elements to define time boundaries. For example, you might only allow access to an Internet destination during business hours, but allow full Internet access afterwards. In this case, you would create one schedule defining your company's work hours, and a second schedule defining all nonwork hours. Schedules are typically combined with other policy elements to define who, what, or which sites or locations are available or restricted during certain times. ISA Server includes two built-in schedules. The first is named Weekends and encompasses all weekend times. The other is named Work hours and includes all time between 9:00 a.m. and 5:00 p.m. Monday through Friday. You can modify these schedules or create your own.

To create a schedule:

1. In the ISA Management console, expand **Policy Elements**, right-click the **Schedules** policy element, point to **New**, and then click **Schedule**.

2. In the New schedule dialog box, name the schedule with a logical name (such as **lunchtime hours** or **MGMT Schedule**) and include a description, if necessary.

3. Below the Name and Description text boxes is a schedule grid. By default, all times are active. Select the times you want by clicking the grid areas and then clicking the Active or Inactive option button. To select all times for a day, click the name of the day. To select all days for a given time, click the name of time. For example, in Figure 6-10, the schedule defines as active times 10:00 a.m. through 4:00 p.m. Monday, Wednesday, and Friday, and all day Tuesday and Thursday. All other times are marked as inactive.

4. After you complete configuring the schedule, click **OK**. The schedule appears in the list.

5. To modify a schedule, double-click the schedule in the list to open the Properties dialog box for that schedule. You can then change the name, description, and the schedule.

6. To delete a schedule, right-click it in the list, and then click **Delete**.

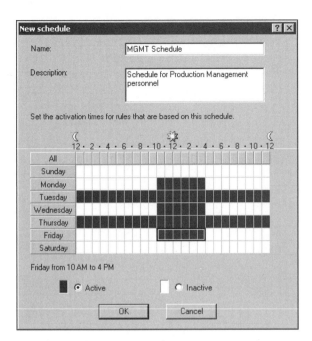

Figure 6-10   Defining a schedule element

Using Bandwidth Priority Policy Elements (Array Only)

You can use **bandwidth priorities** with bandwidth rules to give priority to certain users, groups, or protocols that are passed through ISA Server. Bandwidth priorities are units of bandwidth that, when combined with bandwidth rules, determine the overall percentage of WAN bandwidth granted to users. Bandwidth priorities are based on a scale from 1 to 200, where the number assigned is relative to the other configured bandwidth priorities. For example, you could create three bandwidth priorities, the first named FTP, the second named HTTP, and the third named SMTP. You could then assign FTP a priority of 30, HTTP a priority of 60, and SMTP a priority of 90. Note that when you add the three priorities together, the total amount is 180. This is the number ISA Server uses to find what percentage of bandwidth each protocol is assigned. When combined with bandwidth rules, FTP is assigned approximately 17 percent (30/180) of the overall WAN bandwidth, HTTP is given about 33 percent (60/180), and SMTP is given 50 percent.

ISA Server only uses bandwidth priorities during times of high network traffic when packets are bottlenecking at the server. You could also use these priorities to rank individual users or groups over others. For example, you could prioritize the network administrator's network traffic over all other users.

To create a bandwidth priority:

1. In the ISA Management console, right-click **Bandwidth Priorities** under the Policy Elements node, point to **New**, and then click **Bandwidth Priority**.

2. In the New Bandwidth Priority dialog box, type the name of the new bandwidth priority, a description, and the inbound (traffic entering the network) and outbound (traffic leaving the network) bandwidth. The name you assign the bandwidth priority should reflect how the priority will be used. For example, Figure 6-11 shows a bandwidth priority named FTP that sets the outbound priority of FTP traffic at 175. In addition, the priority for inbound FTP traffic is set to ten.

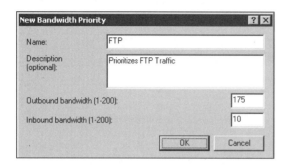

Figure 6-11   Setting bandwidth priorities

3. Once you configure the options for the priority, click **OK** and the bandwidth priority joins the list on the right of the ISA Management console.

After you configure your bandwidth priorities, you need to apply them using a bandwidth rule (discussed in the following section).

Using Destination Set Policy Elements

A **destination set** defines one or more network devices accessed on the local or remote network. Using destination sets with policy rules, you can choose to allow or deny access to the hosts defined within the set. Destination sets can include computer names, IP addresses, domain names, and network paths to local or remote network devices. For example, you could create a destination set named Internet Access that includes the sites *www.microsoft.com/isaserver* and *www.course.com*. You could then create a site and content rule (discussed in the following sections) that grants access to only the Internet Access destination set. This would allow access to only the sites included in the destination set and nothing more. Even subsidiaries of the *www.course.com* and *www.microsoft.com/isaserver* sites would be inaccessible (such as *tech.course.com* or *www.microsoft.com/technet*). Likewise, you could define a destination set of computers internal to your LAN and make them available to Internet users by using a Web publishing rule.

To configure a destination set:

1. In the ISA Management console, right-click the **Destination Sets** node under Policy Elements, point to **New**, and then click **Set**.

2. In the Name text box of the New Destination Set dialog box, shown in Figure 6-12, type a descriptive name of the sites or computers you want the set to contain. You can also enter a description of the set in the Description text box.

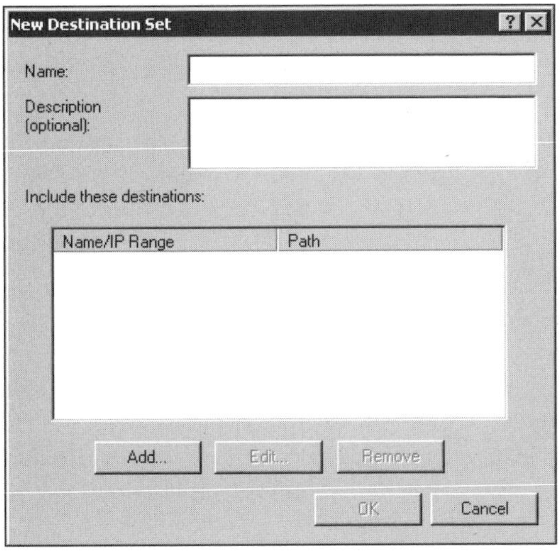

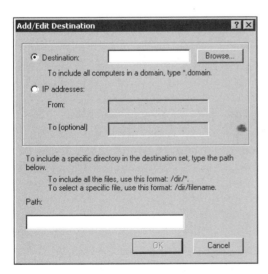

Figure 6-12   Creating a new destination set

3. To begin adding destination addresses, click the **Add** button. The Add/Edit Destination dialog box appears, as shown in Figure 6-13.

Figure 6-13   Adding destination sites and ranges

Enter or select information in this dialog box according to the following descriptions:

- *Destination*—The Destination text box can include a single computer or an entire domain of computers. To specify an individual computer, you must use the Fully Qualified Domain Name (FQDN) of the machine. The \\computer_name syntax is not accepted. If you want to include an entire domain of computers, add an asterisk mark to the beginning of the domain name, i.e., *.microsoft.com, *.com, *.acme.org.

- *IP Addresses*—Use these text boxes to include a single IP address or a range of IP addresses. To include a single IP address, click the **IP addresses** option button, type the single IP address in the From text box, and then click **OK**. To include a range of IP addresses, enter the first address of the range in the From text box and the last address in the To (optional) text box.

- *Path*—The Path text box supplements the Destination or IP address text boxes and allows you to specify a more specific destination than a single computer or IP address. Type a path in the Path text box to restrict or allow specific areas of a Web site or computer to be visible to the network. For example, the destination could be **www.microsoft.com** and the path could be **/isaserver/***. This would include all of **www.microsoft.com/isaserver** in the destination set rather than the full Microsoft Web site.

4. Once you have configured a destination, click **OK**. The destination you specified appears under the "Include these destinations:" table.

5. Continue to add destinations by using the **Add** button until the set contains all desired destinations. When you have finished adding destinations, click **OK**. The destinations appear in the table in the right pane of the ISA Management console. The amount of destination sets you can configure is virtually limitless, but until they are used in an enterprise or array rule, they have no functionality.

Using Client Address Sets

You use client address sets like you use destination sets; however, unlike a destination set, a **client address set** defines the clients that can access resources through ISA Server. A more logical name for client address sets could be source address sets, because they define the source computers attempting to access a resource. Client address sets used with enterprise or array rules and destination sets provide for greater access control. For example, you could create a site and content rule granting access to a particular destination set of addresses, but only for a particular client address set.

To create a client address set:

1. In the ISA Management console, right-click the **Client Address Set** node under Policy Elements, point to **New**, and then click **Sets**. The Client Set dialog box appears.

2. Type a descriptive name in the Name text box and a description in the Description text box, if necessary.

3. To add client IP address ranges, click the **Add** button. Enter the first address of the range in the From text box and the last in the To text box. If you want to add only a single address, type the same address in the From and To text boxes. Then click **OK**.

4. The specified address range appears under the Members table. Continue to add all desired ranges using the **Add** button. Click **OK** when you are finished. Figure 6-14 shows the IP address configuration for the management and marketing departments of a given company.

6

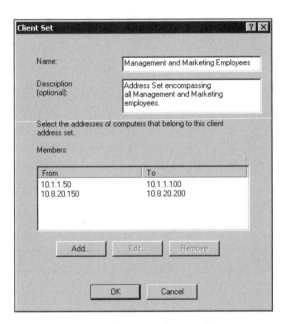

Figure 6-14   Defining a client address set

Using Protocol Definitions

Protocol definitions define the TCP and UDP sub-protocols that ISA Server can use. Protocol definitions are used with protocol rules and server publishing rules to choose what protocols to allow into and out of the network. For example, you could create a protocol rule to deny the marketing group of users access to the Internet when they use the Network News Transfer Protocol (NNTP). ISA Server includes many of the common protocol definitions. Table 6-1 lists some of the commonly used protocol definitions that are included with ISA Server.

Table 6-1 Common Protocol Definitions Included with ISA Server

Protocol Name	Description
AOL	AOL Internet Access
AOL Instant Messenger	AOL Instant Messenger
Archie	Archie
BOOTP	Bootstrap
Chargen (TCP)	Character generator (TCP)
Chargen (UDP)	Character generator (UDP)
Daytime (TCP)	Daytime (TCP)
Daytime (UDP)	Daytime (UDP)
Destination Unreachable	Destination Unreachable
Discard (TCP)	Discard (TCP)
Discard (UDP)	Discard (UDP)
DNS	Domain Name System
DNS (Zone transfer)	Domain Name System (Zone transfer)
DNS Server	Domain Name System (server)
Echo (TCP)	Echo (TCP)
Echo (UDP)	Echo (UDP)
Echo Reply	Echo Reply
Echo Request	Echo Request
Exchange RPC Server	Exchange RPC Server
Finger	Finger
FTP	File Transfer Protocol
FTP Download only	File Transfer Protocol - Download only
FTP Server	File Transfer Protocol (server)
FTP Server - Read only	File Transfer Protocol (server) - Read only
Gopher	Gopher support
H.323	H.323 video conferencing
HTTP	Hypertext Transfer Protocol
HTTP Server	Hypertext Transfer Protocol (server)
HTTPS	Secure Hypertext Transfer Protocol
HTTPS Server	Secure Hypertext Transfer Protocol (server)
ICA	Citrix Intelligent Console Architecture
ICQ	ICQ instant messenger
Ident	Ident username identifier
IKE	Internet Key Exchange
IMAP4	Interactive Mail Access Protocol
IMAPS	Secure Interactive Mail Access Protocol
IRC	Internet Relay Chat

Table 6-1 Common Protocol Definitions Included with ISA Server (continued)

Protocol Name	Description
Kerberos-Adm	Kerberos administration
Kerberos-IV	Kerberos IV authentication
Kerberos-Sec	Kerberos V authentication
LDAP	Lightweight Directory Access Protocol
LDAP GC (Global Catalog)	Lightweight Directory Access Protocol (Global Catalog)
LDAPS	Secure Lightweight Directory Access Protocol
Microsoft SQL Server	Microsoft SQL Server
MSN	MSN Internet Access
MSN Messenger	MSN Messenger
Net2Phone	Net2Phone
Net2Phone Registration	Net2Phone Registration
NetBIOS Datagram	NetBIOS Datagram
NetBIOS Name Service	NetBIOS Name Service
NetBIOS Session	NetBIOS Session
NNTP	Network News Transfer Protocol
NNTPS	Secure Network News Transfer Protocol
NTP (UDP)	Network Time Protocol (UDP)
Parameter Problem	Parameter Problem
POP2	Post Office Protocol v.2
POP3	Post Office Protocol v.3
POP3S	Secure Post Office Protocol v.3
PPTP	Point-to-Point Tunneling Protocol
Quote (TCP)	Quote of the day (TCP)
Quote (UDP)	Quote of the day (UDP)
RADIUS	Remote Authentication Dial-In User Service
RADIUS Accounting	Remote Authentication Dial-In User Service Accounting
RDP (Terminal Services)	Remote Desktop Protocol (Terminal Services)
RealAudio / RealVideo	RealNetworks streaming media (PNM)
RealAudio / RealVideo Server	RealNetworks streaming media (PNM) (server)
Redirect	Redirect messages
RIP	Routing Information Protocol
Rlogin	Remote login
RPC	Remote Procedure Call
RPC port mapper	Remote Procedure Call port mapper (server)
RTSP	Real Time Streaming Protocol

6

Table 6-1 Common Protocol Definitions Included with ISA Server (continued)

Protocol Name	Description
RTSP Server	Real Time Streaming Protocol (server)
SMTP	Simple Mail Transfer Protocol
SMTP Server	Simple Mail Transfer Protocol (server)
SMTPS	Secure Simple Mail Transfer Protocol
SNMP	Simple Network Management Protocol
SNMP Trap	Simple Network Management Protocol - Trap
Source Quench	Source Quench
SSH	Secure Shell
Syslog	Syslog support
Telnet	Telnet
Telnet Server	Telnet Server
TFTP	Trivial File Transfer Protocol
Time (TCP)	Time (TCP)
Time (UDP)	Time (UDP)
Time Exceeded	Time Exceeded
Timestamp Reply	Timestamp Reply
Timestamp Request	Timestamp Request
Whois	Nickname/Whois protocol
Windows Media	Microsoft streaming media
Windows Media Server	Microsoft streaming media (server)

If you are using enterprise policies in your network, all protocol definitions are contained under the enterprise policy elements and must be configured from this area. Any array affected by an enterprise policy pulls its protocol definition database from the enterprise policy elements.

You can use the built-in protocol definitions to configure most rules. However, your company may be using a custom application that needs to have a certain TCP or UDP port open in the firewall that the standard set of built-in protocol definitions does not include. In this case, you can create a custom protocol definition to open the required ports.

To create a custom protocol definition:

1. In the ISA Management console, right-click **Protocol Definitions** under the Policy Elements node, point to **New**, and then click **Definition**. The New Protocol Definition Wizard appears.

2. Enter the name of the protocol definition you want to create (this is typically the name of the application requiring the protocol, such as **Telnet**), and then click **Next**. The Primary Connection Information dialog box appears, as shown in Figure 6-15.

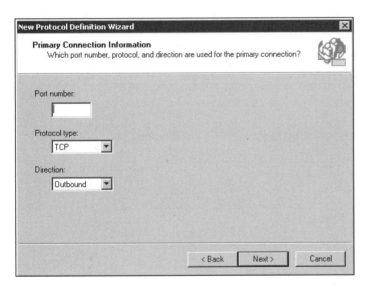

Figure 6-15   Defining protocol and port information

3. In the Port number text box, type the port number the application uses (this is typically found in the application documentation).

4. Click the **Protocol type** list arrow, and then click the applicable protocol (**TCP** or **UDP**).

5. Click the **Direction** list arrow to choose the direction you want the protocol to operate. This is the direction from where ISA Server allows the request to be *initiated*. For example, if you choose **Outbound** for TCP, the connection

can then be initiated from a client inside the network. The remote server the client connects to can communicate back, but ISA Server does not allow the remote server to initiate the connection. When choosing the TCP protocol, you have the option to initiate communications on the **Inbound** or **Outbound** directions. If you choose the UDP protocol, you can choose one of four direction options: **Receive**, **Receive Send**, **Send**, or **Send Receive**. Because UDP does not create a session like TCP, these describe data-flow patterns. For example, if you select **Receive**, that allows the internal LAN to receive but not send UDP requests from the external network. If you choose **Send Receive**, it allows the internal LAN client to send data and then receive from the communicating host. Once you select the port, protocol, and direction, click **Next**. The Secondary Connections dialog box appears.

6. Use the Secondary Connections dialog box to configure any secondary port numbers the application may need to open. Some applications initially connect using a certain port number, but may open other ports once the initial connection is established. FTP is an example of this. You must define all secondary ports the application uses here. In the Do you want to use secondary connections? section, click the **Yes** option button. To define a secondary connection, click the **New** button, type the port ranges, protocol, and direction of the secondary connections, and then click OK.

7. Once you have configured the necessary secondary ports, click **Next**. The Completing the New Protocol Definition Wizard window opens, summarizing the protocol you are about to create. Click **Finish** to add the protocol to the protocol definitions list, as shown in Figure 6-16.

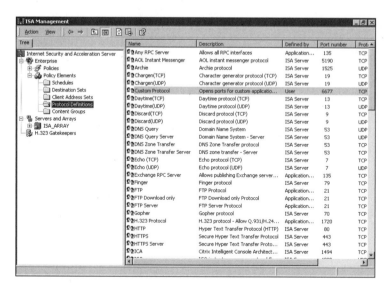

Figure 6-16   Viewing existing protocol definitions

When you select the protocol definitions node, as shown in Figure 6-16, the name, description, and port numbers of all current protocol definitions appear in the right pane of the ISA Management console. In addition, in the Defined by column, ISA Server lists how each protocol definition was created, showing one of three options: User, Application Filter, or ISA Server. The protocol definitions created by the user have been manually added by a network administrator. You can edit or delete all protocol definitions created by the user. To edit or delete these protocol definitions, right-click the protocol definition, and select either Delete to remove it, or Properties to modify it. The protocol definitions provided by application filters are specific to individual applications. While many application filters come installed with ISA Server, some applications may modify the ISA Server configuration and add its own application filters. These application filters may be deleted, but not modified. Finally, protocol definitions defined by ISA Server are predefined and may not be deleted or modified.

Using Content Groups

Content groups define valid file name extensions and **Multipurpose Internet Mail Extensions (MIME)** types. A content group is a list of file types (or MIMEs) and filename extensions that you can use when creating site and content rules or bandwidth rules. When a user opens a Web browser, content begins to download. This content could be a simple text file, or a Web page complete with pictures, streaming audio, Flash animations, or streaming video. Regardless of what a user downloads from the Web, each downloadable item has its own particular content type. Therefore, each type of Web content is identifiable, and you can create filters to allow or restrict that content. This is the function of content groups: to identify all unique file types and extensions, giving network administrators the ability to control the type of content entering or leaving the network. For example, the popularity of streaming audio applications on the Web continues to increase. Suppose many employees at your company are beginning to tune in to online radio stations and download MPEG audio layer 3 (MP3) files rather than listen to the radio because the files provide clearer reception and fewer commercials. Unfortunately, because the employees leave the streaming audio applications open all day, the company's T1 line is becoming increasingly overwhelmed. Using the content groups and site and content rules, you could restrict the use of any audio application simply by restricting the relevant file types and extensions.

ISA Server comes with eleven content groups already installed, as shown in Figure 6-17. These content groups encompass the most common MIME types and file extensions for today's networks.

6

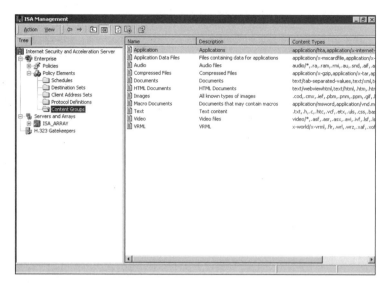

Figure 6-17   ISA Server's built-in content groups

To view the MIME types and file extensions each content group contains, right–click a group, click Properties, and then click the Content Types tab in the Properties dialog box. MIME mappings appear in the list with the syntax of *mime_type/application_type* (i.e. application/x-mspublisher or text/html); file extensions appear as *.extension_type* (i.e. .exe, .mp3, or .jpeg). Depending on which Web server you connect to, different MIME types may have different file extension mappings. Table 6-2 lists the file extension mappings associated with various MIME types when using IIS.

Table 6-2 IIS Default MIME Associations

Filename Extension	MIME Type
.*	application/octet-stream
.acx	application/internet-property-stream
.ai	application/postscript
.axs	application/olescript
.bcpio	application/x-bcpio
.bin	application/octet-stream
.cat	application/vndms-pkiseccat
.cdf	application/x-cdf
.cer	application/x-x509-ca-cert
.clp	application/x-msclip
.cpio	application/x-cpio
.crd	application/x-mscardfile
.crl	application/pkix-crl

Table 6-2 IIS Default MIME Associations (continued)

Filename Extension	MIME Type
.crt	application/x-x509-ca-cert
.csh	application/x-csh
.dcr	application/x-director
.der	application/x-x509-ca-cert
.dir	application/x-director
.dll	application/x-msdownload
.doc	application/msword
.dot	application/msword
.dvi	application/x-dvi
.dxr	application/x-director
.eps	application/postscript
.evy	application/envoy
.exe	application/octet-stream
.fif	application/fractals
.gtar	application/x-gtar
.gz	application/x-gzip
.hdf	application/x-hdf
.hlp	application/winhlp
.hqx	application/mac-binhex40
.hta	application/hta
.iii	application/x-iphone
.ins	application/x-internet-signup
.isp	application/x-internet-signup
.js	application/x-javascript
.latex	application/x-latex
.m13	application/x-msmediaview
.m14	application/x-msmediaview
.man	application/x-troff-man
.mdb	application/x-msaccess
.me	application/x-troff-me
.mny	application/x-msmoney
.mpp	application/vnd.ms-project
.ms	application/x-troff-ms
.mvb	application/x-msmediaview
.nc	application/x-netcdf
.oda	application/oda

6

Table 6-2 IIS Default MIME Associations (continued)

Filename Extension	MIME Type
.ods	application/oleobject
.p10	application/pkcs10
.p12	application/x-pkcs12
.p7b	application/x-pkcs7-certificates
.p7c	application/pkcs7-mime
.p7m	application/pkcs7-mime
.p7r	application/x-pkcs7-certreqresp
.p7s	application/pkcs7-signature
.pdf	application/pdf
.pfx	application/x-pkcs12
.pko	application/vndms-pkipko
.pma	application/x-perfmon
.pmc	application/x-perfmon
.pml	application/x-perfmon
.pmr	application/x-perfmon
.pmw	application/x-perfmon
.pot	application/vnd.ms-powerpoint
.pps	application/vnd.ms-powerpoint
.ppt	application/vnd.ms-powerpoint
.prf	application/pics-rules
.ps	application/postscript
.pub	application/x-mspublisher
.roff	application/x-troff
.rtf	application/rtf
.scd	application/x-msschedule
.setpay	application/set-payment-initiation
.setreg	application/set-registration-initiation
.sh	application/x-sh
.shar	application/x-shar
.sit	application/x-stuffit
.spc	application/x-pkcs7-certificates
.spl	application/futuresplash
.src	application/x-wais-source
.sst	application/vndms-pkicertstore
.stl	application/vndms-pkistl
.sv4cpio	application/x-sv4cpio

Table 6-2 IIS Default MIME Associations (continued)

Filename Extension	MIME Type
.sv4crc	application/x-sv4crc
.t	application/x-troff
.tar	application/x-tar
.tcl	application/x-tcl
.tex	application/x-tex
.texi	application/x-texinfo
.texinfo	application/x-texinfo
.tgz	application/x-compressed
.tr	application/x-troff
.trm	application/x-msterminal
.ustar	application/x-ustar
.wcm	application/vnd.ms-works
.wdb	application/vnd.ms-works
.wks	application/vnd.ms-works
.wmf	application/x-msmetafile
.wps	application/vnd.ms-works
.wri	application/x-mswrite
.xla	application/vnd.ms-excel
.xlc	application/vnd.ms-excel
.xlm	application/vnd.ms-excel
.xls	application/vnd.ms-excel
.xlt	application/vnd.ms-excel
.xlw	application/vnd.ms-excel
.z	application/x-compressed
.zip	application/x-zip-compressed
.aif	audio/x-aiff
.aifc	audio/aiff
.aiff	audio/aiff
.au	audio/basic
.m3u	audio/x-mpegurl
.mid	audio/mid
.mp3	audio/mpeg
.ra	audio/x-pn-realaudio
.ram	audio/x-pn-realaudio
.rmi	audio/mid
.snd	audio/basic

6

Table 6-2 IIS Default MIME Associations (continued)

Filename Extension	MIME Type
.wav	audio/wav
.cmx	image/x-cmx
.cod	image/cis-cod
.dib	image/bmp
.gif	image/gif
.ief	image/ief
.jfif	image/pjpeg
.jpe	image/jpeg
.jpeg	image/jpeg
.jpg	image/jpeg
.pbm	image/x-portable-bitmap
.pnm	image/x-portable-anymap
.ppm	image/x-portable-pixmap
.ras	image/x-cmu-raster
.rgb	image/x-rgb
.tif	image/tiff
.tiff	image/tiff
.xbm	image/x-xbitmap
.323	text/h323
.htm	text/html
.html	text/html
.htt	text/webviewhtml
.sct	text/scriptlet
.stm	text/html
.tsv	text/tab-separated-values
.xml	text/xml
.xsl	text/xml

As new applications and Web file types are developed, you can create new content groups to handle them.

To create a content group:

> 1. In the ISA Management console, right-click the **Content Groups** node under Policy Elements, point to **New**, and then click **Content Group**. The New Content Group dialog box appears, as shown in Figure 6-18.

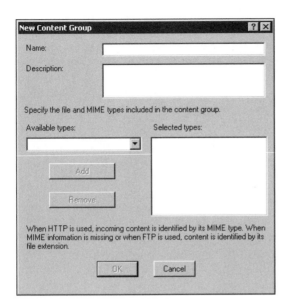

Figure 6-18   Configuring a new content group

2. In the Name text box, type the name of the new content group. In the Description text box you can also type a description, if necessary.

3. To add a MIME type and file extension to the new content group, either click the **Available types** list arrow to select them, or type the information in the Available types text box. Then click the **Add** button.

4. Repeat Step 3 to add other MIME mappings and file extensions to the new content group.

5. Click **OK** after you have added all the MIME mappings and file extensions to the content group.

Using Dial-up Entries (Array Only)

ISA Server can use a variety of methods to connect to the Internet. While most medium- to large-sized companies use high-speed connections such as DSL, Frame Relay, Leased Lines, or ATM, some choose slower and less expensive dial-up connections. Most use such modem-based connections as back-up lines, providing redundancy for the primary connection. Regardless of the server configuration, ISA Server allows you to configure these connections as **dial-up entries**.

Use dial-up entries to configure dial-up connections with ISA Server to connect to an ISP or remote network. Creating a dial-up entry does not create a new dial-up connection complete with name, phone number, and network settings, but rather gives ISA Server the ability to use an existing Windows 2000 dial-up connection. Using routing rules, you can prioritize this connection so it is not used until a failure in the primary connection is detected.

CONFIGURING ENTERPRISE AND ARRAY POLICY RULES

Once you create and configure applicable policy elements, you can begin configuring rules. You base ISA Server rules on corporate policies. For example, corporate policies might dictate that users can access only three specific Internet Web sites during business hours using only HTTP, but have full Internet access using all protocols after work hours. Deployment of this policy would occur in two phases: first, define needed policy elements, and then create the ISA Server rules.

To define the policy elements in this scenario, you create two schedule policy elements, the first defines standard work hours, and the second defines all other times. You use these elements when creating the rules to allow or deny Internet access during set periods of time. In addition to schedules, you need to create a destination set policy element that defines the three Internet Web sites that are valid during work hours. You can use the destination set with the work hours schedule to grant access only to the Web sites you specify. On their own, the schedules and destination sets have no functionality. You must apply them to ISA Server in the form of an enterprise or array policy rule.

Between the enterprise and array policies are two common sets of rules: site and content rules and protocol rules. Many network administrators use only these rules to configure outbound Internet access from the LAN. Site and content rules determine who can access administrator-defined Internet Web sites and when ISA Server should allow access. ISA Server uses protocol rules to grant or deny access based on the protocol used by the client. Each of these rules is configured using the policy elements discussed in the previous section. The following section discusses the configuration of site and content and protocol rules.

Setting Site and Content Rules

As discussed before, site and content rules define who can access a group of specified Web sites and when they can access them. When you install ISA Server, it has no preconfigured site and content rules. Remember, this default configuration denies access to all users entering or leaving the private network. Before ISA Server grants network access, you must configure at least one site and content rule to allow access to at least one Web site. Many network administrators initially configure ISA Server with a site and content rule granting everyone access to all Internet Web sites, and then begin applying restrictions as circumstances require. Other high-security networks prefer to restrict all Internet access, and then grant Internet access on an individual Web site basis.

While ISA Server does not process site and content rules in a certain order, the deny access flag always takes precedence in a grant and deny access rule conflict. For example, the human resources group may need access to a set of Internet sites so they can research competitive salaries. Management does not want other employees to access these Web sites because it could affect their morale. You can grant the human resources group access to the specific destination set, and deny the other groups access to the same set. If a user was a member of both groups, he or she would be denied access to the Web sites because the deny access setting always takes precedence. Furthermore, when ISA Server denies a user access to any location because of a site and content rule, they can be redirected to an alternate URL, which is typically a Web page on an internal Web server that has a generic explanation of why they were denied access.

 If you are redirecting users to an internal or external Web server containing an access denied message, be sure to define a rule allowing access to the redirected URL.

Depending on your scope of management, you can apply site and content rules at either the array or enterprise policy levels. Site and content rules created within the enterprise policies can affect all arrays within the corporate network. These site and content rules should be as general as possible and as strict as the strictest *corporate* policy, such as those blocking access to all pornographic Web sites. Site and content rules created at the array level can apply policies specific to the individual department the array supports.

To create an enterprise or array specific site and content rule:

1. In the ISA Management console, expand the Enterprise Policy or Access Policy nodes depending on where you want to configure the rule (enterprise or array). If you are configuring an enterprise-level rule, expand the Policies node, and then expand the individual enterprise policy you want to configure. If you are configuring an array-level rule, expand the array you want to configure, and then expand the Access Policy node.

2. Right-click **Site and Content Rules**, point to **New**, and then click **Rule**. The New Site and Content Rule Wizard appears.

3. Enter a name for the new site and content rule, such as Restrict Content, and then click **Next**. The Rule Action dialog box appears.

4. Click the **Allow** option button to allow access using the site and content rule, or click the **Deny** option button, if necessary, to deny access. If you are choosing to deny access, you can also click the **If HTTP request, redirect request to this site** check box, and then type an address of a Web server to redirect denied users, as shown in Figure 6-19.

5. Click **Next**. The Rule Configuration dialog box appears, as shown in Figure 6-20. This dialog box allows you to choose one of four separate rule configuration paths. Depending on the action you chose in Step 4, you can allow or deny based on destination (using *destination set* policy elements), the time of day (using *schedule* policy elements), or selected clients (using *client address set* policy elements or Active Directory users and groups). You may also want to choose the custom configuration to create a rule which uses a combination of all three elements and gives the greatest amount of control. (These steps will follow the custom configuration.)

6

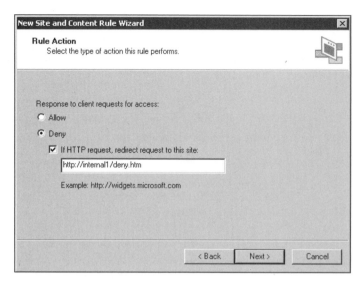

Figure 6-19   Redirecting denied users to an internal server

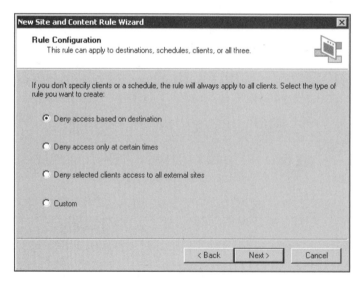

Figure 6-20   Selecting site restriction criteria

6. Click the **Custom** option button, and then click **Next**. The Destination Sets dialog box appears.

7. In the list box, click one of the following options:

   ■ *All destinations*—Allows or denies access (depending on the action you selected in Step 4) to all destinations

- *All internal destinations*—Allows or denies access to all internal network destinations (for example, internal Web servers and mail servers)
- *All external destinations*—Allows or denies access to all external (Internet) network destinations
- *Specified destination set*—Allows or denies access based on a destination set policy element
- *All destinations except selected set*—Allows or denies access to all destinations except the sites listed in a destination set policy element

Choose a destination set or leave the default **All destinations** selection, and then click the **Next** button. The Schedule dialog box appears.

8. Use the Schedule dialog box to select the time of day to allow or deny internal or external network access. To select any schedule policy element you have configured, click the **Use this schedule** list arrow, as shown in Figure 6-21.

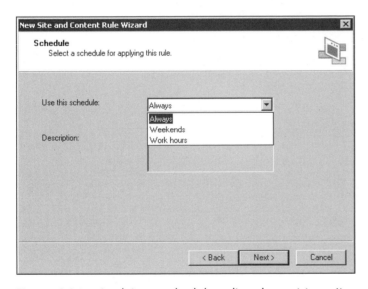

Figure 6-21   Applying a schedule policy element to a site and content rule

9. If you want the rule to apply at all times, select **Always**, if necessary, and then click **Next**. The Client Type dialog box appears, as shown in Figure 6-22.

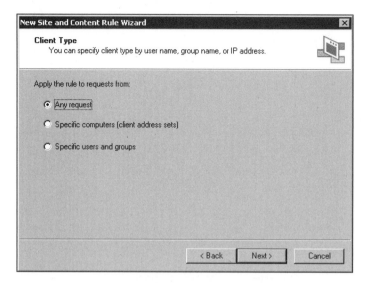

Figure 6-22   Setting client specific restrictions

10. To specify what users or computers the site and content rule affects, click one of the following option buttons:

- *Any request*—Allows or denies any client request based on the other configured rule elements

- *Specific computers (client address sets)*—Allows or denies access based on IP addresses included in a *client address set* policy element

- *Specific users and groups*—Allows or denies access based on Active Directory user or group membership

Then click **Next**. Depending on the option button you select, you may need to configure specific users, groups, or client address sets on the following window. If so, make the appropriate selections, and click the **Next** button.

11. The Content Groups dialog box appears, as shown in Figure 6-23. So far, you have configured site-specific settings. Use the Content Group dialog box to grant or deny access based on the content type.

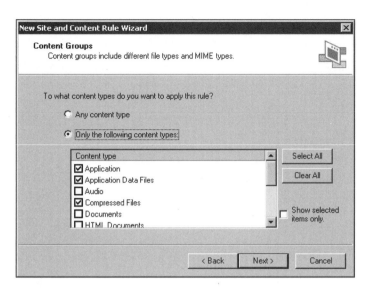

Figure 6-23   Filtering based on content type

 To allow or deny access based on username or group membership, you must install the firewall client on the client machine.

To allow or deny any content type to traverse ISA Server, click the **Any content type** option button. To specify the individual content types you would like to allow or deny, click the **Only the following content types** option button.

12. ISA Server pulls these content types directly from the content group policy elements. Each contains MIME mappings for the file types and extensions. Remember, you can modify this list to include any custom extensions you would like to filter. Click **Next**. The final wizard dialog box appears.

13. Click **Finish** to close the wizard and create the rule.

Setting Protocol Rules

ISA Server uses protocol rules to determine which protocols client computers can use to access the Internet. Because the TCP/IP protocol suite is made up of many sub-protocols, you can allow some protocols and restrict others to ensure the Internet access allocated to the end user is used only for business purposes. For example, when an application transmits using TCP/IP, it must choose between using TCP-based communication (reliable, but slow) and UDP-based communication (unreliable, but fast). Applications that use UDP are typically data streaming types (such as streaming audio, video, and online games), and have a reputation for consuming a lot of WAN bandwidth. To conserve bandwidth, you could limit the use of UDP ports in connecting to the Internet to only business-related applications.

Like site and content rules, protocol rules have no processing order; however, deny protocol rules always take precedence over the allow protocol rules. For example, suppose Troy Leslie, a network user, is a member of both the sales and marketing groups. If you grant the sales group access to use the HTTP protocol, but deny the marketing group, Troy will not have access to the protocol.

You can create protocol rules at both the enterprise and array levels. Remember that array-level rules can only further restrict enterprise rules. For example, you could never create an enterprise protocol rule that denies all TCP-based protocols and then create an array protocol rule allowing HTTP or FTP. Protocol rules use the protocol definition policy elements as building blocks. A protocol rule can never block a protocol that has not already been defined as a protocol definition. You can modify the list of protocol definitions, adding and deleting required protocols, and then use a protocol rule to allow or deny access.

Protocol rules affect both firewall clients and SecureNAT clients. This benefits the network administrator because corporate-wide protocol restrictions can be applied without the administrative expense of installing client software on every user PC.

To create and configure a protocol rule:

1. In the ISA Management console, expand either the Enterprise Policy or Access Policy node depending on the level where you plan to deploy the protocol rule (enterprise or array).

2. Right-click the **Protocol Rules** node, point to **New**, and then click **Rule**. The New Protocol Rule Wizard appears.

3. In the Name text box, type a descriptive name for the new protocol rule, and then click **Next**. The Rule Action dialog box appears. This dialog box sets the tone (to allow or deny access) for the entire rule.

4. Click the appropriate option button to choose whether the rule allows or denies access to the selected protocols, and then click **Next**. The Protocols dialog box appears, as shown in Figure 6-24.

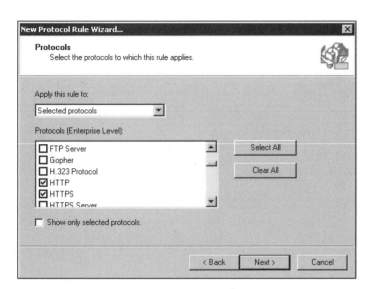

Figure 6-24   Choosing affected protocols

5. To select the protocols you will allow or deny, click one of the following option buttons:

- *All IP traffic*—Allows or denies all TCP/IP related traffic. (This option is rarely used except in organizations that have no Internet protocol restrictions on some or all of their users.)

- *Selected protocols*—Allows or denies the protocols that you select, as shown in Figure 6-24; check the boxes next to the protocols you wish to allow or deny.

- *All IP traffic except selected*—Allows or denies all protocols *except* the protocols you select. Using this selection is a simple way of opening a few protocol ports for access, while denying all others.

Then click **Next**. The Schedule dialog box appears.

6. The Schedule dialog box allows you to apply a time restriction on your protocol rule. For example, you could restrict the HTTP protocol during work hours, but allow access outside of that time. The schedules are based on the preconfigured *schedule* policy elements. Choose a schedule (if necessary), and then click **Next**. The Client Type dialog box appears.

7. To specify what users or computers the site and content rule affects, click one of the following option buttons:

- *Any request*—Allows or denies any client request based on the other configured rule elements

- *Specific computers (client address sets)*—Allows or denies access based on IP addresses included in a *client address set* policy element

- *Specific users and groups*—Allows or denies access based on Active Directory user or group membership; remember, this option restricts the firewall client and does not restrict SecureNAT or Web Proxy clients

Then click **Next**.

8. To configure specific users, groups, or client address sets, click the appropriate options as seen in the previous exercises, if necessary, and then click **Next**.

9. Click **Finish** to close the wizard and create the protocol rule.

Setting Bandwidth Rules

Use bandwidth rules to prioritize certain traffic types during times of high network congestion. Using bandwidth rules, you can rank traffic based on the user or group sending data, the protocol the device is using, the destination to which data is sent, or the content type being downloaded. For example, suppose that between eight and nine every morning, hundreds of users access various news Web sites to download the daily headlines. During this time, the WAN slows significantly, and you notice a performance loss when you use your browser to access various sites. You could set up a bandwidth rule, allocating your client workstation the majority of network bandwidth between eight and nine every morning. By doing this, when ISA Server receives your Web request at the same time as all other employees, your request is answered first.

Bandwidth rules are configured in a specific order. When ISA Server receives a request, it works through the bandwidth rules using top-down processing. When it locates a bandwidth rule that matches the request, the rule is applied and ISA Server stops processing. Because of this, you should move the rules applied most often to the top of the list. To change the order of the bandwidth rules, select the rule you would like to move and use the up or down arrow on the MMC toolbar. See Figure 6-25.

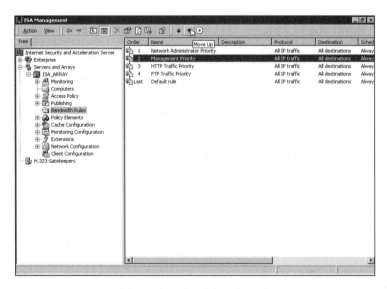

Figure 6-25   Modifying bandwidth rule order

At the bottom of the bandwidth rule list is the **Default rule**. The Default rule applies to all users (provided they reach the bottom of the rule list) and ensures they receive the minimum bandwidth configured in Windows 2000 default scheduling. When configuring bandwidth rules, you should be careful not to create rules that apply to large amounts of people. The bandwidth provided by Windows 2000 default scheduling is a relatively small amount. Increasing this amount can cause the network performance for the majority of users to become tediously slow.

Before you configure bandwidth rules, you must first specify the speed of your network connections. This is called the **effective bandwidth**. You should configure the effective bandwidth to equal the lowest speed connection in your network. For example, if the LAN currently runs at ten megabits per second and uses a 128 Kbps ISDN WAN connection, the lowest connection speed is the ISDN line running at 128 Kbps, and the effective bandwidth should reflect this accordingly.

To configure the effective bandwidth, do the following:

1. Right-click the **Bandwidth Rules** node under the ISA Server array, and then click **Properties**. The Bandwidth Rules Properties dialog box appears.

2. Click the **Enable bandwidth Control** box to insert a check, as shown in Figure 6-26, and then type the speed of the lowest speed connection in kilobits per second (typically the WAN link) in the Effective bandwidth text box. ISA Server then bases its bandwidth calculations on this speed. For example, if you specified a 128 Kbps effective bandwidth and user A was given 60 percent available bandwidth, while user B was given 40 percent (via bandwidth priorities), the effective bandwidth would be 76.8 Kbps for user A and 51.2 Kbps for user B.

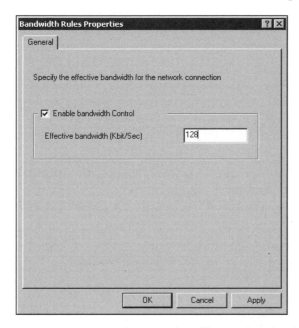

Figure 6-26   Configuring the effective bandwidth

Because bandwidth rules are built using bandwidth priorities, be sure that you have all your bandwidth priorities configured before you configure bandwidth rules.

To configure a bandwidth rule:

1. In the ISA Management console, right-click **Bandwidth Rules** located under the Servers and Arrays node, point to **New**, and then click **Rule**. The New Bandwidth Rule Wizard appears.

2. In the Name text box, type a logical name for the bandwidth rule, and then click **Next**. The Protocols dialog box appears.

3. To configure the protocols (if necessary) to which the bandwidth rule should apply, click the appropriate check boxes to select protocols, and then click **Next**. The Schedule dialog box appears.

4. Choose the schedule during which the bandwidth rule should be active. Then click **Next**. The Client Type dialog box appears.

5. Choose what users, groups, or IP addresses you would like the bandwidth rule to affect. Then click **Next**. (You may need to make additional configuration settings if you chose to apply the rule to users, groups, or IP addresses.) The Destination Sets dialog box appears.

6. If necessary, apply the bandwidth rule to your selected destinations using the process described in prior configurations, and then click **Next**. The Content Groups dialog box appears.

7. Select any specific content you would like to apply the bandwidth rule to, and then click **Next**. The Bandwidth Priority dialog box appears, similar to the one shown in Figure 6-27.

8. Use the Bandwidth Priority dialog box to associate a bandwidth priority policy element with the bandwidth rule. If you do not want to associate a bandwidth priority with the rule, make sure the **Use default scheduling priority** option button is selected. The default Windows 2000 scheduling is used as the priority.

9. If you want to associate a bandwidth priority, click the **Custom** option button and then click the **Name** list arrow to choose the priority you would like to associate. The description and bandwidth settings are displayed in the text boxes below.

10. After you have selected the bandwidth priority, click **Next**, and then click **Finish** to close the wizard and create the bandwidth rule.

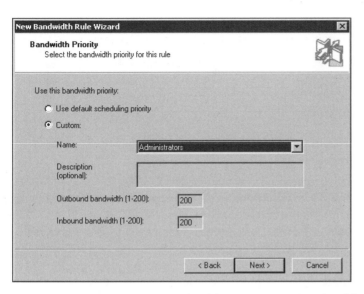

Figure 6-27   Applying a bandwidth priority to a bandwidth rule

6

CHAPTER SUMMARY

❑ The ISA Management console is an MMC snap-in that allows you to configure all ISA Server options.

❑ Enterprise policies are used to apply standard rules to the entire organization and should only be configured to match the strongest corporate policy. Array policies apply to a specific set of ISA Server machines and can further restrict the enterprise policy. Server policies are used on stand-alone ISA Server machines.

❑ By default, ISA Server denies all network traffic entering or leaving the network. Many network administrators configure a default enterprise policy that allows complete access to the Internet and then applies restrictions as necessary.

❑ You can configure more than one enterprise policy and choose which ISA Server arrays they affect. An ISA Server array can only be affected by one enterprise policy.

❑ Policy elements are used in building rules. By themselves they have no functionality.

❑ ISA Server allows you to define the following policy elements: schedules (specifies time ranges), bandwidth priorities (sets priority levels), destination sets (sets a group of destination IP addresses), client address sets (sets a group of client IP addresses), protocol definitions (defines protocols and port numbers), content groups (identifies specific MIME types and file extensions), and dial-up entries (creates dial-up connections on demand).

- There are two primary ISA Server rules to restrict access: site and content rules and protocol rules. Each uses policy elements to allow or deny specified network traffic.

- Bandwidth rules allow you to prioritize network traffic based on time of day, source or destination, protocol type, content type, user, or group membership. Bandwidth rules are used to give certain administratively defined traffic types priority over other traffic types.

KEY TERMS

array policy — A policy that applies to the single ISA Server arrays throughout the network. These policies typically contain the department-specific restrictions specified by the department management.

bandwidth priorities — A policy element allowing you to configure priorities from one to 200 to use with bandwidth rules.

client address set — A policy element allowing you to define ranges of IP addresses to represent internal clients.

content groups — A policy element allowing you to group together different MIME types to use when creating site and content rules.

content rules — The rules in an enterprise policy that define what types of content network users can access.

default rule — The last item in the bandwidth rule list, the default rule applies to all users and ensures they receive the minimum bandwidth configured in Windows 2000 default scheduling.

destination set — Defines one or more network devices accessed on the local or remote network.

dial-up entries — Policy elements defined at the array level to configure ISA Server with dial-on-demand capabilities.

effective bandwidth — The lowest speed of your network connections. Before you configure bandwidth rules, you must first configure the effective bandwidth so ISA Server can match the lowest-speed connection in your network.

enterprise policy — A policy that applies to all ISA Servers in the entire corporate network.

enterprise policy behavior — Settings that determine how ISA Server applies enterprise and array policies for the entire network.

ISA Management console — An MMC snap-in that organizes options for managing every aspect of your ISA Server.

Multipurpose Internet Mail Extensions (MIME) — A specification defined by the IETF in 1992 which allows users to send character sets other than plain ASCII text (such as GIF or WAV files) across the Internet through e-mail.

Policy Elements — The parts of a policy that define the criteria used when deciding to allow or deny a client inbound or outbound access to the LAN or Internet.

protocol definition — A policy element used to define the protocols supported by ISA Server, and the specific protocol configuration.

protocol rules — The rules in an enterprise policy that define what protocol that network users can use to access an Internet or intranet destination.

schedule — A policy element used to define set intervals of time.

server policy — A policy implemented only on stand-alone ISA Server installations.

site rules — The rules in an enterprise policy that define which network users can access a given Internet or intranet destination.

REVIEW QUESTIONS

6

1. F&Y Publishing is attempting to configure global management of ISA Server policies. After analyzing their corporate policies, you suggest creating two enterprise policies to apply to a series of ISA Server arrays. One ISA Server array (management) requires the application of both enterprise policies. What is the best method of configuration?

   a. Open the Properties dialog box for both enterprise policies and check the Management Array check box.

   b. Open the Properties dialog box for the management array and select both enterprise policies.

   c. Create a custom array-level policy for management implementing the settings of both enterprise policies.

   d. Reinstall the management array under the newly configured enterprise policies.

2. What is the default ISA Management view configuration?

   a. advanced

   b. large icons

   c. list

   d. taskpad

3. When you create a new enterprise policy, what arrays are affected by default?

   a. all currently created arrays

   b. only arrays created after the new enterprise policy is implemented

   c. arrays configured in the default enterprise policy list

   d. no arrays are affected by default

4. What configuration setting in the Set Defaults dialog box for enterprise policies allows you to configure array policies that grant more access than is granted through the applied enterprise policies?

   a. Use array policy only.

   b. Use this enterprise policy.

   c. Allow array-level policies that restrict enterprise policy.

   d. There is no setting to allow this.

5. Elite Widgets Inc. has just finished installing ISA Server 2000 on their network. To keep Internet access from overwhelming the WAN, the network administrator creates a schedule policy element and applies a rule denying Internet access between the hours of 8:00 a.m. and 1:00 p.m. After applying the rule, the administrator tests connections and finds that no one can access the Internet, even outside the hours specified in the schedule. The network connections are tested and are found to be in good working order. What is the *most likely* cause of the problem?

   a. The network administrator needs to define at least one allow rule.

   b. Schedule policy elements are typically only used to allow access.

   c. Clients must have the firewall client software installed before access is allowed.

   d. The ISA Server network card has a duplicate MAC address configured.

6. Which one of the following definitions best describes the function of a schedule policy element?

   a. A schedule policy element defines the range of times ISA Server is active.

   b. A schedule policy element defines active and inactive times for use in cre ating rules.

   c. A schedule policy element creates a block of time when Web access is either allowed or denied, depending on the setting you choose in the schedule policy element.

   d. A schedule policy element is used to schedule certain processes to run at a given time.

7. Which of the following defines a ranking system from one to 200?

   a. destination sets

   b. bandwidth rules

   c. client address sets

   d. bandwidth priorities

8. Dorel Ranches has recently installed ISA Server on their 100-user network. They want to give a group of 20 computers full access to the Internet while restricting all others. Which policy element would be most appropriate for this situation?

   a. client address set

   b. destination set

   c. bandwidth priority

   d. dial-up entry

9. A network administrator creates a bandwidth priority named FTP with a priority of 60. What significance does this have?

   a. FTP is allocated 60 percent of all available WAN bandwidth.

   b. FTP is guaranteed 60 of every 200 units of WAN bandwidth.

    c. FTP has a slight priority over all other TCP/IP protocols used on the WAN.

    d. This has no significance in its current configuration.

10. Which of the following is an invalid entry in a destination set?

    a. *www.yahoo.com*

    b. 192.168.5.0 to 192.168.5.200

    c. \\InternalWebServer

    d. *www.microsoft.com/isaserver/updates/ISAServer2000*

11. Which of the following can only be applied at the array level?

    a. schedules

    b. content groups

    c. protocol definitions

    d. bandwidth priorities

12. Which of the following can be granted priority using a bandwidth rule?

    a. individual users

    b. certain content types

    c. protocols

    d. all of the above

13. Buttercup Industries is rolling out ISA Server at their corporate headquarters in New York. They want to restrict all users from using the HTTP protocol to access a group of 80 different Web sites. Which of the following would best fit their needs?

    a. protocol rules

    b. site and content rules

    c. client address sets

    d. bandwidth rules

14. What best defines a protocol definition?

    a. a list of protocols allowed to access the Internet

    b. a prioritized list of protocols that defines which protocol has priority over another

    c. a list of supported protocols combined with rules to grant or deny access

    d. all of the above

15. When creating a protocol rule, you can redirect users to an internal Web server when access is denied. True or false?

6

16. Users at Snuggle Software Inc. have been accessing Web pages and downloading MP3 files to their local computers. The local network administrator wants to block access to all files ending in the .mp3 extension. What policy element would best fit the situation?

    a. protocol definitions

    b. site and content rules

    c. destination sets

    d. content groups

17. Sharp Money Inc. is an investment firm that allows their financial planners Internet access through ISA Server. All internal client computers currently run the Linux operating system and access the Internet via the Web Proxy service. The network has just converted to DHCP rather than static IP addressing; therefore, rather than applying restrictions based on an IP address, the network administrators want to apply restrictions based on user or group membership. How can this best be accomplished?

    a. Use site and content rules and SecureNAT to grant the Linux machines access.

    b. Migrate Linux clients to Windows 2000 Professional, install the firewall client, and use site and content rules.

    c. Create an additional enterprise policy named "user and group restrictions" configured with the appropriate rules and apply it to all ISA Server arrays.

    d. Change the current site and content rules to apply to user and groups rather than IP addresses. Continue using SecureNAT for Linux clients.

18. Client address sets can only contain ranges of IP addresses. True or false?

19. Ginger Kay is the network administrator for Cinematics, a motion picture development corporation. She installs three ISA Servers as stand-alone servers and defines an enterprise policy granting full Internet access. Clients are still unable to access the Internet. What must she do?

    a. Create three individual server policies granting Internet access.

    b. Modify the enterprise properties and select the checkbox for the three individual server names.

    c. Check the event viewer for relevant error messages.

    d. Define the correct policy elements and apply them to the enterprise policies.

20. What is the maximum number of enterprise policies that can be created?

    a. one

    b. two

    c. five

    d. There is no practical limit.

HANDS-ON PROJECTS

Before you can begin configuring rules, you must configure policy elements depicting your company's network configuration. In the following set of projects, you configure every major policy element, and then connect them to create ISA Server bandwidth, protocol, and site and content rules. Most of these policy elements and rules will be configured at the enterprise level. The projects for this and all subsequent chapters use the Advanced view in the ISA Management console. To change to Advanced view, open ISA Management, click the View menu, and then click Advanced. Advanced view is selected when a check mark appears next to its option on the View menu.

Project 6-1

To configure a schedule policy element:

1. Using the ISA Management utility, expand the **Enterprise** node and then expand **Policy Elements**. You see a list of Policy elements shown in Figure 6-28.

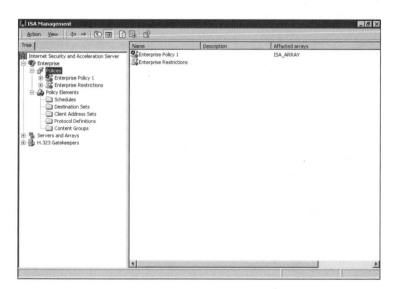

Figure 6-28

2. Right-click **Schedules**, point to **New**, and then click **Schedule**. The New schedule dialog box appears. By default, all times are active.

3. Create a schedule named **Weekend Access** that is only active on Saturdays and Sundays. See Figure 6-29.

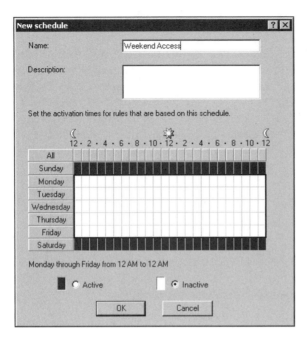

Figure 6-29

4. Click **OK**. The schedule appears in the right pane, called the Results pane.

5. Repeat Steps 1-4 to create an additional schedule for the night employees who work from 8:00 p.m. until 5:00 a.m., Monday through Friday (weekends are inactive periods). Name the schedule **Graveyard Shift**.

Project 6-2

To configure bandwidth priority policy elements:

1. Collapse the **Enterprise** node and expand the **Servers and Arrays** node. Expand the **Policy Elements** node, right-click **Bandwidth Priorities**, point to **New**, and then click **Bandwidth Priority**. The New Bandwidth Priority dialog box appears.

2. In the Name text box, type **Management Personnel**. Assign a description to this priority. Configure the outbound bandwidth equal to **100** and the inbound bandwidth equal to **50**. See Figure 6-30.

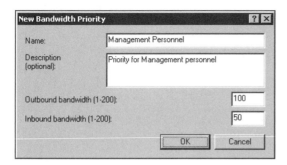

Figure 6-30

6

3. Click **OK**. The Management Personnel bandwidth priority appears in the Results pane.

4. Repeat Steps 1–3 for the following bandwidth priorities:

Name	Outbound Bandwidth	Inbound Bandwidth
Network Administrators	150	100
Human Resources	25	10
FTP	10	5
HTTP	50	10
SMTP	100	100

Project 6-3

To configure destination set policy elements:

1. Collapse the **Servers and Arrays** node and expand the **Enterprise** node. Right-click the **Destination Sets** node under the policy elements, point to **New**, and then click **Set**. The New Destination Set dialog box appears.

2. Add a new destination set named **Restricted Networks**. The Add/Edit Destination window appears, as shown in Figure 6-31.

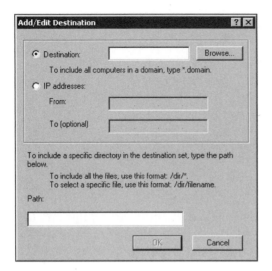

Figure 6-31

3. In the Destination text box, type ***.hackers.com**, and then click **OK**.

4. Repeat Steps 1–3 to add the destinations ***.warez.com** and ***.elite.com**. After you have finished adding all three sites, add the IP range **24.1.254.0** to **24.1.254.255** to the list. When all elements have been added, click **OK**. Then click **OK** again. The destination set appears in the Results pane.

5. Create an additional destination set named **Permitted Networks** and add the following addresses: ***.Microsoft.com**, ***.ISAServer.org**, and the address range **192.168.0.0** to **192.168.255.255**.

Project 6-4

To configure client address set policy elements:

1. Create a client address set named **Internal Clients** set at the enterprise level.

2. Specify that this client address set includes internal addresses from **10.0.0.0** to **10.240.255.255** (all potential internal addresses).

3. Create a client address set named **Management Personnel** with the IP address range **10.241.0.0** to **10.241.255.255**.

Project 6-5

To configure protocol definition policy elements:

1. Create a protocol definition named **Custom Application**.

2. Specify that the protocol definition policy applies to port number **7776**, protocol type **UDP**, and direction **Send Receive**.

3. Indicate that you want to use secondary connections, and then enter a secondary connection range. Specify that the secondary connection ranges from **8777** to **8779**, where **UDP** is the protocol type, and **Send Receive** is the direction. See Figure 6–32.

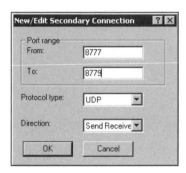

Figure 6-32

The Custom Application protocol definition should appear in the Results pane.

Project 6-6

To create a new content group policy element:

1. Create a content group named **Restricted MIME Types**.

2. Add the **application/x-zip-compressed** MIME type as the available type. See Figure 6–33. The MIME type should appear in the Selected types field.

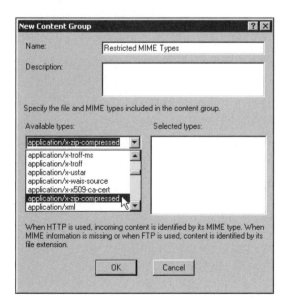

Figure 6-33

3. Add the following MIME types: **audio/mpeg**, **audio/wav**, **image/jpeg**, **image/gif**, and the **.exe** file extension.

4. After you have added the MIME types, the content group should appear in the Results pane.

5. Create a content group named **Permitted MIME Types** that allows the following MIME types: **text/html**, **text/plain**, and **image/bmp**.

Project 6-7

To create a new enterprise policy:

1. Using the ISA Management utility, expand the **Enterprise** node, if necessary. You should see the Policies and Policy Elements nodes listed below Enterprise.

2. Right-click the **Policies** node, point to **New**, and select **Policy**. The New Enterprise Policy Wizard appears.

3. Name the policy **Enterprise Restrictions** and click **Next**. On the following window, click the **Finish** button to close the wizard and create the new enterprise policy. Under the Policies node you should now see the default enterprise policy (Enterprise Policy 1) and the newly created Enterprise Restrictions policy, as shown in Figure 6-34.

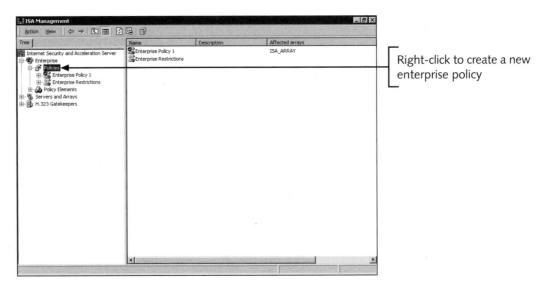

Figure 6-34

Project 6-8

To create and configure a site and content rule:

1. Create a site and content rule at the enterprise level named **Work Related Internet Access**.

2. To grant any Internet access, create an Allow rule.

3. In the Rule Configuration dialog box shown in Figure 6-35, specify that you want to create a custom allow rule.

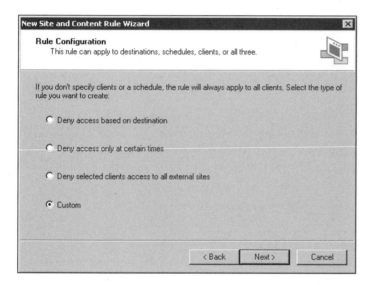

Figure 6-35

4. In the Destination Sets dialog box, specify that the rule should apply to a Specified destination set you defined as **Permitted Networks** (see Project 6-3).

5. In the Schedule dialog box, choose the **Graveyard Shift** (defined in Project 6-1) schedule.

6. Specify that you want this schedule to apply to Specific computers (client address sets).

7. Add the **Internal Clients** client address set (defined in Project 6-4). The names of the client sets should appear in the Include these sets field, as shown in Figure 6-36.

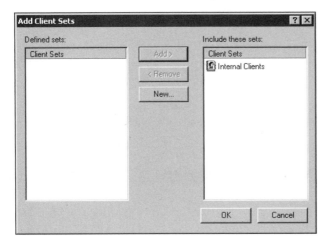

Figure 6-36

8. Choose the **Only the following content types** radio button and select the checkbox next to the **Permitted MIME Types** content group (defined in Project 6-6). When you finish creating the site and content rule, it should appear in the Site and Content Rules Results pane.

Project 6-9

To create and configure a protocol rule:

1. Create a protocol rule at the enterprise level named **Permitted Internet Protocols**.

2. Create this rule as an allow rule.

3. In the Protocols dialog box, choose to apply this rule to **Selected protocols**. From the list of protocols, shown in Figure 6-37, choose to allow **FTP Download only**, **H.323 Protocol**, **HTTP**, **HTTPS**, **NNTP**, and **SMTP**.

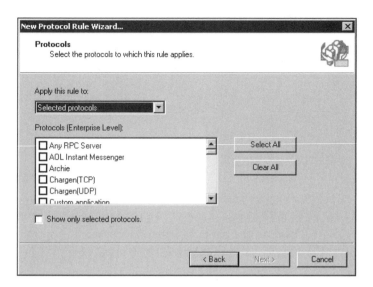

Figure 6-37

4. Choose the **Graveyard Shift** schedule, and the **Specific computers (client address sets)** as the client type.

5. To add the internal clients, click the **Add** button and move the **Internal Clients** client address set from the Defined sets pane to the Include these sets pane.

6. When you finish creating the new protocol rule, it appears in the Results pane.

Project 6-10

To create and configure a bandwidth rule:

1. Create a bandwidth rule named **Management Priority**.

2. Make sure the protocol allows **All IP traffic**.

3. Make sure the schedule **Always** applies.

4. Choose to apply this rule to **Specific computers (client address sets)**.

5. Add the **Management Personnel** client address set.

6. Apply this rule to **All destinations** and **All content groups**.

7. Set a **Custom** bandwidth priority named **Management Personnel**. The description, outbound bandwidth, and inbound bandwidth fields should appear as they do in Figure 6-38.

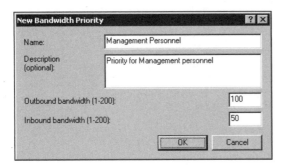

Figure 6-38

8. When you finish creating the bandwidth rule, it should be listed in the first position in the Bandwidth Rules Results pane. This prioritizes all traffic from the management PCs (as defined in the client address set range) over standard user traffic.

CASE PROJECTS

Case Project 6-1

You are a network administrator at Malp Enterprises, a 5,000-user company that has recently decided to deploy ISA Server arrays at each of its 10 office locations. Malp Enterprises does not want every internal user to have full Internet access and they are very concerned about the WAN connection becoming overloaded with Internet traffic. Malp has provided you with a list of one thousand users who should receive full Internet access, three thousand users that should receive access only to the Malp.com external Web site, and one thousand users that should not receive any Internet access at all. Furthermore, Malp would like to restrict the use of non-Internet browser applications (such as Napster, MSN Messenger, and online games). What strategy should you use when preparing the ISA Server rollout? What policy elements and rules need to be created, and at what level (enterprise or array) should they be implemented? What information, if any, do you still need to gather from the Malp Enterprises management team? After you have answered these questions and designed Malp's policy strategy, implement a sample configuration using ISA Server.

Case Project 6-2

Crizal Technology has contracted you to handle the rollout of ISA Server 2000 at their new headquarters in Moscow. Crizal creates cleaning solution for eyeglasses and receives a large number of orders through their e-commerce Web site. Employees at the Moscow location use a custom application (that uses TCP port 54,398) to create new requests and check order status at the warehouse location in Arizona. The Moscow and Arizona locations are connected via an Internet VPN. Crizal wishes to deploy ISA Server at the Moscow location to allow employees to research competing products on the Internet. They would like employees to have access only to competitors' Web sites, while management maintains full access to the Internet. What strategy should you use when preparing the ISA Server rollout? What policy elements and rules need to be created, and at what level (enterprise or array) should they be implemented? What information, if any, do you still need to gather from the Crizal Technology management team? After you have answered these questions and designed Crizal Technology's policy strategy, implement a sample configuration using ISA Server.

Case Project 6-3

You are the network administrator at XL Systems, a company that specializes in developing high-speed LAN switches. You have recently begun to deploy a three-server ISA array at the company. The array is now built and is servicing requests from the Internet, but you want to prioritize certain types of traffic over others. You open the ISA Management console and define Bandwidth Priority policy elements for HTTP, FTP, and Telnet applications. Telnet is configured to receive the highest priority, followed by HTTP, and then FTP. After you have created the bandwidth priorities, you monitor ISA Server for a time and find that all traffic continues to be treated equally. What is the problem?

Case Project 6-4

You are managing multiple ISA Server arrays for DMA Inc., a worldwide company that creates processor chips for computers. DMA's management has two different policies on Internet access, depending on where you are in the world. All European locations would like to allow full Internet access during all times of the day to all employees. However, within the U.S., employees should be restricted to a specific set of destination Internet computers during certain times of the day. How will you be able to accommodate both schools of thought with the least amount of administrative cost? Design a plan showing the necessary policies and policy elements that you need to create.

7

CONFIGURING ISA SERVER FIREWALL COMPONENTS

After reading this chapter and completing the exercises, you will be able to:

♦ Examine network security
♦ Choose the most effective ISA Server firewall strategy
♦ Secure the local ISA Server using Windows 2000 templates
♦ Work with IP routing and packet filtering, and understand their differences
♦ Understand and configure application filters
♦ Understand Web filters

In many organizations, ISA Server is the only line of defense between the Internet and the local network. Thus, ISA Server security is a primary concern for management and network administrators. In Chapter six, you were shown how ISA Server policies provide one way to secure your network. This chapter discusses how to secure ISA Server and the LAN from Internet-based attacks.

Many medium-sized and large corporations typically hire consultants to check the corporation's network security configurations and to make any necessary changes or recommendations. This chapter discusses only the security configuration options for ISA Server, but your company should employ additional measures to secure your internal network resources.

EXAMINING NETWORK SECURITY

Rather than viewing security as simply a matter of configuring a few settings, you should not only develop a strategy for making your network secure, but you should consistently modify and update this strategy to anticipate and prevent new types of hacker attacks. One of your jobs as a network administrator is to stay informed about new security issues that affect your network. Fortunately, this information is usually easy to locate on the Internet. Many Web sites and companies are dedicated to network security, and some of them, such as Microsoft, send e-mail updates that alert you to the latest attack. Microsoft posts all product-specific security issues and updates at *www.microsoft.com/security*.

Microsoft addresses security threats against its software by issuing software updates and service packs. The updates fix the most recently discovered security issues, and the service packs combine many security updates in one release. Be sure to always install the latest ISA Server or Windows 2000-related security updates and service packs on ISA Server. For example, after Microsoft released the Windows 2000 Service Pack 1 (the minimum service pack required to install ISA Server), hackers discovered how to use a buffer overrun attack on the Internet Printing Protocol (IPP) features of Windows 2000 (article Q296576). Such an attack, if successful, gains the hacker full administrative control of the Windows 2000 machine, allowing the hacker to execute any command on the machine. Consequently, Microsoft now includes a patch for this security bug in the Windows 2000 Service Pack 2. This demonstrates the importance of staying current and applying the latest security updates to your network.

You can find article Q296576 at *http://support.microsoft.com/support/ KB/articles/Q296/5/76.ASP*.

Before installing any service packs or security patches, be sure to test them thoroughly in a lab environment.

When hackers attempt to break into a network, rarely do they find an open door on their first attempt. Breaching network security can take weeks or even months. With this in mind, you should think ahead about network security, and use auditing methods. Configure Windows 2000 to watch for security-related events, and record them in log files. Provided that you review the network security log files on a regular basis, you can track when hacking attempts occur, and find out what points of attack the hacker uses. Some hackers even use automated programs that run during the evening and attempt to find weaknesses in a company's firewall. By reviewing the security logs, you can easily identify these programs and stay one step ahead of the hacker. Auditing is discussed thoroughly in Chapter 13.

Above all, ensure the physical security of the ISA Server machine and that of any other critical network equipment. An intruder who gains physical access to a machine can gain complete control of it, even if the computer is protected by built-in Windows security methods. Because of remote manageability through the MMC, many administrators lock ISA Server and other Windows 2000 domain controllers in a server room and disconnect the monitor, keyboard, and mouse from the computer.

CHOOSING A FIREWALL STRATEGY

One of the most significant changes to ISA Server since Proxy Server 2.0 is the integration of viable firewall software. As a result, many network administrators now use ISA Server to secure network communications between the Internet and the internal LAN. If you plan to use ISA Server in this capacity, you must completely plan how to deploy the firewall before installing ISA Server.

In the simplest firewall, ISA Server is configured with two network interface cards, one connecting to the public network and one connecting to the internal LAN. As your design becomes more complex, you can configure additional network cards or ISA Servers to connect to perimeter networks. These small networks are kept separate from the internal LAN to house publicly accessible servers, such as Web, e-mail, and database servers. The standard firewall configurations are discussed in the following sections.

When configuring ISA Server as a firewall, you should disable any unnecessary network services on the server. Any service you leave enabled is a potential target for an intruder. For example, if you are not using ISA Server as a Web server, you should disable the IIS Web services. Also, you should only allow necessary network traffic through the server. Many administrators allow all types of traffic, and then place restrictions where necessary (also known as a **fishnet security** configuration). Instead, you should restrict all types of traffic, and only allow what is necessary for network users, an approach known as **iron wall security**. Remember, it is much better to have network users call you and request certain types of access than to leave potential openings into the network for intruders.

Basic Firewall Methodology

Many smaller networks may use a basic firewall configuration that consists of an individual ISA Server computer or an ISA Server array connected to the Internet and the internal LAN, as shown in Figure 7-1. This configuration is appropriate for small and mid-sized network environments because it is simple: all internal users exist on the LAN and are configured to access the Internet through a single exit point. This configuration is also beneficial if you do not have internal hosts accessible from the Internet, such as Web or e-mail servers.

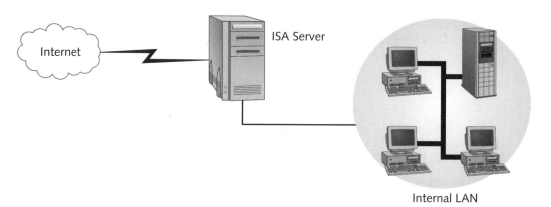

Figure 7-1   A dual-homed ISA Server firewall configuration

Because of its simplistic design, the basic firewall configuration has some inherent disadvantages. First, having one firewall protecting the internal LAN introduces a single point of failure. If the security of the ISA Server machine is compromised, an intruder has access to all internal network servers and clients. The only defensive measure left in place is the internal network security. Second, if you need to provide public access to internal servers, you could compromise the security of the entire internal network. You need to allow Internet users to access certain computers on the LAN, but in doing so you weaken security on the ISA Server computer. Because of this compromise, internal clients are more vulnerable to attack from intruders.

Three-Homed Firewall

To increase network security, you may choose to configure ISA Server in a three-homed firewall configuration. This approach involves installing three network cards in ISA Server, then connecting one to the Internet, one to the internal LAN, and one to the perimeter network, as shown in Figure 7-2. As discussed earlier in this section, the perimeter network contains the devices that are accessible from the Internet, such as Web and e-mail servers. When you configure ISA Server as a three-homed firewall, it treats both the Internet and the perimeter network as public and the internal LAN as a private network. The three-homed firewall is advantageous to network administrators because they can define separate security standards for the internal and perimeter networks. This separation allows greater security for internal clients since there should be no contact from Internet hosts. Any client that does require Internet-initiated connections (such as Web servers) should be assigned to the perimeter network.

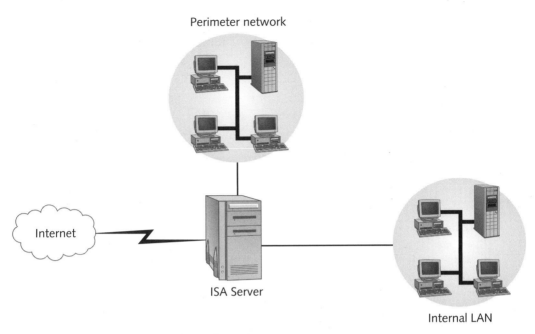

Figure 7-2   A three-homed firewall configuration

When ISA Server is connected to three networks, correct configuration of the Local Address Table (LAT) is crucial to ensuring network security. All IP addresses connected to the internal LAN should be added to the LAT. Any IP address connected to the perimeter network or the Internet should not be included in the LAT. Consequently, ISA Server treats the perimeter network and the Internet as public networks. By default, ISA Server only routes between public and private addresses (in other words, between addresses included in the LAT and excluded from it), so it is necessary to configure IP routing on ISA Server. The configuration of IP routing is discussed later in this chapter.

 Correct configuration of the LAT in a three-homed firewall is critical both in the real world and on the Microsoft certification exam.

Once you configure the LAT on ISA Server, you must enable packet filtering. (This topic is discussed in detail later in the chapter.) Packet filtering allows you to control the types of traffic ISA Server accepts on the external network interface, and can be used in conjunction with IP routing to direct traffic to the correct hosts on the perimeter network. For example, you might have an FTP server on the perimeter network that Internet clients access to download the latest product pricing information. To grant access in a three-homed server configuration, you would enable IP routing because neither the Internet nor perimeter network IP address ranges are included in the LAT.

Next, you would enable packet filtering and create a packet filter that routes FTP packets to the correct perimeter network IP address. When configuring your firewall, allow only the traffic required by the perimeter network or the internal clients.

As with the standard firewall configuration, the disadvantage of using a three-homed firewall is the single point of failure. If the security of ISA Server is compromised, intruders have access to both the perimeter and internal network machines. To eliminate the single point of failure, many network administrators choose to configure a dual ISA Server firewall system.

Dual ISA Server Firewalls

You may choose to configure dual ISA Server firewalls in a back-to-back arrangement. Using this approach, one of the ISA Servers connects to the Internet and the perimeter network, while the other maintains connections to the perimeter network and the internal network, as shown in Figure 7-3. Although this firewall strategy is the most expensive, it is also the most secure; therefore, it is typically used in high-security organizations.

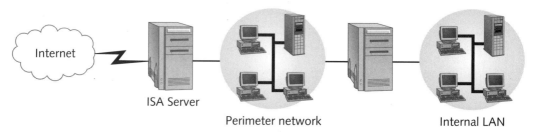

Figure 7-3   Using a dual firewall strategy

Using a dual firewall configuration provides the same advantages as the three-homed firewall strategy, with one significant enhancement: the single point of failure is eliminated. An Internet hacker who compromises the ISA Server machine connected to the Internet would have access to the clients and servers on the perimeter network, but would still have to break through another ISA Server firewall before accessing the internal network. Usually, a network administrator would detect the failure of the external firewall before the hacker could break through the internal firewall. To make matters more difficult for the intruder, the internal firewall has stronger security than the external firewall. Consequently, the attack the hacker used to break the external firewall security would probably fail on the internal firewall.

To configure the dual firewall, you install two ISA Servers in either firewall or integrated mode, and attach them to the correct networks, shown earlier in Figure 7-3. When configuring the LAT of the external ISA Server, include the clients on the perimeter network and the IP address of the internal ISA Server connected to the perimeter network. *Do not* include the NIC IP address of the internal ISA Server attached to the internal network or the address of any clients on the internal network. Doing so could make clients on the internal network accessible from the Internet. When configuring the LAT of the internal ISA Server, include only the addresses on the internal network. The internal ISA Server treats the Internet and perimeter network as public networks.

SECURING THE SERVER

Since ISA Server is only as secure as the underlying Windows 2000 operating system, you should ensure that all Windows 2000 settings are as secure as possible before using ISA Server as a firewall. Microsoft has included the ISA Server Security Configuration Wizard to increase the security of Windows 2000 server components. The wizard allows you to select from three levels of security, shown in Figure 7-4. Each level comes with templates that add security based on how ISA Server is used.

7

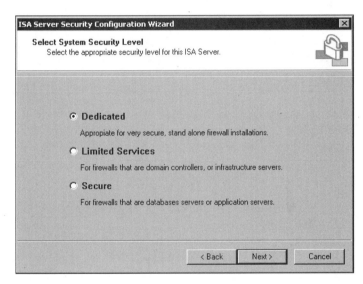

Figure 7-4 Configuring local ISA Server security

The three levels are defined as:

- *Dedicated*—Use this setting if ISA Server is used only as a firewall (installed in firewall mode) and runs no other applications. This setting applies the Hisecws.inf template if ISA Server is used on a stand-alone system or the Hisecdc.inf template if ISA Server is used as a domain controller.

- *Limited Services*—Use this setting if ISA Server is used as a firewall and a cache server (installed in integrated mode) or as a firewall and a domain controller (not recommended). This setting applies the Securews.inf template if ISA Server is used on a stand-alone system or the Securedc.inf template if ISA Server is used as a domain controller.

- *Secure*—Use this setting if ISA Server performs other roles such as running Web, e-mail, or FTP servers. This setting applies the Basicsv.inf template if ISA Server is used on a stand-alone system or the Basicdc.inf template if ISA Server is used as a domain controller.

Before you run the security configuration wizard, be sure the templates you require are located in the *systemroot*\security\templates folder. If the templates are missing, copy them from the Windows 2000 Server CD; otherwise, the wizard fails.

To run the Security Configuration Wizard:

1. Open the ISA Management console, and then expand the **Servers and Arrays** node, if necessary. Expand the appropriate array from the list, and then click the **Computers** node.

2. In the details pane, right-click the server you want to secure, and then click **Secure**. The ISA Server Security Configuration Wizard appears. Click **Next**.

3. Select the security level you want (Dedicated, Limited Services, or Secure) and close the wizard. Be sure you know exactly what changes the security template makes to Windows 2000 before applying a security level. The changes made by the security templates are documented in the Windows 2000 help files.

4. Verify the changes you made by opening the **securwiz.log** file in the ISA Server installation folder.

WORKING WITH PACKET FILTERS AND IP ROUTING

When choosing to allow access through your firewall, you must keep two configurations in mind: packet filtering and IP routing. Packet filtering allows you to control which packets ISA Server accepts or denies on the external interface. IP routing turns your ISA Server into a standard IP-based router. Although each configuration has its own functions, the two are typically used in conjunction to provide secure, yet fully functional, Internet access. The following section discusses the scenarios in which packet filtering and IP routing should be used and the configuration options for each.

Using Packet Filtering vs. Using IP Routing

By using packet filtering and IP routing, you can control the flow of traffic entering or leaving the internal network. Essentially, you can use packet filters to determine what traffic to allow or deny, and use IP routing to move all types of IP-based traffic from one network to another. (Typically, you route traffic from the public network to your internal private LAN or vice versa.) Depending on your network, you might use only packet filtering, only IP routing, or both at once. Use the following information to determine which approach is best for you.

Use IP routing for the following situations:

- *IP protocols other than TCP and UDP*—The ISA Server firewall service supports applications that use the TCP or UDP protocols. Any other IP-based protocols must be routed. If you use any applications that require protocols other than TCP or UDP, you must enable IP routing.

- *Routing between networks not included in the LAT*—If ISA Server connects to two or more networks that are not included in the LAT, you must enable IP routing. For example, the three-homed firewall is connected to the Internet, the perimeter network, and the internal network. The LAT includes IP addresses only from the internal network, so you must enable IP routing to route packets between the Internet and the perimeter network.

Use packet filtering for the following situations:

- *Applications running on the ISA Server computer*—If you decide to run applications other than Web browsers on the ISA Server computer, you need to create packet filters to establish a direct connection to the Internet and open the required ports the applications need to run. For example, if you need to run a Telnet application on ISA Server, you must create a packet filter that allows outgoing traffic on TCP port 25. Installing the firewall client on ISA Server itself is not supported; it is known to cause problems.

- *Protocols other than TCP and UDP*—When a SecureNAT client uses an application that attempts to pass a request to ISA Server on a protocol other than TCP and UDP (such as the Ping utility), ISA Server uses IP routing to send the request to the Internet. However, you must configure packet filters before ISA Server allows the traffic to pass through.

- *Services running on the ISA Server computer*—If you plan to use ISA Server to run other services, such as Web, FTP, or DNS services, you must create packet filters that allow incoming or outgoing requests on the required ports.

- *Routing between networks not included in the LAT*—If you are using IP routing to route requests between networks not included in the LAT, such as in the three-homed firewall configuration, you must create packet filters to open the necessary ports between the networks. For example, if you have an FTP server on the perimeter network, you need to use a packet filter to open port 21 on the interface attached to the Internet.

You can use packet filtering and IP routing separately or in a joint configuration. Use the following guidelines when making your decision.

Packet Filtering Disabled, IP Routing Disabled

Using this configuration keeps ISA Server from applying packet filters to any traffic entering or leaving it. ISA Server cannot route between networks that are not included in the LAT, such as the Internet and a perimeter network in the three-homed configuration, nor can it provide service to SecureNAT clients requesting to use IP protocols other than TCP or UDP. Use this configuration only when the external NIC of ISA Server connects to a trusted network. For instance, you would use this configuration if you were using ISA Server to optimize traffic in a leased line, frame-relay, or ATM-based connection situation.

Packet Filtering Enabled, IP Routing Disabled

Using this configuration enhances security since ISA Server drops all packets sent to the external NICs, unless you create packet filters to explicitly allow the traffic. Unless IP routing is enabled, however, ISA Server does not forward traffic between networks that are not included in the LAT. This limits ISA Server to TCP- and UDP-based traffic; any other applications will not be forwarded.

Packet Filtering Enabled, IP Routing Enabled

This is the most common configuration for ISA Server firewalls. ISA Server gains all the features of a router and can transmit all protocols in the TCP/IP protocol suite; it also can relay data between networks not included in the LAT. At the same time, ISA Server gains the security features related to packet filtering. You can control which types of traffic are allowed through the router and which IP-based hosts can send and receive the data streams.

Packet Filtering Disabled, IP Routing Enabled

Because you must first enable packet filtering before you can enable IP routing, this configuration is not available through ISA Server. However, you can enable this configuration by using the Routing and Remote Access MMC snap-in. This configures ISA Server to be a low-security router. By default, Windows 2000 permits all traffic to flow between network configurations, completely eliminating network security.

Understanding Packet Filtering

Before you begin to configure packet filters, you must understand exactly what filtering criteria the ISA Server packet filters use:

- *Source IP address and port number*—You can allow or deny incoming or outgoing traffic based on the sending device's IP address or the application source port number. However, the source port number is dynamically generated by a network application and can change quite often. For this reason, you typically do not filter based on the source port number.

- *Destination IP address and port number*—You can allow or deny incoming or outgoing traffic based on the IP address of the destination device or the application destination port number. This number is typically static, is considered well-known, and does not change (for example, port 80 for HTTP, port 21 for FTP). Destination port numbers are the most common and effective way of filtering large amounts of network traffic.

- *IP protocol information*—Filtering based on IP protocol information allows you to allow or deny traffic based on the sub-protocol of TCP/IP used on the network. For example, many different types of hacking methods use ICMP to cause Denial of Service attacks. Rather than trying to filter each type of attack, you could simply restrict the use of the ICMP protocol.

Packet filters can be configured to allow or deny traffic based on the criteria discussed above. The deny packet filters always take precedence over the allow packet filters. For example, if you had two conflicting packet filters, one allowing HTTP access and the other denying it, ISA Server would process the deny filter first and deny HTTP traffic. Since ISA Server denies all traffic by default, you should configure deny filters as exceptions to the allow rules. For example, you may decide to allow all Telnet traffic (TCP port 23) to leave your network. However, you have a Cisco router configured as an additional firewall beyond ISA Server. You have found from the ISA Server access logs that some users have been attempting to gain Telnet access to the Cisco firewall. You could implement a deny "exception" packet filter, which disallows access to the Cisco router's IP address.

Each manually configured packet filter falls into the category of **static packet filtering**. Using static packet filters to allow access essentially opens a hole in the firewall for the duration of the packet filter's life. Imagine your firewall as the walls around a castle. If you do not create any openings in the walls, the castle is completely protected from intruders; however, the people inside the castle cannot get the resources they need. You can create holes in the castle walls and allow people to bring resources back to the castle, but the castle then becomes open to outside attack. Static packet filters work in the same way: when you create one, you create an opening that allows traffic both from the internal network to the Internet and from the Internet to the internal network. Unfortunately, these openings also give hackers an opportunity to gain access to the internal network. To allow for higher security standards, ISA Server supports **dynamic packet filtering** in addition to static packet filters.

Dynamic packet filtering resembles a closely guarded gate at a castle wall. People who need to leave the castle must tell the guard where they are going and what resources they plan to bring back. If the wrong person returns or a person returns carrying the wrong resources, the guard denies them access to the castle. Dynamic packet filters work in the same way. Once a user accesses the Internet, a dynamic opening appears in the firewall and allows the Internet to communicate back to the user. However, ISA Server monitors the opening to ensure that only the resource the user requested is returned from the requested network location. Once the request has been fulfilled, ISA Server closes the port. For example, a user might access the default Web page at *www.microsoft.com* using port 80. ISA Server monitors the outgoing request and opens a dynamic port to allow the *microsoft.com* Web server to send the default Web page back to the user. If any Internet resource other than *microsoft.com* attempts to communicate with the user, or if the *microsoft.com* Web server attempts to send any resource other than the default Web page, ISA Server denies the request and closes the port. In addition, once the *microsoft.com* Web server has sent the default Web page, ISA Server closes the port. You should use dynamic filtering rather than static filtering whenever possible.

Default Packet Filters

When you install ISA Server, seven packet filters are created by default, six of which are active. ISA Server uses these default packet filters primarily to deliver communication failures to a client. For example, if a client attempts to connect to a nonexistent IP address on the Internet, the packet sent by the client eventually reaches its TTL and the Internet router that last processes the packet sends an ICMP timeout message to the client. The default packet filter, ICMP timeout in, allows the client to receive the incoming timeout message and the client's browser displays it on the screen.

The seven default packet filters are:

- *DHCP client*—This filter allows ISA Server to receive a DHCP-assigned address. This is the only default packet filter that is not enabled. If the ISP that ISA Server uses requires dynamically assigned IP addresses, you should enable this packet filter.

- *DNS filter*—This filter allows name resolution requests from ISA Server to pass through to an Internet-based DNS server.

- *ICMP outbound*—This filter allows all ICMP messages from ISA Server and the internal network to be sent to the Internet. Without this filter, ISA Server cannot send any ICMP connection error messages to Internet clients.

- *ICMP ping response (in)*—This filter allows ISA Server's external interface to receive responses to any ICMP ping requests. Without this filter, you cannot ping Internet-based hosts.

- *ICMP source quench*—This filter allows ISA Server to receive ICMP source quench messages from Internet-based hosts. A **source quench** is a message from a receiving computer that tells you to slow the transmission of data.

- *ICMP timeout in*—This filter allows ISA Server to receive ICMP timeout messages that notify a client when sent packets have reached their TTL.

- *ICMP unreachable in*—This filter allows ISA Server to receive ICMP unreachable messages, which tell a client the destination host is unreachable.

Microsoft suggests that you keep the default packet filters enabled because they cannot be exploited by hackers and are primarily designed to allow ICMP ping or error messages to be delivered back to clients.

Setting the Packet Filter Global Properties

Before you configure individual packet filters, you should first configure the packet filter global properties. To open the properties dialog box, open the ISA Management

MMC, expand the Servers and Arrays node, expand your server or array, expand the Access Policy node, right-click IP Packet Filters, and then click Properties. The IP Packet Filters Properties dialog box appears, as shown in Figure 7-5.

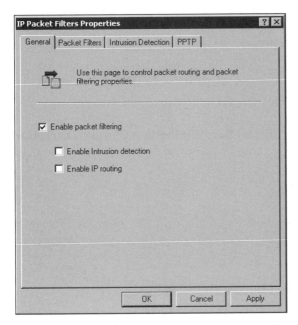

Figure 7-5   The IP Packet Filters Properties dialog box

Use the dialog box to configure the following global options:

- *Enable packet filtering*—Click this check box to turn on packet filtering. You must select this option to allow the configuration of any other options. Remember, as soon as you enable packet filtering, ISA Server drops all packets directed to the external interface.

- *Enable Intrusion detection*—Click this check box to turn on the intrusion detection features of ISA Server, which guard against many common hacking attacks. Intrusion detection features are discussed in Chapter 12.

- *Enable IP routing*—Click this check box to enable the IP routing features of ISA Server discussed earlier in this chapter.

- *Enable filtering of IP fragments* and *Enable filtering IP options*—Set these options in the Packet Filters tab to repel many common Denial of Service attacks, which send many IP fragments or set IP options to incorrect levels. Before selecting these options, ensure that you do not use any applications that use IP fragments or IP options, such as Voice over IP.

- *Log packets from "Allow" filters*—By default, ISA Server only logs packets that activate a deny packet filter. Selecting this option in the Packet Filters tab forces ISA Server to log all requests that activate an allow filter. Beware: selecting this option can result in slow processing times.

- *PPTP through ISA firewall*—Select this option in the PPTP tab to allow PPTP tunnels to pass through the ISA Server firewall.

Creating and Configuring Packet Filters

Now that you have enabled packet filtering, you must create at least one packet filter that allows network access, or all traffic is denied.

To create a packet filter:

1. In the ISA Server MMC, in the Access Policy node, right-click **IP Packet Filters**, point to **New**, and click **Filter**. The New IP Packet Filter Wizard appears.

2. Type a logical name for the packet filter, and then click **Next**. If the ISA Server you are configuring is in an array, the Servers window appears and asks if the packet filter applies to all ISA Servers in the array or only to this server. Choose the appropriate setting based on your network environment, and then click **Next**. The Filter Mode dialog box appears, as shown in Figure 7-6.

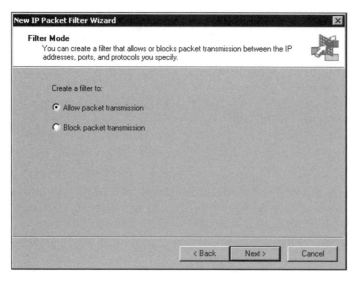

Figure 7-6   Selecting the state of the packet filter

3. Choose whether to allow or deny packet transmission by using the appropriate option button, and then click **Next**. The Filter Type dialog box appears.

4. Select a filter type.

- If you select the **Predefined** option button (the default), you can choose one of the packet filters preconfigured by Microsoft. When you finish, skip to Step nine.

- If you want to create your own packet filter based on custom port assignments, click **Custom**, and then click **Next**. The Filter Settings dialog box appears, as shown in Figure 7-7.

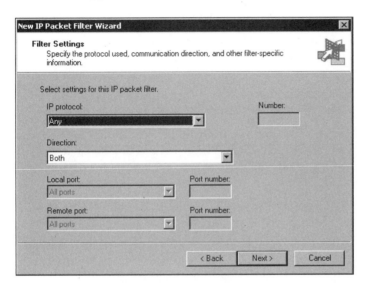

Figure 7-7 Configuring a custom filter

5. In the Filter Settings dialog box, click the **IP protocol** list arrow, and then click the IP-based protocol ISA Server should allow or deny. Selecting **Any** applies the packet filter to any IP-based protocol. If you select the **Custom protocol**, enter the TCP/IP protocol number in the **Number** field. You can find this number in the protocol documentation.

6. Click the **Direction** list arrow, and then click the direction of communication ISA Server should set for the filter. If you select any IP protocol except UDP, you have the following Direction options:

- *Inbound*—Packets entering the internal network are allowed.

- *Outbound*—Packets leaving the internal network are allowed.

- *Both*—Packets traveling in both directions are allowed.

Because UDP is a connectionless protocol and does not use session-based communication, its Direction options differ. If you selected the UDP protocol, you have the following options in the Direction list box:

- *Send only*—Allows traffic to leave ISA Server in the outbound direction

- *Send/Receive*—Allows traffic to leave ISA Server in the outbound direction and receive responses in the inbound direction

- *Receive only*—Allows the traffic to enter ISA Server in the inbound direction

- *Receive/Send*—Allows the traffic to enter ISA Server in the inbound direction and send responses in the outbound direction

- *Both*—Allows full inbound and outbound UDP communication

7. If you selected **ICMP** as the IP protocol, you can apply two additional settings in the Filter Settings dialog box:

   - *Type*—Choose **All types** to apply the filter to all ICMP types, or **Fixed Type** to choose the type (by ICMP type number) of ICMP communication.

   - *Code*—Select **All Codes** to apply the packet filter to all ICMP codes or **Fixed Code** to apply the filter to a specific ICMP code (by ICMP code number). Refer to RFC 792 for a list of all ICMP codes.

8. In the **Local port** and **Remote port** text boxes, define the ports being used on the local and remote networks. These settings are available only for the TCP and UDP protocols. You have the same options for defining the two settings:

   - *All ports*—Apply the protocol filter to all ports within the selected IP protocol.

   - *Dynamic*—Apply the filter to ports 1025 through 5000, the ports typically opened by client applications when connecting to a remote server.

   - *Fixed port*—Apply the packet filter to an individual port number.

   - *Port number*—If you select **Fixed port**, specify which one in the **Port number** field.

The significance of the local and remote ports is related to the direction the packet filter is being applied. If you apply the packet filter in the outbound direction, the local port becomes the local host's source port number and the remote port becomes the local host's destination port number. If you apply the packet filter in the inbound direction, the local port becomes the remote host's destination port number and the remote port becomes the remote host's source port number. For example, if you wanted to allow external clients to access an internal Web server, you would configure the local port to be 80.

9. After selecting the appropriate filter configuration in the Filter Settings dialog box, click **Next**. The Local Computer dialog box appears. Choose the ISA Server IP address or addresses to which the packet filter applies. These can be IP addresses assigned to the ISA Server external interface or to a computer on the perimeter network. Then click **Next**. The Remote Computers dialog box appears.

10. In the Remote Computers dialog box, choose to apply the packet filter to all remote computers or to an individual remote computer, as shown Figure 7–8. Click **Next**, and then click **Finish** to create the packet filter.

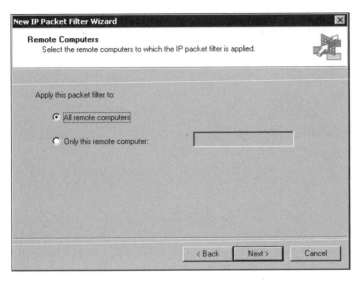

Figure 7-8   Defining the affected remote computers

 When you complete the New IP Packet Filter Wizard, you have the option of applying the filter either to a specific local and remote host or to all local and remote hosts. If you edit the packet filter properties later, you have the additional option of specifying an IP address range of local and remote addresses.

Once you create the packet filter, it should appear in the details pane. You can modify the filter at any time by opening its properties window and changing the settings. In the same window, you can easily enable and disable packet filters without deleting and recreating the entire filter. To disable a packet filter, click the General tab in the properties dialog box, and then click the Enable this filter check box to remove the check, as shown in Figure 7-9. To enable the filter, check the box again, and click OK. Disabled packet filters are displayed in the details pane with a red arrow over them. For an example, see the DHCP client filter in the background of Figure 7-9.

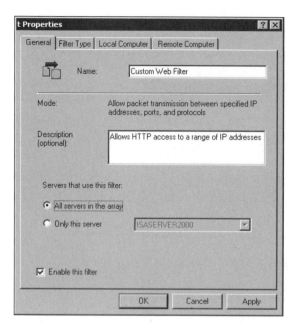

Figure 7-9   Enabling and disabling packet filters

CONFIGURING APPLICATION FILTERS

Packet filters not only check each TCP/IP frame that enters and leaves the internal network, but also make forwarding decisions based on the header information. These features give you precise control over what enters and leaves the network and can repel many common hacking methods. However, packet filters leave the data portion of the frame untouched, leaving networks vulnerable to many other types of attacks. Most firewall products do not offer protection against such attacks and network administrators must typically purchase third-party software to screen data from the Application layer. Fortunately, ISA Server can now screen data at a more advanced level by using **application filters**.

Rather than screening only IP header information, application filters examine the entire session of communication between two devices, such as a file transfer or an e-mail message. These filters can perform program functions such as running a virus scan on incoming data or deleting e-mail attachments. Unlike packet filters, application filters are not limited to screening one protocol at a time; they can watch incoming or outgoing data from multiple protocols.

While many application filters are included with ISA Server, you can also add your own. In other words, your in-house developers can create a custom application filter that meets your company's particular needs. For example, your organization could require that every outgoing e-mail message is tagged with the company logo. You could create a custom application filter that adds the logo attachment to outgoing messages.

During a typical or complete installation, ISA Server installs and enables all application filters, with the exception of the SMTP filter. Each filter provides different functionality and many have different configuration options. To access the available application filters on ISA Server, open the ISA Management console, expand the Servers and Arrays node, expand your array or server name, expand Extensions, and open the Application Filters folder.

The following section discusses the pre-installed application filters, their functions, and, if necessary, their configuration options.

DNS Intrusion Detection Filter

Hackers have developed many attacks that focus on disabling DNS servers because many organizations lose network operation if the DNS server is unavailable. By enabling the DNS Intrusion Detection filter, you can screen for the following attacks, shown in Figure 7-10:

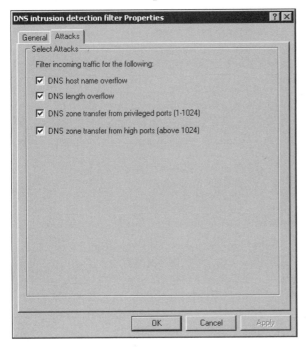

Figure 7-10   Configuring the DNS application filter to prevent hacker attacks

- *DNS host name overflow*—This attack involves sending a DNS hostname response that exceeds a standard, fixed length. Since most applications do not check to verify hostname length, the response causes the internal buffers to overflow and can allow the hacker to execute commands or crash a targeted computer.

- *DNS length overflow*—This attack is similar to the DNS hostname attack, but involves sending an IP address, rather than a hostname, that is longer than four bytes. The result is the same as a DNS hostname overflow.

- *DNS zone transfer from privileged ports (1-1024)*—This attack occurs when a client attempts to gain access to the DNS zone database by sending a zone transfer request on ports 1-1024. Allowing a client to access your entire DNS database opens the door for other, more damaging attacks.

- *DNS zone transfer from high ports (above 1024)*—This is the same attack as the previous one, but it uses ports above 1024.

FTP Access Filter

The FTP Access filter is designed to give SecureNAT clients FTP access beyond the public network. Remember, SecureNAT clients cannot open secondary ports for applications. The FTP Access filter detects the FTP request and dynamically opens the second port that the FTP protocol requires. While you could create a protocol definition to achieve this result, the application filter offers the following additional capabilities:

- The FTP Access filter opens specific secondary connections; the protocol definitions must open a range of secondary connections.

- The FTP Access filter keeps SecureNAT clients hidden by translating the address of the secondary connection. Protocol definitions do not have this ability.

- The FTP Access filter can distinguish between read and write FTP access, allowing you to filter out uploading or downloading to FTP sites.

H.323 Filter

The H.323 filter allows any H.323-based conferencing application (such as Microsoft Netmeeting) to access the Internet through ISA Server. H.323 is the industry-standard protocol for streaming voice, audio, and application sharing. To configure the H.323 filter, open the properties window by double-clicking the H.323 filter, then click the Call Control tab. You can configure the following options, as shown in Figure 7-11.

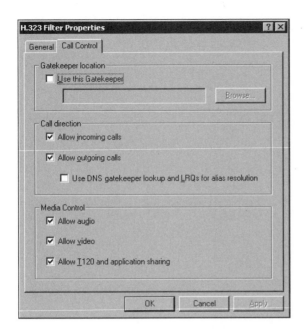

Figure 7-11   Modifying the H.323 filter properties

- *Use this Gatekeeper*—This allows you to specify the computer running the H.323 Gatekeeper service. Gatekeepers are typically used for H.323 access and bandwidth control.

- *Allow incoming calls*—Permits outside network users to call your internal network users

- *Allow outgoing calls*—Permits internal network users to call outside network users

- *Use DNS gatekeeper lookup and LRQs for alias resolution*—Allows you to use DNS to resolve H.323 aliases for outgoing calls

- *Allow audio*—Permits audio-based calls

- *Allow video*—Permits video-based calls

- *Allow T120 and application sharing*—Permits application and data sharing using the T120 protocol standard

HTTP Redirector Filter

Using the HTTP Redirector filter allows ISA Server to redirect Web requests from firewall and SecureNAT clients to the Web proxy service. This filter lets ISA Server cache Web page requests from users who do not have their browser configured to access ISA Server as a Web proxy. This filter also lets you apply site and content rules to firewall and SecureNAT clients. Unfortunately, the HTTP Redirector filter cannot redirect authentication information. If you require authentication for the Web proxy service, the firewall and SecureNAT clients are unable to pass through it.

When configuring the HTTP Redirector filter, you have the options shown in Figure 7-12 and explained in the following list.

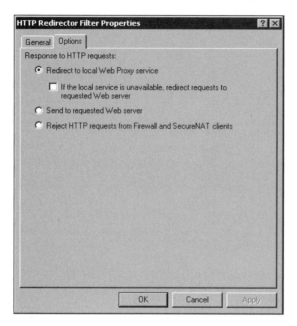

Figure 7-12 Configuring the HTTP redirector filter properties

- *Redirect to local Web Proxy service*—This is the default option, which redirects requests from all clients to the Web Proxy service.

- *If the local service is unavailable, redirect requests to requested Web server*—If you selected the previous redirection option, you also can select this option, which ensures that a failure of the Web Proxy service does not disable all HTTP access.

- *Send to requested Web server*—This keeps the SecureNAT and firewall clients from being routed through the Web Proxy service. This disables caching features for non-Web Proxy clients.

- *Reject HTTP requests from Firewall and SecureNat clients*—This blocks all HTTP requests from SecureNAT and Firewall clients. This prevents non-Web proxy clients from using HTTP to access the Web.

POP Intrusion Detection Filter

The POP Intrusion Detection filter watches traffic passing through ISA Server that was sent with the POP mail protocol. This filter looks for one attack in particular: a POP buffer overflow. Like DNS buffer overflow attacks, hackers who use a POP buffer overflow attempt to overflow the internal buffers of a POP mail server, such as Microsoft Exchange. If successful, the hacker gains unrestricted access to the server.

RPC Filter

The Remote Procedure Call (RPC) filter lets you publish internal RPC servers and make them available to outside clients. RPC servers are discussed in Chapter nine.

SMTP Filter

The Simple Mail Transfer Protocol (SMTP) filter allows you to screen e-mail messages received on TCP port 25. Before you can use the SMTP filter, shown in Figure 7-13, you must install the Message Screener ISA Server component, which is located under the Add-in Services in the ISA Server custom installation category. Instead of overloading the internal Microsoft Exchange server with processing, you can choose to restrict e-mails based on any of the following criteria:

7

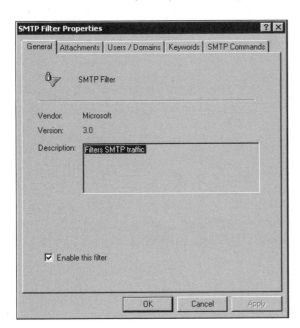

Figure 7-13   Configuring the SMTP filter

- *Attachments*—The Attachments tab lets you create a list of attachment filters based on the attachment name, extension, or size limit. When ISA Server receives a message that matches the attachment criteria, you can configure the filter to instantly delete the message, hold the message, or forward the message to another e-mail address. For example, you could create an attachment filter to discard all e-mails with .vbs attachments, which would keep Visual Basic scripts (a prime virus attachment) from entering the e-mail server.

- *Users/Domains*—The Users/Domains tab lets you create a list of rejected e-mail users and rejected e-mail domains. For example, your company might be receiving bulk e-mail messages from *Sally@CyberSally.com*. You could filter these e-mails in one of two ways: either deny the user "Sally" by adding her to the rejected users list or deny the entire *CyberSally.com* domain by adding it to the rejected domains list.

- *Keywords*—This powerful filtering feature allows you to reject e-mails based on one or many keywords. Simply tell the filter what keywords to reject and where to look for them (either the message body or the message header). For example, if you want to filter any e-mail messages containing the word "poodle" in the message body, click the Keywords tab, and then click Add, as shown in Figure 7-14. Type "poodle" as the keyword, click the Message body option button, and then click OK. ISA Server will now screen for all messages that have "poodle" in the text.

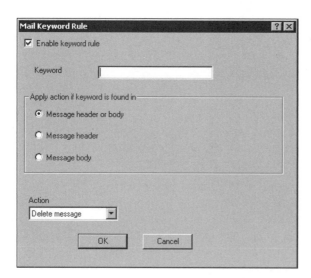

Figure 7-14   Configuring a content-based e-mail filter

- *SMTP Commands*—You can also filter incoming or outgoing e-mails for specific encoded SMTP commands. All e-mail messages transferred using SMTP are encoded with SMTP commands; however, a hacker could configure an individual SMTP command to cause a buffer overrun error on the e-mail server. To prevent this error, ISA Server allows you to define the maximum length for each SMTP command, as shown in Figure 7-15.

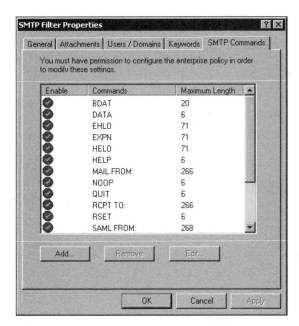

Figure 7-15   Configuring valid SMTP commands and the maximum length allowed by ISA Server

Socks V4 Filter

The Socks V4 filter allows ISA Server to communicate with clients that use the Socks protocol. This protocol is used by many legacy applications for network communication. The only configuration item on the Socks V4 filter is the port number used to communicate. This setting is typically left at the default port, 1080.

Streaming Media Filter

The Streaming Media filter allows network clients to communicate via common streaming media protocols, which are used worldwide for many audio and video applications. Furthermore, the Streaming Media filter allows the configuration of **live stream splitting**, which essentially allows you to "cache" a live video stream on a local Windows Media Technology (WMT) server or WMT server pool, allowing many internal users to access the same audio or video feed without causing multiple downloads across the WAN. ISA Server supports the use of the following streaming media protocols:

- *Microsoft Windows Media (WMS)*—This protocol is used solely by the Windows Media Player application.

- *Progressive Networks Protocol (PNM)*—This protocol is used by the RealPlayer application.

- *Real Time Streaming Protocol (RTSP)*—This protocol is used by RealPlayer G2 and QuickTime 4.

To support live stream splitting on ISA Server, you need to install the Windows Media Service on the ISA Server computer, unless you are connected to a WMT pool, in which case you can install the Windows Media Service administration tool on ISA Server.

To configure live stream splitting:

1. Open the Streaming Media Filter Properties dialog box by double-clicking the filter, and then clicking the **Live Stream Splitting** tab, shown in Figure 7-16.

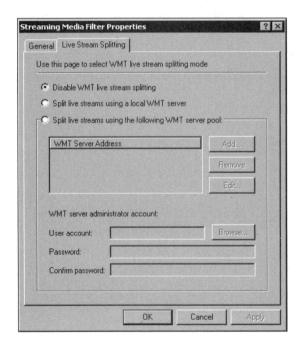

Figure 7-16 Configuring live stream splitting

2. Select one of the following options:
   - *Disable WMT live stream splitting*—Completely disables live stream splitting
   - *Split live streams using a local WMT server*—Splits the media stream on ISA Server itself
   - *Split live streams using the following WMT server pool*—This splits the media streams by using a WMT server pool on the internal network. If you select this option, be prepared with a username and password that has administrative access on the WMT server.

Using ISA Server as a WMT server can cause extremely high processor use and is not recommended.

UNDERSTANDING WEB FILTERS

Web filters were once only available in Internet Information Servers but are now also included with ISA Server. Web filters are nothing more than modified Internet Server Application Programming Interface (ISAPI) filters. ISAPI filters are typically DLL files that filter data traveling to and from the server. These filters monitor HTTP-based traffic for specific events. When the specified event occurs, the Web (ISAPI) filter is triggered, allowing you to monitor or change the data as it travels through ISA Server. The Web filter can modify the data to fit an organization's needs, but it is typically used to provide enhanced logging, custom encryption, custom compression, or additional authentication methods.

ISA Server ships without any installed Web filters, but Microsoft is counting on third-party or in-house development of ISAPI filters that meet an individual organization's needs. For example, GFI (*www.gfisoftware.com*) has produced an ISAPI filter called LANguard, which provides content filtering and anti-virus checking of inbound and outbound network traffic. Finjan Software (*www.finjan.com*) produces SurfinGate, which integrates into ISA Server and blocks malicious code (such as ActiveX or Visual Basic scripts) that are downloaded using the HTTP protocol. These are just a few examples of products that integrate with ISA Server as Web filters.

CHAPTER SUMMARY

❒ When maintaining network security, the best practice is to stay updated. Always install the latest service pack and security updates on the ISA Server machine.

❒ When choosing a firewall strategy, you can select between a standard firewall (one server with two network interface cards), a three-homed server (one server with three or more network interface cards), or dual ISA Server firewalls (two servers with two or more network interface cards).

❒ To secure the Windows 2000 operating system used with ISA Server, start the ISA Server Security Configuration Wizard, which applies Microsoft security templates through one of three modes: Dedicated (hisec templates), Limited Services (sec templates), or Secure (basic templates).

❒ Use the IP routing firewall features to provide routing between networks not included in the LAT and to route protocols other than TCP or UDP. Use the packet filtering features to add security to the IP router or to grant access to external or SecureNAT clients.

- Packet filters screen incoming and outgoing traffic based on the information in the IP header. This allows you to manage traffic based on the source and destination IP address, the source and destination port numbers, and the protocol in use.

- Dynamic packet filtering allows ISA Server to dynamically open ports, which in turn allows external servers to communicate back to internal clients. Once the session ends, the dynamically opened port closes.

- ISA Server contains many default packet filters that allow basic DNS and ICMP messages to pass through the server.

- Application filters are an extendable group of filters that screen for data beyond the IP header information. Application filters perform tasks such as virus checking and e-mail screening.

- Web filters bring the IIS ISAPI filter functionality to ISA Server. This allows the integration of custom DLLs created by third-party vendors to provide additional features such as extended logging, custom encryption, and compression.

KEY TERMS

application filters — Packet filters functioning at the Application layer allow for advanced filtering of data beyond network addresses or port numbers.

dynamic packet filtering — A method of packet filtering that allows ISA Server to dynamically open ports to allow for return transmission of requested data.

fishnet security — A security strategy that grants everyone access to all resources, and then places restrictions where necessary.

iron wall security — A security strategy that denies everyone access to all resources, and then grants permission where necessary.

live stream splitting — A configuration that allows ISA Server to locally store streamed data for multiple clients, thus minimizing the amount of WAN traffic used for audio or video streaming.

source quench — An ICMP-based message that tells the device sending data to slow transmission.

static packet filtering — A method of packet filtering that allows administratively defined ports to be opened on the ISA Server firewall.

REVIEW QUESTIONS

1. The F&Y Publishing firm is a small startup company with 100 on-site employees. The firm is considering ISA Server primarily for its integrated firewall features, but may use caching as well. The ISA Server firewall will be used to protect the internal network from outside attacks and to provide external access to the

internal Web, FTP, and e-mail server. The project budget is limited; what firewall strategy would you recommend to management?

a. basic firewall

b. three-homed firewall

c. dual firewall

d. PIX firewall

2. Which of the following is a valid packet filtering criterion?

a. source port number

b. destination port number

c. destination IP address

d. all of the above

3. Which one of the following servers would you find in a perimeter network?

a. Web server

b. domain controller

c. internal database server

d. all of the above

4. What functionality would you expect to see on a domain controller secured using the Limited Services option in the ISA Server Security Configuration Wizard?

a. Web server

b. e-mail server

c. caching server

d. database server

5. Terminal Processing Systems (TPS) wants to use ISA Server as a firewall and cache server. The internal network clients all use SecureNAT and run a custom application that uses TCP port 15239. TPS is unsure if ISA Server supports the necessary features to run the custom application. What features would you recommend to allow the custom application to access the external network?

a. IP routing

b. packet filtering

c. IP routing and packet filtering

d. The custom application would not be supported.

6. If you needed to send data to the Internet through an ISA Server that used a protocol other than TCP and UDP, what ISA Server feature would you use?

   a. IP routing

   b. packet filtering

   c. IP routing and packet filtering

   d. ISA Server only supports TCP- and UDP-based communication.

7. What is the benefit of using a dual firewall configuration?

   a. the elimination of a single point of failure

   b. the creation of an internal perimeter network

   c. Two levels of security are applied, one for the DMZ and one for the internal network.

   d. all of the above

8. When using a three-homed ISA Server firewall configuration, what networks should be included in the LAT?

   a. the perimeter network only

   b. the internal network only

   c. the perimeter and internal network

   d. only the IP addresses assigned to the ISA Server internal interfaces

9. When using a dual ISA Server firewall configuration, what networks should be included in the LAT of the ISA Server connected to the Internet?

   a. the perimeter network only

   b. the internal network only

   c. the perimeter and internal network

   d. only the IP addresses assigned to the ISA Server internal interfaces

10. When configuring a dual ISA Server firewall, enabling IP routing is required to route between the external network and perimeter networks. True or false?

11. Which of the following default packet filters is *not* enabled by default?

   a. DHCP client

   b. DNS filter

   c. ICMP outbound

   d. ICMP source quench

12. Application filters are used to provide what?

    a. extendable IP header filtering

    b. screening for the entire communication session

    c. restrictions for a predefined list of applications

    d. all of the above

13. What task does the FTP Access application filter perform?

    a. dynamically opens TCP port 20 for SecureNAT clients

    b. applies restrictions to inbound and outbound FTP access

    c. filters FTP access using a Client Address Set policy element

    d. none of the above

14. Mike and Ike's Construction has a corporate office of 300 people in the heart of New York City. Recently, the company has had increased WAN traffic from employees using RealAudio to listen to Internet-based radio stations. What ISA Server feature might the company be interested in?

    a. content caching

    b. packet filters

    c. RealAudio compression

    d. live stream splitting

15. Which of the following criteria *cannot* be filtered using the SMTP application filter?

    a. a word in the text of an e-mail

    b. mail sent from a specific e-mail server

    c. attachments with a .vbs file extension

    d. mail sent from a username of Nathan

16. Which of the following streaming protocols are supported using ISA Server?

    a. Real Time Streaming Protocol (RTSP)

    b. Microsoft Media Stream (MMS)

    c. RealAudio Network Stream (RANS)

    d. all of the above

17. Where would you configure ISA Server to log all traffic that triggers an allow packet filter?

    a. from the individual allow packet filter

    b. in the logging properties window of ISA Server or the ISA Server array

    c. in the logging properties window of the application filters node

    d. from the global packet filter properties window

7

18. What is the primary function of the HTTP redirector?

    a. to redirect denied users to an internal Web server page

    b. to redirect users to approved Web sites

    c. to cache non-Web Proxy users' content using the Web Proxy service

    d. When combined with a site and content rule, it allows the redirection of HTTP content.

19. What application uses the H.323 protocol?

    a. ISA Server firewall client

    b. Microsoft Internet Explorer

    c. Microsoft Netmeeting

    d. none of the above

20. The default DNS packet filters can detect many common DNS buffer overflow attacks. True or false?

HANDS-ON PROJECTS

Project 7-1

To configure local security on the ISA Server machine:

1. Open the ISA Management console, expand the **Servers and Arrays** node and your array, if necessary, and select the **Computers** node. In the details pane, right-click your server name, and then click **Secure**. The ISA Server Security Configuration Wizard appears. Click **Next**. The Select System Security Level dialog box appears.

2. Choose **Secure** as the system security level, if necessary, and click **Next**. (Choosing Limited Services or Dedicated may adversely affect your network communication in future labs.) Select **Finish** to apply the security settings.

3. The ISA Server Security Configuration dialog box appears and applies the Windows 2000 security templates to your machine. When the ISA Server window appears, click **OK**, close the ISA Management window, and restart your computer.

4. Once your computer has restarted, log on, click **Start**, and then click **Run**. Type **C:\Program Files\Microsoft ISA Server\securwiz.log** in the Run text box, and then click **OK**. (Replace "C:" with the drive containing ISA Server, if necessary.) The modified security settings are displayed in the log file.

5. Close Notepad.

Project 7-2

To configure the packet filtering global properties:

1. Open the ISA Management console. Expand the **Servers and Arrays** node, your array, and the **Access Policy** node, if necessary, and open the **Properties** dialog box for IP Packet Filters, as shown in Figure 7–17.

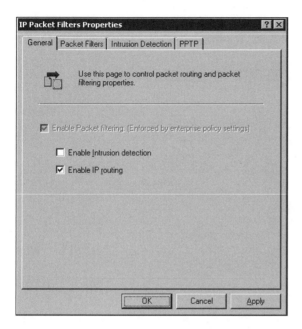

Figure 7-17

2. Click the **General** tab, if necessary, and then click the **Enable packet filtering** and **Enable IP routing** check boxes, if necessary.

3. Click the **Packet Filters** tab, and then enable the filtering of IP fragments and IP options.

4. Click the **PPTP** tab, and then allow PPTP tunnels to pass through ISA Server. Click **OK**.

Project 7-3

To create a predefined HTTP filter:

1. In the ISA Management console, right-click the **IP Packet Filters** node located under the **Access Policy** node, point to **New**, and then click **Filter**.

2. In the New IP Packet Filter Wizard dialog box, type **HTTP Access** for the filter name, and then click **Next**.

3. Ensure the filter applies to **All ISA Server computers in the array**, and then click **Next**.

4. On the Filter Mode page, select the **Allow packet transmission** option button, and then click **Next**.

5. On the Filter Type page, ensure the **Predefined** option button is selected, and then click **HTTP Server (port 80),** as shown in Figure 7-18, and then click **Next**.

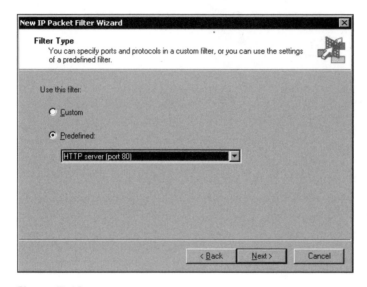

Figure 7-18

6. On the Local Computer page, ensure the **Default IP addresses for each external interface on the ISA Server computer** option button is selected, and then click **Next**.

7. Apply the packet filter to **All remote computers**, and then click **Next**.

8. When you reach the summary screen, review your selections and click the **Finish** button. You have successfully created a packet filter allowing HTTP access.

Project 7-4

To create a custom packet filter:

1. Right-click the **IP Packet Filters** node, point to **New**, and then click **Filter**. The New IP Packet Filter Wizard appears.

2. Name the new packet filter **Allow Limited Web Access**, and click **Next**. The Servers dialog box appears.

3. Click **All ISA Server computers in the array**, if necessary, and then click **Next**. The Filter Mode dialog box appears.

4. Choose to **Allow packet transmission**, if necessary, and then click **Next**. The Filter Type dialog box appears.

5. Choose to create a **Custom** filter, and then click **Next**. The Filter Settings dialog box appears, as shown in Figure 7-19.

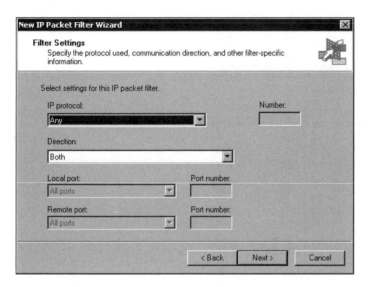

Figure 7-19

6. Click the **IP protocol** list arrow, and then click **TCP**. Click the **Direction** list arrow, and then click **Outbound**. Choose **Dynamic** as the Local port setting, set the Remote port to **Fixed port**, set the port number of the remote port to **80**, and click **Next**. The Local Computer dialog box appears.

7. Apply the packet filter to the **Default IP addresses for each external interface on the ISA Server computer**, if necessary, and then click **Next**. The Remote Computers dialog box appears.

8. Apply the packet filter only to the IP address **30.6.7.110**. Click **Next,** and then click **Finish** to create the packet filter. It appears in the IP Packet Filter details pane.

Project 7-5

Under certain circumstances, you might want to apply a packet filter to only one ISA Server in the array.

To modify the scope of a packet filter:

1. In the ISA Management console, click the **IP Packet Filters** node. You should see the list of defined packet filters appear in the Results pane. Double-click the **Allow Limited Web Access** packet filter you created in Project 7-4.

2. Click the **Local Computer** tab, as shown in Figure 7-20.

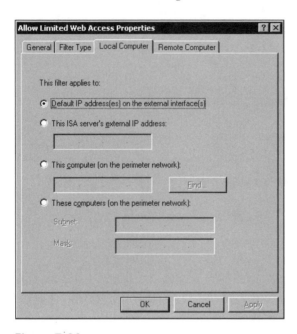

Figure 7-20

3. Click the **This ISA server's external IP address** option button, and enter the IP address assigned to the external interface of your ISA Server.

4. After you finish configuring the IP address, click **OK**. This limits the scope of the **Allow Limited Web Access** packet filter to affect only your server in the ISA Server array.

Project 7-6

To configure the SMTP application filter to screen unwanted e-mail messages:

1. In the ISA Server MMC, expand the **Extensions** node under your server array name, and then select **Application Filters**. A list of predefined application filters appears in the details pane.

2. In the details pane, double-click **SMTP Filter**. The SMTP Filter Properties dialog box appears.

3. Click the **Attachments** tab, and then click the **Add** button. The Mail Attachment Rule dialog box appears, as shown in Figure 7-21.

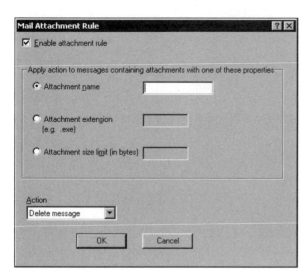

Figure 7-21

4. In the Attachment name text box, type **Virus.vbs**, and then click **OK**. This ensures that any e-mails with the attachment of virus.vbs are deleted.

5. Define attachment filters to delete messages that have **.exe** and **.com** file attachment extensions. Also, limit the size of e-mail attachments to 5 KB.

6. Click the **Users/Domains** tab. Type **Sally** in the Sender's name box, and then click the **Add** button. Sally is added to the list of rejected senders. Type **Junkmail.com** in the Domain name box, and then click the **Add** button. Any future e-mails sent by a username of "Sally" or from *.*Junkmail.com* will be rejected.

7. Click the **Keywords** tab, and then click the **Add** button. In the Mail Keyword Rule dialog box, as shown in Figure 7-22, type **poodles** as the keyword, click **Message body**, and click **OK**. Any future e-mails with the word "poodles" in the body of the message will be deleted.

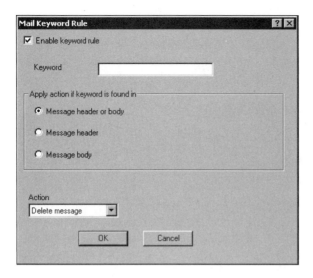

Figure 7-22

8. Click the **SMTP Commands** tab. In the list, double-click the **RSET** command. The SMTP Command Rule dialog box appears. Set the **Maximum Length** of the RSET command to four bytes, and then click **OK**. This prevents the occurrence of any SMTP RSET commands that exceed four bytes.

9. Click **OK** to close the SMTP Filter Properties dialog box.

CASE PROJECTS

Case Project 7-1

The MedHealth Pharmaceutical Company has hired you as a security consultant. The company employs 500 employees at a central location in Mexico, Missouri. The company wants a firewall implementation of ISA Server that grants employees access to the Web and allows them to download device drivers, which are frequently located on FTP sites. The internal network clients use both SecureNAT and the Web Proxy service. Furthermore, MedHealth has an internal Web and e-mail server that hosts the corporate Web site and provides external e-mail access. Due to the confidential nature of their research, airtight security is required on the internal LAN. Determine what additional information you should gather from the client, and then design a thorough firewall implementation and configuration. The design should incorporate any needed ISA Server features and filters.

Case Project 7-2

Worldwide Beef Industries (WBI) provides animal exports for supermarkets worldwide. Recently the WBI firewall was hacked, causing its internal Web servers to crash from a Denial of Service attack. WBI wants to replace the current firewall system using ISA Server, and has hired you to do the job at its three major U.S. locations. WBI currently uses ISA Server only for its caching features and uses a third-party firewall for security. The internal WBI network currently uses only firewall and SecureNAT clients to access the Internet. The company also has a custom database application that uses TCP ports 6701 and 6702 to communicate with the central SQL Server (30.6.9.111) in Mesa, Arizona. The prior firewall system handled this configuration perfectly, and WBI wants the transition to ISA Server to be as seamless as possible. Determine what additional information you should gather from the client, and then design a thorough firewall implementation and configuration. The design should incorporate any needed ISA Server features and filters.

Case Project 7-3

XL Systems has contracted you to design and deploy a new firewall structure for them. After careful analysis, you decide that using a dual ISA Server firewall methodology would be the best design for the company. You install the external ISA Server, configure the LAT to include the IP address ranges for the DMZ and internal network, and create policies granting access to the necessary servers in the DMZ. You then install the internal ISA Server, configure the LAT to include the IP address ranges for only the internal network, and create policies granting DMZ servers access to the necessary servers on the internal LAN. Upon testing your configuration, you find that Internet users can directly access the servers on the internal LAN. What is the problem?

Case Project 7-4

You are a contract network administrator at Elite Systems, Inc. You have just finished installing an ISA Server array and creating the necessary policies. One of the local network administrators on staff asks you to explain the difference between packet filtering and IP routing functions on ISA Server. In your own words, write a definition for each.

8

CONFIGURING ISA SERVER CACHING COMPONENTS

After reading this chapter and completing the exercises, you will be able to:

♦ Understand the process of storing and retrieving cached Internet content

♦ Manage cache storage

♦ Configure an HTTP and FTP cache policy

♦ Configure active caching

♦ Configure scheduled content downloads

♦ Configure CARP and load factors

While ISA Server provides an excellent security and firewall structure, most network administrators use ISA Server because of its caching features. Caching can significantly improve WAN performance by reducing the amount of requests that ISA Server forwards to the Internet. Caching is therefore a feature you can justify to management. When you weigh the cost of deploying an ISA Server system against the cost of increasing the WAN connection speed, the results usually favor ISA Server.

By using the Web Proxy service and the HTTP Redirector application filter, ISA Server supports caching Web and FTP requests from SecureNAT, Firewall, and Web proxy clients. When ISA Server receives a request from an internal network client attempting to access the Internet, it first checks its locally cached files for the resource. If the resource is found in the cache, the requested data is sent back to the client without using additional WAN bandwidth. If the request is not found in the cached files, ISA Server downloads the content from the Internet and stores it in the local cache for the next time an internal client requests the same resource. ISA Server assigns each locally stored resource a time to live (TTL), keeping the cached content from becoming obsolete.

UNDERSTANDING ISA SERVER CACHING FEATURES

ISA Server can cache Web and FTP objects in memory and on disk. The more memory and disk space you allocate to ISA Server caching, the better the system performs. When a user accesses Internet content, ISA Server caches the object directly into an isolated directory in RAM. Based on the popularity of the item, it either remains in the RAM directory or is written to the disk cache. Most user requests are fulfilled by cached content located in RAM, thus ensuring an extremely fast response.

Microsoft has also made significant improvements to the caching system since Proxy Server 2.0. Unlike Proxy Server 2.0, which stored cached content in many different files and locations on the server's hard disk or disks, ISA Server creates one cache file per hard-disk partition. Consequently, ISA Server only needs to have one open file per partition. This increases the efficiency of files stored in the disk cache. Furthermore, ISA Server has a built-in, automatic system to clean up the cache. When the disk cache storage space begins to fill, the cleanup system looks for files that have not been accessed recently and removes them from the disk cache.

Active caching and scheduled content downloads (also called cache prefetching) greatly improve caching efficiency as well. Active caching allows ISA Server to track the TTL of the frequently accessed content stored in RAM and the disk cache. As soon as the TTL of an object nears expiration, ISA Server automatically contacts the Web site and updates the cached content. Updating while the WAN use is low ensures that locally stored content is current when demand increases. Scheduled content downloads allow you to configure ISA Server to automatically download the content of particular Web sites at certain times of the day.

Overall, using ISA Server caching on your network provides the following major benefits:

- Caching reduces the total amount of traffic on the WAN.
- Caching can significantly reduce the response time for Internet content.
- Using active caching allows ISA Server to keep cached content updated.

Processing Requests

Each HTTP or FTP request that ISA Server receives from an internal client is sent to the Web Proxy service, either directly or through the HTTP Redirector application filter. Once the Web Proxy service receives the request, ISA Server puts it through a systematic process to determine whether to return cached or new content to the end user. If ISA Server receives a request for a new, noncached object, the following process occurs:

1. The Web Proxy service receives a Web request from an internal client and checks the cached directory to determine whether the ISA Server machine has a copy of the object in its cache.

2. If the object is not in the cache directory, the Web Proxy service allocates the necessary space in RAM and creates an entry for the object in the RAM cache directory.

3. The Web Proxy service then retrieves the requested object from the Internet and places it into the RAM cache. The Web Proxy service also returns a copy of the object to the requesting internal client.

4. When the system usage is low, ISA Server copies multiple objects from the RAM cache to the disk cache, based on the popularity of the objects. (This is also called a batch update.) The more popular an object is, the longer it remains in the RAM cache.

5. Periodically, ISA Server backs up the entire cache directory in RAM to the disk cache. This allows the RAM cache directory to be completely rebuilt when you reboot the ISA Server computer.

If ISA Server receives a request for content that has already been cached, the following process occurs:

1. ISA Server receives the request and determines that the object is located in either the RAM cache or the disk cache.

2. ISA Server determines whether the object is valid. If it is, ISA Server retrieves it from the RAM cache or the disk cache and returns it to the user. The object is considered invalid if one of the following conditions is true:

   - The TTL specified by the source Web site has expired.

   - The TTL you configured for the object has expired.

   - The TTL that you configured in a scheduled cache content download has expired.

3. If the object is invalid, ISA Server checks the cache configuration to determine whether the expired content should be returned to the user or if the content should be immediately updated from the original Web site or an upstream ISA Server. (Cache configuration is discussed in the following sections.)

8

MANAGING CACHE STORAGE

If you install ISA Server in cache or integrated mode, the installation process prompts you to configure the location and maximum storage size of cached files. After the installation, you may need to change the configuration options for the cached files.

To modify the cache storage settings:

1. In the ISA Management console, expand your server or array, if necessary, expand **Cache Configuration**, and then click **Drives**. In the details pane, you can see the current ISA Servers configured for caching, the total cache

size on all NTFS drives, the disk size of all NTFS drives, and the available storage space remaining on all NTFS drives.

2. Right-click the server you want to modify, and then click **Properties**.

3. The Properties dialog box that opens is the same one you saw during the ISA Server installation. See Figure 8-1.

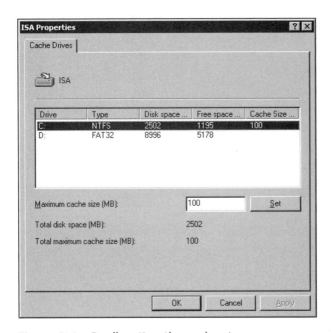

Figure 8-1   Reallocating the cache storage space

4. Choose the drive you want to modify (remember, only NTFS drives can contain cache files), modify the size of the cache using the Maximum cache size text box, click **Set**, and click **OK**. The updated cache size appears in the details pane.

CONFIGURING CACHING POLICIES

You can configure caching policies for both HTTP and FTP content. How you configure the cache policy determines whether ISA Server retrieves the content directly from its cache or from another server, the expiration policy for cached objects, the renewal policies, and the types of content cached by ISA Server. The following sections discuss the configuration of each type of caching.

If ISA Server is installed in Firewall mode, none of these options are available. You must reinstall ISA Server in cache or integrated mode.

HTTP Caching

Configuring HTTP caching authorizes ISA Server to store any HTTP content locally. This type of content typically constitutes the vast majority of the cached content and greatly affects network performance. When you configure the HTTP cache, setting the TTL has the most dramatic effect on network performance. If you configure the TTL of the HTTP objects for a shorter life span, the content returned to the user is more current, but the WAN traffic significantly increases. By configuring the TTL for a longer life span, you risk returning outdated content to the user, but significantly decrease the WAN traffic.

A common practice of many network administrators is to configure a longer TTL for HTTP content, and then configure individual sites that are frequently updated not to cache at all, such as commonly accessed sites with stock tickers, news headlines, or weather reports. By doing so, administrators ensure that users receive fresh content for the dynamic Web sites while lowering the amount of WAN traffic used for relatively static Web sites.

 Through the use of meta-tags, many Web pages can embed an expiration date into the HTTP content. If ISA Server receives content with an embedded expiration date, it sets the TTL to match the expiration date of the object.

8

To configure HTTP caching:

1. In the ISA Management console, expand your server or array node, if necessary, right-click the **Cache Configuration** node, and then click **Properties**. The Cache Configuration Properties dialog box appears. Click the **HTTP** tab. See Figure 8-2.

2. Click the **Enable HTTP caching** check box, if necessary.

3. Select one of the following cache expiration policies:

   - *Frequently (Expire immediately)*—When you select this option, the objects in the cache immediately expire unless an HTTP header meta-tag specifically states the expiration date. Choosing this option can degrade your WAN performance because ISA Server only returns objects from the cache if they specify their own expiration date.

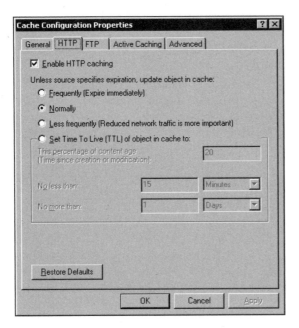

Figure 8-2 Enabling HTTP caching

- *Normally*—This setting is the default policy because it provides the best performance in most situations. Choosing this option allows ISA Server to balance the TTL against the amount of available WAN bandwidth. Objects are updated frequently, but network performance is considered. The exact TTL configuration is shown in the grayed-out boxes of the tab.

- *Less frequently*—Selecting this option increases the amount of time that objects are kept in the cache. Using this option reduces the amount of WAN bandwidth consumed by HTTP requests, but you run the risk of returning outdated content to internal clients. The exact TTL configuration is shown in the grayed-out boxes of the tab.

- *Set Time To Live (TTL) of object in cache to*—Choose this option if none of the preconfigured cache expiration policies meets your needs.

Selecting the final option allows you to configure your own cache TTL policy, as shown in Figure 8-3.

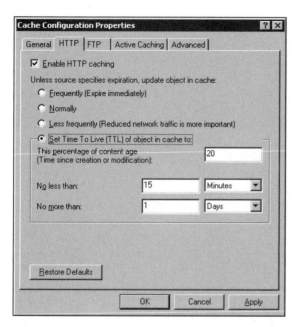

Figure 8-3   Configuring custom TTL settings for the HTTP cache

Set the options in this dialog box according to the following descriptions:

- *This percentage of content age*—Select this option button, and, based on the difference between the last modification date and time and the download date and time, enter a percentage that represents how long an item should be returned from the cache. The last modification date is a field in the HTTP header that specifies when the Web page was last changed in some way on the Web server. For example, suppose a Web page was last modified at 8 a.m. today and is added to the Web cache at 8 p.m. tonight. If you configure the content age percentage at 50%, the item remains in the cache for six hours. If you configure the content age percentage at 100%, the item remains in the cache for 12 hours. Using this option is beneficial because it allows relatively static Web pages (pages not frequently modified) to remain in the Web cache for longer periods of time, as ISA Server assumes they do not change often.

- *No less than*—The time configured in this field is the minimum amount of time an object should remain in the cache. This is a hard-coded time that overrules the percentage configured in the previous field. This keeps content from expiring too quickly; however, configuring this value too high consistently delivers outdated Web pages to internal clients.

- *No more than*—The time configured in this field is the maximum amount of time an object will remain in the cache.

FTP CACHING

In addition to caching HTTP objects, you can also implement FTP caching. This allows commonly accessed FTP content to be stored on the local network. Because ISA Server uses the Web Proxy service to cache both HTTP and FTP content, only requests routed *through* the Web Proxy service are cached. This means that files downloaded via a dedicated FTP program (such as CuteFTP) are not placed in the cache.

 Because items downloaded via FTP tend to have large file sizes, enabling FTP caching can consume a large amount of cache space. Users often download FTP-based content only once; therefore, you may find it more efficient to disable FTP caching.

To enable FTP caching, click the FTP tab in the Cache Configuration Properties dialog box. Click the Enable FTP caching check box, as shown in Figure 8-4, and enter the time in seconds, minutes, hours, days, or in weeks that you want the downloaded item to remain in the cache. Since FTP objects are typically large files, it is best to configure a shorter TTL for them. Otherwise, you may find your entire Web cache consumed by FTP content.

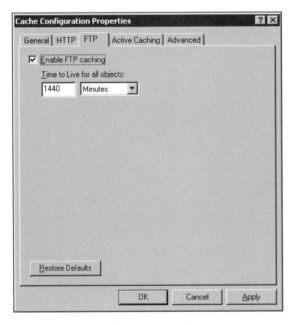

Figure 8-4   Enabling FTP caching

ACTIVE CACHING

When you enable active caching, ISA Server begins to monitor the frequently accessed files in the Web cache. Once it identifies the most popular content, ISA Server begins to automatically refresh the content before the TTL expires, even if there is no current user request for it. This ensures that the most recent and updated content is in the cache when the next internal user attempts to access it.

If you use a dial-up connection to the Internet and you enable active caching, ISA Server attempts to connect to the Internet to refresh content when the TTL nears expiration. To keep this from happening, disable active caching.

To configure active caching:

1. Click the **Active Caching** tab in the Cache Configuration Properties dialog box See Figure 8-5.

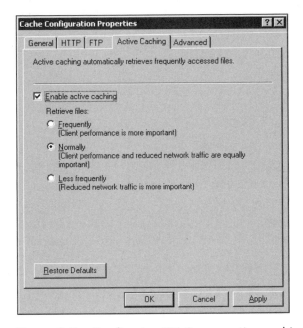

Figure 8-5   Configuring ISA Server active caching

2. Click the **Enable active caching** check box, and then choose one of the following retrieval methods:

  - *Frequently*—This method causes ISA Server to connect to the Internet often to update popular cached files. The cached files are more current, but at a cost of WAN bandwidth.

- *Normally*—Cached objects are updated frequently, but ISA Server also takes into account available WAN bandwidth and processor time. This is typically the best setting for most organizations.

- *Less frequently*—ISA Server refreshes cached objects occasionally, but is primarily concerned with network performance.

3. After you select the file retrieval method, click **OK**.

The active-caching algorithm ISA Server uses to refresh the selected retrieval method is based on the ISA Server processor time and the available WAN bandwidth. When ISA Server is not busy, it refreshes the cached content more often. This minimizes the conflict between the active caching refresh process and users trying to access noncached content.

Active caching can have an adverse affect on your network; if you enable it, be sure to monitor network performance. When you enable active caching, ISA Server assesses the most popular cached content and updates it as the TTL nears expiration. However, this does not guarantee that another user will access the refreshed content, which wastes WAN bandwidth. You should monitor how often internal users access identical cached content to see if you should enable active caching. Monitoring is discussed in Chapter 11.

Advanced and Global Caching Options

The advanced cache settings allow you to configure limitations on the type and size of HTTP content that ISA Server caches.

To configure the advanced caching properties:

1. Click the **Advanced** tab in the Cache Configuration Properties dialog box, as shown in Figure 8-6.

2. Select one or more of the following cache configuration options:

- *Do not cache objects larger than*—This option allows you to limit the size of objects that enter the Web cache. Use this setting if the RAM or hard-disk space used for caching is limited or if users frequently download large files.

- *Cache objects that have an unspecified last modification time*—When Web site administrators configure a Web page, they typically save the date and time the page was last modified. ISA Server uses this information to estimate the length of time that the item should be cached. If the date and time are missing or invalid, ISA Server does not cache the content unless you select this advanced configuration option. When you select this option, ISA Server sets the TTL for the content to the maximum TTL allowed.

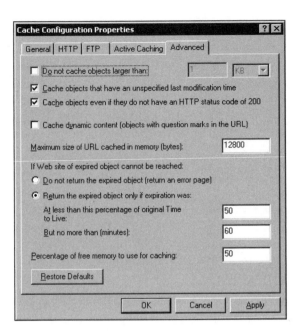

Figure 8-6   Configuring ISA Server advanced caching properties

- *Cache objects even if they do not have an HTTP status code of 200*—When you connect to a Web site and successfully download content, the Web site also returns an HTTP status code of 200. This is essentially a success message. If any other status code is returned, such as 204 (no response) or 404 (page not found), then an error occurred during transmission. Selecting this advanced option enables **negative caching**, which caches the HTTP error message. The next time a user attempts to access the same Web site, the request instantly returns the cached error message. Be careful with this option; if it is selected during a brief Web server failure, an entire Web site might become inaccessible from within your organization for an extended time. For example, if a firewall supporting the *www.microsoft.com* Web site loses power and causes the site to be unavailable for two minutes, and a user within your organization accesses *microsoft.com* during the same period, ISA Server will cache a negative response. Even after the connection to the Web site is restored, your internal users cannot connect until the TTL of the negative cached item expires.

- *Cache dynamic content (objects with question marks in the URL)*—When you select this option, ISA Server caches dynamic Web content. This is content returned as the result of an internal user's interaction with a Web page. For example, if you search for the keywords "ISA Server" using the *www.msn.com* search engine, the Web site dynamically generates a page showing the results of your search. By default, this option is deselected since the Web server usually returns different content each time a user accesses a dynamic Web page.

- *Maximum size of URL cached in memory (bytes)*—Just as the "Do not cache objects larger than" option limits the size of cached items stored in ISA Server, this configuration option limits the size of cached items stored in memory. By default, ISA Server does not store any cached item larger than 12,800 bytes (12.8 Kb) in memory. If you have a larger amount of memory dedicated to caching, you may increase this value as you see fit.

Under "If Web site of expired object cannot be reached" (refer back to Figure 8-6), you have the following configuration options:

- *Do not return the expired object (return an error page)*—If this option is selected and ISA Server cannot contact a requested Web server, the internal user receives an error message rather than expired cached content. It is typically best to deselect this option, since internal users would usually rather receive older content than no content at all.

- *Return the expired object only if expiration was*—Select this option if you want ISA Server to return expired content when the original Web server cannot be contacted. Under this option, you have the following two choices:

  - *At less than this percentage of original Time to Live*—Enter a percentage of the original TTL that reflects the length of time to allow expired content to be returned. For example, if the original TTL of certain Web content were 10 hours and you left this setting at its default value, 50%, ISA Server would return expired content for an additional five hours if the original Web server could not be contacted.

  - *But no more than (minutes)*—Enter a maximum amount of time you want ISA Server to return expired content if the original Web site is unreachable. This hard-coded, maximum time limit is set in minutes, and supersedes the prior percentage configuration. The default time limit is 60 minutes.

- *Percentage of free memory to use for caching*—Type a percentage of free memory you want to use for caching purposes. By default, ISA Server uses 50%. Note that the actual amount of memory used for caching purposes may vary depending on how much *free* memory is available. Microsoft does not allow you to enter a set amount of physical memory to use, since you could prevent the base Windows 2000 operating system functions from receiving the necessary memory to operate. If ISA Server is configured as a dedicated caching-only server, you can safely increase the amount of free memory to use for caching to 80 or 90%. However, if ISA Server is used for application processing or complex firewall functions, it may be best to decrease the amount of free memory dedicated to caching.

CREATING SCHEDULED CONTENT DOWNLOADS

Scheduled content downloads allow you to configure ISA Server to download specified Web sites during scheduled times. Using this approach, you can essentially "pre-cache" Internet content and alleviate WAN traffic during times of heavy network use. Typically, you should schedule downloads during periods of low network use. Just as with active caching, you should monitor Web sites accessed through ISA Server for one to two weeks before configuring scheduled content downloads. This allows you to find the popular Web sites internal users access and the times of day the sites are most frequently accessed. For example, users may frequently access a price list from a business partner's Web site. Since the partner updates the price list daily, you could schedule to cache the updated price list the night or morning before employees arrive at work.

Scheduled content downloads also allow you to cache popular Web sites even when internal users are unable to connect to the Internet. For example, you may restrict Web usage to nonbusiness hours to conserve WAN bandwidth during the day, but schedule downloads of popular Web sites to the ISA Server cache. This allows users to access favorite Internet content during business hours without an Internet connection.

To configure a scheduled content download:

1. In the ISA Management console, expand **Servers and Arrays** and your individual server or array, if necessary. Expand **Cache Configuration**, right-click **Scheduled Content Download Jobs**, point to **New**, and then click **Job**. The New Scheduled Content Download Job Wizard appears, as shown in Figure 8-7.

Figure 8-7   Beginning the Scheduled Content Download Job Wizard

2. Enter a logical name for the scheduled job, and then click **Next**. The Start Time dialog box appears. Enter the starting date and time you want the scheduled download to begin, and click **Next**. The Frequency dialog box appears, as shown in Figure 8-8.

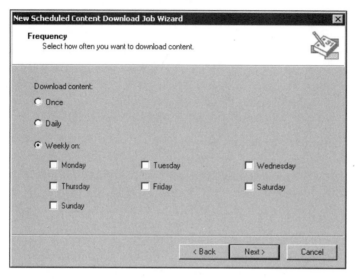

Figure 8-8   Configuring scheduled download frequency

3. In the Frequency dialog box, select how often you want to download content. Click **Once** to download the content only on the scheduled date and time, **Daily** to download content once a day at the scheduled time, or **Weekly on** to select individual days of the week to download content. Once you select the frequency, click **Next**. The Content dialog box appears.

4. In the Content dialog box, enter the URL of the Web site you want to download. In addition, you may choose to download **Content only from URL domain (not sites to which it links)** to restrict the scheduled download to only the specific URL you enter. Or choose **Cache dynamic content** to cache dynamic content from the URL. Once you enter the necessary information, click **Next**. The Links and Downloaded Objects dialog box appears, as shown in Figure 8-9.

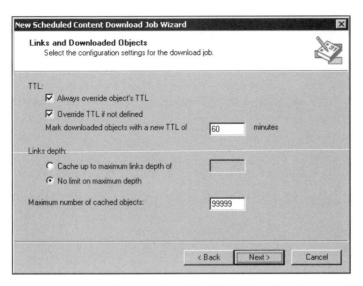

Figure 8-9   Configuring the scheduled download TTL and links depth

5. Configure the following TTL settings in the Links and Downloaded Objects dialog box:

- *Always override object's TTL*—This option allows you to override the TTL on Web pages that contain expiration dates, allowing them to remain in the cache longer. For example, you might schedule a download of *www.msn.com* at 7 a.m. every morning. Since the content of the MSN changes often, the expiration date might be set to 15 minutes. By selecting this option and typing a new TTL in the box below, you override the expiration configured by the Web site.

- *Override TTL if not defined*—This option allows you to override the time configured in the ISA Server cache properties if no expiration date is configured by the Web site.

- *Mark downloaded objects with a new TTL of*—Enter the TTL you want to assign to the scheduled content downloads from this URL. This configuration option overrides any other TTL settings in the global ISA Server cache properties.

6. Configure the following link depth settings in the Links and Downloaded Objects dialog box:

- *Cache up to maximum links depth of*—Select this option and enter the depth in the provided text box. This defines how deep you choose to follow and cache the links on the specified URL. For example, if you enter a maximum link depth of one, ISA Server caches the initial URL entered and follows every link on the Web page one level deep.

- *No limit on maximum depth*—Select this option to cache the initial URL entered and follow every link entered as far as possible.

Selecting **No limit on maximum depth** for a scheduled content download can create excessive network traffic and processor load on the ISA Server computer. For example, if you were to type a URL such as *www.microsoft.com* and select no depth limit, you would cache hundreds of megabytes of content.

- *Maximum number of cached objects*—Enter a numeral (up to 99,999) reflecting the maximum number of objects ISA Server should cache from any one URL in a scheduled download.

7. After you configure the TTL and link depth settings, click **Next**, and then click **Finish** to complete the wizard. The new scheduled download appears in the details pane of the ISA Management console.

8. Repeat this procedure to configure additional scheduled downloads for all necessary URLs.

UNDERSTANDING AND CONFIGURING CARP

When you configure an array of ISA Server computers, you can distribute the cache among them. ISA Server uses the **Cache Array Routing Protocol (CARP)** to create a single logical cache and eliminates the possibility of storing duplicate cached content on multiple array members. CARP uses a hash-based routing technique to route the request through the best server in the array. The hash is a mathematical value derived from the URL of the requested Web content. ISA Server uses this value to determine which server in the array stores the cached content. Web proxy clients can also compute and use this hash value to direct their request to the correct array member.

To configure ISA Server array members to use CARP:

1. In the ISA Management console, right-click the array you want to modify, and then click **Properties**. When the array Properties dialog box appears, click the **Outgoing Web Requests** tab, as shown in Figure 8-10.

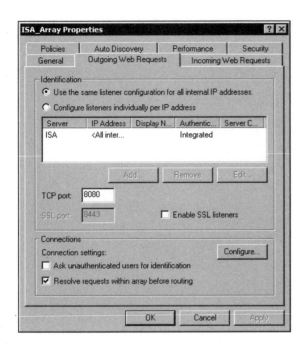

Figure 8-10   Configuring array members to use CARP

    2. Ensure that the **Resolve requests within array before routing** check box is selected, and then click **OK**.

In addition, you can increase or decrease the amount of cache load on each ISA Server in the array. This is beneficial if the ISA Servers in the array have different hardware specifications. For example, you might have an array built with three ISA Servers. The first has significantly more RAM and increased processor power, while the second and third ISA Servers meet minimum installation requirements. By configuring the load factor, you could direct more of the caching work to the first server.

To configure the load factor:

    1. In the ISA Management console, expand your array, if necessary, and then click **Computers**.

    2. In the details pane, right-click the server you want to configure, and then click **Properties**. In the server Properties dialog box, click the **Array Membership** tab, as shown in Figure 8-11.

8

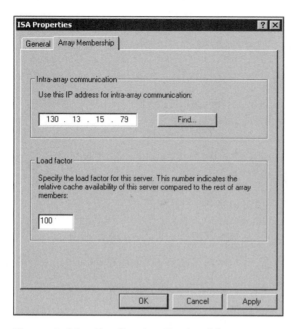

Figure 8-11   Configuring the load factor

3. Type the load factor for the server in the load factor text box. The load factor is an arbitrary number between 1 and 2,147,483,647. The default value is 100. Its significance is in relation to the other configured ISA Server load factors. For example, if you wanted one ISA Server array member to process four times as many cache requests, you would configure the load factor to be 400 while the others remained at the default setting of 100.

USING ROUTING RULES

Routing rules allow you to specify how ISA Server handles requests. When you use routing rules, you can specify the network or server to which you want to route a request, which items the ISA Server should cache and how they are stored, and the Web site redirection. The action to be taken is based on the URL requested by the network user. Routing rules can be useful when you are configuring a chained caching structure or fine-tuning your cache settings. For example, suppose your network users must manually refresh Web pages frequently because the content changes often. After monitoring user access to the Web site, you could create a destination set called Dynamic that contains the sites that are constantly updated. You could then define a routing rule that instructs ISA Server to never cache the sites contained in the destination set.

In another situation, you might find that the WAN connection is becoming overloaded by frequent requests for large, uncachable device drivers used to support network users. Using routing rules, you could redirect these requests to secondary ISA Server machines equipped with a WAN connection dedicated to the driver downloads, while all other user requests are sent through the primary ISA Server computer.

You configure routing rules as a hierarchical list that defines what actions should be taken for specific content types. When ISA Server receives an incoming request for Web content, it evaluates the request according to the routing rule list, beginning from the top and working down. When it finds a routing rule that matches the Web request, ISA Server performs the action defined by the rule.

You can define the order of the rules through the ISA Management console. At the bottom of the list is the Default rule, which is created when you install ISA Server. This rule applies to all destinations and defines the action performed by ISA Server for all Web requests that do not match any other routing rules.

To create a routing rule:

1. In the ISA Management console, expand your array or server name, if necessary, expand the **Network Configuration** node, right-click the **Routing** node, point to **New**, and then click **Rule**. The New Routing Rule Wizard appears.

2. Enter a logical name for the new routing rule, and then click **Next**. The Destination Sets page appears.

3. Select the destination set to which this rule applies, and then click **Next**. Now you also can apply the rule to a broader scope, such as all internal or external destinations.

4. On the Request Action page shown in Figure 8-12, you have the following options:

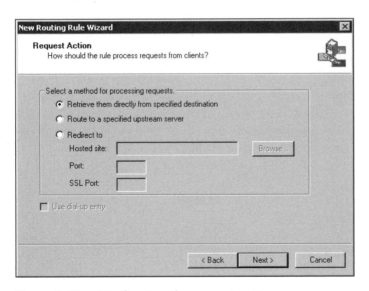

Figure 8-12   Configuring the request action

- *Retrieve them directly from specified destination*—This setting configures ISA Server to attempt to download the Web page in the standard fashion. This does not mean the download bypasses the caching system, but that ISA Server downloads the page directly from the Web.

- *Route to a specified upstream server*—This option lets you send the request to an ISA Server machine or ISA Server array for retrieval. After you select this option and click the **Next** button, you are prompted for the server or array to which to redirect the request, the port numbers to use for connecting, and the account used to authenticate.

- *Redirect to*—This option allows you to redirect requests to another Web site or internal Web server. Redirect when you want to block unproductive or inappropriate Web content from internal network users and redirect them to a Web page describing the company Internet policy.

After you select an option, click the **Next** button. The Cache Retrieval Configuration page appears.

5. On the Cache Retrieval Configuration page, you can configure how ISA Server caches the Web content. In the Search cache for area, you have the following options:

- *A valid version of the object; if none exists, retrieve the request using the specified requested action*—If an ISA Server receives a Web request and a valid cached object of the Web content exists whose TTL has not expired, ISA Server returns the cached object to the user. Otherwise, the content is retrieved directly from the Web or an upstream ISA Server computer.

- *Any version of the object; if none exists, retrieve the request using the specified requested action*—Selecting this option allows ISA Server to return cached content to the user, even if the content is expired. This option saves a large amount of WAN bandwidth because it uses a "cache once, return many" logic, but increases the chance of outdated content being returned to the user.

- *Any version of the requested object. Never route the request*—Selecting this option allows ISA Server to return only cached content. If the requested item is not available in the current cache files, the user receives an error message stating that the object could not be found.

After you select an option, click the **Next** button. The Cache Content Configuration page appears, shown in Figure 8-13.

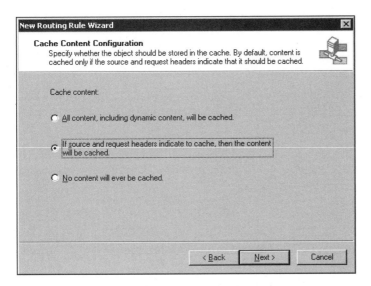

Figure 8-13 Managing the cache configuration

   6. On the Cache Content Configuration page, you can select the types of objects to store in the cache by selecting one of the following options in the Cache content area:

   ■ *All content, including dynamic content, will be cached*—Selecting this option configures ISA Server to ignore all header information and cache even dynamic Web pages.

   ■ *If source and request headers indicate to cache, then the content will be cached*—Choose this option to set ISA Server to cache the content based on the header information. This keeps dynamic content from being cached and allows the source Web server to decide what content your ISA Server caches.

   ■ *No content will ever be cached*—Choose this option to keep any content matching this routing rule from ever being cached. This option should be used for Web sites that have frequent updates.

After you select an option, click the Next button, and then the Finish button to create the routing rule.

After you create the routing rule, it appears in the details pane of the ISA Management console. This pane allows you to see in what order the rules are applied and whether the rules are enabled or disabled. Use these routing rules to optimize the caching and chained routing of your ISA Server computers.

CHAPTER SUMMARY

❑ Caching alleviates WAN traffic by storing Internet HTTP- and FTP-based content locally.

❑ ISA Server can cache downloaded content from any client by using the HTTP Redirector application filter to redirect non-Web proxy clients to the Web Proxy service.

❑ ISA Server caches content downloaded from the Internet directly to RAM, and then moves the infrequently accessed content to the hard disk while keeping the popular content stored in RAM.

❑ Web page authors can affect the amount of time ISA Server stores the page in the cache by configuring expiration meta-tags in the HTTP header.

❑ Active caching allows ISA Server to identify popular, cached Web content and update it when the TTL expires.

❑ Scheduled content downloads allow you to cache popular Web content during times of low network use.

❑ By using CARP, ISA Server efficiently manages the cache on multiple ISA Servers without duplicating cache content.

❑ The ISA Server load factor configuration allows you to place heavier caching loads on servers that have more memory or processing power.

KEY TERMS

Cache Array Routing Protocol (CARP) — The protocol used by ISA Servers array to distribute cached content evenly across array members and ensure content is not duplicated.

negative caching — A feature allowing ISA Server to cache negative Web responses, such as a Web site being unavailable.

REVIEW QUESTIONS

1. When ISA Server downloads and caches Internet content, it is initially stored on which component?

   a. hard disk

   b. RAM

   c. flash memory

   d. The content must be accessed at least twice before ISA Server caches it.

2. Active caching recaches all objects as they expire. True or false?

3. Which of the following HTTP codes represents a success (OK) message?

   a. HTTP 404

   b. HTTP 204

   c. HTTP 200

   d. HTTP 400

4. What method does ISA Server use to cache requests from SecureNAT and Firewall clients?

   a. ISA Server cannot cache SecureNAT or Firewall client requests.

   b. Web routing

   c. proxy client refresh

   d. HTTP Redirector

5. When the ISA Server computer is rebooted or crashes, what happens to the cache files stored in RAM?

   a. They are automatically repopulated using the disk cache files.

   b. The cache automatically rebuilds itself as clients request various Web content.

   c. The RAM cache waits for the next scheduled content download to repopulate.

   d. The files remain in RAM through the reboot.

6. Which of the following caching methods are enabled by default in integrated or cache installation modes?

   a. HTTP caching only

   b. FTP caching only

   c. both HTTP and FTP caching

   d. You must manually enable either caching method.

7. Provided FTP caching is enabled, ISA Server can cache content from all FTP clients. True or false?

8. If you select the "Less frequently" option under the HTTP caching options, which of the following occurs?

   a. The cache content TTL is extended.

   b. The cache content TTL is shortened.

   c. Active caching does not update the cache as often.

   d. none of the above

9. Active caching updates cached content based on what criteria?

   a. total amount of RAM available

   b. content popularity

   c. administratively defined URLs

   d. all of the above

10. Which of the following types of caching is not enabled by default in integrated or cache installation modes?

    a. HTTP caching

    b. FTP caching

    c. dynamic caching

    d. all of the above

11. What is the disadvantage of enabling negative caching?

    a. Content accessed through SecureNAT and Firewall clients is not cached.

    b. Internal clients may be erroneously informed that a Web site is unreachable.

    c. Only administratively defined content is stored in the cache.

    d. none of the above

12. You are the network administrator of Dial-a-Map, a service that allows drivers to call an 800 number and receive directions nationwide. Every week, the map Web site that your internal employees access is updated with all road changes nationwide. What feature should you enable on ISA Server to update the cache files on a weekly basis?

    a. HTTP caching

    b. scheduled content download

    c. active caching

    d. none of the above

13. What is the function of the load factor parameter?

    a. defines the maximum processor load an ISA Server computer dedicates to caching purposes

    b. defines the maximum processor load an ISA Server computer reaches before passing the request to another ISA Server in the array

    c. defines the amount of resources an ISA Server computer dedicates to caching compared with other ISA Servers in the array

    d. defines the maximum amount of RAM dedicated to storing cached Internet content

14. What is CARP used for?

    a. to distribute the cache content between ISA Servers in an array

    b. to keep duplicate cache content from being stored on multiple ISA Servers

    c. to point clients to the correct ISA Server storing relevant cache files

    d. all of the above

15. Active caching allows ISA Server to update cached Internet content before the TTL expires. True or false?

16. ISA Server limits the size of downloaded HTTP content to eight megabytes, by default. True or false?

17. You have configured ISA Server to cache *www.microsoft.com* on a scheduled basis. You soon find that your cache storage is full on ISA Server. What is the problem?

    a. You have configured the maximum depth to be too deep.

    b. The Web site, *www.microsoft.com,* is not configured to support scheduled caching.

    c. Scheduled content downloads can only be legally used on noncommercial Web sites.

    d. none of the above

18. A Web site administrator sets the TTL on pages downloaded from their Web site. Where is this configuration stored?

    a. in the downloaded HTML text

    b. in the HTTP header

    c. in the HTTP trailer

    d. none of the above

19. You can override the TTL configured by Web site administrators using ISA Server features. True or false?

20. If ISA Server is only dedicated to caching functions, how much free memory can you safely commit to cache storage?

    a. 20% to 30%

    b. 40% to 50%

    c. 60% to 70%

    d. 80% to 90%

HANDS-ON PROJECTS

Project 8-1

You have been contracted to install ISA Server in a company with 200 internal users. The company is concerned about decreasing WAN performance and wants to use ISA Server primarily for its caching features, as the company already uses a Cisco firewall for security. The ISA Server computer has more than one gigabyte of available memory. Your goals are to increase performance for internal users and conserve the WAN bandwidth where possible. To accomplish these goals, you perform the following tasks:

- Because ISA Server is a dedicated caching-only server, dedicate 80% of the free memory to caching purposes.

- For Web objects not assigned an expiration date and time via HTML meta-tags, the TTL should be 70% of the object's current age. These objects should not be refreshed more than once every 12 hours, nor become more than three days old before they expire.

- If ISA Server cannot contact a Web site to update the cached files, it should return the expired content for up to 100% of the original TTL. This allows the cached item to be used for twice as long as the original TTL if the Web site cannot be contacted. However, ISA Server should never return expired content that is older than 24 hours (1440 minutes).

To configure Web cache settings on the ISA Server computer:

1. Open the ISA Management console and expand the **Servers and Arrays** node and your array, if necessary. Right-click **Cache Configuration**, and then click **Properties**. The Cache Configuration Properties dialog box appears.

2. In the **HTTP** tab, ensure that the **Enable HTTP caching** check box is selected.

3. Click the **Set Time To Live (TTL) of object in cache to** option button.

4. In the **This percentage of content age** text box, type **70**.

5. In the **No less than** text box, type **12** and then select **Hours** from the list box.

6. In the **No more than** text box, type **3** and then select **Days** from the list box. Your completed HTTP cache configuration should resemble Figure 8-14.

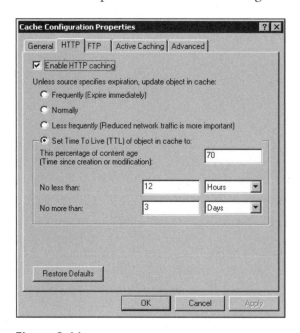

Figure 8-14

7. Click the **Advanced** tab in the Cache Configuration Properties dialog box.

8. Click the **Return the expired object only if expiration was** option button, and enter **100** in the At less than this percentage of original Time to Live text box.

9. Enter **1440** in the But no more than (minutes) text box.

10. Enter **80** in the Percentage of free memory to use for caching text box.

11. Click the **Apply** button.

12. When the ISA Server Warning dialog box prompts you to restart the Web Proxy service, ensure that the **Save the changes, but don't restart the service(s)** option button is selected, as shown in Figure 8-15, and then click **OK**.

Figure 8-15

Project 8-2

Your company has 15 worldwide sites that employ more than 1,500 people. Since there are so many employees, the company phone directory is centrally located at the New York office. The directory is updated every two weeks to include new employees and delete those who have left the company. You want to enable FTP caching to update the phone list biweekly at the other 14 sites.

In addition, you have been monitoring the Web sites accessed over the last month and have noticed that the same few Web sites are consistently accessed by internal employees. You want to enable the active caching features to update the Web sites in the cache before the TTL expires, but at the same time, you want to minimize the effect on the WAN traffic and ISA Server processing time.

To configure FTP caching on the ISA Server computer:

1. In the Cache Configuration Properties dialog box, click the **FTP** tab, as shown in Figure 8-16.

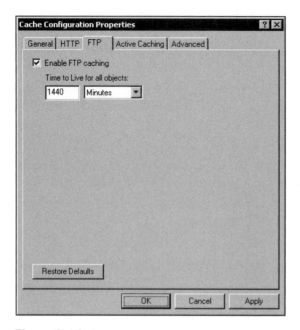

Figure 8-16

2. Ensure that the **Enable FTP caching** check box is selected.

3. In the Time to Live for all objects text box, enter **2**, and then select **Weeks** from the list box.

4. Click the **Active Caching** tab.

5. If necessary, click the **Enable active caching** check box to insert a check mark.

6. Choose to retrieve files **Less frequently** to ensure minimal conflict with the WAN traffic and ISA Server processing time.

7. Click **OK** in the Cache Configuration Properties dialog box to return to the ISA Management console.

Project 8-3

Because of the increased interest in ISA Server within your organization, your internal users want to access the *ISAServer.org* Web site to review daily updates, bulletins, and message board posts. Since your company does not allow Internet access during business hours, you want to create a scheduled content download of the entire *ISAServer.org* Web site to the local cache at 4 a.m. every morning. In addition, since the site contains links to many *Microsoft.com* areas, you want to restrict caching to only the *ISAServer.org* domain.

To configure a scheduled content download on the ISA Server computer:

1. In the ISA Management console, expand your array, if necessary, and then expand **Cache Configuration**.

2. Right-click **Scheduled Content Download Jobs**, point to **New**, and then click **Job**. The New Scheduled Content Download Job Wizard appears.

3. Enter **ISAServer.org, 4 a.m.** as the job name, and then click **Next**. The Start Time dialog box appears.

4. Enter today's date in the Date text box, change the time to **4 a.m.** in the Time text box, and then click **Next**. The Frequency dialog box appears.

5. Click the **Daily** option button, and then click **Next**. The Content dialog box appears.

6. In the **Download content from this URL** field, enter **www.ISAServer.org**, as shown in Figure 8-17.

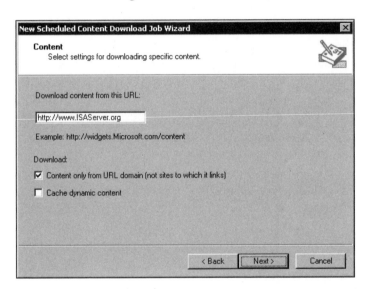

Figure 8-17

7. Click the check box to download **Content only from URL domain (not sites to which it links)**, and then click **Next**. The Links and Downloaded Objects dialog box appears.

8. Since you need to have the cached content available for 24 hours, click both the **Always override object's TTL** and **Override TTL if not defined** check boxes, and then enter a TTL of **1440** minutes in the Mark downloaded objects with a new TTL of text box. See Figure 8-18.

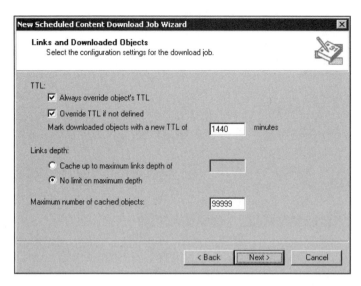

Figure 8-18

9. Ensure that the **No limit on maximum depth** option button is selected, leave the **Maximum number of cached objects** at the default setting of **99,999**, and then click **Next**.

10. When you click **Finish**, the ISAServer.org, 4 a.m. scheduled download appears in the details pane.

Project 8-4

Your company has an array of five ISA Server computers. The company wants to ensure that all Web requests are retrieved from one of the array members using the CARP algorithm before being forwarded to the Web. In addition, the ISA Server machine you use has a superior hardware configuration compared to the other four ISA Server array members. The company wants to configure your ISA Server to handle double the cache load of the other ISA Server computers.

To configure CARP and Load factors on the ISA Server computer:

1. Click the **Computers** node under your array, right-click your server in the details pane, and then click **Properties**.

2. In the Properties dialog box, click the **Array Membership** tab.

3. Since the other ISA Servers are configured with the default load factor of 100, and enter **200** in the Load factor field to allow your machine to double the cache load, and then click **OK**.

4. In the ISA Management console, right-click your array name, and then click **Properties**. The array Properties dialog box appears.

5. Click the **Outgoing Web Requests** tab, ensure that the **Resolve requests within array before routing** check box is selected, and then click **OK**.

Project 8-5

When you initially installed ISA Server, you configured the cache storage to handle 15 clients. Over the last few months, your company has doubled in size. Because of the increased network demands, you need to double your current cache size.

To reconfigure current cache settings, do the following:

1. In the ISA Management console, expand the **Cache Configuration** node under your array, click **Drives**, and double-click your server to open the server Properties dialog box, as shown in Figure 8–17.

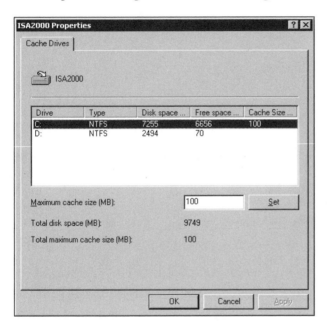

Figure 8-19

2. Set the HTTP cache storage to double its current value, save the settings, and close the server Properties dialog box.

Project 8-6

When you initially installed ISA Server, you did not enable active caching. Now, because your WAN connection is overused, you want ISA Server to monitor the frequently accessed files in the Web cache and update the most popular content. Since the WAN connection is overused, you should configure active caching to *reduce* network traffic and update cached files as *little* as possible. Perform the necessary steps to enable and configure active caching for your company's network scenario.

Project 8-7

An internal user on your network has recently located a HTTP-based Web site that contains Adobe Acrobat (.pdf) documents, each averaging 20 megabytes in size. Each day, the Web site posts a new Acrobat document, which the user downloads and then sends to other internal users via e-mail. Because ISA Server sees the documents as HTTP content, it places the files in cache, yet they are never accessed again. You need to configure limitations on the size of HTTP content that ISA Server caches because your cache storage space is limited. Perform the necessary steps to change the advanced caching properties so that ISA Server does not cache HTTP content exceeding 500 kilobytes in size.

CASE PROJECTS

Case Project 8-1

Your company has just installed ISA Server for the caching functionality. The company has a T1 line that is shared by more than 300 internal clients. During peak hours, WAN traffic is so high that internal users average a 28.8-Kbps download speed from the Internet. After monitoring the network for a week, you have determined that internal users primarily visit 15 major Web sites. One of these Web sites represents more than half the WAN traffic and is only updated once a day. The Web site with the most hits gives free, real-time stock quotes; this Web site also represents the smallest amount of WAN traffic. Answer the following questions:

- How should you configure caching on this network?
- With what hardware should you equip the ISA Server computer?
- Should you enable other caching features besides standard HTTP and FTP caching?
- Will dynamic caching benefit the stock quote site?
- What should the cached TTL configuration be?
- What additional information should you gather before deployment?

Case Project 8-2

Your company has just installed ISA Server for both security and caching functionality. The 200-employee company has a 512-Kbps DSL connection and is noticing significant slowdowns during peak hours. About 50% of the network traffic accesses the *ftp.microsoft.com* FTP site. The company currently has 100 megabytes of storage space allocated for caching purposes and allocates 20% free memory to cache storage. You also notice that Web content is removed from the cache long before the default TTL for cached content expires. Answer the following questions:

- How should you configure caching on this network?

- With what hardware should you equip the ISA Server computer?

- Should you enable other caching features besides standard HTTP and FTP caching?

- What is causing the Web pages to be removed from the cache before the default ISA Server TTL?

- What additional information should you gather before deployment?

Case Project 8-3

You have returned to work from a three-week vacation. As you begin filing through the trouble tickets received while you were gone, you notice that many tickets mention slow Internet access. This was not a problem before you left for vacation. After monitoring ISA Server for a short time, you find that the cache is virtually empty. When an internal user accesses Web content, it is stored in the cache momentarily, and then disappears. Explain what you would do to correct this problem, and why.

Case Project 8-4

You recently installed ISA Server in a midsize investment company. Management is impressed by the increased speed they gain when accessing the Internet; however, many employees complain that the information they download from the Internet is often out of date. Some users report that news articles they downloaded from popular news sites the previous day are not current. Many financial consultants are finding the Internet stock quotes are inaccurate. Explain what you would do to correct this problem, and why.

Case Project 8-5

You are the network administrator of a large company with over 5,000 employees. You are using a new ISA Server array built on three servers to support the bulk of the Internet traffic from internal employees. While the network performance is typically excellent, you have received many complaints from internal users that the Internet connection is very slow from 4:00 p.m. to 5:00 p.m. You monitor the servers in the array at 4:30 and find that the processor usage on all three servers is 100%. The traffic on the WAN is also above normal. What could be causing this problem? Explain possible causes and solutions.

9

CONFIGURING SERVER PUBLISHING

After reading this chapter and completing the exercises, you will be able to:

♦ Develop strategies to safely access internal servers from the Internet

♦ Examine ISA Server publishing capabilities

♦ Develop publishing strategies

♦ Configure Web, e-mail, and generic server publishing

♦ Understand the function and features of the H.323 protocol suite

♦ Configure the H.323 Gatekeeper service

♦ Configure advanced H.323 routing patterns

Although the features of ISA Server that allow clients to access the Internet and improve network security may satisfy smaller businesses, these features are incapable of meeting the needs of medium- and large-sized companies. Such companies must provide external users with access to resources on the internal network. Exposing the internal network to external client access introduces many security concerns. Opening a single port on ISA Server to allow external access creates a security risk not only to the internal servers that the external users access, but to the entire internal network as well. To maintain security, ISA Server supports server publishing.

Server publishing safely provides Internet access to internal servers. When you publish a server to the external users, ISA Server automatically begins checking for common attacks on the internal servers. It also restricts access to only the servers you publish; the rest of your internal clients are not at risk. Furthermore, ISA Server is taking a step into the next generation of Voice over IP (VoIP) systems by supporting the H.323 Gatekeeper service. This chapter discusses both the methodology and configuration of server publishing and H.323 services.

ALLOWING INBOUND ACCESS

Until now, this book has focused on improving the performance and security of internal clients that attempt to access the Internet. While these are prime objectives of ISA Server, companies can also use ISA Server publishing services to provide Internet clients with access to internal Web and e-mail servers without compromising server security or other internal clients. By publishing internal servers through ISA Server, you add an extra layer of security that protects the internal network from potential intruders. ISA Server should be your company's single point of exposure to the Internet; all requests for internal servers should be redirected through ISA Server. You can then apply ISA Server's intrusion detection filters and packet filters to all requests, and secure internal servers from outside attacks.

You can also apply the caching features of ISA Server to requests for internal resources. This approach is similar to caching requests from internal network clients accessing the Internet. When an external user accesses an internal resource, the request is routed through ISA Server. If the request is for an HTTP- or FTP-based resource, you can configure ISA Server to cache the data as it leaves the internal network. This approach is known as reverse caching, and significantly improves the response time to external users because ISA Server immediately responds to the request without routing to an internal server. Reverse caching also improves the load on internal Web and FTP servers because they process fewer requests. Furthermore, reverse caching improves internal network traffic because the request never consumes internal network bandwidth.

ISA Server allows you to publish any type of internal server by creating a **publishing policy**. These policies define the rules ISA Server uses to process requests for internal resources. ISA Server has three wizards to assist you in server publishing: the Web Publishing Rule Wizard, the Mail Server Security Wizard, and the Server Publishing Rule Wizard. Since most corporations are only interested in establishing an Internet presence by publishing their own Web site, Microsoft geared the Web publishing wizard to support HTTP, HTTP-S, and FTP traffic. If your company allows external users to access other types of servers, you can use the server publishing wizard to allow access. You can also make the internal mail server accessible from external networks, thus allowing users to retrieve e-mail from any location that provides an Internet connection. The mail publishing wizard allows you to make internal mail services accessible from the Internet while maintaining secure access policies. The server publishing wizard allows you to publish all other types of internal servers, such as Telnet, SQL, and RPC.

 ISA Server treats the published internal servers as SecureNAT clients. You should not install the firewall client software on any published server. This can lead to unpredictable results.

EXAMINING ISA SERVER PUBLISHING CAPABILITIES

When most people consider publishing internal servers to external users, they think mostly of routing between external and internal networks. While ISA Server provides this capability, it also provides enhancements that improve the security and speed of retrieving internal resources, such as applying application filters and caching features to all incoming HTTP, FTP, and HTTP-S requests for internal servers.

When using the Web publishing wizard, you configure ISA Server to be more of a "middleman" to external users than just a bridge to the internal network. Let's say you want to make your company's internal Web server available to external users. When an external user makes a request to the internal Web server, the request first stops at ISA Server. Instead of passing the request directly to the Web server and allowing the server's response to pass directly to the external user (known as standard routing), ISA Server *emulates* the Web server to external users, making them believe the ISA Server *is* the internal Web server. On the internal network, ISA Server emulates the external user to the internal Web server, as if the request *originated from the ISA Server machine itself*. The Web server then sends the requested data to ISA Server, which caches it (if caching is configured), and then passes the data to the external user. There is no direct contact between the external user and the internal Web server. Microsoft refers to this process as a **reverse proxy**.

While ISA Server can only cache HTTP and FTP requests, you continue to gain the benefits of ISA Server's security features when publishing other TCP/IP-based servers using the server publishing wizard. Because ISA Server hides all internal IP addresses when publishing internal servers, you also protect the IP addressing structure of your internal network from external users.

DEVELOPING PUBLISHING STRATEGIES

Opening your internal network to external users exposes the network to potential security hazards, so your publishing strategy must be carefully considered and well designed. When you enable server publishing, all external users connect to the external network adapter of the ISA Server computer connected to the Internet. From there, depending on the IP address and port number to which external users connect, ISA Server either discards the request or retrieves the data from an internal server.

Each network design requires a different publishing strategy. The one you choose should closely reflect the firewall strategy you designed in Chapter 7. Most networks use one of the strategies described in the following sections.

9

Hosting Services on ISA Server

In small network environments, you may choose to use ISA Server not only for caching and security, but also to host other network services. This strategy is not typically recommended for most network environments, but you can use it if you have a limited network budget.

When you publish resources from the ISA Server computer, you centralize all network services in one location. You then only need to administer and back up one server, and internal network clients and servers are protected from intruders. If the security of ISA Server were compromised, intruders would gain access only to the resources on ISA Server itself. Packet filters defined on ISA Server would allow access to only the services on ISA Server, not to those on the local network.

 Remember, while both server publishing rules and IP packet filters will open ports for communication between local networks and the Internet, you must use IP packet filters instead of publishing rules when you are publishing services that are located on the ISA computer itself.

Publishing from the ISA Server computer also has many disadvantages. First, adding services to ISA Server decreases the performance of all services. For example, hosting multiple services from ISA Server affects not only the services you install, such as Web or e-mail services, but also hampers ISA Server firewall and caching services. Second, hosting multiple services on ISA Server introduces a single point of failure. If the ISA Server machine that forms the bridge between your internal network and the Internet fails, you not only lose Internet access, you potentially lose the Web, e-mail, or database servers.

In addition, when you use ISA Server to publish HTTP or FTP content directly from the server, you lose the load distribution of caching. Typically, when you have a Web server *behind* the firewall rather than *on* the firewall, the Web server has a decreased processing load. After ISA Server caches the content from the internal Web server, ISA Server services all requests for the same content until the TTL expires, greatly easing the load on the internal Web server. Combining both servers on one computer defeats the purpose of caching because ISA Server takes processing power from the Web server.

Finally, this strategy creates major security risks. An intruder who compromises the security of ISA Server can easily break the security of the other installed services because the server's primary defenses are already defeated. Hosting the services on multiple servers allows you to create unique security policies on each machine. Even if an intruder breaks the security of one server, the others remain fully secure.

To summarize the advantages of publishing from ISA Server:

- It provides a low-cost solution.

- All network service is centralized in one location, which allows for easy backup and administration.

- Internal clients and servers gain security since packet filters allow access to only ISA Server itself.

To summarize the disadvantages:

- Performance decreases for all network services running on ISA Server, including its caching and firewall features.

- You have a single point of failure for all network services.

- You defeat the purpose of ISA Server's caching services.

- If ISA Server security is compromised, the security of all locally installed network services is also compromised.

Server Publishing in a Basic Firewall Configuration

When publishing servers in a basic firewall configuration, you configure ISA Server with one network interface connected to the external network and one network interface connected to the internal network, as shown in Figure 9-1. You then use ISA Server publishing wizards to make the internal servers available to the public.

9

Basic firewall publishing

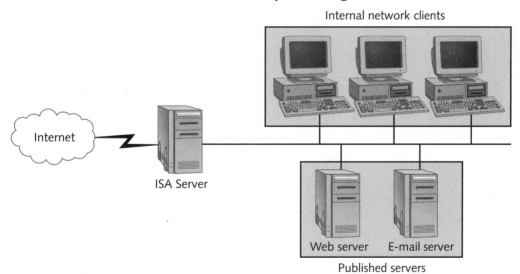

Figure 9-1   Server publishing in a basic firewall configuration

When you publish servers in a basic firewall configuration, you gain the advantage of having ISA Server act as an intermediary between the external and internal networks. This allows ISA Server to be dedicated to firewall and caching purposes, thus keeping performance high. You also gain all the standard security and caching features that ISA Server publishing provides. If you use an array of ISA Server computers in conjunction with back-up WAN connections, you also eliminate a single point of failure bridging the external and internal networks.

The disadvantage of using the basic firewall configuration is that the published internal servers reside on the same network as network clients and local servers. Traffic therefore increases on the internal network because ISA Server retrieves all external requests from servers on the local segment. This configuration also poses a slight security risk for all internal computers. If an intruder compromises the security of ISA Server, the internal network could be exposed because it connects directly to ISA Server. However, internal network clients would only be at risk if the intruder gained complete control of the ISA Server machine.

To summarize the advantages of publishing in a basic firewall configuration:

- The cost is relatively low.
- ISA Server is dedicated to caching and firewall services, resulting in high performance.

To summarize the disadvantages:

- Network traffic increases for the internal network.
- Because ISA Server resides on a directly connected network segment, internal clients incur a slight security risk.

Server Publishing in a Three-Homed Configuration

Publishing in a three-homed configuration, where a single ISA Server machine is attached to three different networks, eliminates the network traffic caused by external users who access internal servers located on the same network segment as the other internal clients. A three-homed configuration contains a separate network segment for servers that are accessible to external users, as shown in Figure 9-2. This configuration offers the same advantages as the basic firewall for about the same price. If possible, you should use this configuration rather than the basic firewall.

Three-Homed publishing

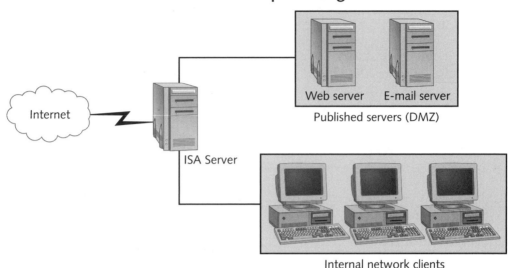

Figure 9-2   Server publishing in a three-homed configuration

To summarize the advantages of publishing in a three-homed configuration:

- Network traffic caused by publishing internal servers is eliminated from the internal network.

- It offers all the advantages of the basic firewall configuration, for about the same price.

To summarize the disadvantages:

- Because ISA Server resides on a directly connected network segment, internal clients incur a slight security risk.

Server Publishing in a Dual ISA Server Configuration

Publishing servers using a dual, or back-to-back, ISA Server configuration is an ideal solution, provided your budget allows for the additional hardware and licensing of an added ISA Server. This configuration allows you to split your internal network into separate network segments, just as in the three-homed configuration. Each internal network segment, such as the DMZ and internal LAN, has a dedicated ISA Server, as shown in Figure 9-3.

Dual ISA Servers (back-to-back) publishing

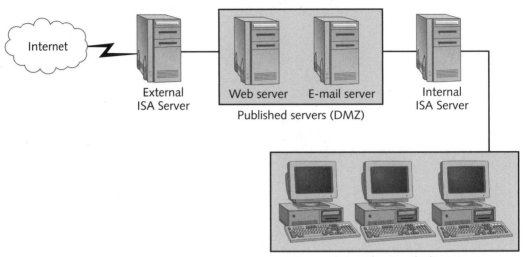

Figure 9-3   Server publishing in a dual ISA Server configuration

This configuration gives you all the advantages of the three-homed configuration, but also gives you increased network security and performance. Network security increases because you have an external and internal ISA Server configured. If an intruder compromises the external firewall, the internal firewall still protects the internal clients. The intruder can begin hacking the servers in the DMZ and the internal ISA Server, but you would probably notice the breach of the external firewall before the intruder could compromise the internal firewall.

When using a dual-server configuration, you should keep all sensitive data on the internal network. If any internal data must be accessible from the Internet, you can either move the server to the DMZ or publish the server's data to the servers in the DMZ. For example, you might have an internal SQL server that contains sensitive corporate data. However, you want to have some data available from the Internet via the internal Web server. To create this configuration, place the Web server in the DMZ, and create a publishing rule on the external server that grants access to the Web server from the Internet. Then create a server publishing rule on the internal ISA Server that allows the servers in the DMZ to access the database server on the internal LAN, as shown in Figure 9-4. Through this configuration, you allow Internet users to access the corporate Web server and select information from the internal database server while maintaining its security.

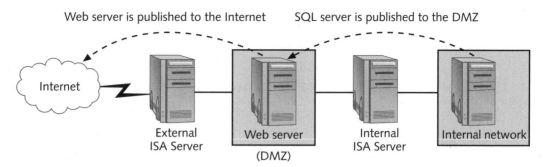

Figure 9-4 Publishing Web servers to the Internet and database servers to the DMZ

To summarize the advantages of publishing in a dual ISA Server configuration:

- It offers increased security for clients and servers residing on the internal network.
- It offers additional secure publishing options.
- It offers all the advantages of the three-homed configuration.

To summarize the disadvantages:

- It is the most expensive publishing option.

CONFIGURING SERVER PUBLISHING

ISA Server contains three wizards designed to publish Web servers, mail servers, and any other TCP/IP-based server. The server publishing design can differ depending on the firewall configuration you select from the choices described in the previous sections. Configuring server publishing in the basic firewall design is the simplest choice: Use the appropriate wizard to publish the necessary server to the Internet. No further configuration should be necessary because ISA Server recognizes the internal and external networks through the local address table (LAT).

When configuring server publishing in a three-homed configuration, you only use server publishing between the internal network and the DMZ, because ISA Server only recognizes the internal network through the LAT. You must enable IP routing between the DMZ and the Internet because ISA Server recognizes both networks as external networks.

Designing server publishing for the dual ISA Server configuration is comparable to designing two basic firewall configurations. The LAT of the external ISA Server should contain only IP addresses from the DMZ, allowing you to publish servers from the DMZ to the Internet. The LAT of the internal ISA Server should contain only IP addresses from the internal network, allowing you to publish servers from the internal network to the DMZ. This configuration permits you to use the server publishing wizards on both the internal and external ISA Server and eliminates the need for IP routing, unless you require applications that use protocols other that TCP or UDP.

Configuring Incoming Web Request Listeners

Before ISA Server responds to any incoming HTTP requests, you must configure listeners on the external interface of ISA Server. A **listener** defines how ISA Server responds to HTTP and SSL requests. If you do not configure any listener ports, ISA Server ignores all incoming HTTP and SSL requests, regardless of how many servers you publish using the Web server publishing wizard. You can configure a single listener that applies to all external ISA Server IP addresses, or you can define individual listener configurations for each IP address.

By default, the listener for incoming web requests opens port 80 on the external interface of ISA Server. You can change this port number if you want; however, clients connecting to ISA Server must then change their browser configuration to connect to the new port number. We recommend changing the port number only in unique situations or in high-security environments.

While configuring listeners, you can also configure authentication for ISA Server. By using authentication, you can restrict access to internal servers based on required usernames and passwords. This authentication is in addition to that required by the published servers and is configured on ISA Server itself. Theoretically, you could require external users to authenticate twice: once on ISA Server and once on the internal servers. However, this is not recommended.

To configure listener ports on the external interface of ISA Server:

1. Open the ISA Management console, expand the **Servers and Arrays** node, right-click your array name, and then click **Properties**.

2. Click the **Incoming Web Requests** tab, shown in Figure 9-5. If you click the **Use the same listener configuration for all IP addresses** option button, ISA Server adds an entry in the configuration table that applies the same incoming TCP port and authentication configuration to all IP addresses bound to the external interface. The incoming TCP and SSL port configuration is shown in the tab.

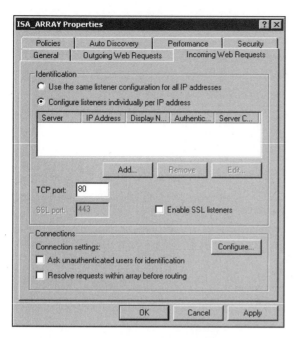

Figure 9-5   Configuring listener ports on the external interface of ISA Server

3. If you click the **Configure listeners individually per IP address** option button, ISA Server clears all listener information from the configuration table and lets you configure each external IP address manually. To add individual listener configurations, click the **Add** button below the configuration table. The Add/Edit Listeners window appears, as shown in Figure 9-6. Using the list boxes, select the ISA Server and external IP address you want to configure. Enter a descriptive name for the listener port configuration. If you want to use certificate security, click the **Use a server certificate to authenticate to web clients** check box, and select the preconfigured certificate. This certificate allows external clients to verify that the Web server represents the corporation it says it does.

9

Figure 9-6 Configuring individual listener ports for each external IP address

4. If you want to configure client authentication, select one or more of the following options in the Add/Edit Listeners dialog box:

- *Basic with this domain*—This option allows clients to send clear-text user-names and passwords to the internal Web server. Use this option only if absolutely necessary and if the external clients do not support encryption.

- *Digest with this domain*—This option allows clients to send digest authentica-tion to ISA Server. Only Windows 2000 clients support digest authentication.

- *Integrated*—This option allows external clients to use either NT Challenge/Response or Kerberos authentication.

- *Client certificate (secure channel only)*—This option allows users to provide client certificates to authenticate. Use this option only if you have precon-figured clients with the necessary client certificates.

Remember, these methods allow the client to authenticate *with ISA Server*, not with the published server. Only basic and anonymous authentication can pass through to the internal Web server. Integrated and digest authentication must terminate at ISA Server.

5. After you configure the listener IP address and authentication settings, click **OK** to return to the Incoming Web Requests tab.

6. If you want to configure connection settings, click the **Configure** button. The Connection Settings dialog box appears, as shown in Figure 9-7. Set the maximum amount of users who can connect through ISA Server at one time, and the amount of idle time ISA Server waits before disconnecting a session. Click **OK** when you finish to return to the Incoming Web Requests tab.

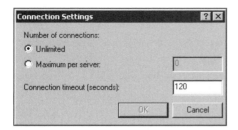

Figure 9-7 Configuring maximum connection and session timeout settings

7. If you want to force all anonymous users to authenticate, click the **Ask unauthenticated users for identification** check box. This setting is global; it cannot be configured differently for each listener. You must either authenticate all anonymous users for all internal Web sites or none at all.

8. If you click **Resolve requests within array before routing**, ISA Server enables CARP for reverse caching. This setting ensures that the internal Web content is not in the cache of any ISA Servers in the array before making a request of the internal Web server.

9. After you finish configuring all required listener ports for all external IP addresses, click **OK** in the Array Properties dialog box.

10. If you made any changes to the listener port configuration, ISA Server prompts you to restart the Web proxy service, as shown in Figure 9-8. Unless you are running in a production environment, click **Save the changes and restart the service(s)**, and then click **OK**. The new listener ports and authentication settings are now configured.

Figure 9-8 Restarting the Web proxy service

Configuring Web Publishing

Use the ISA Server Web publishing wizard to allow external users to access internal Web servers using the HTTP, HTTP-S, or FTP protocols. The wizard also allows you to require authentication of external users who access the Web server, and to allow Web site access only to employees of the company or partner organizations.

ISA Server caches all information transferred from the internal Web server to external users, thus alleviating the load on the Web server. Therefore, the Web publishing wizard is only available if you install ISA Server in cache or integrated mode. If you install ISA Server in firewall mode, you must open the necessary ports manually or publish the Web server using the server publishing wizard.

Before you begin configuring the Web publishing wizard, you need to create a valid destination set. As you learned in Chapter 6, destination sets allow you to restrict the access of internal clients *to* or *from* a specific set of Internet sites. When publishing internal Web servers, you must create destination sets that contain the *external* DNS names that map to specific computers on the internal network. One common mistake occurs when administrators configure the destination set to contain the internal name or IP address of the internal Web server. For example, you want to publish a Web site from your internal network to the Internet. You have registered the domain name *widgets.com* and want to redirect all requests for *www.widgets.com* to the internal Web server named WidgetsWeb. Creating a destination set that contains the WidgetsWeb hostname or internal IP address would not work correctly. Rather, you must create a destination set containing the *www.widgets.com* DNS name or external IP address.

To use a more complex example, you might have two internal Web servers named Sales and Marketing. To configure Web publishing, you first need to create two destination sets. The first contains the *www.widgets.com/sales* Web address, which you use to point to the Sales internal Web server. The second destination set contains the *www.widgets.com/marketing* Web address, which you use to point to the Marketing internal Web server. Once you create the destination sets, use the Web publishing wizard to map the Web addresses defined in the destination sets to the correct internal servers.

 If you configure a destination set that contains a path after the computer name, the Web server must contain the same path. For example, if a client requests *www.widgets.com/sales/figures.htm*, the internal Web server named Sales must contain the path and file /sales/figures.htm.

To configure a Web publishing rule:

1. Open the ISA Management console, expand **Servers and Arrays**, expand your array name, and then expand the **Publishing** node.

2. Right-click **Web Publishing Rules**, point to **New**, and then click **Rule**. The New Web Publishing Rule Wizard appears.

If you cannot create a Web publishing rule, you must modify your array settings first. Right-click your array, click Properties, click the Policies tab, check the Allow publishing rules check box, click OK in the Array Properties dialog box, and then click OK in the ISA Server dialog box.

3. Enter a logical name for the rule, and click **Next**. The Destination Sets page opens, as shown in Figure 9-9.

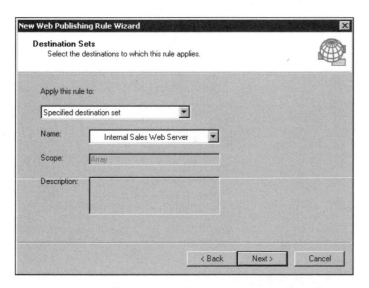

Figure 9-9   Configuring the destination internal Web server

4. On the Destination Sets page, choose the destination set containing the *external* DNS name of the internal Web server. Click **Next** when you finish.

5. The Client Type page allows you to configure clients that can access the internal Web servers. By configuring the permitted client IP addresses through a client address set policy element, you restrict Web server access to those IP addresses. To allow all external users to access the internal Web servers, leave **Any request** selected, as shown in Figure 9-10, and click **Next**.

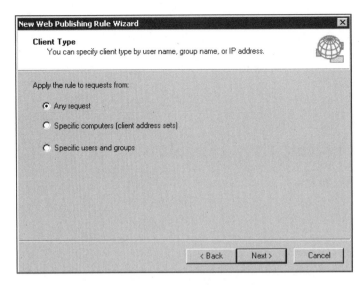

Figure 9-10   Configuring the valid client addresses

6. The Rule Action page appears, as shown in Figure 9-11. Use the page to create a detailed configuration for Web publishing, and then click the **Next** and **Finish** buttons to complete the wizard. You have the following options on the Rule Action page:

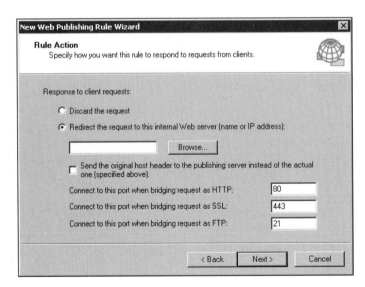

Figure 9-11   Redirecting the Web server request to an internal Web server

■ *Discard the request*—This option configures ISA Server to discard any request directed to the Web sites configured in the applied destination set.

- *Redirect the request to this internal Web server (name or IP address)*—Enter the internal hostname or IP address that maps to the Web address contained in the defined destination set. Click the **Browse** button to search the local network or active directory for the Web server.

- *Send the original host header to the publishing server instead of the actual one (specified above)*—If you select this option, ISA Server sends the original host header to the internal Web server rather than the actual host header. The actual host header contains the name of the actual internal Web server to which ISA Server is connecting, which you specify in the previous text box. The original host header contains the DNS name the external user originally requested. For example, you could have the external DNS name *www.widgets.com* mapped through ISA Server to the WidgetsWeb internal Web server. By checking the box and allowing the original host header to pass through, the internal Web server receives a request directed to *www.widgets.com*. By deselecting the check box, you allow the actual host header to pass through, causing the internal Web server to receive a request directed to WidgetsWeb. It may be useful to pass the original host header through if you are using it in IIS to direct requests to different hosted Web sites. For example, *www.widgets.com* could be directed to the Widgets corporate Web site, while *www2.widgets.com* could be directed to the Widgets sales Web site.

- *Connect to this port when bridging request as HTTP*—This option lets you use different port numbers on the internal Web server. By default, ISA Server tries to connect to the internal Web server on port 80 (default HTTP), but you can change this port for security reasons or to avoid using host headers. To avoid using host headers, you could configure IIS to host a Web site on port 80 and on ports 5000, 6000, and 7000. Then you could configure all IP addresses on the external ISA Server interfaces to point to the same internal Web server, but each on a different port number. Make sure the port numbers to which you redirect are not used by any other services.

- *Connect to this port when bridging request as SSL*—This option is very similar to the previous one, except that it allows you to redirect incoming SSL requests to different ports on the internal Web server. The default redirection port is 443.

- *Connect to this port when bridging request as FTP*—Use this setting to redirect incoming FTP requests to a different port number. The default redirection port is 21.

ISA Server handles Web publishing rules as an ordered list, as shown in Figure 9-12. At the bottom of the list is the Default rule, which cannot be deleted, modified, or reordered, and is configured to deny all incoming Web requests. When ISA Server receives an incoming request, ISA Server begins processing through the list of Web publishing rules to find a rule match. If it finds one, it redirects the request to the internal Web server. If ISA Server does not find a match, it eventually reaches the Default rule

9

at the bottom of the list and discards the incoming request. Because ISA Server processes the list from the top down, you should move the most popular rules to the top of the list using the arrow icons, as shown in Figure 9-12.

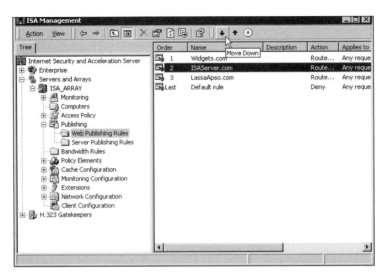

Figure 9-12   Changing the order of Web publishing rules

Configuring Protocol Redirection

When ISA Server receives a request for an internal Web site and finds a match in the Web publishing rules, it bridges the request to the internal Web server using the same protocol the external client used to make the original request. For example, if an external client sends a request via HTTP, ISA Server attempts to access the internal Web server using the HTTP protocol. To improve security or to create easier access for external users, you can configure ISA Server to perform protocol redirection on incoming requests.

Protocol redirection allows you to route HTTP and SSL requests as different protocols. For example, you could receive an incoming HTTP request to download a file on the Web server. Rather than requiring external users to use an FTP client (or type FTP:// before their request in a Web browser), you can redirect the incoming HTTP request to use FTP, as shown in Figure 9-13. Protocol redirection also allows security to terminate or begin at ISA Server. For example, you could require all external users to connect to the internal Web server using SSL (HTTP-S) to ensure the security of internal data routed across the Internet. However, since your company's internal network is known to be secure, you want the SSL to terminate at ISA Server to save processing time on the internal Web server. You could configure protocol redirection to redirect all SSL requests as HTTP for the internal Web server.

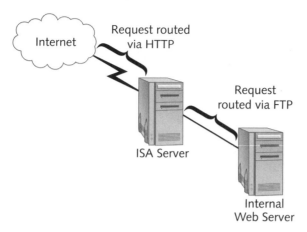

Figure 9-13   ISA Server protocol redirection

To configure protocol redirection:

1. In the ISA Management console, expand the **Servers and Arrays** node, expand your array name, expand **Publishing**, and then click **Web Publishing Rules**.

2. In the details pane, right-click the internal Web publishing rule you want to use for protocol redirection, and then click **Properties**.

3. In the Properties dialog box, click the **Bridging** tab, as shown in Figure 9-14.

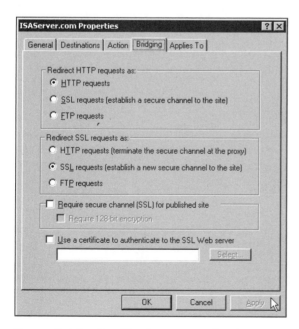

Figure 9-14   Configuring protocol redirection

4. On the Bridging tab, you can **Redirect HTTP requests as** HTTP, SSL, or FTP requests. When ISA Server receives a request via HTTP, it redirects the request to the internal Web servers using the protocol you select. By default, ISA Server redirects HTTP requests as HTTP.

5. Decide whether to **Redirect SSL requests as** HTTP, SSL, or FTP requests to the internal Web servers.

6. Click the **Require secure channel (SSL) for published site** check box if you want to require all external clients to connect to ISA Server via SSL. You can also **Require 128-bit encryption** if you require SSL.

7. If you redirect external requests to use the SSL protocol and the internal Web server requires certificates for authenticating client requests, click the **Use a certificate to authenticate to the SSL Web server** check box, click the **Select** button to choose the client certificate, and then click **OK.**

Configuring Mail Server Publishing

Since many companies make their internal mail servers available on the Internet, ISA Server includes a specific wizard for publishing mail servers. Publishing a mail server to the Internet allows external users to send and receive e-mail anywhere in the world and saves long distance costs to provide dial-up e-mail access. Publishing the mail server through ISA Server gives you the added benefits of packet and application filters. These filters eliminate many common attacks on mail servers, which are typically prime targets for hackers. In addition, the application filters let you screen incoming e-mail for viruses, eliminate large file attachments, and filter e-mail based on keywords. (Configuration of the SMTP application filter is discussed in Chapter 7.)

Microsoft ISA Server can publish any mail server that supports the SMTP protocol. This includes Microsoft Exchange 5.5, Exchange 2000, and non-Microsoft products such as Novell Groupwise and Lotus Notes.

To publish an internal mail server:

1. In the ISA Management console, expand the **Servers and Arrays** node, expand your array, and expand the **Publishing** node. Right-click **Server Publishing Rules**, and then click **Secure Mail Server**.

2. When the Mail Server Security Wizard appears, click **Next** on the welcome screen.

3. In the Mail Services Selection window, choose the internal mail services you want to make available to the Internet by clicking the **Default Authentication** or **SSL Authentication** check boxes, as shown in Figure 9-15. ISA Server creates a separate mail publishing rule for each service you select. If you choose to allow incoming SMTP services, you can also **Apply content filtering** by clicking its check box. This selection enables the message screening features of ISA Server, which are discussed in the following section. After you select the mail services, click **Next**.

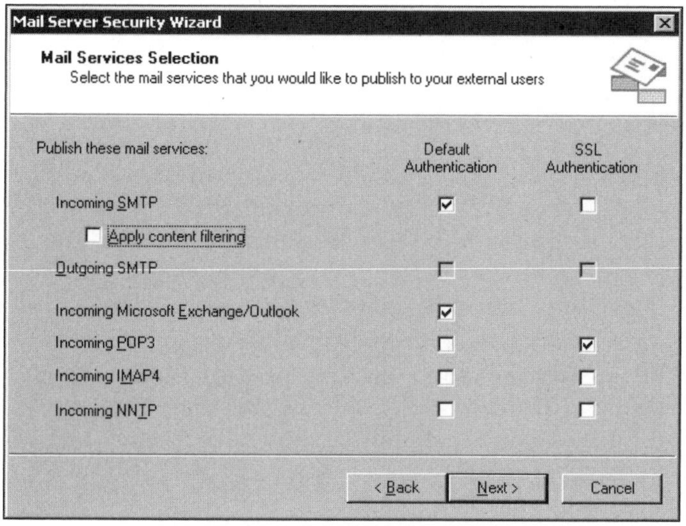

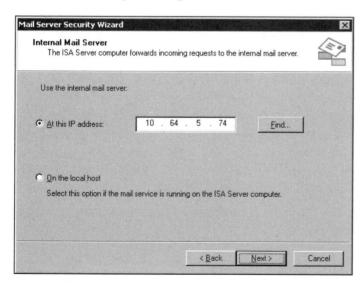

Figure 9-15   Choosing the mail services to publish

4. In the ISA Server's External IP Address dialog box, enter the external IP address you want ISA Server to use to listen for incoming mail requests. You can click the **Browse** button to list all external IP addresses in the array. After you enter the address, click **Next**.

5. In the Internal Mail Server dialog box, enter the IP address of the internal mail server, as shown in Figure 9-16. If the mail server is running on the same computer as ISA Server (which we do not recommend), click the **On the local host** option button, and then click **Next**. Click **Finish** to create the mail publishing rules.

Figure 9-16   Choosing the internal mail server to publish

ISA Server places all mail rules—one for each server protocol you publish—in the details pane of the Server Publishing Rules node.

Configuring the Message Screener

When you configure ISA Server for mail publishing, you might also want to configure the Message Screener. The Message Screener allows you to use features in the SMTP application filter to analyze incoming SMTP traffic and forward, delete, or redirect the messages based on message attachments or keywords. If you do not install the Message Screener, you can still filter SMTP message criteria such as sender name or domain, but you cannot filter based on file attachments or keywords. You install the Message Screener as an Add-in service while installing ISA Server. Because the Message Screener increases processor use when screening e-mails, we highly recommend that you run it on a separate computer on the internal network, unless you expect very light SMTP traffic.

When you turn on SMTP content filtering (by clicking the Apply content filtering check box in the mail publishing wizard), ISA Server forwards all incoming SMTP traffic to the SMTP server. You can configure the SMTP server to run on the ISA Server computer if SMTP traffic is exceptionally light, or on a separate computer if you expect moderate to heavy traffic. The Message Screener service (installed on the SMTP server) retrieves the SMTP application filter settings you configured on ISA Server and processes all messages accordingly. This may include dropping selected incoming e-mails and delivering others to the internal mail server.

The configuration of the SMTP application filter settings is discussed in Chapter 7.

Configuring the Message Screener on the ISA Server computer itself is different from configuring the Message Screener on a separate computer. Both procedures are explained next.

To run the Message Screener service from the ISA Server computer:

1. On the ISA Server computer, install IIS, including the SMTP Service component if it is not already installed. This is the minimum requirement to run the Message Screener service.

2. Open the Internet Services Manager console (in the **Administrative Tools** submenu), expand your server, right-click the **Default SMTP Virtual Server**, and then click **Properties**.

3. On the **General** tab, use the **IP address** list box to select the internal IP address of the ISA Server computer, as shown in Figure 9–17. Click **OK** when you finish.

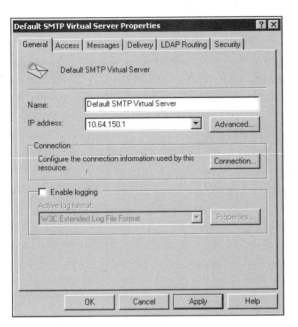

Figure 9-17   Configuring the internal ISA Server address to receive incoming SMTP mail

4. Expand the **Default SMTP Virtual Server** node, right-click **Domains**, point to **New**, and then click **Domain**.

5. In the New SMTP Domain Wizard, choose to create a **Remote** domain, and then click **Next**.

6. On the Select Domain Name page, shown in Figure 9-18, enter your local domain name (for example, **widgets.com**) in the **Name** text box to receive mail destined only for your domain. Next, click **Finish**. Your local domain name appears in the details pane.

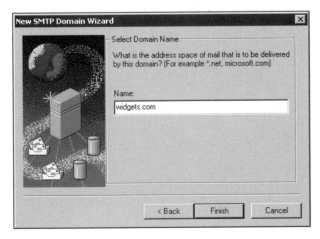

Figure 9-18   Configuring IIS to receive SMTP mail only for the local domain

7. In the details pane, double-click the domain you created in the previous step. The domain Properties dialog box appears.

8. In the Route domain section of the General tab, click the **Forward all mail to smart host** option button. Enter the DNS name or IP address of the internal mail server, as shown in Figure 9-19, and then click **OK**.

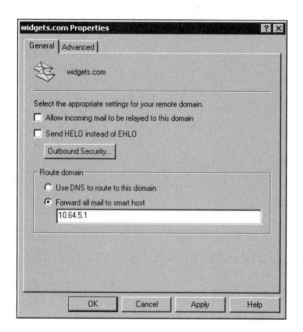

Figure 9-19   Configuring IIS to forward screened messages to the IP address of the internal mail server

9. If you have not already done so, run the ISA Server installation utility, click **Add/Remove Components** from the menu, click **Add-in services**, click **Change Option**, click the check box and click **OK** to install the **Message Screener** service, as shown in Figure 9-20.

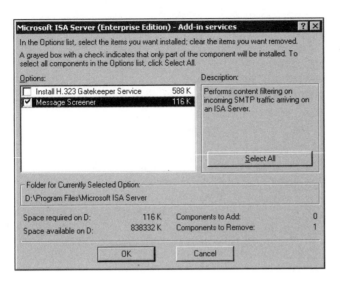

Figure 9-20   Installing the Message Screener service

10. Create a server publishing rule using Mail Server Security Wizard to publish the internal IP address of the ISA computer.

11. If you have not already done so, configure and enable the SMTP application filter.

To run the Message Screener service from a separate computer:

1. On the designated computer, install IIS, including the SMTP Service component. This is the minimum requirement to run the Message Screener service.

2. In the Internet Services Manager console (in the **Administrative Tools** submenu), expand your server, right-click the **Default SMTP Virtual Server**, and then click **Properties**.

3. On the **General** tab, ensure that the IIS Virtual SMTP server is configured to receive incoming mail on **All Unassigned** IP addresses, and then click **OK**.

4. Expand the **Default SMTP Virtual Server** node, right-click **Domains**, point to **New**, and then click **Domain**.

5. In the New SMTP Domain Wizard, choose to create a **Remote** domain, and then click **Next**.

6. On the Select Domain Name page, enter your local domain name (such as **widgets.com**) in the Name text box to receive mail destined only for your domain, and then click **Finish**. Your local domain name appears in the details pane.

7. In the details pane, double-click the domain you created in the previous step. The domain Properties dialog box appears.

8. In the Route domain section of the **General** tab, click the **Forward all mail to smart host** option button. Enter the DNS name or IP address of the internal mail server, and then click **OK**.

9. Run the ISA Server installation utility and install only the Message Screener service. You do not need to install any other ISA Server components unless they are required for other purposes.

10. If you installed ISA Server as a stand-alone server, or if the computer running the Message Screener service does not belong to the same Active Directory forest as the ISA Server computer, you must run the SMTPCred.exe utility, which is on the ISA Server CD in the \isa\i386 directory. The utility prompts you to specify the type of ISA Server, refresh interval, and authentication data, as shown in Figure 9-21. Configure these settings, and click **OK** to establish communication with ISA Server.

Figure 9-21   Configuring ISA Server authentication through the SMTPCred.exe utility

11. Since ISA Server communicates with the Message Screener using the Distributed Component Object Model (DCOM), you must configure the DCOM settings on the Message Screener computer. Click **Start**, click **Run**, and type **dcomcnfg.exe** in the Run dialog box.

12. In the Distributed COM Configuration Properties dialog box, shown in Figure 9-22, double-click the **VendorData Class** application.

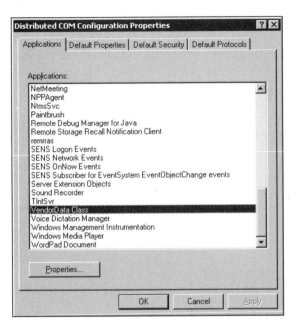

Figure 9-22   Distributed COM Configuration Properties dialog box

13. On the **Security** tab of the VendorData Class Properties dialog box, click **Use custom permissions** for all three option buttons, as shown in Figure 9-23.

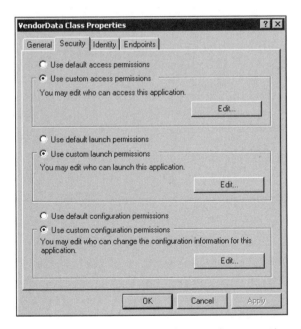

Figure 9-23   Configuring the VendorData Class DCOM application to communicate with ISA Server

14. For each of the three settings in the VendorData Class, click the **Edit** button. The Registry Value Permissions dialog box appears, as shown in Figure 9-24. Click the **Add** button to add the **Everyone** group with the **Allow Access** permission setting. After you configure the Everyone group for all three areas of the VendorData Class, click **OK** to close the Properties dialog box. Then click **OK** to close the Registry Value Permissions dialog box.

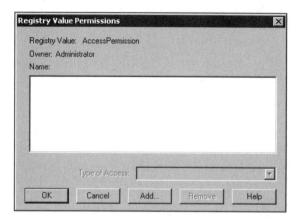

Figure 9-24   Granting permissions to the Message Screener service

15. On ISA Server, create a server publishing rule using the Mail Server Security Wizard to publish the IP address of the computer running the Message Screener service.

16. Restart the ISA Server machine to complete the process. Next, open the ISA Management console, expand the **Monitoring** node under your array, and click **Sessions**. You should see an active firewall session with the SMTP Message Screener computer. ISA Server should now forward all incoming mail to the Message Screener computer, which will screen the messages and forward the appropriate ones to the internal mail server.

As you can see, configuring the Message Screener on a separate computer can be a complex, time-consuming job. Microsoft plans to automate the process in future releases of ISA Server.

Generic Server Publishing

Thus far, you have seen ISA Server's ability to publish internal Web and mail servers to the Internet. However, you may have other internal servers, such as database servers, chat servers, and newsgroup servers, that you want to make available to external users. To accommodate this need, ISA Server includes a generic server publishing wizard that allows you to publish any other TCP/IP-based internal server. Using this wizard is beneficial because it creates all the necessary packet filters for incoming requests to ISA Server.

To publish an internal server using the generic server publishing wizard:

1. In the ISA Management console, expand your array, expand the **Publishing** node, right-click **Server Publishing Rules**, point to **New**, and then click **Rule**.

2. On the Welcome page of the New Server Publishing Rule Wizard, enter a logical name for the server publishing rule, and then click **Next**.

3. On the Address Mapping page, enter the IP address of the internal server and the external IP address of the ISA Server machine you want to map, as shown in Figure 9-25. Click **Next** when you finish.

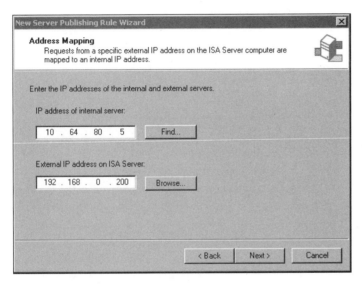

Figure 9-25   Mapping the internal server IP address to the external ISA Server IP address

4. On the Protocol Settings page, choose the protocol you want to publish from the list, as shown in Figure 9-26. After you choose the protocol, click **Next**.

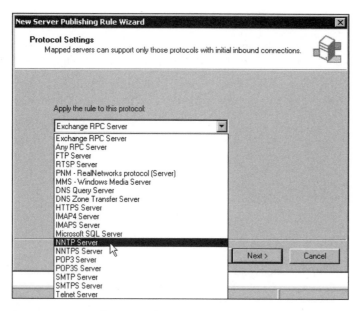

Figure 9-26   Choosing the protocol to publish

The list shows the protocols you have defined on ISA Server. If the list does not include the protocol you need, ensure that you have created a definition for the protocol.

5. In the Client Type dialog box, choose either to allow **Any request** to reach the published server, or to restrict the published server to **Specific computers** by using client address sets. Click **Next**, and then click **Finish** to complete the wizard and publish the internal server.

ISA Server opens all required port numbers on the external interface for the published servers. You do not need to create packet filters to allow traffic to pass through.

If you plan to publish Web, SMTP, NNTP, or FTP services on internal servers, be sure the IIS installed on the ISA Server computer is not running the duplicate service. This causes conflicts with ISA Server when rerouting those port numbers to internal servers.

UNDERSTANDING H.323 SERVICES

H.323 is a multimedia protocol that includes voice, video, and data conferencing for use over packet-switched networks. H.323 is an emerging, fast-growing standard that allows Voice over IP networks to function in today's industry. Two major networks currently tie worldwide communication together: the Internet and the **Public Switched Telephone Network (PSTN)**. In the near future, these networks will likely merge into a single, global network. Just as TCP/IP ties all major computer communication together on the Internet, the H.323 protocol suite is poised to become the protocol that unifies all voice and video streaming devices.

Many companies, such as Cisco Systems, have already produced IP telephones capable of connecting directly to an RJ-45 Ethernet cable, obtaining a DHCP-assigned IP address, and registering with a central call manager. Because WAN bandwidth has evolved to allow phone calls with streaming audio, large companies have already begun to use H.323 clients within their enterprise networks. Long distance costs between branch offices are virtually eliminated. For example, Intel has several U.S. corporate offices and many branch offices around the world. Since Intel already pays the cost for WAN connections between all offices, it could use the H.323 protocol to route all phone calls over the WAN and save thousands of dollars in long distance charges. You can also keep the PSTN connections intact in case the WAN goes down or runs low on bandwidth.

Identifying H.323 Components

You can use hundreds of devices to build an H.323 network, ranging from IP telephones to H.323 routers. Overall, you can divide these devices into four major categories:

- *Terminals*—Terminals are the client endpoints on the LAN that provide real-time, two-way communications. These devices consist primarily of end-user equipment such as IP telephones, which are designed to work over IP-based networks; video phones, which allow streamed video to be displayed; and soft phones, which are software-based telephones, such as Microsoft Netmeeting.

- *Gateways*—Gateways interface H.323 to other networks, such as the PSTN, H.320 (ISDN) networks, or other H.323 networks. These devices are only required if you plan to use H.323 beyond the local subnet. ISA Server does not include an H.323 gateway.

- *Gatekeepers*—Gatekeepers are optional H.323 components that provide address resolution, access control, and bandwidth control. You can typically find gatekeepers in enterprise-scale H.323 networks since they manage the WAN traffic. You can use gatekeepers to restrict users from calling certain locations or telephone numbers, or to ensure that maximum WAN bandwidth is not exceeded, causing poor quality for all voice calls. The address resolution feature lets you place calls based on a user's e-mail address. Microsoft ISA Server includes an H.323 gatekeeper service.

- *Multipoint Control Units*—The Multipoint Control Unit supports conference calls between three or more terminals.

9

USING THE ISA SERVER H.323 GATEKEEPER SERVICE

You can use the ISA Server H.323 Gatekeeper service to maintain a directory of all internal H.323-based clients. This service allows external H.323 clients to contact the ISA Server H.323 gatekeeper to validate and access internal H.323 users. For example, you might run Microsoft Netmeeting on your PC, which you have connected to an internal network behind an ISA Server firewall. You can configure Microsoft Netmeeting to register an account name (such as *Jeremiah.Cioara@course.com*) or an internal phone number (such as 4805551212) with the ISA Server gatekeeper. After you configure both the internal Netmeeting client and the ISA Server gatekeeper, all external and internal users registered with the gatekeeper can reach you based on your account name or phone number, rather than the IP address of your machine.

You can think of the ISA Server gatekeeper as the phone book of your H.323 client base. Whenever ISA Server receives an H.323 incoming call, it opens the phone book to find the dialed-user's phone number (IP address). Since the ISA Server Gatekeeper service only manages the phone book for the internal network, it has a limited knowledge of phone entries in the enterprise network. To expand the entries to include all H.323 users in the enterprise WAN, you can configure ISA Server for your internal network to reference the phone books of other ISA Servers managing other internal networks.

Figure 9-27 shows an example network composed of three branch offices: Arizona, Michigan, and Nebraska. Each office has multiple ISA Server gatekeepers managing the H.323 directory database for its respective location. If an H.323 user in Arizona (*Chris.Ward@arizona.widgets.com*) attempts to call a user in Michigan (*Lynn.Davidson@michigan.widgets.com*), the ISA Server gatekeeper in Arizona routes the call to the ISA Server machine in Michigan. This scenario would also require the configuration of call routing rules, which are discussed in the following section.

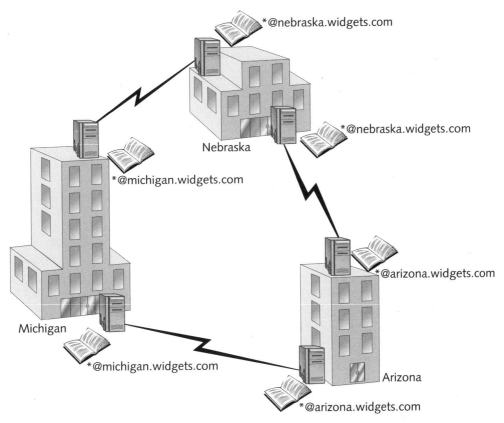

*@nebraska.widgets.com

*@nebraska.widgets.com

Nebraska

*@michigan.widgets.com

*@arizona.widgets.com

Michigan

*@michigan.widgets.com

Arizona

*@arizona.widgets.com

9

Figure 9-27   Using ISA Server Gatekeeper services to manage H.323 traffic

Configuring the H.323 Gatekeeper Service

Initially configuring and managing the ISA Server Gatekeeper service is easy. First, ensure that you installed the gatekeeper service and management options when you installed ISA Server. If you skipped the installation of these components, you can add them by starting the installation utility and clicking Add/Remove Components from the menu. If you have the H.323 Gatekeeper service and management items installed, you must add the local (or remote) ISA Server computer as an H.323 gatekeeper. To do so, open the ISA Management console, right-click the H.323 Gatekeepers node, and click Add gatekeeper. The Add Gatekeeper dialog box appears, as shown in Figure 9-28. If you are working from the ISA Server machine that you want to add as the H.323 gate-keeper, click the This computer option button. Otherwise, click Another computer, and enter the hostname or IP address of the remote ISA Server.

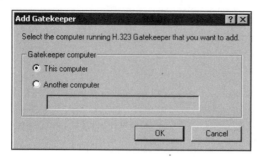

Figure 9-28   Configuring ISA Server as an H.323 gatekeeper

After making your selection, click OK. The selected ISA Server machine appears under the H.323 Gatekeepers node, meaning that you have successfully installed and configured the ISA Server Gatekeeper service for the local network. Once you add this particular ISA Server to the list of H.323 gatekeepers, ISA Server creates and starts all the necessary gatekeeper services and directories. This simple configuration allows the gatekeeper to maintain a directory of all internal clients and allow them to dial using account names or phone numbers rather than IP addresses. The next step is to configure internal H.323 clients to use the ISA Server Gatekeeper services and, if necessary, configure gateway-to-gateway calling to expand the size and scope of the H.323 calling directory. These steps are discussed in the following sections.

Configuring Netmeeting H.323 Clients

A Microsoft Netmeeting client is one example of an H.323 client capable of combining voice, video, and data sharing in one application. By connecting a microphone and video camera to your computer, you can video conference with thousands of Netmeeting users around the world. Since Microsoft included Netmeeting in Windows 2000, it has become one of the leading H.323 applications in the industry.

The easiest way to use a Netmeeting client is to dial someone using the IP address assigned to their computer. While this is a simple way to make an occasional call, managing an entire phone directory based on IP addresses can be a painstaking process, especially since many addresses frequently change due to DHCP. Using Netmeeting clients in a large-sized H.323 environment requires the use of a dynamic name-to-IP address H.323 database, such as that offered with ISA Server's gatekeeper service. You can configure Netmeeting to register an account name or internal phone number with the gatekeeper service each time it runs. Doing so ensures that the H.323 client database is consistently updated to reflect new IP address assignments or name changes in the internal network.

To configure Microsoft Netmeeting to interface with the ISA Server gatekeeper service:

1. Open Netmeeting. In a default Windows 2000 installation, you open Netmeeting by clicking **Start**, pointing to **Programs**, pointing to **Accessories**, pointing to **Communications**, and then clicking **NetMeeting**.

 If this is your first time running Microsoft Netmeeting, you will see a series of basic configuration dialog boxes. After you respond to these dialog boxes, Netmeeting will start.

2. Click **Tools** on the menu bar, and then click **Options**. The Options dialog box appears, as shown in Figure 9-29.

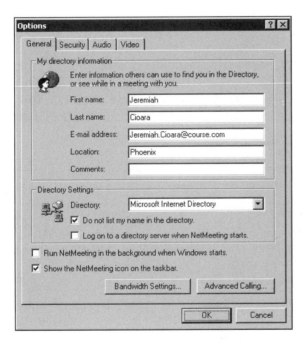

Figure 9-29   The Netmeeting Options dialog box

3. At the bottom of the Options dialog box, click the **Advanced Calling** button.

4. The Advanced Calling Options dialog box appears, as shown in Figure 9-30.

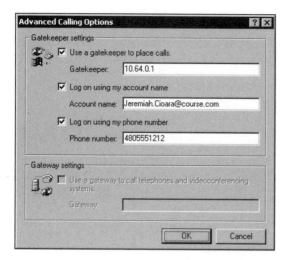

Figure 9-30 Configuring Microsoft Netmeeting to register with the ISA Server gatekeeper

Click one of the following options:

- *Use a gatekeeper to place calls*—Choose this option to ensure a Netmeeting client on the internal network uses the ISA Server Gatekeeper service (and user database) when placing calls. Enter the IP address of the ISA Server's *internal* interface or DNS hostname.

- *Log on using my account name*—Select this option and enter the username or e-mail address you want to register with the ISA Server Gatekeeper service. Users can then reach you by calling your username or e-mail address.

 Only users who are configured to access your ISA Server gatekeeper directly or another ISA Server connected via call routing rules can resolve internal clients based on username or e-mail address.

- *Log on using my phone number*—Select this option and enter the phone number you want to register with the IOS gatekeeper service. Anyone who has configured Netmeeting to use your ISA Server gatekeeper to place calls can then reach you via the configured phone number.

 Do not use dashes or spaces when entering the Netmeeting phone number.

- *Use a gateway to call telephones and videoconferencing systems*—Select this option to have Netmeeting clients on the external network (the Internet) access the H.323 client database on the ISA Server gatekeeper. Internet clients can then place calls to Netmeeting clients on the internal network. To configure this option, click the check box, and type the IP address of the *external* interface of the ISA Server.

 You cannot select *Use a gatekeeper to place calls* and *Use a gateway to call telephones and videoconferencing systems* simultaneously because you use them to configure internal or external Netmeeting clients, respectively.

5. To verify registration, open the ISA Management console, expand the **H.323 Gatekeepers** node, expand the ISA Server computer with which the client registered, and then click **Active Terminals**. The Netmeeting clients appear in the details pane, as shown in Figure 9-31.

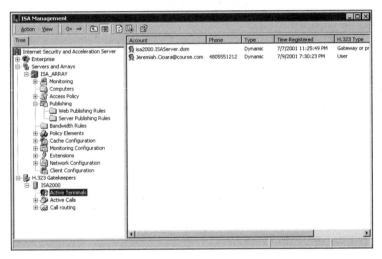

Figure 9-31   Viewing registered H.323 clients

CONFIGURING ADVANCED H.323 GATEKEEPER ROUTING FUNCTIONS

Although configuring an ISA Server gatekeeper to maintain a local H.323 database is relatively simple, configuring multiple H.323 networks and gatekeepers quickly makes the design more complex. ISA Server includes an automated configuration system, allowing you to connect multiple gatekeepers and route voice and video calls among them. You must understand four items to successfully configure gateway-to-gateway routing: destinations, phone number rules, e-mail address rules, and IP address rules.

Setting Destinations

Destinations are comparable to the ISA Server policy elements discussed in Chapter 6. By themselves, destinations have no functionality, but when combined with phone number, e-mail, or IP address rules, they allow ISA Server to route the H.323 call to the correct destination. Configuring the destinations themselves defines potential H.323 devices where ISA Server could route an H.323 request.

To configure gatekeeper destinations:

1. In the ISA Management console, expand **H.323 Gatekeepers**, expand your server, expand **Call routing**, right-click the **Destinations** node, and then click **Add destination**.

2. When the New Destination Wizard welcome screen appears, click **Next**.

3. The Destination Type page opens, shown in Figure 9-32.

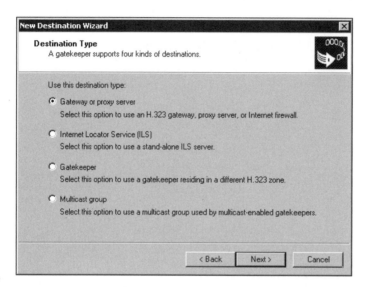

Figure 9-32   Configuring ISA Server gatekeeper destinations

Click an option to create one of the following destinations:

- *Gateway or proxy server*—If you plan to use the ISA Server gatekeeper to call other networks, you can configure an H.323 gateway as a destination to route the request. You can use non-Microsoft gateways provided they meet the H.323 RFC standards.

- *Internet Locator Service (ILS)*—This option allows you to connect to a server running the Site Server ILS service. This service transforms a computer into a central hub for call processing. Since you can dedicate the server to this function, it can register and manage many calls at once.

169. 254. 214. 188

 You should not configure ISA Server to point to any Internet-based ILS servers.

- *Gatekeeper*—The gatekeeper option allows you to forward requests to another H.323 gatekeeper. This could be another ISA Server managing a different group of clients, or a third-party H.323 gatekeeper such as a Cisco 2600 series router.

- *Multicast group*—This option allows you to configure ISA Server to send multicast messages to find a possible destination database. All H.323 gate-keepers listen for possible queries on the multicast address 224.0.1.41. For example, your ISA Server could search for the H.323 account *Lisa.Walker@course.com*. If you configure ISA Server to use a multicast destination, it sends a query for the account name to 224.0.1.41. All other H.323 gatekeepers receive the message, and if one has the account in the H.323 client database, it responds with the appropriate IP address to your ISA Server.

4. Once you select the destination type, click **Next**.

5. The Destination Name or Address page prompts you for the DNS name or IP address of the gateway, ILS server, or gatekeeper you want to specify as a destination. Enter the DNS hostname or IP address, and click **Next**.

6. On the Destination Description page, type a logical description of the destination and click **Next**. It is common practice to enter the range of H.323 clients supported as the description (e.g., the 602 area code or the xxx@widgets.com domain).

7. Click **Finish** to end the wizard and create the destination. The configured destination appears in the details pane of the ISA Management console.

Setting Phone Number Rules

You can use phone number rules to route calls based on the number a user dials on an H.323 client to a specific destination. (You configured destinations in the previous section.) For example, you might use internal H.323 phone numbers to identify Netmeeting clients around the world in your enterprise network. When configuring the H.323 phone numbering scheme, you could identify all Netmeeting clients in the Tokyo office by beginning their phone numbers with 333. The Michigan office's phone numbers could all begin with 444, Arizona's with 555, and so on. By implementing phone number rules, you could forward the H.323 call to a different destination based on the phone number prefix.

To create a phone number routing rule:

1. Under the **Call routing** node of the H.323 gatekeeper, right-click **Phone number rules**, and then click **Add routing rule**.

2. Click **Next** on the New Routing Rule Wizard welcome screen.

3. On the Name and Description page, enter a unique name and description to identify the routing rule, and then click **Next**.

4. On the Prefix or Phone Number page, shown in Figure 9-33, enter the prefix or phone number you want to match and route to a configured destination. If you enter an entire phone number rather than just the prefix, deselect the **Route all phone numbers using this prefix** check box. This allows you to forward an individual phone number to a specific destination. Click **Next** when you finish.

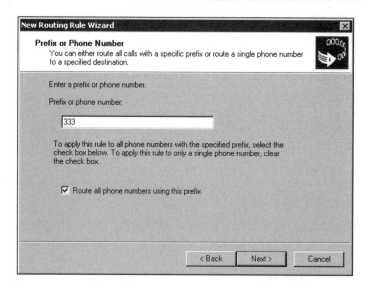

Figure 9-33   Configuring a phone number routing rule prefix

5. On the Destination Type page, choose the type of destination you want to receive the calls affected by this routing rule, shown Figure 9-34, and click **Next**.

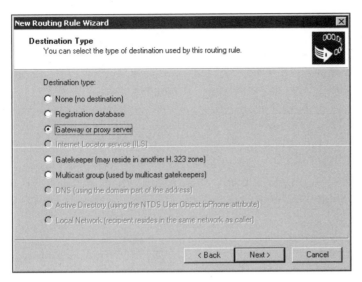

Figure 9-34   Selecting the destination for numbers affected by the configured phone prefix

9

6. The Destination Name page shows a list of configured destinations based on the type you selected in the previous step. Choose the destination you want to receive the calls, and click **Next**.

7. On the Change a Phone Number page, add or remove digits from the beginning of the phone number, if necessary, as shown in Figure 9-35. For example, you can remove the locally configured access codes for the locations described in the previous example and add the actual area codes instead.

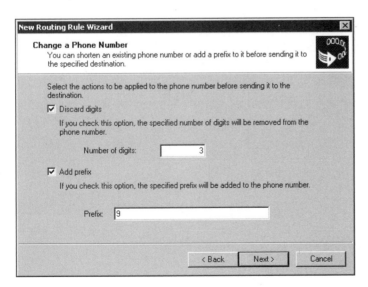

Figure 9-35   Modifying the H.323 client's dialed number

Click one of the following options:

- *Discard digits*—Clicking this option allows you to specify the number of digits to discard from the *beginning* of the dialed phone number. For instance, you could discard the local access codes from the previous example by entering **3** in the **Number of digits** field.

- *Add prefix*—Clicking this option allows you to add a prefix to the beginning of the dialed number. For example, the gateway that interfaces your H.323 network to the PSTN could require a 9 before the phone number to get an outside line.

8. After changing the phone number, click **Next**. The Routing Rule Metric dialog box appears.

9. Define a routing rule metric that specifies the order in which the rules are carried out. For example, you might have two routing rules to reach Tokyo. The preferred rule calls Tokyo through the IP WAN, saving all long distance charges. The secondary rule calls Tokyo through the PSTN. Using this order, ISA Server always attempts to reach Tokyo over the IP WAN first. If the IP WAN is down, the call is rerouted to the PSTN. Enter the order of the rule in the **Metric** field, and click **Next**.

10. Click **Finish** to create the routing rule.

Once you complete the rule wizard, the new routing rule appears in the details pane of the ISA Management console, as shown in Figure 9-36. Notice that a default routing rule named Local already exists. This rule routes all calls that do not have a specifically configured rule to the local ISA Server registration database, which eliminates the need to create routing rules for registered local numbers.

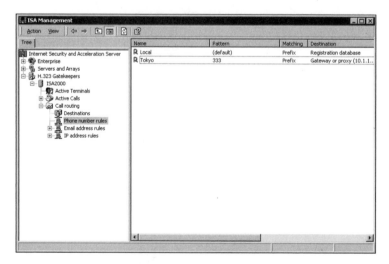

Figure 9-36   List of phone number rules

Setting E-mail Address Rules

E-mail address rules allow you to route calls based on a user's e-mail address rather than their phone number. Instead of configuring phone number patterns to match, you configure the e-mail domain name to match.

To configure an e-mail address rule:

1. Under the **Call routing** node of the H.323 gatekeeper, right–click **Email address rules**, and then click **Add routing rule**.

2. Click **Next** on the New Routing Rule welcome page.

3. On the Name and Description page, specify a logical name and description for the rule, and click **Next**.

4. On the Domain Name Suffix page, shown in Figure 9-37, enter the DNS domain name for all e-mail addresses you can reach with this routing rule, and then click **Next**. For example, to route all requests for users who end their e-mail address with @course.com, enter **course.com** in the **DNS domain name** text box. If you want to create a routing rule for an individual e-mail address, enter it in the text box, and deselect the **Route all e-mail addresses that include this general DNS domain name** check box. ISA Server must then match the e-mail address in the text box *exactly* before it applies the rule.

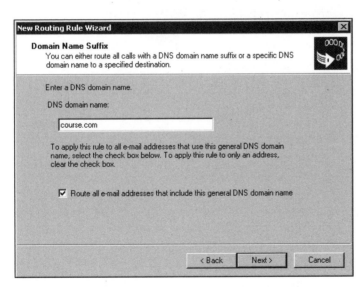

Figure 9-37   Configuring the e-mail domain suffix

5. On the Destination Type page, choose the *type* of destination device you have configured for this routing rule, and then click **Next**.

6. On the Destination Name page, select the *individual* destination device you have configured for this routing rule, and then click **Next**.

7. On the Routing Rule Metric page, enter the order of preference for this rule, and then click **Next**.

8. Click the **Finish** button to complete the wizard and create the e-mail routing rule.

Setting IP Address Rules

IP address rules allow you to route calls based on the IP address the internal user attempts to dial. When a user attempts to place a call to a specific IP address, ISA Server checks the IP address rules to see if a destination is configured for a particular subnet, and then routes the call appropriately. For example, you could configure an IP address rule for ISA Server to route all 182.0.0.0 IP addresses to the Missouri gateway. If a user then places a call to the IP address 182.50.3.85, ISA Server would route it directly to Missouri.

Configuring an IP address rule is very similar to configuring phone number or e-mail address rules, as described in the previous sections. Instead of configuring phone number patterns or e-mail domain names, however, you configure IP address subnets, as shown in Figure 9-38.

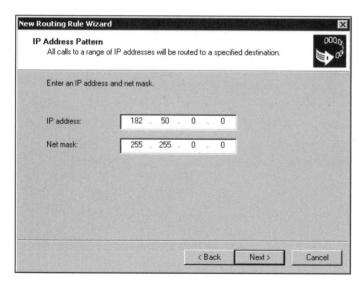

Figure 9-38 Configuring IP address rules

CHAPTER SUMMARY

- ISA Server contains three publishing wizards for making internal resources available to the external network: the Web Publishing Rule Wizard, which is designed to publish HTTP, HTTP-S, and FTP services; the Mail Server Security Wizard, which you use to publish SMTP, IMAP, and POP services; and the Server Publishing Rule Wizard, which lets you publish any other TCP/IP-based server.

- Reverse caching is the process of storing HTTP, HTTP-S, or FTP content from internal Web servers locally on ISA Server.

- Before you can use Web publishing rules, you must first configure a listener on the external ISA Server interface. A listener defines how ISA Server should handle incoming HTTP or HTTP-S requests. You can also configure listeners to require users to authenticate before accessing the internal Web server.

- Before you configure the Web publishing wizard, you should create a destination set containing the *external* DNS name for the internal Web server. The Web publishing wizard allows you to map this DNS name to an internal server.

- By using protocol redirection, you can route incoming HTTP, HTTP-S, or FTP requests to the internal network using a different protocol.

- Before you can use the SMTP application filter, you must configure ISA Server or one of your internal computers with the Message Screener service.

- The generic server publishing wizard allows you to publish any server using a TCP/IP protocol defined in the protocol definitions policy elements.

- The H.323 Gatekeeper service allows ISA Server to keep a database of locally registered H.323 clients by account name or phone number.

- Using H.323 routing rules and destinations, you can route calls to external H.323 devices based on the phone number, e-mail address, or IP address dialed by the internal Netmeeting client.

KEY TERMS

listener — A configuration that tells the ISA Server external interface how to respond to incoming requests.

Public Switched Telephone Network (PSTN) — The standard telephone network, also called the Plain Old Telephone Service (POTS).

publishing policy — A policy configured on ISA Server to grant secure access to internal servers.

reverse proxy — A device such as ISA Server that services requests from external users attempting to reach resources on the internal network.

REVIEW QUESTIONS

1. When publishing a server through the Web publishing wizard, what three types of access are granted to the internal server?

    a. HTTP, SMTP, and FTP

    b. FTP, HTTP-S, and HTTP

    c. HTTP, SMTP, and HTTP-S

    d. none of the above

2. Why would you want to use ISA Server to publish an internal Web server?

    a. It allows the use of access lists to restrict open ports.

    b. It can perform reverse caching.

    c. By default, it redirects all HTTP requests as HTTP-S to improve security.

    d. all of the above

3. Messenger Guy Inc. provides overnight package delivery services throughout California for a reasonable price. The company consists of six employees and is located in San Diego. It wants to install an internal Web server to accept Web-based ordering and use ISA Server for firewall protection. Because the company is new, its budget is limited. What publishing strategy would you suggest?

    a. hosting services on ISA Server

    b. basic firewall configuration

    c. three-homed configuration

    d. dual ISA Server configuration

4. What ISA Server feature must you configure before publishing is possible?

    a. incoming packet filters

    b. outgoing packet filters

    c. dynamic packet filters

    d. listeners

5. Which type of authentication is considered pass-through authentication, meaning it passes through ISA Server to the internal Web server?

    a. basic

    b. digest

    c. integrated

    d. client certificate

6. Before using the Web publishing wizard, you must configure a destination set containing what information?

    a. the IP addresses of the clients you expect to access the internal Web server

    b. the internal hostname or IP address of the internal Web server

c. the external FQDN or IP address of the internal Web server

d. the internal IP address of ISA Server

7. Before using the Web publishing wizard, you can configure a client address set containing what information?

a. the IP addresses of the clients you expect to access the internal Web server

b. the internal hostname or IP address of the internal Web server

c. the external FQDN or IP address of the internal Web server

d. the internal IP address of ISA Server

8. A client can access an internal Web server using HTTP, but ISA Server can translate the request to FTP for the internal network. What is this feature called?

a. protocol proxy

b. protocol redirection

c. protocol translation

d. tunneling

9. Which one of the following mail server platforms can ISA Server publish using the Mail Publishing Wizard?

a. Novell Groupwise

b. Microsoft Exchange 5.5

c. Lotus Notes

d. all of the above

10. You have enabled the SMTP application filter to screen all incoming mail for the keyword "XXX." A week later, an internal user reports that he is still receiving e-mails containing "XXX" in the message body. You check the SMTP application filter and it seems to be working correctly. What should you check next?

a. Verify that the internal mail server has the SMTP application filter installed locally.

b. Verify that the Message Screener service is installed and working.

c. Ensure that the internal user is not using a modem to retrieve e-mail.

d. Ensure that the ISP is not forwarding junk e-mail to your local server.

11. You want to publish an internal server that runs a custom application using TCP port 5678. What should be your first step?

a. Create a protocol definition for the custom application.

b. Enable protocol redirection for the internal server, allowing ISA Server to redirect the request to the correct port.

c. Use the generic server publishing wizard to make the server available to the public.

d. none of the above

12. It is best to run the Message Screener service on ISA Server, which allows ISA Server to screen the message before it reaches the internal mail server. True or false?

13. You are attempting to publish an internal Web server to the Internet. You configure the internal IIS server to listen for Web requests on TCP port 9000 for security reasons, and then configure ISA Server to redirect the incoming requests to the internal Web server on TCP port 9000. You then configure a listener on the internal interface of ISA Server to accept requests on port 80, so Internet users won't need to change their browser configuration. Internet users complain that they cannot connect to the internal Web server. Where does the problem lie?

    a. on the internal Web server port configuration

    b. on the ISA Server port configuration

    c. on the ISA Server listener configuration

    d. on the external users' browser configuration

14. If you were using Microsoft's Network Monitor to capture packets coming from ISA Server and destined for the internal Web server, what would the source IP address be?

    a. the IP address of the external user

    b. the IP address of the internal ISA Server interface

    c. the IP address of the external ISA Server interface

    d. the IP address of the last Internet router the request passed through

15. Which of the following are H.323 gatekeeper functions?

    a. address resolution

    b. bandwidth control

    c. access control

    d. all of the above

16. To which of the following IP addresses do all H.323 Gatekeepers listen?

    a. 224.0.1.5

    b. 224.0.1.144

    c. 224.0.1.14

    d. 224.0.1.41

17. What is the primary reason you should use the ISA Server Gatekeeper service?

    a. to interface with the PSTN

    b. to maintain a local H.323 client directory

    c. to allow compression between the G.711 and G.723 audio codecs

    d. to route packets to Internet-based ILS servers

18. What is the function of an H.323 destination?

a. It defines external H.323 devices to use when creating rules.

b. It acts as the default gateway for all internal H.323 clients behind ISA Server.

c. It defines the H.323 destination clients that users can reach on the internal network.

d. none of the above

19. When using the Discard digits option in the H.323 phone number rule, you can configure ISA Server to remove digits from which section of the dialed phone number?

a. the beginning

b. the end

c. anywhere in the number

d. It depends on the number dialed.

20. You are using Netmeeting on the internal network to dial other Netmeeting users on the Internet. You configure Netmeeting to register your e-mail address as your account name with ISA Server. While some users can dial you by using your e-mail address, most cannot. What is the most likely reason?

a. They are using the improper version of Netmeeting.

b. They are not located behind another H.323 gateway.

c. They have not configured their default gateway as your ISA Server.

d. You have improperly registered the Netmeeting client.

HANDS-ON PROJECTS

Project 9-1

You are employed by Nexus Sound Corporation, a speaker manufacturer specializing in home theater sound systems. Nexus has recently installed ISA Server to improve access speeds on the internal network. To improve slumping sales, Nexus has decided to build an e-commerce division, allowing customers to order Nexus products from anywhere in the world. The Web server has been built and tested, and is ready for use. You must allow HTTP and HTTP-S access to the internal Web server for sales, which, for security reasons, is configured to respond to requests on TCP ports 9000 and 9001 for all external clients. To ensure high performance, the company wants to allow only 100 users to access the internal Web server at a time. Nexus also wants to set the HTTP session timeout to 60 seconds, so that users who take time to read the speaker descriptions do not prevent others from accessing the Web site.

Before you can publish internal Web servers with the Web publishing wizard, you must configure a listener port on the external interface of ISA Server. To configure a listener port:

1. Open the ISA Management console, expand the **Servers and Arrays** node, right-click your array name, and then click **Properties**.

2. Click the **Incoming Web Requests** tab, and then click the **Configure listeners individually per IP address** option button.

3. Click the **Add** button below the listener configuration table to open the Add/Edit Listeners dialog box. Using the list boxes, select your ISA Server and the external IP address of your server. In the **Display Name** text box, enter **Sales Web Server**. Your configuration should look like the one in Figure 9-39.

Figure 9-39

4. After you configure the listener IP address and authentication settings, click **OK** to return to the Incoming Web Requests tab.

5. Click the **Enable SSL listeners** check box, and then click **OK**. Leave the default SSL port as 443.

6. Click the **Configure** button to open the Connection Settings window. Click the **Maximum per server** option button, set the maximum amount of sessions to **100**, and set the **Connection timeout** to **60** seconds, as shown in Figure 9-40. To return to the Incoming Web Requests tab, click **OK** when you finish.

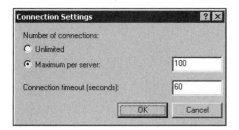

Figure 9-40

7. To allow anonymous access to the internal Web server, deselect the **Ask unauthenticated users for identification** check box.

8. To enable CARP for reverse caching, click the **Resolve requests within array before routing** check box. Click **OK**.

9. Click **OK** in the array properties window to finish configuring the listener port for the internal Web server for sales. When the ISA Server Warning window appears, click **Save the changes and restart the service(s)**, and then click **OK**.

Project 9-2

Before you can use the Web publishing wizard to make the Nexus sales Web server available to the public, you must configure a destination set that contains the FQDN or external IP address for the Web site.

To configure the necessary destination set:

1. In the ISA Management console, expand **Servers and Arrays**, expand your array name, and then expand the **Policy Elements** node.

2. Right-click the **Destination Sets** node, point to **New**, and then click **Set**.

3. In the New Destination Set dialog box, enter **Sales Web Server** in the **Name** box, and then click the **Add** button.

4. In the **Destination** text box, enter **Sales.Nexus.com**, as pictured in Figure 9-41, and click **OK**.

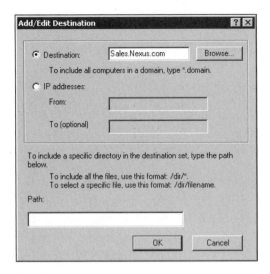

Figure 9-41

5. Click **OK** in the New Destination Set dialog box. The destination set appears in the details pane of the ISA Management console.

Project 9-3

Now that you have configured the necessary listener port and destination set on ISA Server, you must use the Web publishing wizard to make the sales Web server available to external users.

To publish the sales Web server:

1. In the ISA Management console, expand **Servers and Arrays**, expand your array name, and then expand the **Publishing** node.

2. Right-click **Web Publishing Rules**, point to **New**, and then click **Rule**. The New Web Publishing Rule Wizard appears.

3. Enter **Sales Web Server** for the rule name, and then click **Next**.

4. On the Destination Sets page, click **Specified destination set** from the **Apply this rule to** list box. In the **Name** list box, click the **Sales Web Server** destination set you just created, and then click **Next**.

5. On the Client Type page, click the **Any request** option button, if necessary, to allow access to the internal Web server for sales, and then click **Next**.

6. On the Rule Action page, click the **Redirect the request to this internal Web server** option button, and then click the **Browse** button. Choose the ISA Server machine from the list of computers in your domain, and then click **OK**.

You could redirect the request to ISA Server if the published Web server were running on ISA Server itself. If you were configuring ISA Server in an actual environment, you would typically redirect the request to an internal Web server.

7. Change the HTTP port ISA Server connects to on the internal Web server to **9000** and the SSL port to **9001**, to match the configuration of the internal Web server for sales.

8. Click **Next**, and then click **Finish** to complete the Web publishing wizard and publish the sales Web server.

Project 9-4

Due to declining sales at Nexus Sound Corporation, management is considering layoffs for 50% of the workforce. Employees have heard rumors and are becoming restless. Since many Nexus employees are technically savvy, management is concerned they may be able to monitor network traffic and capture customer credit card information being sent from the Web site. Currently, all traffic is redirected from ISA Server as unencrypted HTTP traffic, which can be interpreted easily by a network monitor application. Management wants you to secure all traffic between ISA Server and the internal Web server. You decide to redirect all incoming requests as 128-bit HTTP encryption.

To configure protocol redirection:

1. In the ISA Management console, expand the **Servers and Arrays** node, expand your array name, expand **Publishing**, and then click **Web Publishing Rules**.

2. In the details pane, right-click the **Sales Web Server** publishing rule, and then click **Properties**.

3. On the **Bridging** tab, redirect HTTP requests as **SSL requests (establish a secure channel to the site)**. In addition, ensure that ISA Server is configured to redirect SSL requests as **SSL requests**.

4. Click the **Require secure channel (SSL) for published site** check box to select it, and then click **Require 128–bit encryption**, as shown in Figure 9-42. Click **OK** to close the publishing rule Properties dialog box.

9

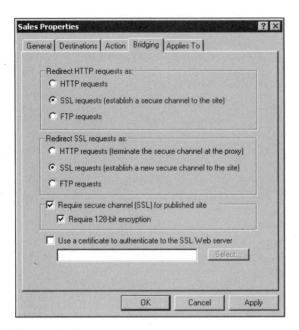

Figure 9-42

Project 9-5

Nexus management has decided that rather than cutting half its workforce, it could cut costs by allowing those employees to telecommute rather than work in the office. Before employees can work at home and retrieve company e-mail from their home Internet connections, you must publish the internal mail server, which currently runs POP and SMTP services.

To publish an internal mail server:

1. In the ISA Management console, expand the **Servers and Arrays** node, expand your array, and then expand the **Publishing** node. Right-click **Server Publishing Rules**, and then click **Secure Mail Server**.

2. When the Mail Server Security Wizard appears, click **Next** on the welcome screen.

3. In the Mail Services Selection dialog box, click the **Default Authentication** check boxes for the **Incoming SMTP** and **Incoming POP3** mail services, as shown in Figure 9-43, then click **Next**.

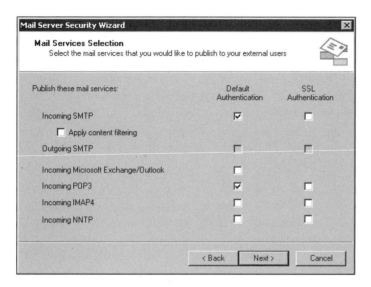

Figure 9-43

4. In the ISA Server's External IP Address dialog box, enter the external IP address of your ISA Server, and then click **Next**.

5. In the Internal Mail Server dialog box, choose to run the mail services **On the local host,** and then click **Next**. Click **Finish** to create the rules and publish the internal mail server. The POP3 and SMTP publishing rules appear in the details pane of the ISA Management console.

 You could run the mail services on the local host if the published mail server were running on the ISA Server machine itself. If you were configuring ISA Server in an actual environment, you would typically redirect the request to an internal mail server.

Project 9-6

Since Nexus Sound Corporation allows many of its users to telecommute, you must make the internal SQL server database available to external users. This allows users to enter their sales figures at the end of each day.

To configure generic server publishing to publish the SQL server:

1. In the ISA Management console, expand your array, expand the **Publishing** node, right-click **Server Publishing Rules**, point to **New**, and then click **Rule**.

2. On the Welcome page of the New Server Publishing Rule Wizard, enter **SQL Database Publishing** as the server publishing rule name, and then click **Next**.

3. On the Address Mapping page, enter the IP address of the external and internal ISA Server interfaces, and then click **Next**.

As mentioned in the previous projects, in an actual environment the SQL Server would typically be a separate internal server, not the ISA Server machine itself.

4. On the Protocol Settings page, click **Microsoft SQL Server** from the list of protocols, and then click **Next**.

5. In the Client Type dialog box, allow **Any request** to reach the published SQL server, and click **Next**. Click **Finish** to complete the wizard and successfully publish the internal SQL server.

Project 9-7

Nexus Sound Corporation allows half its workforce to telecommute, but has determined that the telecommuters' long distance calls to the office cost too much. Nexus has decided to eliminate these costs by installing an IP telephony network, allowing off-site employees to dial the office using Microsoft Netmeeting. To save confusion, management wants to allow users to dial each other by using the same phone number they used on the PSTN service. You must configure the ISA Server gatekeeper service to manage a database of all Nexus employees and track them by their current phone numbers. To improve efficiency, you also decide to assign account names to the Netmeeting clients, thus allowing users to place calls based on e-mail addresses.

To configure the H.323 Gatekeeper service:

1. Collapse all nodes in the ISA Management console, right-click the **H.323 Gatekeepers** node, and then click **Add gatekeeper**.

2. In the Add Gatekeeper dialog box, ensure that the **This computer** option button is selected, and click **OK**.

Your server appears under the H.323 Gatekeepers node, meaning that you have successfully started the gatekeeper services on your ISA Server. You must now configure a Microsoft Netmeeting client to test the configuration.

To configure Microsoft Netmeeting to interface with the ISA Server gatekeeper service:

1. Open Microsoft Netmeeting.

2. Click **Tools** on the menu bar, and then click **Options**. The Options dialog box appears.

3. Click the **Advanced Calling** button.

4. The Advanced Calling Options dialog box appears. Click **Use a gatekeeper to place calls**, and type the IP address of the internal ISA Server interface.

5. To assign the account name, click **Log on using my account name**, and enter **Remote.Client@NexusSound.com** in the text box.

6. To assign the phone number, click **Log on using my phone number**, and enter **5551212** (with no spaces or dashes), as shown in Figure 9-44. Click **OK** to close the Advanced Calling Options dialog box, and then click **OK** to close the Options dialog box.

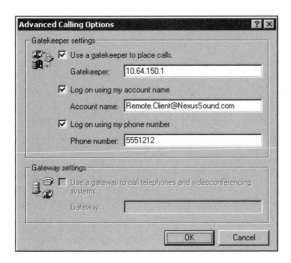

Figure 9-44

7. To verify registration, open the ISA Management console, expand the **H.323 Gatekeepers** node, expand your ISA Server, and click **Active Terminals**. The registered Netmeeting client appears in the details pane.

CASE PROJECTS

Case Project 9-1

You are employed by Logi-Secure, a company based in Texas that specializes in hosting secure e-commerce sites for other companies. Within the Texas office, the company has two internal mail servers, 50 internal Web servers, and a single internal server running a custom database application that uses TCP port 44512. Logi-Secure wants to use ISA Server to publish the internal servers to the Internet. Because confidential information is stored on the server that runs the custom database application, the company wants that server to be accessible only from a certain group of IP addresses. Because security is critical for all Web sites, Logi-Secure wants to force 128-bit encryption, authentication for anonymous clients, and ISA Server to redirect all requests in the HTTP-S protocol. Logi-Secure also wants to screen all e-mail attachments for viruses before they reach either of the internal e-mail servers. Draw a network topology diagram for the customer, and answer the following questions:

- How are you going to design this publishing scenario?

- How many external IP addresses would you recommend for Logi-Secure?

- How many ISA Servers would you suggest?

- Are there any extra requirements for the e-mail screening, or can ISA Server handle it using the SMTP application filter?

- Do you need to gather any other information from your employer?

Case Project 9-2

Robert Barr is the network administrator of Retinas Unlimited, a corporation specializing in repairing retina eye damage. Robert needs to make the internal Web server available to external users to allow them to place orders online. In addition, the Web server must access the SQL database to maintain order status. The SQL database contains confidential customer information and should not be accessed directly by any external clients. Draw a network topology diagram for the customer, and answer the following questions:

- How can Robert ensure the SQL database is not compromised?

- How many external IP addresses does he need?

- How should the LAT be structured?

- How many ISA Servers does he need?

- What additional information does Robert need to gather from his employer?

Case Project 9-3

Chris Ward is the network administrator at Sticky Inc., a manufacturing company that specializes in the creation of custom sticky notes printed with company logos. The Sticky management team wants to publish the current intranet server on the Internet to allow potential Sticky clients to place their orders without phoning a sales representative. Chris has used the Web publishing wizard to publish the necessary server to the Internet; however, external users are unable to connect to the Web site. What is the problem? Create a step-by-step outline describing the process of publishing a Web server.

Case Project 9-4

Carlos Leyva is the network administrator for HalfLife Technology, a company that stores radioactive chemicals. Recently HalfLife converted to a VoIP telephone network and is using ISA Servers at each office location as H.323 gatekeepers. Users within the offices can make calls to each other by e-mail address using the Microsoft Netmeeting application, but Internet users are unable to communicate with internal users by e-mail address. What is the most likely cause of this problem? How can you fix it?

10

CONFIGURING ISA SERVER VIRTUAL PRIVATE NETWORKING

After reading this chapter and completing the exercises, you will be able to:

♦ Determine the benefits of using VPN services

♦ Use ISA Server as a VPN server

♦ Configure VPN servers in ISA Server

♦ Configure VPN clients

As the Internet experienced explosive growth in the mid to late 1990s, the worldwide infrastructure of networks increased significantly. The hundreds of networks that built the foundation of the Internet soon expanded to thousands more networks. Overall, the Internet exists today as a web of interconnecting networks that provide a full mesh-style WAN connection between every location. Virtual private networking allows you to harness the power of the existing Internet infrastructure while minimizing WAN costs.

Because virtual private networking uses the public Internet infrastructure, security can be a primary concern for companies deciding to use this technology to connect the parts of their network. This chapter discusses the fundamentals of virtual private networking, how to configure ISA Server to support VPN connections, and how to ensure data security when transmitting data across the Internet connection.

DETERMINING THE BENEFITS OF VPNS

A virtual private network allows you to extend your internal network across a public network, such as the Internet. A VPN configuration provides many benefits. First, rather than leasing expensive lines to connect two locations, companies can use the Internet to link their networks. Second, VPNs provide access to the internal LAN for network users around the world at a low cost. Figure 10-1 shows a typical VPN configuration. This configuration is commonly called a hub-and-spoke topology, with the Internet acting as the hub, or backbone, of the network. Because this configuration only requires every user and corporate office to have Internet access, which can typically be provided by a local ISP, you can keep long distance and WAN costs to a minimum.

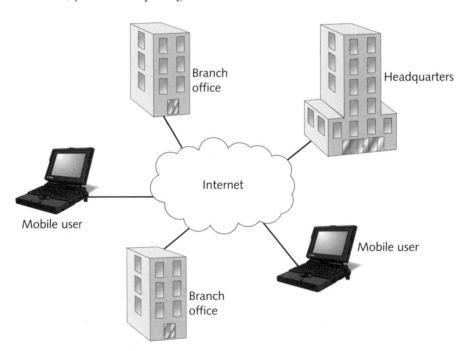

Figure 10-1   A VPN hub-and-spoke topology

On the other hand, using a VPN across the Internet exposes traffic from your internal LAN to the public. This should set off internal alarms for any network administrator considering VPN use. Because of the security risk, a VPN server should encrypt all traffic sent across the public network, and likewise, the receiving VPN server should decrypt all the data. By using strong encryption, you can secure the internal data before sending it across the WAN. This way, if a hacker is using a packet sniffer to collect data sent across the Internet, your company's network traffic appears as garbage in the packet sniffer display.

USING ISA SERVER AS A VPN SERVER

ISA Server supports VPN configurations that allow both the temporary connection of remote clients, such as mobile or home users, and the continuous connection of corporate offices worldwide. When you use ISA Server to maintain the VPN, the connections are invisible to the users. Once connected, they access network resources as if they had local access to the network.

ISA Server relies on the Routing and Remote Access Service (RRAS) in Windows 2000 to support all VPN connections. Therefore, before you can configure VPN services in ISA Server, you must install the RRAS service in Windows 2000. It is not necessary to manually configure VPN settings through the RRAS snap-in because ISA Server manages the configuration for you.

Because ISA Server uses RRAS to support the VPN connections, ISA Server can use both the Point-to-Point Tunneling Protocol (PPTP), and its successor, the Layer 2 Tunneling Protocol (L2TP). Each of these protocols **encapsulates** packets from the internal network with TCP/IP header information that is valid on the Internet. By encapsulating the internal network data, Internet routers view it as any other public Internet communication. The public TCP/IP packet header and trailer contain only the necessary information to route the packet from the VPN server to the VPN client across the Internet, as shown in Figure 10-2. Once a VPN device receives an encapsulated packet, the device strips off the public TCP/IP header and trailer and accesses the internal network data. Because it is normally encrypted, only the sending and receiving VPN servers or clients can read the internal network data contained in the encapsulated packet.

10

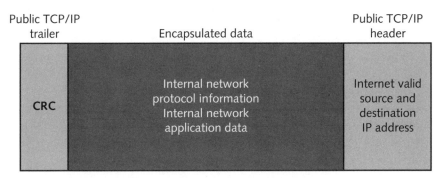

Public TCP/IP trailer	Encapsulated data	Public TCP/IP header
CRC	Internal network protocol information Internal network application data	Internet valid source and destination IP address

Figure 10-2   Architectural view of an encapsulated packet

Using protocol encapsulation to send data across the Internet allows two types of network communication at the same time (communication on the public and private network). You may commonly hear this type of communication called **tunneling**. This term refers to using the Internet as a highway or a tunnel to move data from one internal network to another. Tunneling is similar to transporting an undercover agent from one building to another. The agent leaves one building and is encapsulated in a car with dark, tinted windows. As he travels across the public road system, everyone believes him to be a standard citizen driving a car. Once he reaches the destination building, he leaves the car and delivers the top-secret information.

The type of encapsulation you use (PPTP or L2TP) depends on the protocols your clients support. The major difference between the two encapsulation protocols is the type of encryption they use. PPTP uses a proprietary PPP encryption standard, while L2TP uses the industry standard IPSec encryption. Because IPSec is a stronger and more flexible encryption method, L2TP is the preferred protocol; however, because L2TP is more recent than PPTP, not all clients may support it. Table 10-1 compares PPTP features to L2TP features.

Table 10-1   PPTP vs L2TP

PPTP	L2TP
Internetwork must be IP-based	Internetwork can be IP, frame relay, X.25, or ATM-based
No header compression	Header compression
No tunneling authentication	Tunneling authentication
Uses a proprietary encryption called Microsoft Point to Point Encryption (MPPE)	Uses the industry standard IPSec encryption

CONFIGURING VPN SERVERS WITHIN ISA SERVER

Because ISA Server builds upon the standard RRAS VPN configuration, ISA Server includes configuration options and methods that are different from the standard Windows 2000 VPN configuration. While you can configure ISA Server to allow incoming VPN requests from VPN clients, as you can in Windows 2000, you can also create a permanent VPN between two sites running ISA Server. For example, you can create a constantly connected VPN between the corporate headquarters and a branch office. This essentially combines the two separate, internal networks into a seamless virtual network.

Configuring a VPN to Accept Client Connections

In the most basic VPN configuration, you can configure ISA Server to allow incoming VPN requests from remote clients. This allows mobile and home office users to use an Internet connection to access the internal network from any location. Using ISA Server to complete this process automatically configures all necessary Windows 2000 RRAS settings.

Manually configuring the Windows 2000 RRAS VPN settings can cause unexpected results. It is best to allow ISA Server to make all necessary configuration changes.

Once you configure ISA Server to accept VPN clients, you must then configure the VPN clients to access ISA Server. This is discussed in the following section.

To configure ISA Server to accept VPN client connections:

1. In the ISA Management console, expand your array, if necessary, right-click **Network Configuration**, and then click **Allow VPN client connections**.

2. On the ISA VPN Server Wizard Welcome page, click **Next**.

3. ISA Server configures the settings for you. On the Completing the ISA VPN Server Configuration Wizard dialog box, click the **Details** button.

4. The ISA VPN Server Summary page, shown in Figure 10-3, displays all the changes ISA Server must make to allow VPN access. To return to the completion page, click the **Back** button. Click **Finish**.

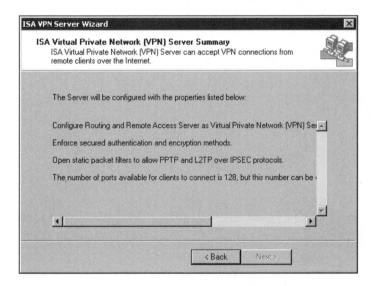

Figure 10-3   Enabling ISA Server for VPN client access

After you configure ISA Server to accept incoming VPN connections, you should also configure an address pool in the Routing and Remote Access console. Configuring an address pool allows ISA Server to assign VPN clients an IP address automatically. Otherwise, you must manually configure each of the VPN clients with a static address to use when connecting through the VPN.

To create a VPN address pool:

1. Click **Start**, point to **Programs**, point to **Administrative Tools**, and then click **Routing and Remote Access**.

2. Under the Routing and Remote Access node, right-click your server, and then click **Properties**.

3. Click the **IP** tab on the Properties dialog box, click the **Static address pool** option button, and then click **Add** to enter a new range.

4. Enter the start and end IP address of the new range you would like to assign to the VPN clients, and then click **OK**.

5. Click **OK** to close the Properties dialog box. ISA Server now dynamically allocates IP addresses from your defined range to VPN clients as they connect.

Once you allow the VPN connections and define the VPN address pool, you must give your internal users the necessary permissions to connect to the VPN. Windows 2000 considers users connecting through the VPN as dial-up users. By default, Windows 2000 denies all users dial-in privileges. Before any users can connect, you must allow dial-in access to at least one user account. If you are running a Windows 2000 domain and have installed ISA Server in an array, you can grant dial-in access from the Active Directory Users and Computers console. If you have ISA Server configured as a stand-alone server, you can grant dial-in access from the Local Users and Computers console on ISA Server.

CONFIGURING VPN CLIENTS

After configuring ISA Server to allow VPN clients to connect, you must now configure all mobile and home users to attach to ISA Server as a VPN client. This chapter covers configuring a Windows 2000 VPN client. If you are using another client OS, you may need to download a third party VPN solution to allow client VPN access. Table 10-2 describes the tunneling protocols supported by the various Windows-based operating systems.

Table 10-2   Supported Tunneling Protocols

Virtual private networking client	Supported tunneling protocols	Unsupported tunneling protocols
Windows 2000	Point-to-Point Tunneling Protocol (PPTP) and Layer 2 Tunneling Protocol (L2TP)	
Windows NT version 4.0	PPTP	L2TP
Windows 98	PPTP	L2TP
Windows 95	PPTP with the Windows Dial-Up Networking 1.3 Performance & Security Upgrade for Windows 95	L2TP

To configure a Windows 2000 VPN client:

1. Open the Windows 2000 Control Panel, and then double-click the **Network and Dial-up Connections** icon.

2. In the Network and Dial-Up Connections window, double-click **Make New Connection**.

3. On the Network Connection Wizard Welcome page, click **Next**.

4. In the Network Connection Type dialog box, shown in Figure 10-4, click the **Connect to a private network through the Internet** option button, and then click **Next**.

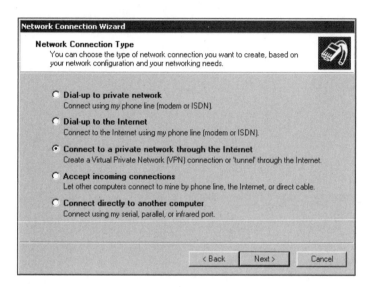

Figure 10-4   Configuring a client VPN connection

5. Enter the hostname or IP address of the VPN server for your ISA VPN Server, and then click **Next**.

6. You can now choose to make this VPN connection available for all users of this workstation by selecting the **For all users** option button, or just the current user by selecting the **Only for myself** option button. Make this selection, and click **Next**.

7. If you would like to enable Internet Connection Sharing for the VPN connection, click the **Enable Internet Connection Sharing for this connection** box to insert a check, and then click **Next**.

8. Finally, enter a logical name for this VPN connection, and then click **Finish**.

9. The newly created VPN connection appears in the Network and Dial-up Connections window, as shown in Figure 10-5. If the Connect dialog box appears, use it to connect to the VPN Server. Double-click the icon, enter your username and password for the connection, and then click **Connect**. Provided your Internet connection is available, the client should connect successfully.

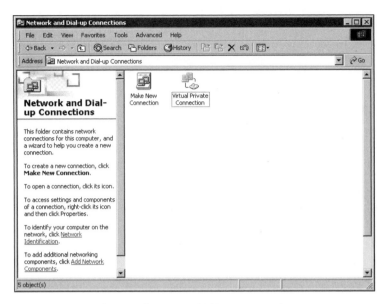

Figure 10-5 The newly created VPN connection

Configuring the Local Server VPN

The Local Server VPN wizard allows you to begin configuring permanent VPN connections from a central ISA Server to other remote ISA Servers. The Local VPN Wizard creates and configures all the dial-on-demand interfaces that are required to receive connections from remote ISA Server networks. This wizard also creates the necessary packet filters that are specific to the protocols you selected to allow VPN connections in both the inbound and outbound directions. In addition, the wizard sets the static routes to forward the traffic through the tunnel from the local network to the remote network. You typically run this wizard at the central office (most often the headquarters) or the building with the largest internal network, as all remote ISA Servers attempt to connect to the ISA Server computer configured with this wizard.

The Local VPN Wizard creates a **VPN configuration settings (.vpc) file**. The .vpc file contains all the settings for the remote VPN servers, and is required when you configure the servers. Depending on the location of the remote servers, it may be best to save it to a removable media, such as a floppy disk or a CD, or you may place it in a network location, and allow access from anywhere in the network. Security of the .vpc file is critical. Think of this file as one of the keys to the VPN. If an intruder has access to this file, the security of your entire internal network could be compromised.

Using the Local VPN Wizard only configures the local server VPN. Afterwards, you must set up the remote VPN servers. Once you complete this process, you will have two-way, tunneled communication between two internal networks, essentially allowing them to be used as one network.

To configure a local VPN server:

1. In the ISA Management console, expand your array, if necessary, right-click **Network Configuration**, and then click **Set Up Local ISA VPN Server**.

2. On the Welcome page for the Local ISA VPN Wizard, click **Next**.

3. On the ISA Virtual Private Network (VPN) Identification page, enter a short description of the local network and the remote network, as shown in Figure 10-6. Based on these descriptions, ISA Server generates a name for the VPN connection with the syntax *LocalNetwork_RemoteNetwork*. Click **Next**.

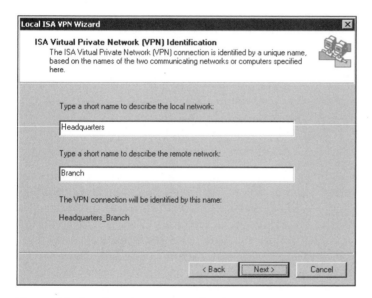

Figure 10-6   Creating a name for the VPN connection

4. On the ISA Virtual Private Network (VPN) Protocol page, choose one of the following three options, as shown in Figure 10-7:

- *Use L2TP over IPSec*—Selecting this option button forces ISA Server to only use L2TP tunneling and IPSec encryption.

- *Use PPTP*—Select this option button if either endpoint does not support IPSec. Your connection is established using PPTP. (IPSec is preferred because it is more secure than PPTP.)

- *Use L2TP over IPSec, if available. Otherwise, use PPTP*—Select this option button if you are uncertain about the features of the remote VPN server. When selected, ISA Server attempts to connect via L2TP over IPSec, but if it is not available, it resorts to PPTP.

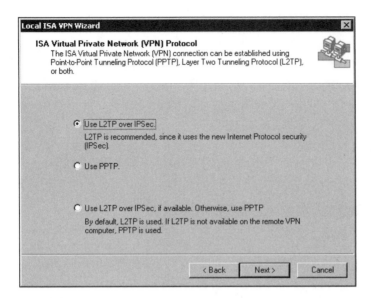

Figure 10-7   Selecting the preferred tunneling protocol

Click the appropriate option button, and then click **Next**.

5. The Two-way Communication page, shown in Figure 10-8, allows you to choose whether to let the remote VPN server initiate the VPN connection, or to let only the local VPN server initiate the connection. By default, only the local VPN server can start the communication. To allow the remote VPN server to start the VPN, click the **Both the local and remote ISA VPN computers can initiate communication** check box, enter the IP address and hostname (or domain name, if the remote VPN server is a domain controller) of the remote VPN server, and then click **Next**.

6. On the Remote Virtual Private Network (VPN) Network page, enter the range of IP addresses you want to make accessible to the VPN on the remote network, and then click **Next**. Remember, *only* the IP addresses you enter here are accessible remotely.

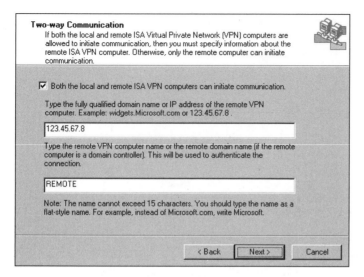

Figure 10-8   Allowing two-way VPN initiation

7. On the Local Virtual Private Network (VPN) Network page, select the external IP address the remote ISA Server should connect to, and then enter the range of IP addresses you would like to make available to the VPN on the local network, as shown in Figure 10-9. Then click **Next**.

10

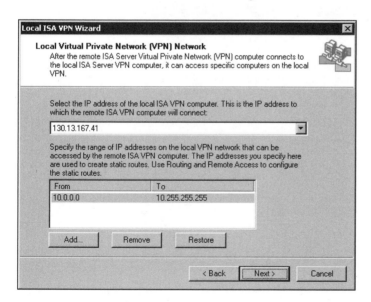

Figure 10-9   Configuring the local network ranges acessible from the VPN

8. On the ISA VPN Computer Configuration File page, enter the location and filename for the generated .vpc file, and then type a password for the file. You need both this file and the password when configuring a remote VPN server.

9. Click **Next**, and then **Finish** to complete the Local ISA VPN Wizard.

Configuring the Remote Server VPN

Once you configure the local VPN server, you must complete the process by configuring the remote VPN server. The Remote ISA Server VPN configuration wizard will use the .vpc file created on the Local ISA Server to configure the dial-on-demand interfaces, IP packet filters, and any static routes.

To configure a remote VPN server:

1. In the ISA Management console, expand your array, if necessary, right-click **Network Configuration**, and then click **Set Up Remote ISA VPN Server**.

2. On the Remote ISA VPN Wizard Welcome page, click **Next**.

3. On the ISA VPN Computer Configuration File page, shown in Figure 10-10, type the path to the .vpc file in the File name text box, or click the **Browse** button to select the file. In the Password text box, type the password generated on the local VPN server. Then click **Next**.

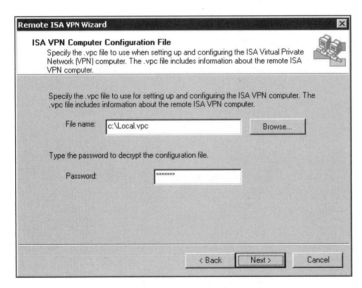

Figure 10-10   Configuring the .vpc file on the remote VPN server

4. On the Completing the ISA VPN Configuration Wizard page, click the **Details** button to review the configuration details in the .vpc file before you configure the remote VPN server. Then click **Finish**. ISA Server uses the .vpc file and password to establish a connection with the local VPN server.

When you configure ISA Server to use IPSec/L2TP, the IPSec driver is enabled on ISA Server; both the Authentication Header (AH) and the Encapsulating Security Payload (ESP) are controlled by the IPSec driver, and not by the packet filter driver on ISA Server.

CHAPTER SUMMARY

- ◘ Virtual private networks can be used to significantly reduce WAN and long distance costs.

- ◘ Because the VPN servers send internal network data across the Internet, you should use heavy encryption and security standards.

- ◘ ISA Server supports configurations allowing remote users to connect via a VPN when necessary, and also supports permanent VPN connections between corporate offices.

- ◘ ISA Server uses the Windows 2000 Routing and Remote Access service as the foundation for running the VPNs, and adds enhanced features and configurations.

- ◘ When you encapsulate internal network packets and forward them across the Internet, you are creating a tunnel through the Internet for your company's private traffic. Most Internet routers cannot tell the difference between a tunneled packet and a standard Internet packet.

- ◘ ISA Server supports tunneling using the PPTP and L2TP tunneling protocols. It is recommended to use L2TP whenever possible to enable the stronger, IPSec encryption standard.

- ◘ When configuring a local VPN server, the ISA Server generates a .vpc file. Remote VPN servers need access to this file to gain their complete VPN configuration.

10

KEY TERMS

encapsulate — The process of adding a public network header and trailer to an internal network packet, allowing it to cross the Internet in a tunnel.

tunneling — Sending private data across a public network backbone, such as the Internet, and disguising it to look like public network traffic.

virtual configuration settings .vpc file — A file generated by the Local VPN Wizard, which stores all VPN configuration and is used to configure the remote VPN server.

REVIEW QUESTIONS

1. Which of the following is a benefit of using VPNs to access the internal network from a remote location?

    a. decreased WAN costs

    b. increased security

    c. increased connection stability

    d. all of the above

2. What VPN-related concept surrounds internal network data with Internet valid TCP/IP header and trailer information?

    a. framing

    b. encapsulation

    c. tunneling

    d. none of the above

3. A hub-and-spoke topology describes what?

    a. a LAN switch topology with clients attached using Ethernet cable

    b. a WAN topology where all sites connect to a central backbone

    c. a WAN topology allowing for increased security

    d. none of the above

4. If you are implementing a VPN, what should be your primary concern?

    a. WAN bandwidth

    b. the number of configured PPTP/L2TP ports

    c. implementing the correct packet filters to allow access

    d. encrypting all transmitted traffic

5. Which of the following tunneling protocols uses proprietary encryption?

    a. SLIP

    b. PPTP

    c. L2TP

    d. T2TP

6. The Windows 2000 RRAS service must be configured before using the ISA Server VPN wizards. True or false?

7. S&L Publishing would like to design a VPN solution that allows their clients to connect to the internal network from anywhere in the world. The solution should also provide high encryption levels. What configuration would you recommend?

   a. Use the Allow VPN Client Connections selection from the ISA Server management console and use L2TP tunneling.

   b. Use the Allow VPN Client Connections selection from the ISA Server management console and use PPTP tunneling.

   c. Use the Set Up Local ISA VPN Server selection from the ISA Server management console and use L2TP tunneling.

   d. Use the Set Up Local ISA VPN Server selection from the ISA Server management console and use PPTP tunneling.

8. What is the function of a .vpc file?

   a. It is used to store all configuration settings for the local VPN server for backup purposes.

   b. It is the Virtual Private Configuration file, which contains all IP addresses for the internal network.

   c. It is the Virtual Private Configuration file, which contains the encryption configuration for the WAN.

   d. It is required when configuring the remote VPN server to connect to the local VPN server.

9. What device(s) will read the source and destination network address of the internal network in the encapsulated data?

   a. each Internet router the packet passes through

   b. only the local VPN server

   c. both the local and remote VPN servers

   d. none of the above

10. You can add additional VPN PPTP or L2TP ports through the Windows 2000 RRAS console. True or false?

11. What is contained in the VPN address pool?

   a. valid IP addresses that users connect to for VPN access

   b. the range of IP addresses used on the internal network

   c. the range of IP addresses assigned to VPN clients

   d. none of the above

12. ISA Server can accept L2TP and PPTP connections at the same time. True or false?

10

13. Which of the following is not a benefit of L2TP?

    a. header compression

    b. virus detection

    c. tunnels authentication

    d. uses IPSec encryption

14. The Windows 2000 server platforms include client VPN software for Windows 95/98/NT clients. True or false?

15. In the default configuration, which VPN server can start the VPN connection?

    a. only the local server

    b. only the remote server

    c. both the local and remote server

    d. ISA Server can only accept VPN client connections

16. What tool do you use to grant individual users permission to establish a VPN connection?

    a. the ISA Management console

    b. Active Directory Users and Computers

    c. Routing and Remote Access

    d. none of the above

17. You should configure Windows 2000 to accept VPN connections through the Routing and Remote Access console when ISA Server is installed. True or false?

18. What concept is Microsoft Point to Point Encryption (MPPE) associated with?

    a. L2TP

    b. IPSec

    c. PPTP

    d. NTFS

19. When an encapsulated packet leaves ISA Server, what source IP address is located in the header of the packet?

    a. the IP address of the internal client

    b. the IP address of the public interface of ISA Server

    c. the IP address of the destination server

    d. the IP address of the private interface of ISA Server

20. Active Directory users placed in the Power Users group are granted dial-up access. True or false?

HANDS-ON PROJECTS

To successfully configure and test a VPN server, you must have two devices: the VPN server and a VPN client. In the following labs, team up with another classmate. This allows you to set up the client and server sides of a VPN, and then test the configuration. In Projects 10-1 and 10-2, both you and your partner can configure a VPN server to accept incoming connections, and VPN clients to make the connection. In Projects 10-3 and 10-4, you must designate one ISA Server to be the local VPN server and the other ISA Server to be the remote VPN server. If you are the remote VPN server, you must allow your partner to complete the local VPN configuration before you can configure the remote VPN server.

Project 10-1

LLJ Incorporated would like to allow their 50 remote employees to connect to the company's internal network through the Internet, rather than having them directly connect to the office using a modem. Configure ISA Server to allow client connections using both PPTP and L2TP.

To configure ISA Server to receive incoming VPN client requests:

1. In the ISA Management console, expand your array, if necessary, right-click **Network Configuration**, and then click **Allow VPN client connections**.

2. On the ISA VPN Server Wizard Welcome page, click **Next**.

3. On the Completing the ISA VPN Server Configuration Wizard page, click the **Details** button to verify the configuration.

4. Click the **Back** button, and then click the **Finish** button.

5. The ISA Virtual Private Network (VPN) Wizard dialog box opens, as shown in Figure 10-11, and prompts you to start the Routing and Remote Access service.

10

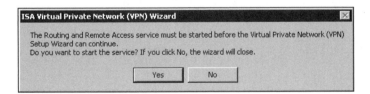

Figure 10-11

Click the **Yes** button. The RRAS service should start.

6. Minimize the ISA Management console, click **Start**, point to **Programs**, point to **Administrative Tools**, and then click **Routing and Remote Access**.

7. In the **Routing and Remote Access** node of the RRAS console, right-click your server, and then click **Properties**.

8. In the Properties dialog box, click the **IP** tab, as shown in Figure 10-12. Click the **Static address pool** option button, and then click **Add** to enter a new range.

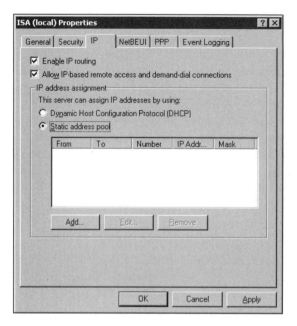

Figure 10-12

9. In the Start IP address text box, type **172.16.5.1**, and then type **75** in the Number of addresses text box. ISA Server enters the necessary end IP address for the range. Verify the IP address pool configuration, and then click **OK**. The new range appears in the Properties dialog box.

10. Click **OK** to close the Properties dialog box. ISA Server now dynamically allocates IP addresses from within the allowable range to VPN clients as they connect.

11. Close the Routing and Remote Access console, and open the Active Directory Users and Computers console from the **Administrative Tools** program group.

12. In the Active Directory Users and Computers console, expand your server name, right-click the **Users** node, point to **New**, and then click **User**.

13. In the New Object – User Wizard, configure the following, as shown in Figure 10-13, and then click **Next**.

- First Name: **Victor**

- Initials: **P**

- Last Name: **Newman**

- Full Name: **Victor P. Newman**

- User logon name: **VPN**

- User logon name (pre-Windows 2000): **VPN**

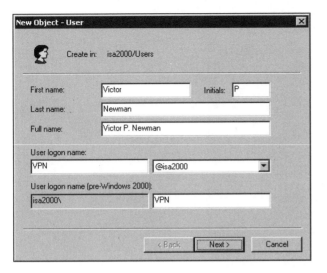

Figure 10-13

14. In both the **Password** and **Confirm Password** text boxes, type **VPN**, and then click **Next**. Click **Finish** to create the new user. The Victor P. Newman user appears in the details pane of the Users node.

15. Double-click the **Victor P. Newman** user account to open the Properties dialog box.

16. Click the **Dial-in** tab, if necessary, click the **Allow access** option button, as shown in Figure 10-14, and then click **OK**. Close the Active Directory Users and Computers console.

10

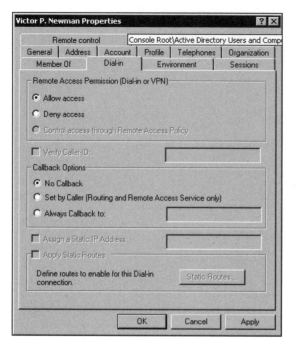

Figure 10-14

You have successfully configured ISA Server to accept incoming VPN calls from Victor P. Newman.

Project 10-2

To configure a Windows 2000 VPN Client and connect to the VPN server:

1. On the Windows 2000 desktop, right-click the **My Network Places** icon, and then click **Properties**.

2. In the Network and Dial-Up Connections window, double-click **Make New Connection**.

3. On the Network Connection Wizard Welcome page, click **Next**.

4. In the Network Connection Type dialog box, click the **Connect to a private network through the Internet** option button, and then click **Next**.

5. For the hostname or IP address of the VPN server, enter the external IP address of your partner's ISA Server, and then click **Next**.

6. Choose to make this VPN connection available **For all users**, and then click **Next**.

7. To keep Internet Connection Sharing for this connection disabled, click **Next**.

8. Enter **Intra-Classroom VPN** for the VPN connection name, and then click **Finish**.

9. The newly created Intra-Classroom VPN connection appears in the Network and Dial-up Connections window. Double-click the new VPN icon, and then click the **Properties** button below the username and password text boxes.

10. In the VPN Properties dialog box, click the **Networking** tab.

11. Click the **Type of VPN server I am calling** list box, click **Point-to-Point Tunneling Protocol** (**PPTP**), and then click **OK**.

12. In the Connect Intra-Classroom VPN dialog box, enter **VPN** as your username and password for the connection, as shown in Figure 10-15, and then click **Connect**.

Figure 10-15

13. Your server connects to your partner's VPN server. Open a command prompt and type **ipconfig**. You should see a network interface assigned to the VPN, and the IP address configuration defined by your partner.

Project 10-3

PTR Construction has a corporate office in California and a branch office in New York. Management has decided to use VPN technology to lower the cost of dedicated WAN connections between the two sites. The VPN configuration in California should be able to handle the connection if New York uses L2TP or PPTP. You must first begin by configuring the local VPN server in California.

Only perform this exercise from one of the student servers. This exercise requires a blank, formatted floppy disk.

To configure the Local Server VPN:

1. Open the ISA Management console, expand your array, if necessary, right-click **Network Configuration**, and then click **Set Up Local ISA VPN Server**.

2. On the Welcome page of the Local ISA VPN Wizard, click **Next**.

3. On the ISA Virtual Private Network (VPN) Identification page, type **California** for the description of the local network, and **New York** for the description of the remote network, and then click **Next**.

4. On the ISA Virtual Private Network (VPN) Protocol page, click the **Use L2TP over IPSec** option button, if available. Otherwise, click the **Use PPTP** option button to allow either PPTP or L2TP connections to New York. Click **Next** to continue.

5. On the Two-way Communication page, select the **Both the local and remote ISA VPN computers can initiate communication** check box. Enter the IP address of your partner's ISA Server (external interface) in the first text box, and your partner's down-level (non-DNS style) domain name in the second text box, and then click **Next**.

6. On the Remote Virtual Private Network (VPN) Network page, click the **Add** button, type the range of addresses for your partner's internal network, and then click **Next**. Remember, *only* the IP addresses you enter here are accessible remotely.

 In this lab environment, you probably have only the IP address of the internal network interface to use as a client on the internal network. For the local and remote ranges, you can either add just the IP address of the internal network interface of your ISA Server, or enter a range of IP addresses that includes the internal network interface.

7. On the Local Virtual Private Network (VPN) Network page, select the external IP address of your ISA Server, and enter the range of IP addresses you would like to make available to the VPN on the local network, as shown in Figure 10-16. Then click **Next**.

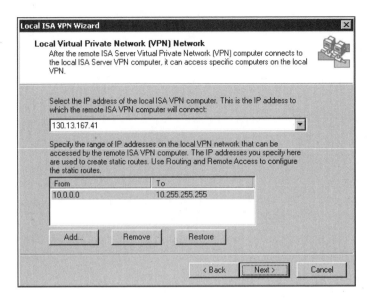

Figure 10-16

 Notice that ISA Server populates the addresses accessible on the local network with the entries from the LAT.

8. On the ISA VPN Computer Configuration File page, enter **A:\RemoteCFG** for the filename of the generated .vpc file (ISA Server adds the .vpc file extension for you), and then type **VPN** in the Password and Confirm password text boxes, as shown in Figure 10-17. Insert the blank floppy disk in the floppy disk drive, and then click **Next**. ISA Server copies the .vpc file to the disk.

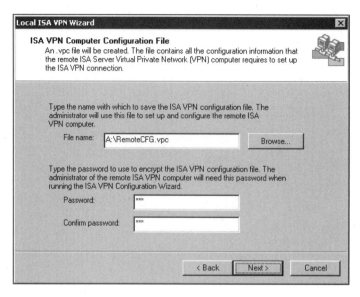

Figure 10-17

9. Click **Finish** to complete the Local ISA VPN Wizard.

Project 10-4

Only perform these steps on the server not used in the prior exercise. You need the floppy disk containing the .vpc file from Project 10-3.

To configure the Remote Server VPN:

1. Insert the floppy disk from Project 10-3 into your floppy disk drive.

2. In the ISA Management console, expand your array, right-click **Network Configuration**, and then click **Set Up Remote ISA VPN Server**.

3. On the Welcome page of the Remote ISA VPN Wizard, click **Next**.

4. On the ISA VPN Computer Configuration File page, type **A:\RemoteCFG.vpc** in the File name text box, type **VPN** in the Password text box, and then click **Next**.

5. On the Completing the ISA VPN Configuration Wizard page, click the **Details** button.

6. The configuration displayed in the Details window should mirror the local VPN server configuration. Click the **Back** and **Finish** buttons to complete the Remote VPN wizard.

7. The VPN between the two ISA Servers should activate. Open a command prompt and use the **ping** command, followed by the internal IP address of your partner's ISA Server, to test the VPN connection.

It can take between 30 seconds to five minutes for the VPN to activate.

Project 10-5

Using the Web site *http://www.ssh.com/tech/crypto/* as a reference, type a one to two page report on the mechanics of cryptography. Relate this to applications with VPNs and ISA Server.

Project 10-6

Using the Web as a resource, type a one page report on two or three different VPN clients available for the Windows 95, 98, or NT operating systems. Outline the advantages, disadvantages, and the protocols supported by each client type.

CASE PROJECTS

Case Project 10-1

Peabody Distributors is a company that rents warehouse space to other vendors and handles product fulfillment for their customers. Peabody is based in Massachusetts, but also has a large site in Florida. They are currently using ISA Server at both locations to provide caching and firewall services. To cut costs, they would like to use virtual private networking rather than leased lines between the Massachusetts and Florida sites. This solution should also allow Peabody's customers to establish VPN client connections to the internal network so they can verify product counts and access the internal Peabody intranet server. Management expects no more than 70 client connections at any one time. Create a network diagram of the Peabody Distributors current and proposed WAN solutions. How should Peabody Distributors configure ISA Server at both locations? Do both locations need to allow client VPN access? How many addresses should be configured in the VPN address pool? What other information do you need to gather from the Peabody Distribution management?

Case Project 10-2

Joshua Char is a network administrator at a large company named Brace Technology. Brace Tech. is deploying a VPN solution using Microsoft ISA Server to manage incoming connections. They have over 200 remote employees, some of which use Windows 98 while others use Windows 2000 Professional. ISA Server is configured to support the L2TP protocol and to accept incoming VPN client connections in the ISA Management console. All users are granted dial-in privileges in the Active Directory Users and Computers. Upon initial deployment, Joshua discovers that only half of the remote clients are able to connect. What is the most likely cause of the problem?

10

Case Project 10-3

Benjamin Johnson is the network administrator at Plactronics Inc., a software distribution company. He has just finished configuring ISA Server to accept incoming connections from VPN clients using the PPTP and L2TP protocols. Most remote employees are using Windows 2000 as their primary operating system, but others are using Windows NT 4.0 Workstation at their home offices. When users connect to the VPN, they are given the message "Access Denied." What is the most likely cause of the problem?

Case Project 10-4

Megan Nedbolk is the network administrator of Tiagro, a large pharmaceutical company. Since Tiagro has many vendors worldwide, they would like to provide VPN access to outside clients. Megan configures ISA Server as a Local VPN server accepting connections using both the PPTP and L2TP protocols. She then grants the necessary user accounts dial-in privileges. Most vendors are using Windows 98 and NT, but a few have Windows 2000. When clients attempt to connect to the server, they receive an error message stating the connection could not be established. What is the most likely cause of the problem?

11

ISA SERVER CLIENT CONFIGURATION

After reading this chapter and completing the exercises, you will be able to:

♦ Understand the advantages and disadvantages of the three types of ISA Server clients

♦ Configure a SecureNAT client

♦ Configure a Web Proxy client

♦ Install and configure a Firewall client

After you install and configure ISA Server, you can begin to configure its internal clients. The client configuration you choose may require little or no work, or you may need to install client software on every PC in the enterprise network. Although Windows 2000 can help you configure ISA Server clients, the process may still be complex. To avoid problems and unnecessary complications, you must plan the configuration before you install ISA Server.

Each client configuration offers advantages and disadvantages, so you must consider the requirements of your organization before configuring ISA Server clients. Overall, ISA Server supports three different client types: SecureNAT, Firewall, and Web Proxy. This chapter discusses each configuration and how to install Firewall clients.

EXAMINING AND CONFIGURING ISA SERVER CLIENTS

Before choosing an ISA Server client type, you must first weigh the advantages and disadvantages of each configuration. A single client configuration for all computers typically does not work, because most modern networks run in a heterogeneous environment. Microsoft Windows machines often share network bandwidth with Macintosh, mainframe, and UNIX-based devices. Microsoft Proxy Server 2.0 could only support non-Windows clients through a Web Proxy service, so users could only interact with the Proxy Server through their Web browsers. Any other Internet-based applications, such as e-mail, Telnet, and even the Ping utility, would not work. ISA Server addresses these shortcomings with expanded client support.

You can configure a client as more than one type of client. This approach is often required to provide full application support for internal clients. For example, you can configure a client as a firewall client, which allows you to place restrictions based on username or group membership, but only allows TCP- and UDP-based protocol requests. You can also configure the same client to be a SecureNAT client, which supports the rest of the TCP/IP protocol suite. In addition, you can configure the same client to be a Web proxy client, which forwards requests directly from the client's Web browser to the Web Proxy service on ISA Server, allowing full use of CARP and server redundancy.

Ultimately, you should configure the client platforms that best suit your network environment. The following sections list the advantages, disadvantages, and capabilities of each client type. Consult these sections when you are determining which types of platforms to use.

CONFIGURING SECURENAT CLIENTS

Network address translation allows you to use IP addresses from the private addressing spaces on your internal network and still access the Internet through IP address translation, as shown in Figure 11-1. Because NAT is an RFC-based standard, it is platform independent. When Windows 2000 runs NAT services, any TCP/IP-based client can connect to the Internet through the Windows 2000 server. SecureNAT uses the Windows 2000 network address translation service, but also incorporates ISA Server policies into incoming and outgoing requests.

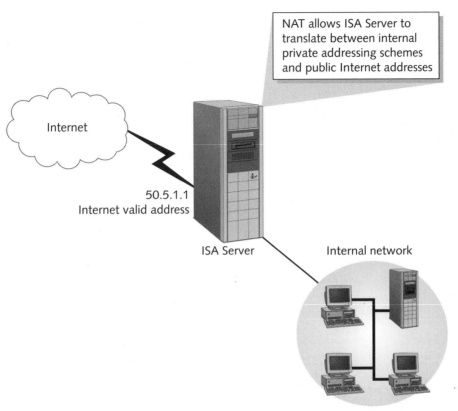

NAT allows ISA Server to translate between internal private addressing schemes and public Internet addresses

Internet

50.5.1.1
Internet valid address

ISA Server

Internal network

172.16.X.Y private addressing space

Figure 11-1   Implementing NAT services

As network requests pass through ISA Server, it translates the destination address from private to public (or vice versa for requests for internal resources) through NAT services. After ISA Server translates the address, it applies any rules that you configure to the incoming request. This allows you to filter requests from any TCP/IP-based device. Because SecureNAT clients do not authenticate to ISA Server, all applied rules can only filter requests based on the IP address or hostname of the source and destination devices. User and group restrictions do not apply to SecureNAT clients. For example, a user may log on to a SecureNAT client with the IP address 10.25.1.10 and a username of SusanF, then access the Web site *www.course.com*. When applying rules to this SecureNAT client, you could allow or deny the request based on the source IP address or the Web site, but not on the username SusanF.

Configuring SecureNAT clients requires no client installation and can even be done through DHCP services. Simply direct the default gateway of the client to ISA Server to complete the client configuration. The client directs all requests for resources not located on the internal network to ISA Server, which then performs

IP address translation, applies any applicable ISA Server rules, and forwards the request to the correct external network. SecureNAT clients can use any subprotocol of the TCP/IP protocol suite (such as TCP, UDP, or ICMP) to access the Internet, thus allowing the use of nearly any application by a client device to do so. However, some applications may have difficulty operating through a NAT server.

The following list summarizes the advantages of using SecureNAT clients.

- SecureNAT clients provide a platform-independent solution.
- No installation of client software is required.
- Configuration is extremely easy through DHCP.
- SecureNAT clients support all TCP/IP subprotocols.

The following list summarizes the disadvantages of using SecureNAT clients.

- You are unable to restrict network access based on user or group membership.
- Some network applications may have difficulty operating through a NAT server.

Configuring Web Proxy Clients

Some companies provide Internet access solely to allow employees access to the World Wide Web using a Web browser. The design of Web proxy clients allows you to redirect Internet requests originating from the Web browser to ISA Server, while redirecting all other external network traffic to another default gateway.

For example, you might have a network that has three boundary routers, as shown in Figure 11-2. The first router is ISA Server, which connects the Arizona network to the Internet. The second and third routers connect the Arizona and Michigan networks through a dedicated connection. You might want the Arizona internal clients to use the IP address of the second router as the default gateway, but still access the Internet through the ISA Server machine when using their Web browsers. By configuring the Arizona internal clients as Web proxy clients, only the network requests originating from their Web browsers are received by ISA Server. The clients forward all other network requests to the second router connecting to Michigan.

You can configure any Web browser that is HTTP 1.1 compliant as a Web proxy client. Because HTTP 1.1 is an industry standard, any modern Web browser on any operating system meets this requirement. Thus, Web Proxy clients are completely platform independent.

The difficulty with Web proxy clients is that redirection only applies to the Web browser itself. Therefore, Web proxy clients only support the HTTP, HTTPS, and FTP protocols. Other applications cannot access the Internet through ISA Server, except for a few media streaming applications, such as RealAudio and the Windows Media Player, both of which have added support for the Web Proxy service. You must manually configure these applications on each machine.

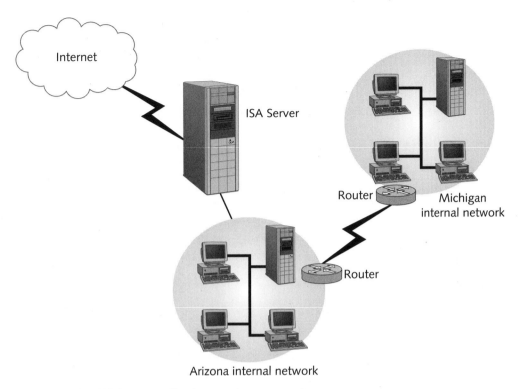

Figure 11-2   Web proxy client scenario

Because Web proxy clients forward requests directly to the Web Proxy service on ISA Server, ISA Server can cache all client requests. This allows Web proxy clients to gain all the speed benefits the caching service offers. ISA Server applies all configured rules and filters to Web proxy client requests, like any other request. Because the Web proxy client does not interface directly with Windows, no authentication information passes from the client to ISA Server. Therefore, you must configure rules and filters for Web proxy clients to allow or deny traffic based on IP address or port numbers rather than user or group membership.

The following list summarizes the advantages of using Web proxy clients.

- You can redirect requests from a single application to ISA Server, while all other requests are directed to the default gateway.

- Web browsers can take advantage of ISA Server caching features without becoming a full ISA Server client.

- Because any HTTP 1.1-compliant Web browser supports proxy configuration, Web proxy clients are platform independent.

The following list summarizes the disadvantages of using Web proxy clients.

- Administrative costs are high because each Web proxy application must be manually configured.

- Web proxy clients support only the HTTP, HTTPS, and FTP protocols.

- You cannot restrict clients based on user or group membership.

Basic Configuration of a Web Proxy Client

The most basic Web proxy client configuration requires you to manually configure each client Web browser to access the hostname or IP address assigned to the ISA Server internal network card. Because each browser platform has a different method of configuring proxy server support, you need to find the method that fits the platform your clients use. Internet Explorer is one of the most popular Web browser platforms, so we use it in the following example of how to configure Web proxy client support.

To manually configure a Web proxy client using Internet Explorer:

1. Open Internet Explorer.

2. Click **Tools** on the menu bar, and then click **Internet Options**.

3. In the Internet Options dialog box, click the **Connections** tab, and then click the **LAN Settings** button.

4. In the Local Area Network (LAN) Settings dialog box, click the **Use a proxy server** check box, enter the hostname or IP address of the ISA Server's internal network interface, and then enter the Web Proxy service port number, as shown in Figure 11-3. This redirects any HTTP, HTTPS, or FTP request from the Web browser to ISA Server, even if the address is included on the local subnet. If you want to keep Internet Explorer from forwarding requests for clients on the internal network to ISA Server, click the **Bypass proxy server for local addresses** check box.

5. After entering the necessary information, click **OK** in the LAN Settings and Internet Options dialog boxes. Internet Explorer should now forward all requests through ISA Server's Web Proxy service.

 The default port number for the Web Proxy service on ISA Server is 8080.

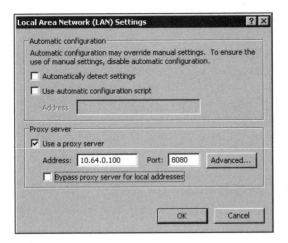

Figure 11-3   Configuring Internet Explorer as a Web proxy client

You can configure ISA Server itself as a Web proxy client by configuring the Web browser to access the IP address of the internal network interface. Do not configure it to access the external IP address or hostname of ISA Server.

Using an Automatic Configuration Script for a Web Proxy Client   11

You do not need to install additional software to configure a Web proxy client, but you do need to configure each Web browser manually. A manual configuration creates a static entry on the client that points the Web browser to an individual ISA Server, which introduces three potential problems:

- If a single, statically configured ISA Server fails, the Web proxy clients configured to access that server lose Internet service.

- There is no easy way to provide for load balancing. For example, if you have two ISA Servers, you must manually configure half the Web proxy clients to access the first server, and half to access the second server. Because there is no easy way to find which clients are assigned to which servers, you would have to keep a spreadsheet of client assignments that required constant updating.

- If the configuration of ISA Server changes, you must manually update every Web proxy client to reflect this change. For example, you might change the internal port ISA Server uses to receive incoming Web proxy requests from 8080 to 7070 for security reasons. However, you would have to manually configure each Web proxy client on the internal network to reflect the new port assignment.

Using an automatic configuration script can address each of these concerns, and because the script is automatically built and updated by ISA Server, very little administrative work is needed. Using an automatic configuration script allows Web proxy clients to take advantage of CARP, or Cache Array Routing Protocol, which distributes the load between all ISA Servers in the array. An automatic configuration script also addresses the single point of failure by allowing you to configure a backup route to use if the original ISA Server becomes unavailable. Finally, if any major configuration changes occur, such as to the internal port number ISA Server uses to accept client requests or backup routes to other ISA Servers, the configuration script is updated. The next time the client attempts to access network resources through ISA Server, the updated script is sent to the client.

Configuring a Web proxy client to use an automatic configuration script occurs in two phases. First, you configure ISA Server with the correct settings, which allows ISA Server to create a script with the desired configuration before a client downloads it. Next, you configure the clients to access the script.

 Every ISA Server you install generates a default automatic configuration script. Configuring Web proxy clients to access this script allows them to connect to the Internet through the ISA Server machine where the script resides. However, the settings may not be optimal.

To set up the automatic configuration script on ISA Server:

1. In the ISA Management console, expand the **Servers and Arrays** node and your array name, if necessary.

2. Click the **Client Configuration** node. In the results pane, double-click **Web Browser**.

3. In the Web Browser Properties dialog box, shown in Figure 11-4, enter the **DNS name** of the ISA Server machine you want the Web proxy client to access initially.

   Note that you cannot use this dialog box to modify the port number on which ISA Server receives incoming requests; you configure this listener port number from the Outbound Listening page of the Server Properties dialog box. If you change the port number of the outbound listener, it is reflected here as well. Below the port number is the Automatic configuration section, which allows the Web proxy client to configure itself with an automatic script and no administrative intervention. See the following section for details.

4. Click the **Direct Access** tab, as shown in Figure 11-5.

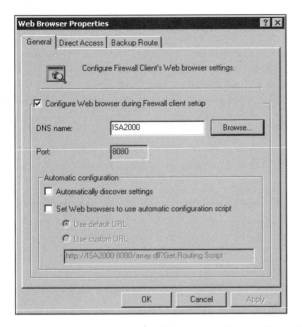

Figure 11-4   Setting up the automatic configuration script

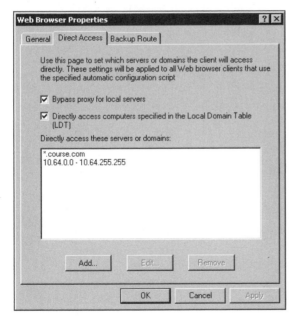

Figure 11-5   Configuring the LAT for Web proxy clients

11

Because all requests from a Web proxy client are forwarded directly from the Web browser to the ISA Server Web Proxy service, the client does not check the LAT to find if the address or domain name resides on the local network segment. The Direct Access page allows you to build a LAT for Web proxy clients and keep requests for resources on the local network from forwarding to ISA Server. To do so, click the **Bypass proxy for local servers** check box, click the **Add** button, and then enter the local IP address ranges and domain names. If you have already added all the local domains to the Local Domain Table in the ISA Management console, you can avoid entering redundant information here by clicking the **Directly access computers specified in the Local Domain Table (LDT)** check box.

5. Click the **Backup Route** tab, shown in Figure 11-6, and configure fault tolerance for the Web proxy clients. Click the **If ISA Server is unavailable, use this backup route to connect to the Internet** check box.

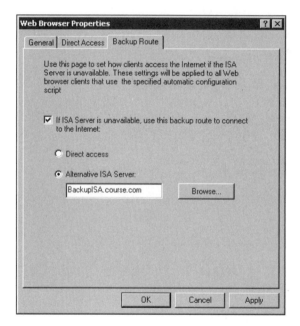

Figure 11-6   Configuring Web proxy clients for ISA Server fault tolerance

6. Choose a redundancy option according to the following descriptions:
   - Click the **Direct access** option button if the internal Web proxy clients have a redundant connection themselves, such as a modem connection. This allows the Web browser to access the local modem rather than failing once it finds ISA Server is unavailable.
   - Clicking the **Alternative ISA Server** option button allows you to configure a backup ISA Server if the primary one is unreachable.

7. When you finish, click **OK**.

After you configure the automatic configuration script on the server side, you can begin configuring each Web proxy client to access the script. Again, these steps differ on each Web browser platform. The following steps focus on a common platform, Internet Explorer.

To enable a Web proxy client running Internet Explorer to use an automatic configuration script:

1. Open Internet Explorer.

2. Click **Tools** on the menu bar, and then click **Internet Options**.

3. In the Internet Options dialog box, click the **Connections** tab, and then click the **LAN Settings** button.

4. In the Local Area Network (LAN) Settings dialog box, click the **Use automatic configuration script** check box, and then enter the **Address** of the automatic configuration script, as shown in Figure 11-7. The default location of this script is *server_name:port/array.dll?Get.Routing.Script*, where *server_name* is the hostname of the ISA Server machine the client should access, and *port* is the internal listening port number for Web requests. The default port number is 8080.

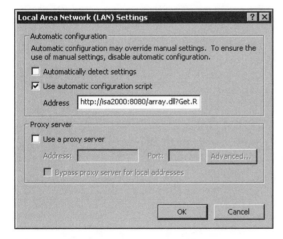

Figure 11-7   Configuring the Web proxy client for an automatic configuration script

5. After you enter the automatic script configuration, click **OK**. The next time you attempt to access a Web page from the client, it downloads the automatic configuration script from the specified ISA Server and applies the configuration specified on the server.

Using Automatic Discovery for a Web Proxy Client

While using an automatic configuration script solves many issues facing the static Web proxy client configuration, it still causes a heavy administrative load because you must manually configure each internal network client to access the script. Given the size of today's networks, this daunting task could take days, weeks, or even months to complete. In addition, you must reconfigure any computer that you move to a new area of the network and connect to a different ISA Server.

To address this issue, Microsoft has introduced automatic discovery features in recent versions of Internet Explorer (version 5.0 and later). Automatic discovery allows Internet Explorer to dynamically locate the ISA Server machine anywhere on the network rather than requiring manual configuration. This feature allows you to move any client to any area of the network without the need for reconfiguration. When the Web browser boots up, it queries either a DHCP or DNS server to find the ISA Server machine it should use. The answer is returned through a **Web Proxy Auto Discovery (WPAD)** entry in either database. Once the Web browser receives information for the preferred server, it can access the Internet through the configured ISA Server machine without your intervention.

Before you enable automatic discovery, you must configure a WPAD entry on the DNS and DHCP server, and configure ISA Server to support automatic discovery. While the Web proxy client queries only one of the servers for the WPAD information, you should configure both servers with a WPAD entry; some client types attempt to access DNS and others use DHCP. Table 11-1 lists the various Windows platforms and the types of servers they attempt to query.

Table 11-1   Server Types Queried for WPAD Information

DNS Server	DHCP Server
Windows XP	Windows XP
Windows 2000	Windows 2000
Windows NT 4.0	Windows 98
Windows 98	Windows ME
Windows ME	
Windows 95*	
* Automatic discovery only works if DNS is statically configured for Windows 95 clients.	

To configure the DNS server and DHCP server to support automatic discovery for Web Proxy clients:

1. On the DNS server in your domain, click **Start**, point to **Programs**, point to **Administrative Tools**, and then click **DNS**.

2. In the DNS console, expand your server and the **Forward Lookup Zones**, if necessary. Right-click your zone name, and then click **New Alias** to create a CNAME record.

3. In the New Resource Record dialog box, enter **WPAD** in the Alias name text box. In the Fully qualified name for target host text box, enter the FQDN of the ISA Server machine or array, as shown in Figure 11-8.

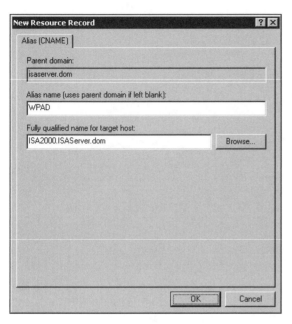

Figure 11-8   Configuring the WPAD entry on the DNS server

4. Click **OK** to save the record. The DNS server is now configured to support automatic discovery. Close the DNS window.

5. On the DHCP server, click **Start**, point to **Programs**, point to **Administrative Tools**, and then click **DHCP**.

6. Right-click your DHCP server, and then click **Set Predefined Options**.

7. In the Predefined Options and Values dialog box, click the **Add** button.

8. In the Option Type dialog box, enter **WPAD** in the Name text box, click the **Data type** list arrow, click **String**, and then enter **252** in the Code text box. Your configuration should look like Figure 11-9. After entering the necessary values, click **OK** to return to the Predefined Options and Values dialog box.

9. Configure the DHCP WPAD entry to point to the ISA Server machine or array name. If you configured the DNS server with the WPAD entry, enter **http://WPAD/wpad.dat** in the String text box, as shown in Figure 11-10. Otherwise, enter **http://*server_name*/wpad.dat**, where *server_name* is the name of the ISA Server machine.

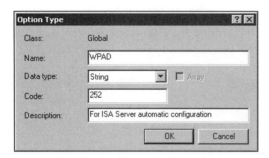

Figure 11-9   Configuring the WPAD entry on the DHCP server

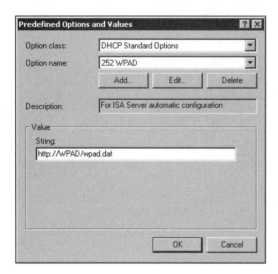

Figure 11-10   Modifying the DHCP WPAD entry

10. After configuring the DHCP WPAD option, click **OK**.

 In a classroom environment, you probably won't be able to perform the following step because you have not configured a scope. Read the rest of the procedure for reference.

11. In the original DHCP console, expand the DHCP server, then expand the scope that provides IP addresses to the internal network. Right-click the **Scope Options** folder, and then click **Configure Options**. In the Scope Options dialog box, scroll down the **Available Options** list until you reach option **252 WPAD**. Click its check box, as shown in Figure 11-11, and then click **OK**. This allows the DHCP scope that provides internal addresses to pass the WPAD parameter to clients requesting IP addresses. If multiple IP address scopes provide addresses to the internal network, repeat this step for all internal scopes.

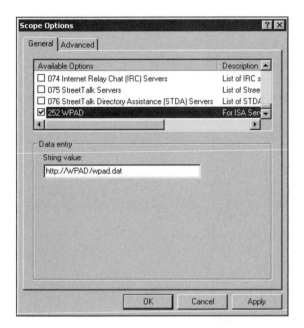

Figure 11-11   Configuring the IP address scope to allocate the WPAD option

12. After you add the WPAD option to all internal scopes, close the DHCP console. The DHCP server and DNS server are now configured to support automatic client discovery.

Once the Web proxy clients obtain the address of ISA Server from the DHCP or DNS server, they attempt to connect to ISA Server and download their configuration. After you configure DNS and DHCP to support automatic discovery, you must publish the automatic discovery information on ISA Server.

To publish automatic client discovery information on ISA Server:

1. In the ISA Management console, expand the **Servers and Arrays** node, if necessary. Right-click your array or server, and then click **Properties**.

2. In the Properties dialog box, click the **Auto Discovery** tab, shown in Figure 11-12.

3. To make the automatic discovery information available to the clients, click the **Publish automatic discovery information** check box, and then click **OK**. You will need to restart ISA Server services before these changes take effect.

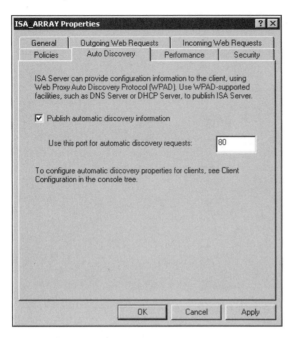

Figure 11-12   Configuring ISA Server to support client automatic discovery

INSTALLING AND CONFIGURING FIREWALL CLIENTS

The easiest way to place restrictions in ISA Server is by Active Directory users and groups. Most administrators configure nearly all Windows 2000 policies, NTFS restrictions, and applications based on the ADS database. You should continue the configuration trend with ISA Server, if possible. Installing the Firewall client on the internal computers allows you to place restrictions in ISA Server based on user or group membership. This is much more efficient than placing restrictions based on the client IP address, especially considering that a machine's internal IP address can change if you use DHCP services to assign it.

You can install the Firewall client on the Windows 2000 Professional or Server platforms, and on Windows 95 OSR2, Windows 98, Windows NT 4.0 Workstation and Server, and Windows Millennium Edition. The Firewall client is not supported on non–Windows platforms, which is its primary disadvantage. In heterogeneous internal client environments, most network administrators do not run the Firewall client because they cannot apply policies that encompass all machines. For example, you might run a network consisting of 500 Windows 2000 Professional clients and 500 Linux-based clients. While you could install the Firewall client on the Windows 2000 machines and create restrictions based on Active Directory users and groups, you would still need to create restrictions based on IP address and port numbers for the Linux-based clients. Rather than create two separate sets of restrictions, most administrators would rather apply IP address and port-based restrictions to all internal clients.

To support Windows 95 OSR1 and Windows 3.1 platforms, you can install the Proxy Server 2.0 client and configure it to access ISA Server.

In addition, the firewall client only supports the TCP and UDP protocols, although it does offer a solution for using others. If you use a protocol other than TCP or UDP (such as SMTP, NNTP, or ICMP), the client forwards the request to ISA Server as a SecureNAT client, assuming that the client's default gateway is configured as the internal network interface of the ISA Server machine. While you lose the ability to place restrictions based on Active Directory users or groups when using a protocol other than TCP or UDP, you do not lose client functionality.

The following list summarizes the advantages of using firewall clients.

- Firewall clients allow you to create rules and restrictions based on username or group membership.
- Firewall clients support all TCP- and UDP-based applications.

The following list summarizes the disadvantages of using firewall clients.

- Software installation is required on all client computers.
- You cannot install the firewall client on versions of Windows before Windows 95 or on non–Windows platforms.

Because the firewall client requires a client installation, you have several options for installation:

- Installing from a shared folder location
- Installing from a Web location
- Installing through a Windows 2000 group policy

Each installation option is explained in the following sections. The default installation of the firewall client creates a folder called C:\Program Files\Microsoft Firewall Client on the client computer. This folder contains key files and application logs that you should be aware of for configuration and troubleshooting purposes. They are as follows:

- *Chkwsp32.exe*—This MS-DOS application can check the status of the connection between the firewall client and ISA Server, along with the version number of the firewall client in use. Figure 11-13 shows the result of using the Chkwsp –f switch, which displays all diagnostic information for the client. You can display a list of switches by typing Chkwsp /? at a command prompt.

11

```
C:\WINNT\System32\cmd.exe                                              _ 8 X
C:\Program Files\Microsoft Firewall Client>chkwsp32 -f                       ▲

*****************************************************************
****          Firewall client Diagnostic Information          ****
*****************************************************************

WAIT...

CONFIGURATION:
        Firewall client - Configuration Location: C:\Documents and Settings\All
Users\Application Data\Microsoft\Firewall Client\
        Proxy Name (IP Addr):
                ISA2000
        WINSOCK 2.0: Firewall client is a Layered Service Provider
        IP:     Installed

WAIT...

32-bit Firewall client:
        Winsock Name: C:\WINNI\System32\wsock32.dll
        Version: 5.0.2195.1207
        Description: Windows Socket 32-Bit DLL
        Version Type: FREE
        Layered Service Provider version: 3.0.1200.50
        Client version of control protocol: 11

ISA SERVER:
        Testing against server: 10.64.150.1 ( isa2000.isaserver.dom )
        Version: 3.0.1200.0
        Version Type: FREE
        Server version of control protocol: 11
        Windows version: 5.0
        Windows build number: 2195

_____

Client control protocol version MATCHES the server control protocol

C:\Program Files\Microsoft Firewall Client>                                ▼
```

Figure 11-13   Using Chkwsp.exe to troubleshoot the firewall client

- *Firewallc.txt*—This text file contains a log of the firewall client installation. If you have installation problems with the firewall client, you can use this log file for troubleshooting purposes.

- *Mpcver.txt*—This short text file contains the version of the installed firewall client.

- *Mspclnt.ini*—This file stores all the configuration settings for the firewall client. The client initially downloads these settings after the installation completes, then updates them each time the computer is restarted, or every six hours.

- *Msplat.txt*—This is a copy of the ISA Server's LAT, which the client stores locally. This file is updated whenever the LAT is modified on ISA Server.

- *Setupbin*—This folder contains all the setup files used to install the firewall client. If you need to reinstall or uninstall the firewall client, double-click the Setup_A.exe utility in this folder.

Do not install the firewall client on ISA Server itself. This can cause unpredictable results and may cause ISA Server to stop working.

Installing a Firewall Client from a Shared Folder

When you install ISA Server using the default settings, the Setup program creates a folder named C:\Program Files\Microsoft ISA Server\Clients, and copies the firewall client installation files to that folder. The Setup program shares the folder using the share name MSPClnt. You can connect to this shared folder on the ISA Server machine from any client on the internal network and install the firewall client software.

To install the firewall software from the shared folder:

1. On the Windows 2000 taskbar, click **Start**, and then click **Run**.

2. In the Run dialog box, type ***ISAServer*\\MSPClnt**, where *ISAServer* is the name of the ISA Server machine.

3. When the list of files in the shared folder appears, double-click **Setup.exe**. Follow the on-screen instructions to install the firewall client.

Installing a Firewall Client from a Web Location

If you are running an intranet server, it may be easiest to install the firewall client through the Web server. You might remember that the installation of Microsoft Proxy Server 2.0 automatically modified the configuration of Internet Information Services (IIS) on the local server, to include a virtual folder that contained the proxy client installation files. Because many administrators use the local Web server as a production server, they delete the MSPClnt virtual folder created by Proxy Server 2.0 immediately after installation. Therefore, Microsoft decided to disallow modifying the configuration of IIS during the installation of ISA Server. Instead, Microsoft now includes the required files in case you want to manually configure IIS to distribute the firewall client.

 The following steps assume you are using the default installation path for ISA Server and IIS. If you modified the installation path for either service, use the modified path(s) during the appropriate steps.

To allow Microsoft IIS to distribute the ISA Server firewall client:

1. Double-click the **My Computer** icon on the desktop and navigate to the C:\Program Files\Microsoft ISA Server\CLIENTS\WEBINST folder.

2. Copy the **Default.htm** and **Setup.bat** files to the folder that stores the Web pages for the local IIS server. If you use the default IIS installation, this folder is C:\inetpub\wwwroot. If necessary, click **Yes** to replace the existing Default.htm file.

3. From a client machine, open a Web browser, connect to the internal Web server, and display the Default.htm page. The Web page matches the one displayed in Figure 11-14.

Figure 11-14   Installing the firewall client through a Web page

4. If you are using Internet Explorer on the client machine, click the **Firewall Client software** link, click the **Run this program from its current location** option button in the File Download window, and then click **OK**. The Firewall client installation begins.

5. If you are using Netscape, save the Setup.bat file to the local hard drive, and then run the file from there.

 The Setup.bat file contains nothing more than a URL that points to the shared folder location of the firewall client software. If you want to store the Firewall client somewhere other than the ISA Server machine, just edit the Setup.bat file and redirect the URL to the new location.

Installing a Firewall Client through a Windows 2000 Group Policy

One of the most convenient ways to install the firewall client software is through the Windows 2000 group policy. This allows you to use the software on client machines on a scheduled basis, as they boot up, or once a user logs on. When you install ISA Server, it also installs the Firewall Client Windows Installer package MS_FWC.msi in the same folder as the client software. Use a Windows 2000 group policy to deploy the application on client PCs through your preferred method.

 For more information on installing software through Windows 2000 group policies, go to *support.microsoft.com/support/kb/articles/Q302/4/30.ASP.*

Using Automatic Configuration for the Firewall Client

While you can automate the installation of the firewall client by using Windows 2000 group policies, you may still find yourself configuring the client manually after the installation. Fortunately, the firewall client uses the same automatic configuration methods as the Web proxy client. As with Web proxy clients, you must define WPAD entries on the DNS and DHCP servers, and configure ISA Server to publish the automatic configuration information using the process described in the prior sections. In addition, you should configure settings specific to the firewall client in the ISA Management console. These settings determine to which ISA Server machine or ISA Server array the firewall client should connect, and the applications supported on the firewall client.

To set the firewall client configuration parameters on ISA Server:

1. In the ISA Management console, expand the **Servers and Arrays** node and the server or array name, if necessary.

2. Click the **Client Configuration** node under your array, then double-click **Firewall Client** in the results pane. The Firewall Client Properties dialog box appears.

3. On the General tab, enter the **DNS name** of the ISA Server machine or array (or the individual **IP address** of the ISA Server machine) to which you want the firewall clients to connect, as shown in Figure 11-15. If you want to enable automatic discovery for the firewall clients, click the **Enable ISA Firewall automatic discovery in Firewall Client** check box.

11

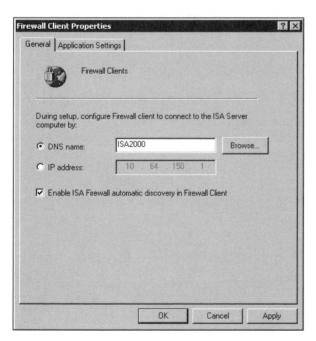

Figure 11-15   Enabling firewall client automatic discovery

4. On the Application Settings tab, shown in Figure 11-16, ISA Server displays all the applications that require special configuration on the firewall client. Most applications work correctly with the firewall client without requiring special settings. Configurations for the listed applications are sent to the firewall client in the mspclnt.ini configuration file. If you install an application on the client machines that requires special configuration, you can modify this list by clicking the **New** button and adding the configuration. ISA Server automatically updates the mspclnt.ini file, triggering an update to be sent to the firewall clients.

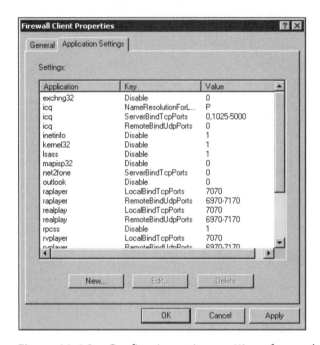

Figure 11-16   Configuring unique settings for a select group of applications

5. After making any changes, click **OK** to complete the automatic configuration of the firewall clients.

By configuring the Web Browser component under the Client Configuration node, you can apply the same settings to the firewall client's Web browser as the ones discussed for the Web proxy client configuration.

CHAPTER SUMMARY

❑ Before you install a server client, you should develop a configuration strategy and learn about the configurations of each client type.

❑ ISA Server supports three client types: SecureNAT, Web proxy, and firewall clients.

❑ You can configure a single client as multiple client types, such as a firewall and SecureNAT client. This allows the client to take advantage of all ISA Server features and support all TCP/IP application types.

❑ SecureNAT clients are the easiest to configure, are supported on all client platforms, and provide support for any TCP/IP-based application. However, if you use SecureNAT clients, you cannot place restrictions based on Active Directory username or group membership.

❑ Web proxy clients can redirect requests from the Web browser to the Web Proxy service on ISA Server. Thus, the clients take advantage of the caching features of ISA Server without redirecting requests for all installed applications. Web proxy clients provide support for only the HTTP, HTTPS, and FTP protocols.

❑ Firewall clients require a software installation on the client PC, and are only supported on Windows platforms. They provide support for any TCP- or UDP-based applications and allow you to place restrictions based on Active Directory username and group membership.

❑ To simplify the installation of the firewall client, Microsoft includes the MS_FWC.msi file with ISA Server. You can deploy this Windows Installer package to all internal computers through a Windows 2000 group policy.

❑ To avoid manual configuration, you can use the automatic discovery features of ISA Server to allow Web proxy and firewall clients to "configure themselves." The clients learn the location of the ISA Server computer using a DNS or DHCP WPAD entry, then contact ISA Server to obtain configuration information.

KEY TERMS

Web Proxy Auto Discovery (WPAD) — An entry in the DNS or DHCP server that directs firewall and Web proxy clients to ISA Server for automatic configuration information.

REVIEW QUESTIONS

1. F&Y Publishing has just installed an ISA Server array consisting of three servers that connect to the Internet. The F&Y internal network has 250 Windows 2000 Professional client machines and 500 Linux-based machines. The applications F&Y uses are all TCP- and UDP-based. What client type would work best in this scenario?

   a. SecureNAT client only

   b. Web proxy client only

   c. Firewall client only

   d. SecureNAT and firewall clients installed on all PCs

2. Which of the following client types supports the TCP, UDP, and ICMP protocols?

   a. SecureNAT

   b. Web proxy

   c. Firewall

   d. Firewall and SecureNAT

3. Web proxy clients take advantage of the CARP protocol when configured statically. True or false?

4. Nathan Sealaff owns a small insurance company. He has a single DSL connection to the Internet with a single ISA Server. All internal machines run on Windows 98. Nathan wants to allow users access to the Web through their browsers, but wants to keep users from using other applications, such as online games, to access the Internet from their computers. What client type should Nathan use?

   a. SecureNAT

   b. Web proxy

   c. Firewall

   d. Firewall and SecureNAT

5. You need to convert 500 internal PCs to Web proxy clients. What would be the most efficient method to configure the clients?

   a. Windows 2000 group policy

   b. third-party imaging software, such as Ghost or Image Cast

   c. automatic discovery

   d. manual configuration

6. Before you can configure a Web browser as a Web proxy client, what must you check?

   a. that DNS name resolution is working properly

   b. that the browser is CERN compliant

   c. that the browser is using Internet Explorer 5.0 or later

   d. that the browser is HTTP 1.1 compliant

7. You must configure a separate version of the LAT for Web proxy clients because they do not access the ISA Server LAT. True or false?

8. Which client platform does SecureNAT support?

   a. Windows

   b. Linux

   c. Macintosh

   d. all of the above

9. What is the function of the WPAD entry?

   a. It allows Web proxy clients to support TCP- and UDP-based protocols.

   b. It points automatic discovery clients to the ISA Server's hostname or IP address.

   c. It delivers automatic discovery information to the clients.

   d. none of the above

10. What default port number does ISA Server use to receive incoming requests from Web proxy clients?

    a. 80

    b. 880

    c. 800

    d. 8080

11. Shannon is using a Web proxy client to access the Internet. She can access any Internet resource without a problem. Whenever she tries to connect to an intranet server, the request fails. What is the most likely cause of the problem?

    a. The client IP address is not configured correctly.

    b. The default gateway is not configured correctly.

    c. The LAT for Web Proxy clients is not configured correctly on ISA Server.

    d. The LAT stored on Shannon's machine does not include the IP addresses of the intranet servers.

12. Joshua's computer is configured as a SecureNAT and firewall client. You create a rule on ISA Server to allow Joshua access to the Internet using all TCP/IP protocols, based on his Active Directory username. A week later, Joshua reports that he cannot ping any Internet hosts. What is the most likely cause?

    a. The client does not support any ICMP protocols.

    b. SecureNAT clients do not support rules based on username or group membership.

    c. The computer should be configured as a Web proxy client.

    d. none of the above

11

13. When you configure a Web proxy client using an automatic configuration script, what advantage(s) do you gain?

    a. support for all TCP- and UDP–based protocols

    b. support for the Cache Array Routing Protocol

    c. elimination of any manual client configuration

    d. all of the above

14. What is the default location of the Web proxy automatic configuration script on ISA Server?

    a. *server_name:port/array.dll?Get.Routing.Script*

    b. *server_name:port/*

    c. *server_name/MSPclnt*

    d. none of the above

15. Manually configuring a client using an automatic configuration script allows you to specify a backup route in case the primary ISA Server fails. True or false?

16. What is contained in the mspclnt.ini file?

    a. a list of rules ISA Server has applied to a firewall client

    b. the LAT table from ISA Server, stored locally on the client

    c. the configuration settings for the firewall client

    d. none of the above

17. Which of the following client types *cannot* use automatic discovery features?

    a. SecureNAT

    b. Web proxy

    c. Firewall

    d. all of the above

18. Which of the following is a valid method for installing the firewall client software?

    a. through an intranet server

    b. by accessing the default share created during ISA Server installation

    c. through a Windows 2000 group policy

    d. all of the above

19. Which of the following platforms cannot use the firewall client?

    a. Windows 2000 Datacenter

    b. Windows 98

    c. Windows 95 OSR1

    d. Windows NT 4.0

20. Which of the following DHCP option codes is associated with the WPAD entry?

a. 150

b. 252

c. 354

d. 250

HANDS-ON PROJECTS

Project 11-1

You can perform this project only if you have a client PC attached to the same network as the internal network interface of the ISA Server machine. Perform this exercise from the client PC. The following steps are written for a Windows 2000 Professional client; if you are using another platform, you may need to modify your actions for the specific client.

To configure a Windows 2000 Professional client as a SecureNAT client:

1. Right-click the **My Network Places** icon on the desktop, and then click **Properties**.
2. In the Network and Dial-up Connections window, right-click the icon for the network adapter card connected to the internal LAN, and then click **Properties**.
3. In the Local Area Connection Properties dialog box, double-click **Internet Protocol (TCP/IP)**.
4. In the Internet Protocol (TCP/IP) dialog box, configure the **Default gateway** and **Preferred DNS server** IP address to **10.5.1.1** (or the IP address assigned by your instructor) to point to the internal network interface of the ISA Server machine.
5. After entering the IP address information, click **OK** to close both the Internet Protocol (TCP/IP) and NIC Properties dialog boxes. The client should now be able to access the Internet through ISA Server as a SecureNAT client.

Project 11-2

You can perform this project from an internal client or from ISA Server itself.

To configure a static Web proxy client:

1. Double-click the **Internet Explorer** icon on the desktop.
2. Click **Tools** on the menu bar, then click **Internet Options**.
3. In the Internet Options dialog box, click the **Connections** tab, and then click the **LAN Settings** button.

4. In the Local Area Network (LAN) Settings dialog box, click the **Use a proxy server** check box, enter **10.5.1.1** (or the IP address assigned by your instructor) in the **Address** text box, and enter **8080** in the **Port** text box. Click the **Bypass proxy server for local addresses** check box, as shown in Figure 11-17, and click **OK**.

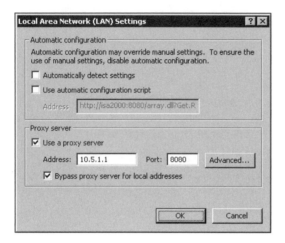

Figure 11-17

5. Click **OK** in the Internet Options dialog box. Internet Explorer should now forward all requests through ISA Server's Web Proxy service.

Project 11-3

You can perform this project from an internal client or from ISA Server itself.

To configure a Web proxy client using an automatic configuration script:

1. On ISA Server, open the ISA Management console, and expand the **Servers and Arrays** node and your array name, if necessary. Click the **Client Configuration** node, then double-click **Web Browser** in the results pane.

2. In the Web Browser Properties dialog box, ensure that your ISA Server's DNS name is entered in the **DNS name** text box, and click the **Direct Access** tab.

3. Ensure that the **Bypass proxy for local servers** and **Directly access computers specified in the Local Domain Table (LDT)** check boxes are selected, as shown in Figure 11-18, and click the **Add** button to create the LAT for the Web Proxy clients.

4. In the Add/Edit Server dialog box, enter **10.0.0.0** in the From text box, enter **10.255.255.255** in the To text box, and then click **OK**. The range you specify appears in the **Directly access these servers or domains** field of the Direct Access tab.

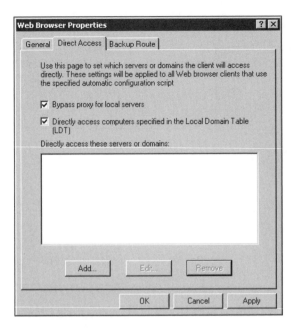

Figure 11-18

5. Click the **Backup Route** tab, and then click the **If ISA Server is unavailable, use this backup route to connect to the Internet** check box. Ensure that the **Direct access** option button is selected, and click **OK**.

6. Minimize the ISA Management console, and then double-click the **Internet Explorer** icon on the desktop (or on the internal client computer, if available).

7. Click **Tools** on the menu bar, then click **Internet Options**.

8. In the Internet Options dialog box, click the **Connections** tab, and then click the **LAN Settings** button.

9. In the Local Area Network (LAN) Settings dialog box, deselect the **Use a proxy server** check box.

10. Click the **Use automatic configuration script** check box and type **http://10.5.1.1:8080/array.dll?Get.Routing.Script** in the **Address** text box, as shown in Figure 11-19. Click **OK** when you finish.

11. Click **OK** in the Internet Options dialog box. Internet Explorer should now download the automatic configuration script and forward all requests through ISA Server's Web Proxy service.

11

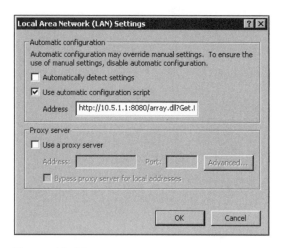

Figure 11-19

Project 11-4

You can only perform this project if you have a client PC attached to the same network as the internal network interface of ISA Server. Perform the following steps from the client PC. Do not attempt to install the firewall client software on ISA Server.

To install and configure the firewall client on an internal Windows client:

1. On the Windows 2000 taskbar, click **Start**, and then click **Run**. In the Run dialog box, enter **\\10.5.1.1\mspclnt**. The contents of the mspclnt shared folder on ISA Server should appear.

2. Double-click the **Setup.exe** icon in the folder. The Microsoft Firewall Client Install Wizard appears, as shown in Figure 11-20. Click **Next**.

3. The wizard prompts you for the destination folder. If you want to modify the default installation folder of C:\Program Files\Microsoft Firewall Client, click the **Change** button. Otherwise, click **Next**.

4. Click the **Install** button to begin the installation. After ISA Server copies the necessary files, click the **Finish** button to complete the installation.

5. The Firewall client icon appears in the system tray, as shown in Figure 11-21. Double-click the **Firewall client** icon.

Figure 11-20

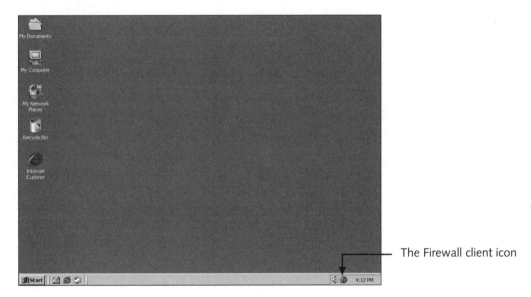

The Firewall client icon

Figure 11-21

6. The Firewall Client Options dialog box appears, as shown in Figure 11-22. Ensure that the name or IP address of your ISA Server appears in the **Use this ISA Server** text box, and click **OK**. You can now access the Internet using any TCP- or UDP-based application.

Figure 11-22

Project 11-5

You can only perform this project if you have a client PC attached to the same network as the internal network interface of the ISA Server machine. Perform the following steps from the client PC.

Using Windows Explorer, browse to C:\Program Files\Microsoft Firewall Client. Verify the existence of the following files. If you have time, open and review the contents of each.

 Depending on the features you have deployed with ISA Server, you may or may not have all of the listed files.

- *Firewallc.txt*
- *Mpcver.txt*
- *Mspclnt.ini*
- *Msplat.txt*

Project 11-6

Now that you have configured ISA Server or an internal client as a Web Proxy or Firewall client, you can verify the connection to the server. You can only perform this exercise if you have an active Internet connection.

To verify the client connection:

1. In the ISA Management console, under your array, expand the **Monitoring** node, and click **Sessions**.

2. From the internal client or ISA Server, open your Web browser and connect to a Web location. If you have configured the client correctly, you should see the new session appear under the **Sessions** node in the ISA Management console. You may need to refresh your view.

CASE PROJECTS

Case Project 11-1

Brian McCann is the network administrator of Watts, a company that provides ultraviolet lighting systems for businesses around the country. Brian has recently installed an ISA Server array to connect the internal network to the Internet. The internal network contains 500 client PCs. Nearly all of these PCs run Windows NT Workstation 4.0, but a few also run Macintosh for graphics design purposes. Brian wants to configure the clients in the simplest fashion. He also wants to design ISA Server rules to restrict access based on the Active Directory groups he already uses within the company. What would be the best client type(s) for the Watts internal network? How should Brian install this client type to allow for the least amount of administrative load? What potential issues can arise from this scenario? What additional information does Brian still need to gather?

Case Project 11-2

Alex Murawski is the network administrator of Jipps, a nationwide convenience store chain. There are over 50 locations across the nation. Each location has a dedicated ISDN connection to the corporate headquarters and typically between two and five PCs requiring Internet access. The PC's use this connection to check for new product pricing information on the Jipps intranet server and to verify pricing on competitors' Web sites. The platforms used at the convenience stores are typically Microsoft or Linux. What would be the best client type for the Jipps locations? How should Alex deploy this client type to allow for the least amount of administrative load? What additional information does Alex still need to gather?

11

Case Project 11-3

Michelle Abram is the network administrator for a small consulting firm located on the California coastline. She has just deployed ISA Server for the firm's 40 employees. Because of company policy, Michelle has created a site and content rule to deny users in the Employee Active Directory group access to all nonwork related Web sites. After monitoring the network for a short time, Michelle learns that all employees can reach any Internet Web site. What client type(s) are the employees using? Identify three workable solutions to this problem.

Case Project 11-4

Christopher Simson is the network administrator of Elaborate Equity, Inc., a large Missouri-based company that specializes in lucrative investments. He has recently deployed an ISA Server array consisting of five servers at the corporate office. Recently, Christopher has received a number of complaints that employees are unable to access the external mail server through the firewall. Christopher verifies that the clients have access to the e-mail server, but the clients are still unable to connect. What client type(s) are the employees using? Identify a solution to this problem that does not require a major reconfiguration of the network.

MONITORING AND TUNING ISA SERVER 2000

After reading this chapter and completing the exercises, you will be able to:

- ♦ Plan a monitoring and reporting strategy
- ♦ Enable intrusion detection
- ♦ Configure intrusion detection
- ♦ Configure ISA Server responses
- ♦ Monitor and capture network activity in logs
- ♦ Use ISA Server reporting features
- ♦ Monitor current ISA Server activity
- ♦ Test the monitoring configuration

After you install and configure ISA Server, you must monitor and tune the server. This process can take days, weeks, or even months. Unfortunately, Microsoft offers no small, medium, or large company template that you can download and apply to ISA Server to optimize its performance. Likewise, consultants who move between companies have found no standard formula for optimizing ISA Server. Every environment is different, and performance depends on too many variables to make a generic solution feasible.

For example, administrators know that a company's size is an important variable that creates many questions for configuration: How many employees does the company have? Will the company grow significantly within the next year? How often do the employees access the Internet? While size is a significant variable, it is only one of many you must address when configuring ISA Server for a specific environment.

In Chapter 4 you learned how to plan for the installation of ISA Server. Now you must plan a monitoring and reporting strategy. You can examine thousands of areas in ISA Server, so planning which ones you should monitor is critical to your success. Attempting to monitor ISA Server without planning is like driving through a foreign city without a map; you may eventually reach your destination, but a map makes the task much easier.

Planning a Monitoring and Reporting Strategy

Creating a monitoring and reporting plan can be time consuming. You could easily configure ISA Server to log every access and performance-related event, but the log files would be so huge that you could never sort through them. Monitoring too many events can be as useless as monitoring none at all. Extensive monitoring also creates a considerable load on ISA Server, which decreases the performance of all clients.

When creating a monitoring and reporting strategy, divide your plan into five major steps:

1. Choose the type of information to collect.

2. Determine the most critical information.

3. Document your strategy.

4. Develop an emergency response strategy.

5. Create a schedule for reviewing and archiving log files.

Each step is described in detail in the following sections.

Step 1. Choosing the Type of Information to Collect

The type of monitoring and reporting strategy you develop depends on the information you need to collect. If you initially use ISA Server as a caching server, you are probably most interested in monitoring performance. However, if you use ISA Server as a firewall server, you probably want to monitor security. There are three categories of monitoring:

- *Alerts*—Alerts allow you to monitor critical ISA Server information. For example, if a hacker tries to break through the ISA Server firewall using a Denial of Service attack, you would probably want ISA Server to send you an e-mail alert or page you. Likewise, you could configure ISA Server to alert you if an overwhelming amount of HTTP-based traffic flooded ISA Server and slowed performance.

- *Performance trends*—ISA Server includes a number of methods to analyze performance trends during given time intervals. You can take a snapshot of performance levels at a given point in time, or you can watch performance levels over a long period to better understand daily peaks and valleys.

- *Security trends*—Typically you use alerts to notify you of security attacks, but you can use the security monitors to watch other firewall-related events. For example, you might want to print a monthly report of internal users who attempted to access restricted Internet content, or you can analyze external users who tried to access restricted resources on the internal network.

By identifying the type of information you want to gather, you can significantly reduce the number of monitoring areas. After the initial installation and configuration of ISA Server is complete, you may want to monitor all areas of ISA Server use; however, it is much better and easier to choose one area at a time. The area you initially monitor should reflect the primary purpose of ISA Server. If you installed it primarily to speed Internet access, monitor the performance areas first; if you are using ISA Server to increase security, monitor the security areas first.

Step 2. Determining the Most Critical Information

After selecting the major category of information you want to monitor, you must choose the critical aspects within that area. For example, if you monitor ISA Server performance, you might initially focus on average processor time and memory usage. If you find that the system uses more memory than you expected, you can begin to monitor more specific areas that deal with memory usage, such as cache memory storage and the TTL on the cache stored in memory. If you monitor security on ISA Server, you might start in a broad area, such as the number of packets denied by the packet filters on ISA Server. If the number continues to increase and then spikes during evening hours, you can enable more detailed logging that tracks the source IP addresses and port numbers from which the denied requests originate.

Overall, the goal of your monitoring strategy is to start with broader areas, then focus on details after you identify the larger problems. Starting with a detailed logging of all ISA Server activities creates excessive data and makes problems more difficult to isolate. By monitoring the broader areas of ISA Server, you can review the log files more easily and identify potential problems before they occur.

12

Step 3. Documenting Your Strategy

After you decide which areas to monitor, you should document your strategy with both soft copy and hard copy. Besides providing a record of your plan, documentation allows you to create a **baseline**, a record of network activity during normal operations. Network administrators often fail to create a baseline, and then attempt to monitor ISA Server only after performance problems arise. While monitoring without a baseline does return the current performance levels, the administrator has no idea what the levels should be during normal operation, which renders the capture useless. Before you monitor any new area, you should create a baseline.

Step 4. Developing an Emergency Response Strategy

As part of your monitoring and reporting plan, you should also develop an emergency response strategy to follow once a problem occurs. Many new network administrators neglect this step, only to realize during a crisis just how important it is. Amid the stress of a network failure, many people tend to act impulsively or rely on trial and error in an attempt to solve the problem. This is why you should develop an emergency response strategy before problems occur, while you can think clearly.

Depending on the type of company you work for, a loss of Internet connectivity can create a minor inconvenience or a major crisis. A hard copy of your emergency response plan should be available at all times, and it should detail the steps to follow in case of network failure. These steps can differ depending on your network configuration, but they typically include a detailed checklist of every major network component, beginning with the most volatile.

Step 5. Creating a Schedule for Reviewing and Archiving Log Files

The final step of developing a monitoring and reporting strategy is to create a schedule for reviewing and archiving log files. Make sure you follow this schedule. Many administrators develop thorough monitoring strategies, but then fail to review the log files on a regular basis. When they do finally review the files and realize how much data has accumulated, they delete the files and reset all the logs. Network administrators who follow this system are better off not configuring logging in the first place.

If you are logging high-level data, you can probably review the log files once a week. However, if you log detailed information for troubleshooting purposes, you should review the files daily because they tend to grow quickly.

After you review the log files, you should archive them. You can use archived log files to track trends or for legal purposes. For example, within the last few months, your company might have added 30 employees to the staff. By reviewing log files from periods before your company hired the additional employees, you can see exactly how much extra load they have added to ISA Server. This information not only helps you generate a new baseline of normal operation, it helps you determine how many more users ISA Server can handle before you must upgrade.

ENABLING INTRUSION DETECTION

While monitoring the performance of ISA Server allows you to watch for trends and potential problems, most performance issues occur over an extended time. Unless your service is configured incorrectly or you installed background third-party applications, your resource load on ISA Server should remain relatively steady, allowing you to see gradual increases or decreases in resource use. On the other hand, intruders commonly strike without warning and with great potency. Hackers often know what weaknesses to look for and exploit in Internet firewall software.

ISA Server includes an intrusion detection system that allows you to generate log files, create trigger events, and send administrative alerts when ISA Server detects an attack. You can respond immediately to a hacker who attempts to attack the ISA Server machine itself or a server on the internal network. For example, you could configure a script to run when ISA Server detects an attack; the script could log the IP address of the intruder, then either page you or shut down the firewall service (eliminating all network access), depending on the time of day.

Most firewall attacks occur at the Network layer of the OSI Model and exploit natural weaknesses in the TCP/IP protocol itself. These are considered packet-level attacks. Other attacks occur at the Application layers of the OSI model and single out applications and services, such as DNS or IIS. The following sections list common Network and Application layer attacks that ISA Server guards against.

Network Layer Attacks

- *All Ports Scan*—This type of attack uses port scanning software to check for any open TCP or UDP ports on ISA Server. Each open port number is logged to the intruder's PC. The hacker then attempts to attack through the open port numbers.

- *Enumerated Port Scan*—Using this common probing mechanism, a hacker attempts to see what services are running on a system by sending data to each port and waiting for a response.

- *IP Half Scan*—This attack finds open ports and services while avoiding detection. Repeated attempts to connect are sent to each port, but the connection is never established.

- *Land Attack*—Establishing a TCP-based session requires a three-way handshake. Land attacks send a packet requesting to establish a session in which the source and destination IP address and port number are identical. Some TCP implementations continuously loop, attempting to establish a session with a non-existent computer, and eventually crash.

- *Ping of Death*—Using the Internet Control Message Protocol (ICMP) to send an echo request packet to a target, the hacker attaches a large amount of information to the ping. When the target attempts to respond to the ping packet, it overflows its buffers and crashes.

12

Application Layer Attacks

- *DNS host name overflow*—This attack involves sending a DNS hostname response that exceeds a standard, fixed length. Because most applications do not check to verify hostname length, the response makes the internal buffers overflow, which can allow the hacker to execute commands or crash a targeted computer.

- *DNS length overflow*—This attack is similar to the DNS hostname attack, but involves sending an IP address, rather than a hostname, that is longer than four bytes.

- *DNS zone transfer from privileged ports (1-1024)*—This attack occurs when a client attempts to attain the DNS zone database by sending a zone transfer request on ports 1-1024. A client who accesses your entire DNS database can unleash many other more damaging attacks.

- *DNS zone transfer from high ports (above 1024)*—This is the same attack as the previous one, but it uses ports above 1024.

- *POP buffer overflow*—This attack attempts to gain control of a POP mail server by overflowing the server's internal buffer.

- *UDP Bomb*—Modification of UDP packets can corrupt data in certain fields, which can cause older operating systems to stop working.

- *Windows Out-of-Band Attack*—This method attempts to send an out-of-band, Denial of Service attack in a series of messages to open computers. The receiving computer typically loses all network connectivity or crashes.

CONFIGURING INTRUSION DETECTION

Most network administrators turn on all intrusion detection features on ISA Server, which allows them to detect all major types of attack. In most situations, this causes no problems; however, some custom applications attempt to connect through ISA Server in a way that resembles an attack. For example, some client applications can connect to a server on multiple TCP or UDP port numbers, depending on which port is available. When the application is run, it attempts to connect on the first available port; if the port is closed, the application moves to the next port. This process continues until the application locates an available port number. Depending on its configuration, ISA Server may interpret this application as an intruder attempting an All Ports Scan attack, and then alert you to the intrusion. To avoid this potential problem, you can enable or disable individual types of intrusion detection.

To configure Network layer intrusion detection:

1. In the ISA Management console, expand the **Servers and Arrays** node, your server or array, and, if necessary, the **Access Policy** node, right-click **IP Packet Filters**, and then click **Properties**. The IP Packet Filters Properties dialog box appears.

2. In the **General** tab, click the **Enable packet filtering** and **Enable Intrusion detection** check boxes if they are not already selected.

3. In the **Intrusion Detection** tab, click the packet-level attacks you want ISA Server to detect, as shown in Figure 12-1. If you click the **Port scan** check box, you have additional options:

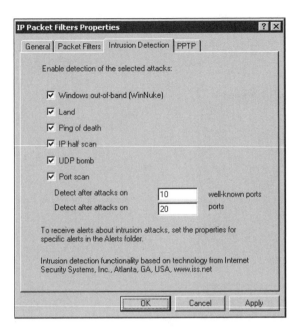

Figure 12-1   Configuring Network layer intrusion detection

- *Detect after attacks on <n> well-known ports*—Enter the number of well-known ports that an intruder can scan before ISA Server generates an event. ISA Server considers TCP and UDP ports from 0 to 2048 to be well-known. These ports are most vulnerable to an intruder attack because most network services are run from them. Setting this number too low can generate false alerts; setting it too high can allow intruders to escape detection. The default configuration is to generate an event after detecting 10 consecutive scans on the well-known port ranges.

- *Detect after attacks on <n> ports*—Enter the total number of ports an intruder can scan before ISA Server generates an event. This includes both the well-known port number range (0-2048) and the dynamic port number range (anything above 2048). The default configuration is to generate an event after detecting 20 consecutive scans on any port number ranges.

4. After you configure the necessary intruder detection options, click **OK**.

While Network layer attacks are more common, the number and complexity of Application layer attacks continue to increase. Therefore, ISA Server includes two application filters that intercept common DNS and mail server attacks.

To configure DNS intrusion detection:

1. In the ISA Management console, expand the **Servers and Arrays** node and your server or array, and, if necessary, expand the **Extensions** node, and then click the **Application Filters** node.

2. In the details pane, double-click the **DNS intrusion detection filter**.

3. In the Properties dialog box, click the **Attacks** tab. Next, click the individual filters you want to enable, as shown in Figure 12-2, and then click **OK**.

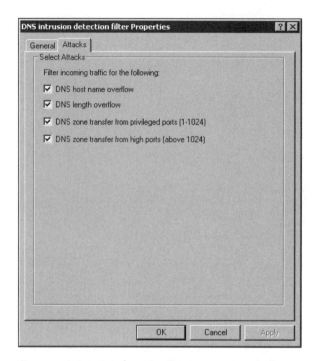

Figure 12-2   Configuring DNS intrusion detection

There is only one major type of attack on POP mail servers. Enabling the POP intrusion detection filter allows ISA Server to scan for the attack.

To enable the POP intrusion detection filter:

1. In the ISA Management console, expand the **Servers and Arrays** node, your server or array, and the **Extensions** node, if necessary, and then click the **Application Filters** node.

2. In the details pane, double-click the **POP intrusion detection filter**.

3. In the **General** tab of the POP intrusion detection filter Properties dialog box, click the **Enable this filter** check box to insert a check mark, and then click **OK**. POP intrusion detection is now configured.

CONFIGURING ISA SERVER RESPONSES

After you configure the type of intruder detection that ISA Server performs, you should configure how it responds to the attack. By default, ISA Server logs the event to the event viewer and continues running normally. However, most attacks occur outside normal business hours, when a network administrator is not available to respond. If ISA Server is only configured to log attacks to the event viewer, a hacker could spend an entire evening attempting to compromise the ISA Server itself, or one of the internal clients. Fortunately, ISA Server allows you to configure a more immediate response to attacks.

To configure ISA Server responses, you must first identify the significant network **events** that occur. An event is any abnormal condition that ISA Server detects during operation. For example, when a hacker attempts an All Ports Scan attack, ISA Server records it as an event. Likewise, if a dial-on-demand connection fails to connect, ISA Server also records an event.

In its default configuration, ISA Server records any major network event to the Windows 2000 Event Viewer; however, it does nothing to immediately respond to the event. Your job as administrator is to configure a response to each relevant event area. Because so many events can occur, you must first identify which ones warrant an immediate response. Table 12-1 lists the ISA Server events and briefly describes them. Before you configure ISA Server to respond to any events, look through the table and highlight the events that you think demand a fast response.

Table 12-1   ISA Server Events

Event	Description
Alert action failure	The action associated with this alert failed
Asymmetric installation	A component that was configured for the array is missing on this server
Cache container initialization error	The cache container initialization failed and the container was ignored
Cache container recovery complete	The recovery of a single container was completed
Cache file resize failure	There was a failure to reduce the cache file size
Cache initialization failure	The Web cache proxy was disabled because of global failure
Cache recovery completed	The cache content recovery was completed
Cache write error	There was a failure to write cached content to the cache
Cached object ignored	During cache recovery, an object with conflicting information was detected, and ignored
Client/server communication failure	Communication between the Firewall client and the firewall service of ISA Server failed

12

Table 12-1   ISA Server Events (continued)

Event	Description
Component load failure	There was a failure to load an extension component
Configuration error	The ISA Server configuration is invalid
Dial-on-demand failure	Failed to create a dial-on-demand connection because there is no answer or the line is busy
DNS intrusion	A host name overflow, length overflow, zone high port, or zone transfer attack occurred
Event logging failure	There was a failure to log the event information to the system event log
Failed to retrieve object	The object <URL> could not be loaded
Intra-array credentials	The intra-array credentials were incorrect
Intrusion detected	An external user attempted an intrusion attack
Invalid dial-on-demand credentials	Invalid dial-on-demand credentials were detected
Invalid ODBC log credentials	The specified user name or password for this ODBC database is invalid
IP packet dropped	An IP packet not allowed by the policy was dropped
IP protocol violation	A packet with invalid IP options was detected and dropped
IP spoofing	The IP packet source address is not valid
Log failure	The log failed
Network configuration changed	A network configuration change that affects ISA Server was detected
OS component conflict	There is a conflict with an operating system component: network address translation (NAT) editor, Internet Connection Sharing (ICS), or Routing and Remote Access
Oversize UDP packet	ISA Server dropped a User Datagram Protocol (UDP) packet because it exceeded maximum size, as specified in the registry key
POP intrusion	Detected a Post Office Protocol (POP) buffer overflow
Report summary generation failure	Received an error while generating a report summary from log files
Resource allocation failure	There was a resource allocation failure, e.g., the system ran out of memory
RPC filter - server connectivity changed	The connectivity to the publishing RPC service changed
Server publishing failure	The server publishing rule cannot be applied
Service initialization failure	There was a service initialization failure
Service not responding	An ISA Server function terminated or stopped unexpectedly

Table 12-1   ISA Server Events (continued)

Event	Description
Service shutdown	A service stopped properly
Service started	A service started properly
SMTP filter event	A Simple Mail Transfer Protocol (SMTP) filter event occurred
SOCKS configuration failure	The port specified in SOCKS properties is in use by another protocol
SOCKS request was refused	A SOCKS request was refused due to policy violation
The server is out of array's site	All members of the array must be in the same site, but this server is in a different site
Unregistered event	An unregistered event was raised
Upstream chaining credentials	The upstream chaining credentials are incorrect
Web proxy routing failure	The Web Proxy service of ISA Server failed to route the request to an upstream proxy server
Web proxy routing recovery	Web Proxy resumed routing to an upstream proxy server
WMT live stream splitting failure	The streaming application filter encountered an error during Windows Media Technology (WMT) live stream splitting

After identifying the significant event areas, you can customize an ISA Server response for each.

To configure ISA Server event responses:

1. In the ISA Management console, expand the **Servers and Arrays** node and your server or array, and, if necessary, expand **Monitoring Configuration**, and then click **Alerts**. A list of all ISA Server events appears in the details pane, as shown in Figure 12-3.

12

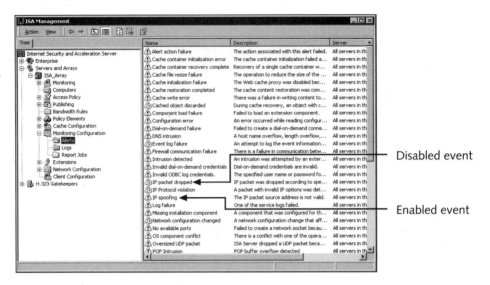

Disabled event

Enabled event

Figure 12-3 Recognized ISA Server events

2. In the details pane, double-click an event that requires an immediate response, such as **DNS intrusion**. The event Properties dialog box appears.

3. The **General** tab shows the event's name and description, and lets you enable or disable the event, as shown in Figure 12-4. By clicking the **Enable** check box, you configure ISA Server to recognize this event. You must check this box before you can configure any other actions in the dialog box. While you may be tempted to enable all ISA Server events, you must realize that doing so increases your processor use. When you install ISA Server, some events are enabled by default, and others are disabled. Disabled events are indicated with circled red arrows, as shown in Figure 12-3.

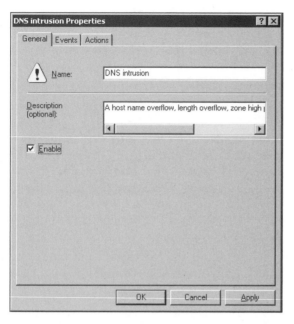

Figure 12-4   Configuring general event information

4. After you enable the event, click the **Events** tab, and configure the following options, as shown in Figure 12-5.

12

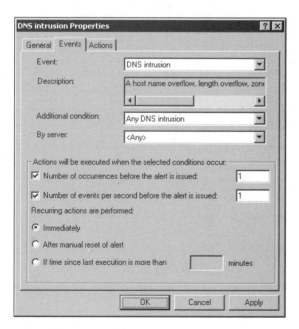

Figure 12-5   Configuring event responses

- *Event*—This list box shows all the events defined by ISA Server. If you want to change the complete event configuration, use this list box. For example, instead of applying this event to DNS intrusion, you can apply it to the Service shutdown event.

- *Description*—This area displays a brief description of the event.

- *Additional condition*—This list box displays additional keys for the selected event. You can use additional conditions to focus the event for more detailed information. For example, the DNS intrusion event has five possible additional conditions: **Any DNS intrusion**, **Hostname overflow**, **Length overflow**, **Zone high port**, and **Zone transfer**. By default, the **DNS intrusion** event monitors **Any DNS intrusion**, which encompasses all four types of DNS intrusion attacks. However, if you want to configure a certain action for only one type of DNS intrusion, you can select it as an additional condition.

- *By server*—Use this list box to select the ISA Server machine in the array to which this event should apply, or choose **<Any>** to apply the event to all ISA Servers in the array.

5. In the **Actions will be executed when the selected conditions occur** section of the Events tab, you have the following options:

   - *Number of occurrences before the alert is issued*—You can specify how many times the event is triggered before ISA Server performs the configured action.

   - *Number of events per second before the alert is issued*—You can specify how many times the event occurs within a second before ISA Server performs the configured action. If you click this check box and the previous one, ISA Server must meet *both* criteria before it performs the configured action.

6. In the **Recurring actions are performed** section of the Events tab, click one of the following radio buttons:

   - *Immediately*—If you select this option, the action executes immediately after the specified conditions occur.

   - *After manual reset of alert*—If you select this option, the action executes after the administrator manually resets the alert. This keeps the event from running more than once if multiple instances of the event occur.

   - *If time since last execution is more than <n> minutes*—If you select this option, you can specify how long ISA Server should wait between alert executions. For example, if a DNS intrusion attack triggers an action that sends an e-mail message to the administrator, you can use this option to keep consecutive attacks from flooding the e-mail server with messages.

7. Click the **Actions** tab, and configure the following options, as shown in Figure 12-6.

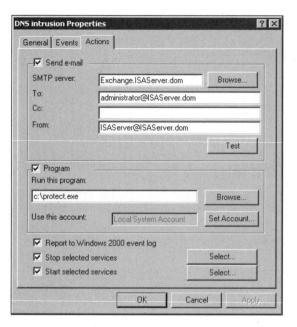

Figure 12-6   Configuring event actions

- *Send e-mail*—Click this check box to have ISA Server send an e-mail alert to you or another network administrator. If you select this option, you must specify the **SMTP server** hostname or IP address, as well as the recipient(s) of the e-mail. In the **From** text box, you can specify the e-mail sender, which allows you to quickly identify ISA Server e-mail alert messages.

- *Program*—Click this check box to run a specified program when an event triggers ISA Server. Such a specified program might do anything from shutting down multiple services to paging the network administrator, as long as the program runs in Windows 2000. Enter the name of the program in the **Run this program** text box. You can also specify a Windows 2000 user account to run the program. By default, the Local System Account runs the program, which allows it to access all Windows 2000 resources.

- *Report to Windows 2000 event log*—This is the only check box selected by default for enabled events. Deselecting this option turns off logging to the Windows 2000 event log.

- *Stop selected services*—Click this check box, then click the **Select** button to stop any of the services listed in Figure 12-7. Be careful with this option. While it does keep the intruder from attempting continued attacks, it also eliminates services for internal network clients.

- *Start selected services*—Click this check box, then click the **Select** button to start any of the services listed in Figure 12-7.

Figure 12-7 Stopping or starting ISA Server services upon an event trigger

8. After you configure all event properties, click **OK** to save your changes. ISA Server begins tracking and recording any relevant events.

After an event occurs, you may be required to reset the event trigger. You can think of this trigger as a mousetrap. ISA Server has "caught" a network intruder or service failure, and now you must reset the trap.

To view and reset event triggers and alerts:

1. In the ISA Management console, expand the **Servers and Arrays** node and your server or array, and, if necessary, expand **Monitoring** (not Monitoring Configuration), and then click **Alerts**.

2. In the details pane of the MMC, review the recorded events captured by ISA Server. The events are organized by date and time.

3. To reset a trigger and remove it from the list, right-click the alert, and click **Reset**.

UNDERSTANDING AND CONFIGURING LOGGING

You should configure event triggers and alerts for occurrences that require immediate response, but not for events that are considered typical operating procedures. To record regular events, you should use ISA Server logging.

Logging allows you to record incoming and outgoing requests and how ISA Server responds to them. Once you configure logging, ISA Server generates log files for each server in the array. These files contain information about general network access and security-related activity. You can generate log files in a variety of formats, which allows you to review trends in ISA Server usage, performance, and security.

ISA Server can generate log files for three different areas:

- *Packet filter logs*—Records packets passing through ISA Server. These are useful for reporting overall traffic trends and activity.

- *Firewall service logs*—Records the access attempts of internal clients using the Firewall service.

- *Web Proxy service logs*—Records the access attempts of internal clients using the Web Proxy service.

ISA Server can generate log files in three different formats. Because scrolling through long files can be painstaking work, most network administrators use a reporting application to generate graphs and statistics from the log data. The type of application you use can dictate the format of the log files. ISA Server reporting features are discussed later in this chapter.

The three types of log file formats are:

- *ISA format*—Use this format only with a reporting application that can read ISA Server-formatted log files. If you attempt to read these log files without a reporting application, you will find them nearly illegible, because the files are stored with data only. There is no information about what the data represents.

- *ODBC database*—Use this format to save the logs to a database application that supports the Open Database Connectivity (ODBC) standards, such as Microsoft SQL Server.

- *W3C format*—Use this format with a reporting application that can read **World Wide Web Consortium (W3C)** formatted log files. The W3C is an agency founded in 1994 that develops standards for the World Wide Web. W3C was founded by Tim Berners-Lee, the creator of the Web. W3C logging follows the Web standards. These files are easier to read in a raw text editor than in the ISA format, because they include data and headers that describe each data set.

By default, logging for all three services is enabled in the W3C format. Use the ISA Management console to control what services are logged, what information is logged from each service, and the logging format.

To configure ISA Server logging options:

1. In the ISA Management console, expand the **Monitoring Configuration** node under your server or array, and click the **Logs** node. The details pane lists the three logging areas: **Packet filters**, **ISA Server Firewall service**, and **ISA Server Web Proxy Service**.

2. Double-click the logging area you want to configure. For this example, use **Packet filters** logging.

3. In the **Log** tab of the Packet filters Properties dialog box, you have the following options, as shown in Figure 12-8.

12

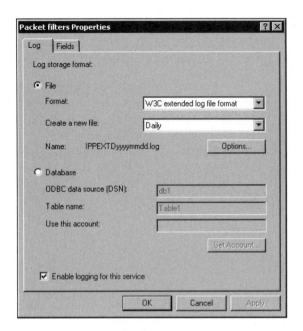

Figure 12-8   Configuring logging properties

- *File*—Click the **File** option button to log to a text file. If you select this option, you can configure the format of the log file, how often ISA Server creates a new log file, and the file naming convention. By clicking the **Options** button, you can also assign a location to the log files, compress log files, and limit the number of old log files kept in storage, as shown in Figure 12-9.

- *Database*—Click the **Database** option button to log to an ODBC-compliant database. If you choose this option, you must configure the ODBC data source (the server to receive the logged data), the database table where information is stored, and the account to use when connecting to the ODBC server.

- *Enable logging for this service*—Click this check box to enable or disable all logging for the selected service.

Figure 12-9   Configuring advanced file logging properties

4. Click the **Fields** tab, and select the individual fields you want to include in the ISA Server logs, as shown in Figure 12-10. To configure all the fields, click the **Select All** button.

12

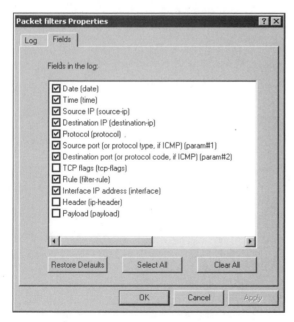

Figure 12-10   Choosing fields to log

Because each service has different capabilities, not all fields are available for every logging service. For example, the Authorization status field is not available for packet filter logs, because packet filters neither require nor view authentication information.

5. After selecting the fields you want to log, click **OK**. ISA Server logging is enabled.

Table 12-2 provides a complete list of fields you can log in ISA Server.

Table 12-2   ISA Server Logging Fields

Field position	Descriptive name (field name)	Description
1	Client IP (c-ip)	The Internet Protocol (IP) address of the requesting client.
2	Client user name (cs-username)	The account of the user making the request. If ISA Server Access Control is not being used, ISA Server uses "anonymous."
3	Client agent (c-agent)	The client application type sent by the client in the Hypertext Transfer Protocol (HTTP) header. When ISA Server is actively caching, the client agent is ISA Server. For Firewall service, this field includes information about the client's operating system.
4	Authentication status (sc-authenticated)	Indicates whether the client has been authenticated with ISA Server. Possible values are "Y" and "N."
5	Date (date)	The date the logged event occurred.
6	Time (time)	The time the logged event occurred. In W3C format, this is Greenwich mean time.
7	Service name (s-svcname)	The name of the logged service. ■ **w3proxy** indicates outgoing Web requests to the Web Proxy service. ■ **fwsrv** indicates Firewall service. ■ **w3reverseproxy** indicates incoming Web requests to the Web Proxy service.
8	Proxy name (s-computername)	The name of the computer running ISA Server. This computer name is assigned in Windows 2000.
9	Referring server name (cs-referred)	If ISA Server is used upstream in a chained configuration, this field indicates the name of the downstream server that sent the request.
10	Destination name (r-host)	The domain name for the remote computer that provides service to the current connection. For the Web Proxy service, a hyphen (-) in this field may indicate that an object was retrieved from the Web Proxy server cache and not from the destination.

Table 12-2   ISA Server Logging Fields (continued)

Field position	Descriptive name (field name)	Description
11	Destination IP (r-ip)	The network IP address for the remote computer that provides service to the current connection. For the Web Proxy service, a hyphen (-) in this field may indicate that an object was sourced from the Web proxy server cache and not from the destination. One exception is negative caching; in that case, this field indicates a destination IP address for which a negative-cached object was returned.
12	Destination port (r-port)	The reserved port number on the remote computer that provides service to the current connection. This is used by the client application that initiates the request.
13	Processing time (time-taken)	This field indicates the total time, in milliseconds, that ISA Server needs to process the current connection. The interval begins when the server receives the request and ends when results are returned to the client and the connection is closed. For cache requests that were processed through the Web Proxy service, processing time measures the elapsed server time needed to fully process a client request and return an object from the server cache to the client.
14	Bytes sent (cs-bytes)	The number of bytes sent from the internal client to the external server during the current connection. A hyphen (-), a zero (0), or a negative number in this field indicates that this information was not provided by the remote computer or that no bytes were sent to the remote computer.
15	Bytes received (sc-bytes)	The number of bytes sent from the external computer and received by the client during the current connection A hyphen (-), a zero (0), or a negative number in this field indicates that this information was not provided by the remote computer or that no bytes were received from the external computer.
16	Protocol name (cs-protocol)	Specifies the application protocol used for the connection. Common values are HTTP, File Transfer Protocol (FTP), Gopher, and Secure Hypertext Transfer Protocol (HTTPS). For Firewall service, the port number is also logged.
17	Transport (cs-transport)	Specifies the transport protocol used for the connection. Common values are Transmission Control Protocol (TCP) and User Datagram Protocol (UDP).

12

Table 12-2   ISA Server Logging Fields (continued)

Field position	Descriptive name (field name)	Description
18	Operation (s-operation)	Specifies the application method used. For Web Proxy, common values are GET, PUT, POST, and HEAD. For Firewall service, common values are CONNECT, BIND, SEND, RECEIVE, GHBN (GetHostByName), and GHBA (GetHostByAddress).
19	Object name (cs-url)	For the Web Proxy service, this field shows the contents of the URL request. This field applies only to the Web Proxy service log.
20	Object MIME (cs-mime-type)	The Multipurpose Internet Mail Extensions (MIME) type for the current object. This field may also contain a hyphen (-) to indicate that the field is not used or that a valid MIME type was not defined or supported by the remote computer. This field applies only to the Web Proxy service log.
21	Object source (s-object-source)	Indicates the source used to retrieve the current object. This field applies only to the Web Proxy service log.
22	Result code (sc-status)	In this field, values of less than 100 indicate a Windows (Win32) error code. Values between 100 and 1,000 indicate an HTTP status code. Values between 10,000 and 11,004 indicate a Winsock error code.
23	Cache info (s-cache-info)	This number reflects the cache status of the object, which indicates why the object was or was not cached. This field applies only to the Web Proxy service log.
24	Rule #1 (rule#1)	This field reflects the rule that either allowed or denied access to the request, as follows: ■ If an outgoing request is allowed, this field reflects the protocol rule that allowed the request. ■ If an outgoing request is denied by a protocol rule, this field reflects the protocol rule. ■ If an outgoing request is denied by a site and content rule, this field reflects the protocol rule that would have allowed the request. ■ If an incoming request is denied, this field reflects the Web publishing or server publishing rule that denied the request. ■ If no rule specifically allowed the outgoing or incoming request, the request is denied. In this case, the field is empty.
25	Rule #2 (rule#2)	This field reflects the second rule that either allowed or denied access to the request. ■ If an outgoing request is allowed, this field reflects the site and content rule that allowed the request.

Table 12-2   ISA Server Logging Fields (continued)

Field position	Descriptive name (field name)	Description
		■ If an outgoing request is denied by a site and content rule, this field reflects the rule. ■ If no rule specifically allowed the outgoing or incoming request, the request is denied. In this case, the field is empty.
26	Session ID (sessionid)	This field identifies a session's connections. For Firewall clients, each process that connects through the Firewall service initiates a session. For secure network address translation (SecureNAT) clients, a single session is opened for all the connections that originate from the same IP address. This field is not included in the Web Proxy service log; it applies only to the Firewall service log.
27	Connection ID (connectionid)	This field identifies entries that belong to the same socket. For each connection, outbound TCP usually has two entries that indicate when the connection is established and terminated. UDP usually has two entries for each remote address. This field is not included in the Web Proxy service log; it applies only to the Firewall service log.

Because packet-filter logging can track all incoming and outgoing traffic, ISA Server allows you to log individual types of traffic that interest you. For example, a new online game might have become popular among office employees. Because the game consumes considerable WAN bandwidth, you decide to create a packet filter that blocks the port number the game attempts to access. You can then enable logging only for the packet filter that blocks the online game from accessing the Internet. This allows you to identify the IP address of internal clients that attempt to use the online game, without having to sort through hundreds of other traffic types in the log files.

By default, ISA Server enables logging for any packet filters that deny network traffic. This default setting minimizes the amount of logging ISA Server performs, because most network traffic is allowed. You can configure ISA Server to log permitted network traffic in addition to denied traffic, but only if you have a good reason; doing so can add a considerable load to ISA Server and decrease your overall performance.

To configure ISA Server to log all permitted network traffic:

1. In the ISA Management console, right-click the **IP Packet Filters** node, expand the **Access Policy** node under your server or array, and click **Properties**.

2. In the IP Packet Filters Properties dialog box, click the **Packet Filters** tab, click the **Log packets from 'Allow' filters** check box, and click **OK**.

12

If you want to decrease the load on ISA Server by limiting which packet filters are logged, you can enable logging on a filter-by-filter basis.

To turn filtering on or off on a per-filter basis:

1. In the ISA Management console, expand the **Access Policy** node under your server or array, and then click the **IP Packet Filters** node.

2. From the list of current packet filters in the details pane, double-click the packet filter you want to configure.

3. In the **General** tab of the packet filter Properties dialog box, click to deselect the **Log any packets matching this filter** check box, as shown in Figure 12-11. (If this check box does not appear in the tab, you must first enable logging of permitted network traffic, as explained in the previous procedure.) Click **OK** when you finish.

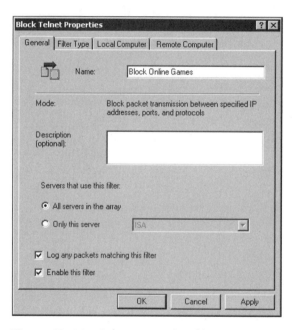

Figure 12-11   Selecting packet filters to commit to the log file

CONFIGURING AND USING REPORTS

Viewing an ISA Server log file in text format can strain your eyes and your patience. Instead, ISA Server includes a reporting application that allows you to generate a summary report for each ISA Server log file. These reports can use a text-only format or generate colorful charts and graphs, depending on the type of report you configure. Furthermore, these reports are saved as Web pages, so you can store them on an intranet Web site for future reference.

Configuring Log Summaries

The first step in generating reports is to configure log summaries. This allows ISA Server to analyze many daily, weekly, or even monthly log files, and generate a summary report of the major events that occurred during the period you specify. Before you can generate reports, you must first summarize all log files you want to include.

To configure log summaries:

1. In the ISA Management console, expand your server or array, expand **Monitoring Configuration**, right-click **Report Jobs**, and then click **Properties**.

2. In the Report Jobs Properties dialog box, click the **Log Summaries** tab.

3. Ensure that the **Enable daily and monthly summaries** check box is selected, as shown in Figure 12-12, and then configure the correct location for the log files under the Location of saved summaries. You can also configure the number of daily and monthly summaries that ISA Server stores in the **Daily summaries** and **Monthly summaries** fields. Click **OK** when you finish.

Figure 12-12   Configuring log summaries

 ISA Server generates log summaries each day at 12:30 a.m. You must have at least one daily summary before you can create a report.

Organizing Report Jobs

After you configure the log summaries, you must organize and create the report jobs. The report jobs allow ISA Server to analyze the log summary files and create the Web-based reporting data.

To create a report job:

1. In the ISA Management console, expand the **Monitoring Configuration** node under your server or array, right-click the **Report Jobs** node, point to **New**, and then click **Report Job**.

2. On the **General** tab, enter a logical name and description for the report job.

3. On the **Period** tab, choose the time frame you want the report job to capture.

4. On the **Schedule** tab, determine when the first report should be generated, and how often it should recur afterward, as shown in Figure 12-13.

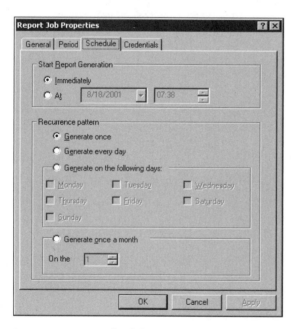

Figure 12-13   Scheduling report jobs

5. On the **Credentials** tab, configure a user account that has access to run the report job. This user account should have local administrative privileges on every ISA Server in the array.

6. After configuring the report job, click **OK**. The new report job appears in the details pane.

Viewing and Saving Reports

Once you configure a report job to run, it creates five Web-based reports that you can view from any Web browser. As you view the reports, you can choose any of the following options:

- *Summary*—Includes a set of reports that illustrate network traffic usage, sorted by application. Summary reports combine data from the Web Proxy service and Firewall service logs.

- *Web Usage*—Includes a set of reports that display top Web users, common HTTP responses and object types, and browsers used. Web Usage reports are based on the Web Proxy service logs. Figure 12-14 shows an example of a Web Usage report.

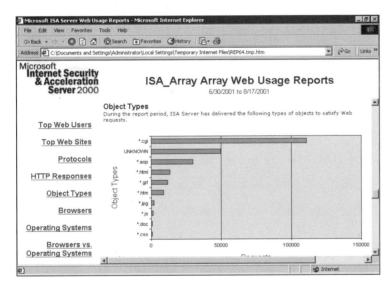

Figure 12-14   A Web Usage report

- *Application Usage*—Includes a set of reports that illustrate Internet application usage in a company, including incoming and outgoing traffic, top users, client applications, and destinations. Application Usage reports are based on the Firewall service logs.

- *Traffic and Utilization*—Includes a set of reports that illustrate total Internet usage by application, protocol, and direction. They also show average traffic and peak simultaneous connections, cache hit ratios, and errors. Traffic and Utilization reports combine data from the Web Proxy and Firewall service logs.

- *Security*—Includes a set of reports that list attempts to breach network security. They can help identify attacks or security violations after they have occurred. Security reports are based on the Web Proxy service, Firewall service, and packet filter logs.

To view generated reports:

1. In the ISA Management console, expand the **Monitoring** node under your server or array, and then expand the **Reports** node.

2. Under the Reports node, click the report type that you want to view.

3. In the details pane, all the report jobs appear, along with the date and time they were generated. To view a report, double-click the report job you want to see. The report job appears in your Web browser in the selected format.

After viewing the report, you may want to archive it for later reference. ISA Server allows you to save individual reports in HTML format or save all reports as a Microsoft Excel workbook.

To save generated reports in HTML format:

1. In the ISA Management console, expand the **Monitoring** node under your server or array, if necessary, expand the **Reports** node, and select the report type you want to save.

2. In the details pane, all generated reports are displayed. Right-click the report job you want to save, and click **Save As**.

3. In the Save As dialog box, enter a report name, and click **Save**.

To save generated reports in Excel workbook format:

1. In the ISA Management console, expand the **Monitoring** node under your server or array, if necessary, and then click the **Reports** node.

2. In the details pane, all generated reports are displayed. Right-click the report job you want to save, and click **Save As**.

3. In the Save As dialog box, enter a report name, and click **Save**.

MONITORING CURRENT ISA SERVER ACTIVITY

The reporting and logging functions of ISA Server allow you to gather and analyze data for traffic that has already occurred. While this data is helpful for trend analysis and security, it does not explain current activity on ISA Server. For example, if your network users begin to complain that Internet access is suddenly too slow, log summaries and daily reports can not help you solve the problem. You need to know what is happening, *now*.

ISA Server offers a few tools to monitor current activity, but the primary tools you need are included with Windows 2000. Performance Monitor and Network Monitor allow you to analyze all major ISA Server activity. After you install ISA Server, new counters are added to the Performance Monitor to record current bandwidth use, caching statistics, and active security measures. Network Monitor is useful for discovering which types of traffic are passing through ISA Server. Using both tools together allows you to quickly diagnose and address most performance issues.

Using the ISA Server Performance Monitor

When you install ISA Server, it adds several objects to the Windows 2000 Performance Monitor. You can use these new objects to monitor performance in all significant areas of ISA Server, to log performance information, and to set alerts. For example, you could configure the Performance Monitor to alert you when the number of packets rejected by a filter exceeds a certain amount. By installing ISA Server, you add the following performance objects to the Performance Monitor:

- *ISA Server bandwidth control*—These counters allow you to monitor current usage of inbound and outbound bandwidth on ISA Server. Use these counters to detect potential bandwidth bottlenecks.

- *ISA Server cache*—You can determine the effectiveness of ISA Server caching by using these counters to monitor the memory, disk, and URL activity associated with the cache.

- *ISA Server Firewall service*—These counters monitor connections associated with the Firewall service, and help you determine overall ISA Server usage.

- *ISA Server packet filter*—These counters are useful for monitoring packet filtering activity, such as dropped packets and incoming connections made through the packet filters.

- *ISA Server Web Proxy service*—Use these counters to determine the number of users and rate at which ISA Server transfers data to remote and upstream servers.

Each performance object includes many counters. Usually the name of the counter is descriptive enough to identify it, but if you need to read a description, select the counter and click the Explain button.

If you use the default installation of ISA Server, it also installs the ISA Server Performance Monitor. This application is no different from the default Windows 2000 Performance Monitor; however, it adds the most critical ISA Server counters automatically when you open the application. By using this utility, you can instantly view all significant areas of ISA Server performance.

To open the ISA Server Performance Monitor, click Start, point to Programs, point to Microsoft ISA Server, and then click ISA Server Performance Monitor. The utility should open with the ISA Server counters already selected, as shown in Figure 12-15.

12

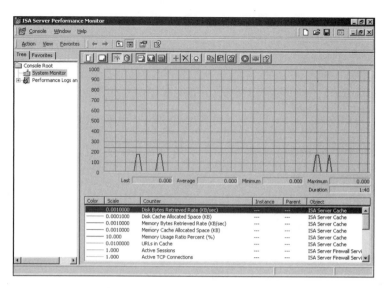

Figure 12-15   The ISA Server Performance Monitor

Managing Active Sessions with the ISA Management Console

The ISA Management console allows you to view all active connections running through ISA Server. You can use the console with other monitoring functions to locate dead or unattended connections. For example, an internal user might listen to a radio station using RealAudio, then leave on vacation without closing the application. This causes a constant stream of uncached data to access the WAN connection (what many network administrators call a "leaky client"). Using the Performance Monitor or ISA Server reporting functions, you can locate these leaks in the network bandwidth, and then use the ISA Management console to disconnect the necessary sessions.

To disconnect a client session:

1. In the ISA Management console, expand your server or array, expand the **Monitoring** node, and then click **Sessions**. The active sessions are listed in the details pane.

2. In the details pane, right-click the applicable session, and then click **Stop**. The session is immediately disconnected.

Some client applications automatically reconnect to the server when the session is disconnected. In this case, you must use more restrictive measures on an individual client basis.

TESTING YOUR CONFIGURATION

When you finish configuring ISA Server, you should test and verify your configuration before subjecting it to full production. You should test both security and performance to ensure that the server can handle the significant load internal clients generate when accessing the Internet while simultaneously dealing with any possible intruder attacks.

The ideal environment for testing ISA Server is a lab with an Internet connection and two client PCs. You should have one client PC connected to the external network device and one attached to the internal network device, as shown in Figure 12-16. You then have an internal network client to test the caching configuration from the internal network, and an external network client to test the firewall configuration from the external network.

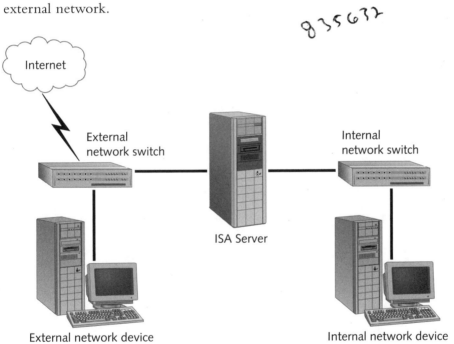

Figure 12-16   The ideal ISA Server testing configuration

Ideally, the external network client should be configured with a third-party application that assesses security. You can buy the application or download it from the Internet, then run intruder attacks on ISA Server and generate a report that assesses its security level. Likewise, the internal network client should be equipped with an application that allows a single internal client to emulate traffic patterns found on a typical internal network.

If you cannot configure a complete lab environment, you can use a few shortcuts to test the ISA Server configuration. Rather than using two external clients, you can use a single client PC with a dial-up Internet connection. This allows you to emulate internal network traffic and test external security from a single client device, as shown in Figure 12-17.

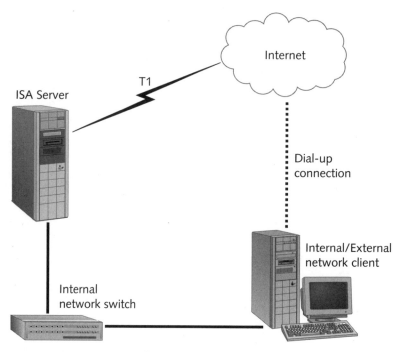

Figure 12-17   The "budget" ISA Server testing configuration

In addition, you can use the following Windows 2000 utilities to test ISA Server security:

- *Telnet*—You can use the Windows 2000 Telnet utility to test for open TCP ports on ISA Server. At a command prompt, use the syntax `telnet ip_address port`, where `ip_address` is the IP address of ISA Server and `port` is the port number you want to test. If Telnet reports that it could not establish a connection, ISA Server is blocking that port number; however, if Telnet opens a session, even briefly, ISA Server allows connections to the port.

- *Netstat*—This command-line utility lets you view open TCP/IP connections, their associated port number, and the status of your server connections. To see all supported syntax for Netstat, enter `netstat /?` at a command prompt.

CHAPTER SUMMARY

- ❑ You must monitor ISA Server to find its optimal configuration and detect any potential performance issues before they become a serious problem.

- ❑ Before you begin monitoring ISA Server, you should develop a detailed plan that describes which areas you want to monitor, the schedule for reviewing the log files, and a troubleshooting plan for emergencies.

3⊢

❐ Configuring intruder detection allows ISA Server to detect, record, and respond to external network attacks. ISA Server protects against most common Network and Application layer attacks.

❐ You can configure alerts that allow ISA Server to respond immediately to intruder attacks. These alerts can include instantly e-mailing the administrator, running a program, or stopping ISA Server services when an attack is detected.

❐ ISA Server can create log files in three formats: ISA, W3C, and ODBC. Because the log files are difficult to read in a text editor, most network administrators use a reporting application to analyze and generate reports on the log files.

❐ By default, ISA Server only logs packet filters that deny network traffic. This alleviates the processor load and reduces the amount of log files.

❐ When you create a report job, ISA Server generates reports for all five reporting categories. You can save these reports individually as HTML pages, or save all of them in a Microsoft Excel workbook.

❐ Windows 2000 provides several tools, including Performance Monitor and Network Monitor, which allow you to monitor all levels of current activity on the ISA Server.

❐ You can use Telnet, a command-line utility in Windows 2000, to connect to various TCP port numbers on ISA Server and test the firewall configuration.

KEY TERMS

baseline — A record of network activity during normal operation

events — Conditions detected by ISA Server during normal operation

World Wide Web Consortium (W3C) — An agency founded in 1994 that develops standards for the World Wide Web. W3C was founded by Tim Berners-Lee, the creator of the Web.

12

REVIEW QUESTIONS

1. What is the first step in creating a monitoring plan for ISA Server?

   a. developing an emergency response strategy

   b. documenting your strategy

   c. determining the most critical information

   d. choosing the category of information you want to collect

2. Which of the following is a valid reason for monitoring ISA Server?

   a. to collect security trend data

   b. to create alerts

   c. to collect performance trend data

   d. all of the above

3. Which of the following intruder attacks is designed to locate open ports and services by establishing sessions, while avoiding detection?

   a. All Ports Scan

   b. Enumerated Port Scan

   c. IP Half Scan

   d. Land Attack

4. Which of the following ranges does ISA Server consider well-known ports?

   a. 1-80

   b. 1-1023

   c. 1-1024

   d. 1-2048

5. Which of the following describes conditions that are outside normal ISA Server operations?

   a. baseline figures

   b. records

   c. errors

   d. none of the above

6. When a packet filter violation occurs, where does ISA Server record the event by default?

   a. Windows 2000 Event Viewer

   b. ISA Server Reports

   c. in an e-mail notification

   d. none of the above

7. Which of the following is not a valid log file?

   a. Web Proxy service logs

   b. ISA service logs

   c. Firewall service logs

   d. packet filter logs

8. Which of the following applications can monitor and report on real-time activity?

    a. ISA Server reporting

    b. ISA Server Performance Monitor

    c. Telnet

    d. ISA Server log files

9. When are ISA Server daily reports generated?

    a. 8 a.m.

    b. 9 a.m.

    c. 10:30 p.m.

    d. 12:30 a.m.

10. What type of attack is a POP buffer overflow?

    a. a backdoor attack

    b. a Network layer attack

    c. an Application layer attack

    d. none of the above

11. ISA Server logs all traffic denied by packet filters by default. True or false?

12. Which utility allows you to see current sessions running on ISA Server?

    a. Netstat

    b. Ping

    c. Telnet

    d. Internet Explorer

13. Which of the following logging formats would be easiest to read with a basic text editor?

    a. ISA format

    b. W3C format

    c. ODBC format

    d. They are all equally difficult to read without using a reporting application.

14. Sarah Wiley has just installed ISA Server intruder detection and logging features on her network. She notices that processor use is unusually high during business hours. What is the most likely cause of the problem?

    a. ISA Server is logging many more intruder detection attacks than before.

    b. Sarah has configured ISA Server to log all traffic allowed through the packet filters.

    c. Sarah has configured ISA Server to log all traffic denied by the packet filters.

    d. none of the above

12

15. What area of ISA Server does the Windows 2000 Telnet application allow you to verify?

    a. performance

    b. availability

    c. security

    d. all of the above

16. What formats are supported when saving ISA Server reports?

    a. .txt and .doc

    b. .asp and .htm

    c. .xls and .asp

    d. .htm and .xls

17. Alerts are configured for many critical ISA Server events by default. True or false?

18. Logging to the Windows 2000 Event Viewer is configured on ISA Server by default. True or false?

19. What must you create before you monitor performance?

    a. a schedule for reviewing security logs and reports

    b. a network baseline

    c. log summaries

    d. all of the above

20. What type of data does the Windows 2000 Network Monitor find?

    a. the detailed header information and protocol of a TCP packet

    b. the average network bandwidth used by internal clients

    c. the frequency of security attacks on ISA Server

    d. none of the above

HANDS-ON PROJECTS

Project 12-1

J&C Publishing has just completed installing ISA Server, primarily for its firewall and security features. J&C's security policy requires that ISA Server notify you of all intrusion attempts. Furthermore, J&C wants to stop all related ISA Server functions if an attack is detected on its DNS or POP e-mail server. Because this is a new ISA Server installation, management wants you to create daily reports that detail network activity, and archive the reports on a regular basis.

To configure intruder detection on ISA Server:

1. In the ISA Management console, expand the **Servers and Arrays** node, expand your array, expand the **Access Policy** node, right-click **IP Packet Filters**, and then click **Properties**. The IP Packet Filters Properties dialog box appears.

2. In the **General** tab, ensure that the **Enable packet filtering** and **Enable Intrusion detection** check boxes are selected.

3. In the **Intrusion Detection** tab, click all check boxes to enable intruder detection for all Network layer attacks.

4. Enter **5** in the **Detect after attacks on <n> well-known ports** text box. Enter **10** in the **Detect after attacks on <n> ports** text box, as shown in Figure 12-18. This allows ISA Server to trigger intruder detection after an application scans five well-known port numbers or 10 total ports.

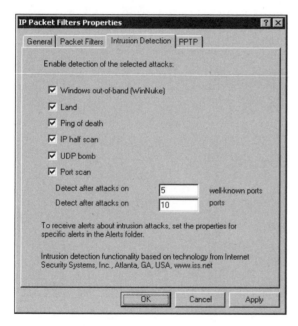

Figure 12-18

5. Click **OK** to close the IP Packet Filters Properties dialog box. In the ISA Management console, expand the **Extensions** node, and then click the **Application Filters** node. In the details pane, double-click the **DNS intrusion detection filter**.

6. On the **General** tab, ensure that the **Enable this filter** check box is selected.

7. On the **Attacks** tab, ensure that all four DNS attacks are selected, and then click **OK** to close the dialog box.

8. In the details pane, double-click the **POP intrusion detection filter**.

9. On the **General** tab, ensure that the **Enable this filter** check box is selected, and then click **OK**. You have successfully enabled Network and Application layer intruder detection on ISA Server.

Project 12-2

To configure ISA Server event alerts:

1. In the ISA Management console, expand the **Monitoring Configuration** node under your array, and click the **Alerts** node. All ISA Server events appear in the details pane of the console.

2. In the details pane, double-click the **DNS intrusion** event.

3. On the **General** tab, ensure that the **Enable** check box is selected.

4. On the **Events** tab, select your server from the **By server** list box. Click the **Number of occurrences before the alert is issued** check box, and enter **1** in the applicable text box. Ensure that the **Immediately** radio button is selected in the **Recurring actions are performed** area, as shown in Figure 12-19.

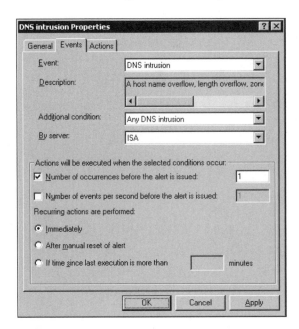

Figure 12-19

5. On the **Actions** tab, click the **Send e-mail** check box. Enter **Exchange2000** in the **SMTP server** text box, **administrator@course.com** in the **To** text box, and **ISAServer@course.com** in the **From** text box. Ensure that the **Report to Windows 2000 event log** check box is selected, click the **Stop selected services** check box, and then click the corresponding **Select** button, as shown in Figure 12-20.

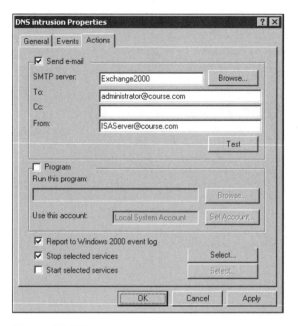

Figure 12-20

6. In the Select ISA Server services dialog box, select the **Firewall** service and click **OK**.

7. Click **OK** in the DNS intrusion Properties dialog box. You have successfully configured an alert for any DNS-related intruder detection services.

12

Project 12-3

To configure log files and summaries on ISA Server:

1. In the ISA Management console, expand the **Monitoring Configuration** node under your array, and click the **Logs** node.

2. In the details pane, double-click the **Packet filters** log component.

3. On the **Log** tab, select the **ISA Server file format** from the **Format** list box, and ensure that a new log file is created **Daily**.

4. On the **Fields** tab, click the **Select All** button to select all logging areas, and click **OK**.

5. Repeat Steps 1 through 4 for the **ISA Server Firewall service** and **ISA Server Web Proxy Service** logging properties.

6. Under the **Monitoring Configuration** node of the ISA Management console, right-click the **Report Jobs** node, and click **Properties**.

7. On the **General** tab of the Report Jobs Properties dialog box, ensure that the **Enable Reports** check box is selected.

8. On the **Log Summaries** tab, ensure that the **Enable daily and monthly summaries** check box is selected. In the Number of summaries saved area, change the **Daily summaries** to **35** and the **Monthly summaries** to **12**, as shown in Figure 12-21. Click **OK** to finish configuring logging and log summaries on ISA Server.

Figure 12-21

Project 12-4

To configure ISA Server reporting:

1. Under the **Monitoring Configuration** node in the ISA Management console, right-click the **Report Jobs** node, point to **New**, and click **Report Job**.

2. On the **General** tab of the Report Job Properties dialog box, name the new report job **Daily Report**, and ensure that the **Enable** check box is selected.

3. On the **Period** tab, ensure that the **Daily** option button is selected.

4. On the **Schedule** tab, shown in Figure 12-22, configure ISA Server to generate a report **Immediately** after you set up the new report job. In the Recurrence pattern section, click the **Generate every day** option button to print daily reports after the first one.

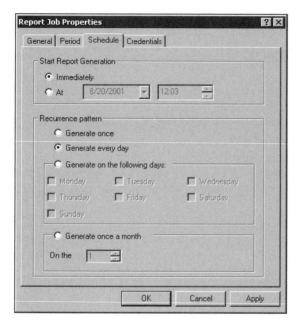

Figure 12-22

5. On the **Credentials** tab, click the **Browse** button to view the Select user list. Double-click the **Administrator** account from the list of users. ISA Server enters the necessary data in the **Username** and **Domain** text boxes. Enter the user's password in the **Password** text box, and then click **OK**. The new report job appears in the details pane.

12

Project 12-5

To view and save reported data:

1. In the ISA Management console, expand the **Monitoring** node under your array, and then expand the **Reports** node. The five report formats are listed in the console tree.

2. Click the **Summary** node. The Daily Report you created in the previous exercise appears in the details pane. Double-click the **Daily Report**.

3. In Internet Explorer, browse through the Summary report and review its contents. When you finish, close Internet Explorer.

4. Repeat Steps 1 through 3 for the remaining four report formats.

5. After reviewing the various report formats, right-click **Daily Report** in the details pane, and click **Save As**. Create a folder on your hard disk named **Saved_Reports**, and save the Summary report in the new folder as **Individual_Report.htm**. Notice that the report is saved in HTML format.

6. Click the **Reports** node in the ISA Management console. Right-click **Daily Report** in the details pane, and click **Save As**. Browse to the **Saved_Reports** folder, and save the file as **All_Reports.xls**. Notice that the reports are saved as a Microsoft Excel Workbook.

Project 12-6

If your environment has the necessary equipment, configure a full ISA Server lab environment for your server. This test environment should include at least one client device and an Internet connection for ISA Server. Practice generating network traffic from the client machine; you can open multiple instances of Internet Explorer to emulate multiple clients. Test ISA Server security using the Telnet and Netstat command-line utilities.

CASE PROJECTS

Case Project 12-1

Michelle Plumb is the network administrator of Gizmo Industries. She has just deployed an ISA Server array consisting of three servers, and enabled caching and intruder detection. Recently the Gizmo help desk installed a simple application to all internal clients by using a Windows 2000 group policy. The application detects whether any of the help desk administrators have an IRC chat utility open on their computers. If so, a chat connection is opened between the employee and the help desk. If not, the employee is redirected to send an e-mail to the help desk. Ever since the application was installed, Michelle has been overwhelmed with intruder detection alerts. What is the most likely cause of the problem? How can Michelle solve it while maintaining equal levels of security on ISA Server?

Case Project 12-2

Nathan Sielaff is the network administrator for Isotopes, Inc. He has recently configured intruder detection and monitoring on ISA Server. For the first few weeks of monitoring, everything seemed normal, but lately he has noticed a steady decline of available WAN bandwidth. After exploring the potential problem areas, he discovers that many internal clients are running a streaming audio application. He disconnects all internal client sessions, but finds they are soon reestablished within a few seconds. What is happening, and how can Nathan solve this problem?

Case Project 12-3

Jennifer Maddison is the network administrator for CJI Software. She has configured ISA Server to respond to the DNS intrusion event by stopping the Firewall service after the Number of occurrences before the alert is issued is 15, and the Number of events per second before the alert is issued is also 15. While reviewing the Event Viewer log, she notices hundreds of recorded DNS intrusion attacks; however, the Firewall service was never stopped. What is the problem, and how can Jennifer correct it?

Case Project 12-4

Benjamin Jacobson is the network administrator for Half-Life, Inc., a nationwide company that manages the disposal of radioactive waste. Recently, many sessions from anonymous employees have been established to Internet hosts using port numbers in the range of 5000 to 35000. Benjamin suspects the internal users are playing online games during business hours. List two ways you can view the active sessions running through ISA Server. Include complete syntax, if necessary.

12

13

TROUBLESHOOTING MICROSOFT
ISA SERVER 2000

**After reading this chapter and completing the exercises,
you will be able to:**

♦ Understand the fundamentals of troubleshooting

♦ Know the troubleshooting tools and resources you can use

♦ Troubleshoot common installation problems

♦ Troubleshoot common cache problems

♦ Troubleshoot firewall and access problems

♦ Troubleshoot client problems

As much as you want everything to go right the first time, it rarely does. Despite your best efforts, some aspect of your ISA Server installation will probably require troubleshooting. Extensive planning does lead to a smooth implementation, but it can never guarantee flawless performance; there is always potential for a loose Ethernet connection, a missing security patch, or a bug in the software. Being familiar with troubleshooting tools and strategy allows you to solve problems more quickly and with less frustration.

This chapter introduces you to several troubleshooting tools that can help you solve problems with ISA Server. These tools can prove invaluable in identifying and solving any problem you might face with ISA Server.

Understanding the Fundamentals of Troubleshooting

At some point as a network administrator, you will need to troubleshoot your company's systems and software. Your task as a troubleshooter is to locate and eliminate problems. Troubleshooting can become one of the most frustrating and time-consuming parts of your job. Many people view network troubleshooting as a double-edged sword; although it can be painful at first, it can also produce some of the most valuable knowledge of your career. Fortunately, most problems with ISA Server result from incorrect configuration or user error. The software does not contain many inherent problems.

This chapter explores many of the tools you can use to troubleshoot ISA Server and quickly diagnose a problem. Before learning about these tools, however, you should know the fundamental steps of troubleshooting. You can follow these basic steps to work through any situation:

1. *Gather information*—During this phase, you gather data relevant to the problem. This applies to network troubleshooting just as in daily life. For example, you may come home to find water leaking from under your front door. After opening the door, you trace the leak to the bathroom. All of this information is relevant. In the network environment, the network might slow down or fail intermittently, or internal servers might crash. While no solutions are apparent at this point, you naturally proceed to the second step.

2. *Analyze the information*—Review the information you gathered during the first step, and begin analyzing potential solutions. To continue the previous example, you might find that someone left water running in the bathtub, or discover a break in the water line. In a network environment, you might find that servers are crashing because of Denial of Service attacks.

3. *Develop and implement a solution*—After analyzing the problem, you need to fix it. The solution to the leak in the prior example is to stop the water flow, which may be as simple as turning off the faucet or as complex as repairing a broken water line. In the network environment, you might easily fix a problem by enabling the DNS intrusion detection filter. Other problems may require more complex solutions, such as installing client software on all internal PCs.

4. *Reassess the state of the network*—After you implement your solution, you must test its effectiveness by reassessing the state of the network. Check to make sure that the problems no longer occur. If the problems are not completely resolved, you need to try another solution.

5. *Document the incident*—After you resolve the problem to your satisfaction, you should document both the original problem and the solution. This documentation is critical for resolving network problems quickly and effectively. Many companies have searchable databases that store troubleshooting records when employees in the IT department resolve and document network incidents.

Once you learn the general process of troubleshooting, you can focus on the resources that help solve your problems.

TROUBLESHOOTING TOOLS AND RESOURCES

The power of the Internet makes troubleshooting much simpler. In addition to information on the Internet, Windows 2000 and ISA Server have many built-in troubleshooting tools to assist you.

Windows 2000 Tools

Windows 2000 includes resources to help you troubleshoot any difficulties in using it. Since ISA Server uses Windows 2000 as its base operating system, you can also use these resources to solve problems with ISA Server.

Network Monitor

As you saw in Chapter 12, the Network Monitor application records network traffic passing through ISA Server at extremely detailed levels. This tool can prove invaluable when you troubleshoot network problems.

 Microsoft calls the version of Network Monitor included with Windows 2000 a "lite" version that can monitor traffic on the local network. The full version, which is included with Microsoft Systems Management Server (SMS), can monitor remote computers attached to other networks.

The Network Monitor allows you to capture frames traveling across the network and analyze the data at each layer of the OSI model. The capture view of Network Monitor, shown in Figure 13-1, is a real-time display of current network activity in a format similar to the Performance Monitor.

13

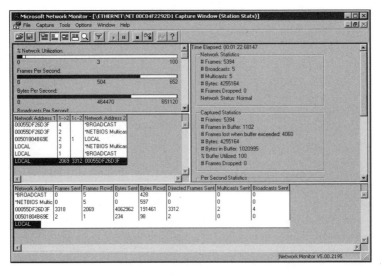

Figure 13-1   The Network Monitor capture view

Although you as network administrator view general network statistics, the Network Monitor records every frame of data that crosses the network. Once you stop capturing network data, you can view all the recorded traffic in detail, as shown in Figure 13-2.

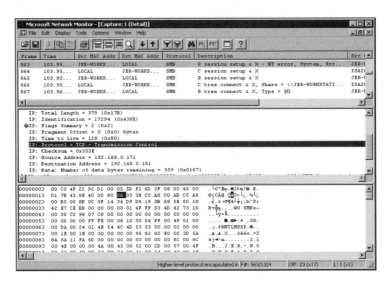

Figure 13-2   The Network Monitor detail view

    Avoid capturing network traffic for long periods. Busy networks can have thousands of frames that cross the network segment every second.

Because the capture files recorded by the Network Monitor can be overwhelming, you can use **capture filter** and **display filter** options to control how much data the application records or displays on the screen. If you apply a capture filter, you can specify the device to use for data capture, or the type of data you want to capture. If you apply a display filter, ISA Server captures all network data from the attached segment, but displays only records that match the filter criteria.

Event Viewer

The Windows 2000 Event Viewer records all events that deal with installed applications, security, and system functions. When Windows 2000 or ISA Server is not working correctly, the Event Viewer is typically the first place you look. The Event Viewer is divided into three categories:

- *Application Log*—This log file stores all events related to applications installed on Windows 2000. To store these records, the application must be configured to write data to the Event Viewer. Generally speaking, Microsoft-coded applications record their events to this log file, but third-party applications do not. ISA Server writes most application and security events to this event log.

- *Security Log*—This log file stores any security-related events. As you learned in Chapter 12, ISA Server 2000 creates a separate log file where it stores all performance and security records; however, Windows 2000 records all security information to the Security Log file. Because Windows 2000 captures and stores any NTFS or logon violations, the file can alert you to hackers who attempt to break ISA Server security. You should review both ISA Server and Windows 2000 security log files on a regular basis.

- *System Log*—The system log stores information related to Windows 2000 components, including system services and device drivers. Since ISA Server installs additional system services, Windows 2000 stores many ISA Server events in this log file.

If you have the DNS service installed, Windows 2000 creates a separate DNS category that logs all DNS-related events, as shown in Figure 13-3.

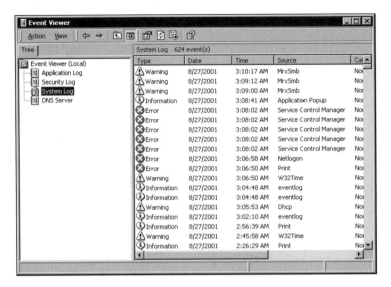

Figure 13-3   The Windows 2000 Event Viewer

From the default summary view, shown in Figure 13-3, you can see that recorded events are organized by the most recent date and time. In the list of Application or System events, you can find three types of messages:

- *Information*—The Information log records significant "success operations." For example, you may configure the event log to write an Information event whenever a service starts successfully.

- *Warning*—The Warning log records atypical events. These events are not necessarily service or driver failures, but might be potential problems. For example, if ISA Server is configured as a DHCP client, and cannot obtain an IP address, the event is written as a Warning.

- *Error*—The Error log records device or service failures. These events typically represent a significant problem. For example, if an ISA Server function fails to start, an Error event is recorded.

From the summary view of the Event Viewer, you can see a list of past events. If you want more detail about an event, double-click it. The Event Properties dialog box appears, as shown in Figure 13-4. You can often begin to troubleshoot the event based on the information in the Description field. For example, in Figure 13-4, the ISA Server control failed to start because it could not access the storage of the current array during service initialization. You know that ISA Server stores array information in Active Directory, so you should check the Windows 2000 domain controller and the intermediate network connections.

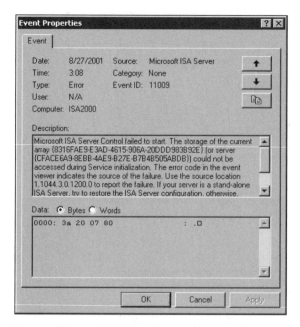

Figure 13-4   Viewing the event properties

Sometimes the description in the Event Viewer can be quite cryptic. In this case, note the **Event ID** in the Event Properties dialog box. You can use this ID when searching for related information on the Web or communicating with Microsoft technical support. For example, Figure 13-4 shows Event ID 11009. If you perform a search on the Microsoft Web site with this Event ID, you find article Q282035. This article describes a failure of ISA Server to communicate with the domain controller because of incorrect LAT configuration.

Additional Troubleshooting Resources

In addition to using the built-in Windows 2000 tools to troubleshoot ISA Server, you have plenty of other resources. ISA Server includes many troubleshooting tools itself, and you can find even more on the Web. By using a combination of these tools, you should be able to troubleshoot any problem with ISA Server.

ISA Server Help Files

ISA Server includes a wealth of information in its Help files. You can search these files and quickly find an answer to most common problems. Furthermore, the Help files are organized by topic to walk you through the following areas, as shown in Figure 13-5.

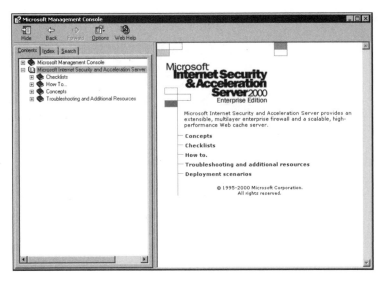

Figure 13-5   ISA Server Help file categories

- *Checklists*—This topic category contains verification checklists for common ISA Server tasks such as installation, migration from Proxy Server 2.0, configuring SecureNAT clients, and creating an access policy. These checklists are excellent guides for new ISA Server administrators to follow.

- *How To*—This topic category can help you configure every major ISA Server feature, including access policies, H.323 Gatekeepers, bandwidth rules, and monitoring and reporting.

- *Concepts*—Use this topic category to review major ISA Server concepts, such as an overview of firewall functions, ISA Server features and architecture, authentication, and Internet security. These topics are conceptual overviews rather than configuration procedures.

- *Troubleshooting and Additional Resources*—This is where you spend most of your time when troubleshooting ISA Server. The troubleshooting topic contains explanations for many common problems and is divided into categories, including access policies, caching, dial-up entries, and publishing. Below the troubleshooting help topics are the additional resources, which include a glossary of terms, definitions of Performance Monitor counters, and ISA Server registry entries. An especially important resource is the list of event messages, shown in Figure 13-6.

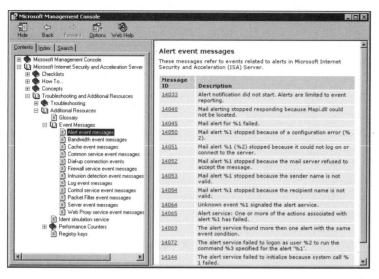

Figure 13-6   A list of common ISA Server Event IDs broken down by category

This list thoroughly defines most ISA Server Event IDs in the Event Viewer. The initial event display separates the listed Event IDs into common categories. If you want to see a more detailed explanation of any single Event ID, click the hyperlinked number. Each Event ID includes the event message from the Event Viewer, an explanation of the occurrence in plain English, and the user action, which tells you how to fix the problem, as shown in Figure 13-7.

13

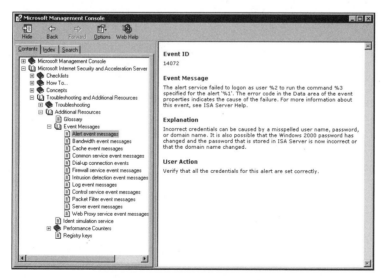

Figure 13-7   A more detailed description of a specific Event ID

Web Resources

The Help files included with ISA Server are good for troubleshooting many common problems; however, they are static, unchanging data. For any recent updates, you should turn to the Web. Microsoft provides an extensive, searchable database of resources on its Web site; three areas in particular provide search options for ISA Server:

- *www.microsoft.com/isaserver*—From this location, you can search two major resources, shown in Figure 13-8: The ISA Server Web site, which primarily provides marketing information describing the features and capabilities of ISA Server, and the ISA Server Information on TechNet, which provides current technical articles for ISA Server. To access these resources, click Advanced Search on the ISA Server Web site. You can also download a 120-day evaluation copy of ISA Server.

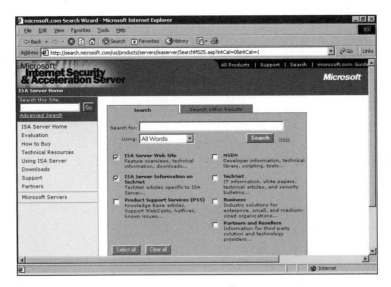

Figure 13-8   Microsoft's Web resource dedicated to ISA Server

- *support.microsoft.com*—This link takes you to the Microsoft Knowledge Base, which is the most extensive search utility on the Microsoft Web site. You can select the product you want to find from a list box, and then type a question. The search engine is structured to accept questions in plain English, such as "How do I install ISA Server?" Searching this database is the easiest way to find Q-articles.

- *www.microsoft.com/technet*—This link allows you to search the online version of TechNet, a centralized resource of the latest security bulletins, white papers, and deployment guides.

In addition to the Microsoft Web resources, you have many third-party Web resources as well. The most prominent is *www.isaserver.org,* which contains tutorials, bug reports, newsgroups, and links to third-party ISA Server applications.

TROUBLESHOOTING COMMON PROBLEMS

Now that you have been introduced to tools and resources that can help you troubleshoot ISA Server, you can learn about common issues that network administrators encounter while using ISA Server. The following sections highlight many of these problems. However, these sections are hardly exhaustive; because of the complex configuration of ISA Server, many more issues can arise. To resolve these issues, use the resources listed in the previous sections.

Troubleshooting Installation Problems

Although the installation of ISA Server is straightforward, a small oversight before installation can make it fail. Be sure to review the pre-installation checklist in Chapter five or the ISA Server online Help before you attempt to install ISA Server. This checklist can solve most of the common installation problems described in the following sections.

ISA Server Cannot Join an Existing Array

This is the most common issue during installation. Before you attempt to install ISA Server into an array configuration, ensure that the following conditions are met:

- The ISA Server Enterprise Schema is installed into Active Directory.

- The ISA Server machine joining the array is a member of the same Windows 2000 domain as the ISA Server machines in the target array before ISA Server was installed.

- The ISA Server machine joining the array is a member of the same Active Directory site as the ISA Server machines in the target array before ISA Server was installed.

- You have permission to access the Active Directory schema.

- A Windows 2000 domain controller is accessible from the ISA Server machine joining the array.

ISA Server Does Not Meet Minimum Installation Requirements

Before ISA Server can successfully install, you must ensure that the installation server meets the minimum hardware and software requirements. Do not try to cut corners on

13

the hardware requirements; this can cause instability with ISA Server. To review, the minimum installation requirements for ISA Server Enterprise Edition are as follows:

- Windows 2000 Server, Advanced Server, or Datacenter with Service Pack 1 or later installed
- at least one Windows 2000-compatible NIC connected to the internal network and included in the LAT
- a 300-MHz or faster Pentium II or compatible processor
- 256 MB of RAM
- at least 20 MB of available hard disk space
- If you want to enable caching, at least one partition must be formatted with the NTFS file system.

You Cannot Select a Partition for Cache File Storage

Remember that for performance and security reasons, ISA Server requires at least one partition to be formatted with the NTFS file system before it can store cached Internet content. If the partitions are formatted with the FAT or FAT32 file systems, they are unavailable for selection during installation. Before you run the installation utility, change at least one partition to NTFS using the command-line Convert utility.

ISA Server Services Fail to Start Following Installation

After you install ISA Server and reboot the server, you may notice that ISA Server services fail to start. This problem is typically caused by one of two configuration issues:

- ISA Server does not have enough memory (RAM) installed to support its services.
- The IP address of the internal NIC is not included in the LAT, or the Active Directory domain controllers are unreachable. Either situation causes ISA Server services to fail on startup, since ISA Server stores its array configuration in Active Directory.

ISA Server Cannot Renew a DHCP Lease After Installation

After you install ISA Server, you will find that the server cannot renew any IP addresses obtained through DHCP. In addition, once you release your existing address, you cannot obtain a new one. If you reboot the server, it will gain a new, DHCP-assigned address, but will still be unable to renew the address. The problem is that DHCP addresses are obtained through a UDP broadcast, and the default configuration of ISA Server blocks all UDP ports. ISA Server obtains an IP address upon reboot because the DHCP request is sent before the ISA Server functions can fully load.

To resolve this issue, you must enable the DHCP client packet filter. It is the only built-in packet filter that is disabled by default. To enable the filter, expand the Access Policy node under your server or array, and click IP Packet Filters. In the details pane, right-click the DHCP client packet filter, and then click Enable. ISA Server should no longer have problems obtaining or renewing an IP address.

Troubleshooting Caching Problems

While caching is a simple feature to configure in ISA Server, it can create a few complications. You can assure minimal caching problems by verifying that the hard-disk space and TTL parameters are configured correctly. To ensure that the proper amount of hard-disk space is available, use the standard cache formula of 100 MB + 0.5 MB cache space per user. For example, if ISA Server handles 1000 clients, you should have a minimum cache storage space of 100 MB + 0.5(1000) = 600 MB.

The TTL parameters make up the other set of cache configuration issues. Setting these parameters too high saves WAN bandwidth, but causes ISA Server to return outdated content to requesting clients. In extreme cases, news articles and stock quotes that are days old can be returned to client browsers. On the other hand, setting the TTL parameters too low defeats the purpose of caching, since ISA Server clears the cached content almost as quickly as it receives it. To reconfigure the TTL parameters, expand your server or array in the ISA Management console, right-click Cache Configuration, and click Properties. In the Advanced tab of the Cache Configuration Properties dialog box, shown in Figure 13-9, you can reconfigure the cache TTL properties. See Chapter eight for a detailed discussion of these properties.

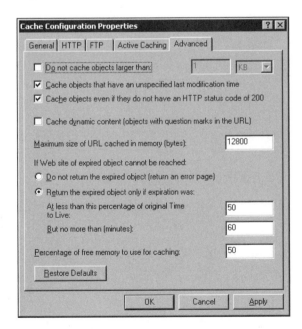

Figure 13-9   Reconfiguring ISA Server cache TTL properties

After the original release of ISA Server, Microsoft discovered a caching security problem that allows an intruder to run a potentially damaging script on internal client PCs. Microsoft has released a patch for this bug. For more information, search for Q295389 on the *support.microsoft.com* Web site.

The following sections describe other common caching problems you might encounter.

Web Proxy Service Fails to Start

If the Web Proxy service does not start, the cache files might be corrupted. While this rarely happens, you should be aware of the possibility. (If you notice the cache becoming corrupt more frequently, you may want to replace the hard disk you use for caching.) To start the Web Proxy service, first clear the current cache files by taking one of the following two actions:

- In the ISA Management console, expand the Cache Configuration node under your server or array. Click the Drives node, remove the current drives used to store cache files, and reconfigure new ones. The new drives can be the same drives you were using before. By deleting and recreating the cache storage drives, you clear the current cached files.

- ISA Server stores all cached content in .cdat files. A new .cdat file is created for every 10 GB of cache storage space required. To clear the cached content, stop the Web Proxy service; if necessary, use Windows 2000 to search for all .cdat files (*.cdat) on the hard disks, and delete the files. Restart the Web Proxy service.

ISA Server Consumes Too Much Available Memory for Caching Purposes

If you use ISA Server for multiple purposes (such as a firewall, domain controller, or mail server), you may not want caching to use too much available memory on the server. To adjust the amount of memory used for caching, open the ISA Management console, right-click the Cache Configuration node under your server or array, and click Properties. In the Advanced tab of the Cache Configuration Properties dialog box, change the Percentage of free memory to use for caching to the amount you want.

All Cached Web Sites Are Not Available Offline

One of the benefits of caching is that internal users can access cached Internet content, even if the Internet connection is down. However, you may notice that users receive "error 502 bad gateway" or "unable to connect" messages on browsers when connecting to certain Web sites. These errors can occur if the Web sites contain pages that ISA Server does not cache by default. Enabling ISA Server to cache dynamic content typically solves the problem, but can create many problems of its own. Make sure you research the benefits and drawbacks of dynamic caching before you enable it. Chapter eight has a discussion of dynamic caching for readers to begin their research. You can also access *support.microsoft.com/support/kb/articles/q275/2/32.asp* for a more detailed explanation of this problem.

Cache Initialization Failure

You can receive a "cache initialization failure" or "cache container initialization error" message if you choose to use all the available hard-disk space on a partition when installing ISA Server. ISA Server allows you to select all available disk space for cache storage, but does not account for the amount of disk space it needs to install. You can pass the built-in check during installation, but once ISA Server reboots, you receive the error message. To fix this problem, resize the cache space to account for remaining free disk space.

Troubleshooting Firewall and Access Problems

Most firewall and access problems result from simple misconfiguration or a misunderstanding of what each client platform provides. The following sections describe the most common firewall and access problems.

Clients Cannot Use a Non-TCP or Non-UDP Protocol

This problem is typically discovered when a client cannot ping external hosts. The Ping utility uses the ICMP protocol, and ISA Server handles only TCP and UDP requests by default. To allow other protocols, you must enable IP routing on ISA Server. Open the ISA Management MMC, expand the Access Policy node under your server or array, right-click IP Packet Filters, and click Properties. In the IP Packet Filters Properties dialog box, shown in Figure 13-10, click the Enable IP routing check box.

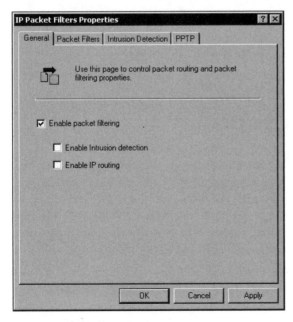

Figure 13-10   Enabling IP routing

User is Granted Access, Although a Site and Content Rule Explicitly Denies Access

After you create a site and content rule that denies access to a specific user or group, you might find that you can still access explicitly denied Web sites through Internet Explorer. This can happen if you configure ISA Server to allow anonymous Web access and the user is configured as a Web Proxy client. Even if you have the Firewall client software installed on the client PC, the authentication information is not sent if ISA Server does not request it.

To solve this problem, choose not to enable anonymous Web access or to create rules based on nonauthentication criteria. If you deny anonymous Web access and users do not have the Firewall client installed, they are prompted to enter their username and password any time they attempt to access the Web. Once they enter the authentication information, ISA Server verifies access and allows or denies the request.

Clients Can Still Access a Protocol After a Rule Is Disabled

After you disable a rule that grants access to a specific protocol, you might find that internal users can still pass through ISA Server using the protocol. For example, if you disable the rule allowing access with the File Transfer Protocol (FTP) while a user is downloading .mp3 music files from an FTP site, the user can still transfer the files.

The problem is that the internal user's FTP session never disconnected. ISA Server denies access from the external or internal network during creation of a session, but does nothing to check sessions already in progress. To apply the new protocol restrictions to a user downloading files via FTP, expand the Monitoring node under your server or array in the ISA Management console, and click Sessions. Find the user in the list of current connections, right-click the current FTP session, and click Abort Session to eliminate the FTP connection. The next time the user tries to connect to the FTP site, ISA Server applies the new protocol restrictions and denies access.

Troubleshooting Client Problems

Because of their sheer numbers, internal clients tend to be involved with most problems in ISA Server. Some client problems result from incorrect configuration, but end users cause the lion's share. People are more computer literate than ever before, and they experiment more with their office PCs. As a result, network administrators use remote monitoring and access software such as Terminal Services or PC Anywhere to monitor user activities. If problems arise, this increasingly popular software can save enormous amounts of troubleshooting time and allow you to reconfigure a user's PC remotely.

Aside from user issues, you should be aware of several other scenarios for client troubleshooting. The following sections describe some common problems.

Client Cannot Connect Directly to the Internet

After you configure a client as a Firewall client, it will be unable to connect to the Internet directly using a modem or any other connection method. This is by design; the ISA Server Firewall client redirects all outgoing requests from the client to ISA Server, even if there is a secondary network connection. To allow the client to connect to the Internet via a secondary method, you must disable the Firewall client software. Click Start, point to Settings, point to Control Panel, and then click Firewall Client to open the Firewall Client Options dialog box, as shown in Figure 13-11. To disable the Firewall client software, deselect the Enable Firewall Client check box and click OK.

Figure 13-11   The Firewall Client Options dialog box

The Client Web Browser Cannot Authenticate

This problem occurs frequently if you use a non–Microsoft Web browser such as Netscape or Mosaic. ISA Server can be configured with four different authentication methods: Basic, Digest, Integrated Windows, or Client Certificate. If you configure ISA Server to support only Integrated Windows (which is one of the more secure authentication methods), non-Microsoft Web browsers will be unable to authenticate to ISA Server and users will be denied access. Most Web browsers can support Digest or Basic authentication levels. To solve this problem, find the highest authentication level supported by all internal clients, and enable it on ISA Server.

13

Firewall Client Connections are Slow to Connect or Cannot Connect to Intranet Servers

Most slow connections are related to DNS. If you configure your clients to access an external DNS server, you open yourself to two major problems:

- The Firewall client attempts to access a Web server and the external DNS server is unavailable.
- The Firewall client attempts to access a server on the intranet.

If the external DNS server is unavailable, the client will either be unable to resolve the DNS hostname and will receive an error message in the Web browser window, or the client will time out while attempting to connect to the external DNS server and will be connected to a secondary DNS server. The latter result causes the seemingly slow Internet connection.

Likewise, if the Firewall client attempts to access a server on the intranet, and is configured to access an external DNS server, one of two results occur:

- The external DNS server does not have the mapping to the intranet server, and the request fails.
- The external DNS server does have a mapping to the intranet server and returns the *external* IP address used to reach the intranet server. When the internal client attempts to access the intranet server, the request goes to ISA Server's external interface, which forwards the request to the internal server. Once the internal server realizes the request is from a client on the local segment, it attempts to reach the client directly. Since the client is expecting a response from ISA Server and not the internal server, the access attempt is ignored and the client fails to connect.

You can solve all these DNS problems by configuring one or more internal DNS servers that contain valid records for any intranet server. Once you set up the internal DNS server, configure all the Firewall clients to access the server for DNS name resolution. Internal clients should no longer be delayed by waiting for DNS responses.

CHAPTER SUMMARY

- Windows 2000 comes with a Network Monitor utility that lets you analyze incoming and outgoing network traffic at detailed levels. You can use it to find information in individual packets.
- Windows 2000 and ISA Server both write any service-related events to the Windows 2000 Event Viewer. All Windows 2000 events are stored under the System log, and ISA Server events are stored under the Application log.

❑ When troubleshooting ISA Server problems, write down the Event IDs for the errors you find in the Event Viewer. ISA Server Help files contain a detailed list of most common Event IDs.

❑ ISA Server Help files contain valuable resources such as configuration checklists, step-by-step configurations, and a list of common troubleshooting problems.

❑ The *support.microsoft.com* Web site searches current Q-articles for any product you specify. These articles are valuable for finding the latest ISA Server bug reports and patches.

❑ Most ISA Server problems result from incorrect configuration, not from bugs in ISA Server 2000.

❑ Many problems can result if the LAT is incorrectly configured or the internal network card cannot reach a domain controller. Ensure the LAT contains only internal client computers and servers in the address table.

❑ If your internal clients have trouble reaching servers on the intranet or have slow connection speeds, try configuring an internal DNS server that contains valid records for all internal servers.

KEY TERMS

capture filters — You can use these filters with the Windows 2000 Network Monitor to screen data captured from the network.

display filters — You can use these filters with the Windows 2000 Network Monitor to filter data displayed in the capture results.

Event ID — The Event ID is stored in the Windows 2000 Event Viewer for each recorded event. You can reference this ID on the Microsoft Web site or in ISA Server Help files for detailed information about a given problem.

13

REVIEW QUESTIONS

1. After you successfully troubleshoot a situation, what should you do?

   a. Apply patches to ensure that the problem does not occur again.

   b. Document the problem and solution.

   c. nothing

   d. Uninstall ISA Server.

2. Upon booting ISA Server, you see the message "One or more devices failed on startup." Where should you look first for the problem?

   a. ISA Management console

   b. Network Monitor

   c. Event Viewer

   d. *support.microsoft.com* Web site

3. Which of the following is the primary resource for ISA Server Q-articles?

   a. ISA Server Help files

   b. *www.microsoft.com/isaserver*

   c. *support.microsoft.com*

   d. *technet.microsoft.com*

4. Where could you expect to find a warning message about a Ping of Death attack on ISA Server?

   a. Event Viewer System log

   b. Event Viewer Application log

   c. Event Viewer Security log

   d. none of the above

5. Michael is reviewing an ISA Server error message in the Event Viewer. Unfortunately, the description is very cryptic. Where is the *best* place to find more information about the event?

   a. ISA Server Help files

   b. *technet.microsoft.com*

   c. *support.microsoft.com*

   d. *www.microsoft.com/isaserver*

6. Benjamin is looking for a step-by-step procedure on configuring an H.323 Gateway. Where is the *best* place to find this information?

   a. ISA Server Help files

   b. *technet.microsoft.com*

   c. *support.microsoft.com*

   d. *www.microsoft.com/isaserver*

7. If you want to download a 120-day evaluation copy of ISA Server, where should you visit?

   a. *www.isaserver.org*

   b. *technet.microsoft.com*

   c. *support.microsoft.com*

   d. *www.microsoft.com/isaserver*

8. If ISA Server is unable to join an array, what should you check first?

   a. Event Viewer

   b. *support.microsoft.com*

   c. access to the c$ share on the domain controller

   d. network connectivity

9. Jennifer is attempting to install ISA Server as a caching server, but cannot select any cache storage partitions. What is the most likely cause of the problem?

  a. The hard disk has bad sectors.

  b. The partitions are formatted with the wrong file system.

  c. The enterprise schema has not been installed.

  d. Jennifer is not logged on with administrative privileges.

10. If your Web Proxy service refuses to start, but all other ISA Server functions are performing normally, what should you do?

  a. Open the Services administrative tool and manually start the Web Proxy service.

  b. Redirect users to the Firewall service using the HTTP Redirector.

  c. Clear the cache.

  d. Download the latest ISA Server service pack.

11. ISA Server is unable to obtain a DHCP address. What is the *best* way to solve this problem?

  a. Open UDP ports 60-70.

  b. Open UDP ports 114-117.

  c. Enable the DHCP client packet filter.

  d. all of the above

12. None of your internal users can check e-mail from an external e-mail server. You have configured ISA Server to allow full access to the Internet. What should you do next?

  a. Use the mail publishing wizard.

  b. Enable IP routing.

  c. Download the patch contained in article Q385113 on the *support.microsoft.com* Web site.

  d. none of the above

13. You have disabled anonymous access on your server. When your clients attempt to access Web content, they are prompted with an authentication dialog box. When they enter their username and password, they receive an "authentication failed" message. What is the *easiest* way to solve this problem?

  a. Ensure that users are granted proper access on ISA Server.

  b. Install Internet Explorer on all client machines.

  c. Enable only basic authentication on ISA Server.

  d. none of the above

13

14. When you attempt to access *www.isaserver.org* from an internal client, it takes 15 seconds for Internet Explorer to display the Web page. How can you solve this problem?

    a. Use an internal DNS server as the primary server in the client configuration.

    b. Disable intruder detection on ISA Server.

    c. Use Performance Monitor to ensure that ISA Server is not overwhelmed.

    d. You can't; all SecureNAT clients have a 15-second delay when accessing external content.

15. Within the Windows 2000 Network Monitor, what tools can you use to screen the amount of data recorded or displayed in the capture report?

    a. input and output filters

    b. allow and block filters

    c. Message Screener

    d. none of the above

16. You have 7,150 internal clients using ISA Server. What is the minimum amount of cache storage space you should use?

    a. 0.1 GB

    b. 3.5 GB

    c. 3.7 GB

    d. 4.5 GB

17. When you want to delete all cached files on a partition, what file extension should you search for?

    a. *.cdat

    b. *.cac

    c. *.dat

    d. *.cda

18. According to Microsoft, what is the minimum amount of memory (RAM) you should have before installing ISA Server?

    a. 64 MB

    b. 128 MB

    c. 256 MB

    d. 512 MB

19. You find that you cannot open any applications on ISA Server because the server is out of memory. How can you adjust the amount of memory ISA Server uses for caching purposes?

    a. through the Windows 2000 Services administrative tool

    b. in the ISA Management console under the cache drive configuration

    c. in the Performance tab of the Windows Task Manager

    d. none of the above

20. When installed into an array with three other servers, where does ISA Server store its configuration?

    a. on a Windows 2000 domain controller

    b. in the \ISAShare folder of the primary array server

    c. in the installation folder (by default, \Program Files\Microsoft ISA Server)

    d. in the Windows 2000 registry

HANDS-ON PROJECTS

Project 13-1

Use the Windows 2000 Web resources discussed in this chapter to find information or downloads on the following items:

▫ A patch for the Code Red worm that can attack Microsoft IIS through ISA Server

▫ A 120-day evaluation copy of ISA Server Enterprise edition

▫ A security patch for ISA Server Web Proxy service

▫ The Q271471 and Q295389 articles

▫ The most recent Windows 2000 Service Pack release

▫ An article about the error message "Could Not Register Smtpfltr.dll" when installing ISA Server

Project 13-2

To use Network Monitor:

1. In Windows 2000, click **Start**, point to **Programs**, point to **Administrative Tools**, and click **Network Monitor**.

2. In the Microsoft Network Monitor window, click **Capture** on the menu bar, and then click **Start**. The capture begins.

3. Minimize the Microsoft Network Monitor window and open a command prompt.

4. In the command prompt window, ping your partner's server IP address, the IP address of another attached client, or the IP address of your default gateway. You should see four success messages.

13

Network Monitor does not record any data if you attempt to ping a loopback address or the IP address of the internal or external interface.

5. Close the command prompt window, and restore the Network Monitor utility.

6. Click **Capture** on the menu bar, and then click **Stop and View**. The output should be similar to that shown in Figure 13-12. If you are on a busy network, you may see additional recorded data.

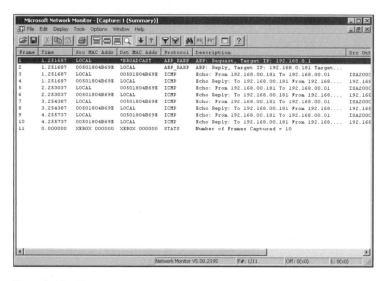

Figure 13-12

7. To make the data easier to read, you can apply a display filter. Click **Display** on the menu bar, and then click **Filter**.

8. In the Display Filter dialog box, double-click the **Protocol == Any** variable.

9. In the Expression dialog box, click the **Disable All** button to filter all protocols. All protocols move to the Disabled Protocols list.

10. Click the **ARP_RARP** protocol in the Disabled Protocols list, and then click the **Enable** button. The only protocol in the Enabled Protocols list should be ARP_RARP (Address Resolution Protocol/Reverse Address Resolution Protocol), as shown in Figure 13-13. Click **OK**. You have applied a display filter that screens all data except the ARP_RARP data type.

ISA Server uses ARP to determine the MAC address associated with the IP address of the host you pinged.

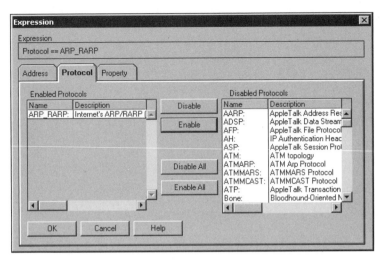

Figure 13-13

11. You should see two entries in the capture summary window. Double-click each of the two entries and each field to record the following data:

Data Field	Frame 1	Frame 2
ETHERNET: Source Address		
ETHERNET: Destination Address		
ARP_RARP: Sender's Protocol Address		
ARP_RARP: Target's Protocol Address		
Frame: Total frame length		

12. When you complete the exercise, close the Network Monitor application. Choose to save the capture or close without saving.

Project 13-3

To use the Event Viewer:

1. In Windows 2000, click **Start**, point to **Programs**, point to **Administrative Tools**, and then click **Event Viewer**.

2. The Event Viewer window displays messages under the System and Application logs. Cross-reference at least one informational message, one warning message, and one error message using the Web resources or help files discussed in this chapter.

13

Project 13-4

Using ISA Server help files, search for help on the following topics:

- A checklist for installing and configuring Firewall clients
- Event IDs 14010 and 14143
- Common registry keys used in performance tuning
- How to configure publishing
- ISA Server deployment scenarios
- How to configure monitoring and reporting
- A list and description of all caching performance counters
- A glossary of common ISA Server terminology
- An overview of ISA Server destination sets and SecureNAT clients
- A definition of an RPC filter

Project 13-5

Using the necessary resources, find a step-by-step walkthrough to configure live stream splitting for a media streaming application filter. Use this walk-through to implement live stream splitting on your ISA Server, which can save valuable WAN bandwidth when multiple internal users access the same media stream.

Project 13-6

Open the Network Monitor utility, and start a network capture. From ISA Server or a client PC's Web browser, access *http://www.course.com*. Once the page has fully loaded, return to the Network Monitor utility, and view the captured data. Apply a display filter that allows you to view only HTTP traffic. Scroll through the captured data, and find the Web server software that the *www.course.com* Web site uses and the date/time the content was last modified. Notice that all captured data is displayed in clear text. In an enterprise network environment, what problems could this pose? What feature, if any, would you be able to implement on your ISA Server to help this issue?

Begin a new capture in Network Monitor, electing not to save the old data. From ISA Server or a client PC's Web browser, access *https://www.microsoft.com*. After the page has completed loading, return to the Network Monitor utility, and view the captured data. By viewing the captured data, is it possible to find the same information you found on the *www.course.com* Web site? Why or why not?

CASE PROJECTS

Case Project 13-1

Juan Salista is the network administrator of Wireless Enterprises, a company that develops wireless network equipment. He has recently installed an ISA Server array consisting of three servers. A user on the internal network has been downloading and installing hacking utilities and attacking the ISA Server's internal network interface card. When Juan reviews the log files, he determines that the user must be changing IP addresses, since the detected attacks come from many different ones. What application or utility allows Juan to find the MAC address of the internal user?

Case Project 13-2

Susan Femmler is the network administrator of Hassle Inc., a debt collection agency. She has recently installed ISA Server, primarily to allow Hassle employees to send e-mail messages to clients, but also to protect the network from intruder attacks. Because employees should only use the Internet to send e-mail and access a handful of Web sites, she creates a site and content rule that denies employee access to all but three Web sites. After monitoring the network for a short time, she finds that employees can still access all Internet content. What is the problem, and how can Susan fix it?

Case Project 13-3

Carrie Davidson is the network administrator of Michigan Bears, a company that manufactures stuffed animals. The company uses ISA Server primarily for its firewall features. When Carrie arrived to work on Monday, she noticed a number of warning messages in the Event Viewer with Event IDs of 15007 and 15006. What is causing these warning messages? What should be Carrie's next step?

13

Case Project 13-4

Joshua Cara is the network administrator for Snowflake Petroleum Products. The company has recently installed ISA Server to improve Internet performance and make Web content available if the Internet connection fails. On Thursday, the Internet connection went down for three hours. Most commonly accessed Web content was available offline, but many other Web pages that users commonly visited were not available. After reviewing the log files, Joshua found that a few of these Web sites were accessed less than five minutes before the connection failure. What is the most likely reason ISA Server did not cache this content? Can Joshua force ISA Server to cache the missing Web pages?

A

Exam Objectives Tracking for MCSE Certification Exam #70-227: Installing, Configuring, and Administering Microsoft Internet Security and Acceleration (ISA) Server 2000, Enterprise Edition

The following table lists the exam objectives for MCSE Certification Exam #70-227: Installing, Configuring, and Administering Microsoft Internet Security and Acceleration (ISA) Server 2000, Enterprise Edition, and where these objectives are covered in the book. While nothing can replace a thorough understanding of the ISA Server product and hands-on experience, you can use this reference to prepare for your certification exam.

Exam Objectives for MCSE Certification Exam #70-227

Objective	Chapter: Section
Installing ISA Server	
Preconfigure network interfaces.	**Chapter 3: Configuring Network Connectivity**
Verify Internet connectivity before installing ISA Server.	**Chapter 3: Configuring Network Connectivity** Chapter 4: Internet Connectivity Considerations Chapter 5: Pre-Installation Checklist
Verify name resolution to the Internet.	**Chapter 3: Configuring Network Connectivity** Chapter 4: Internet Connectivity Considerations Chapter 5: Pre-Installation Checklist
Install ISA Server.	**Chapter 5: Installing ISA Server 2000**
Construct and modify the local address table (LAT).	Chapter 4: The Need for Planning **Chapter 5: Installing ISA Server 2000**
Calculate the size of and configure the cache.	Chapter 5: Installing ISA Server 2000 **Chapter 8: Managing Cache Storage**
Upgrade a Microsoft Proxy 2.0 Server computer to ISA Server.	**Chapter 5: Upgrading Microsoft Proxy Server 2.0 to ISA Server 2000**
Back up the Proxy 2.0 Server configuration.	**Chapter 5: Pre-Installation Checklist**
Troubleshoot problems that occur during setup.	**Chapter 13: Troubleshooting Common Problems**
Configuring and Troubleshooting ISA Server Services	
Configure and troubleshoot outbound Internet access.	Chapter 5: Testing the Configuration: Allowing Outgoing Web Requests **Chapter 6: (all of the chapter)** Chapter 13: Troubleshooting Common Problems
Configure ISA Server hosting roles.	**Chapter 9: Publishing Strategies**
Configure ISA Server for Web publishing.	**Chapter 9: Configuring Server Publishing**
Configure ISA Server for server proxy.	**Chapter 9: Configuring Server Publishing**
Configure ISA Server for server publishing.	**Chapter 9: Configuring Server Publishing**
Configure H.323 Gatekeeper for audio and video conferencing.	**Chapter 9: Using ISA Server H.323 Gatekeeper Service**
Configure gatekeeper rules.	**Chapter 9: Using ISA Server H.323 Gatekeeper Service**
Configure gatekeeper destinations by using the Add Destination Wizard.	**Chapter 9: Using ISA Server H.323 Gatekeeper Service**
Set up and troubleshoot dial-up connections and Routing and Remote Access dial-on-demand connections.	**Chapter 6: Defining and Configuring Policy Elements**
Set up and verify routing rules for static IP routes in Routing and Remote Access.	**Chapter 6: Defining and Configuring Policy Elements**

Exam Objectives for MCSE Certification Exam #70-227(continued)

Objective	Chapter: Section
Configure Virtual Private Network (VPN) access.	**Chapter 10: Configuring VPN Servers within ISA Server**
Configure ISA Server computer as a VPN endpoint without using the VPN Wizard.	**Chapter 10: Configuring VPN Servers within ISA Server**
Configure ISA Server computer for VPN pass through.	Chapter 10: Configuring VPN Servers within ISA Server **Chapter 7: Working with Packet Filters and IP Routing**
Configuring, Managing, and Troubleshooting Policies and Rules	
Configure and secure the firewall in accordance with corporate policies.	**Chapter 7: Examining Network Security**
Configure the packet filter rules for different levels of security, including system hardening.	Chapter 7: Working with Packet Filters and IP Routing **Chapter 7: Securing the Server**
Create and configure access control and bandwidth policies.	**Chapter 6: Configuring Enterprise and Array Policy Rules** Chapter 7: Working with Packet Filters and IP Routing
Create and configure site and content rules to restrict Internet access.	**Chapter 6: Configuring Enterprise and Array Policy Rules**
Create and configure protocol rules to restrict Internet access.	**Chapter 6: Configuring Enterprise and Array Policy Rules**
Create and configure routing rules to restrict Internet access.	**Chapter 6: Defining and Configuring Policy Elements**
Create and configure bandwidth rules to control bandwidth usage.	**Chapter 6: Configuring Enterprise and Array Policy Rules**
Troubleshoot access problems.	**Chapter 13: Troubleshooting Common Problems**
Troubleshoot user-based access problems.	**Chapter 13: Troubleshooting Common Problems**
Troubleshoot packet-based access problems.	**Chapter 13: Troubleshooting Common Problems**
Create new policy elements. Elements include schedules, bandwidth priorities, destination sets, client address sets, protocol definitions, and content groups.	**Chapter 6: Defining and Configuring Policy Elements**
Manage ISA Server arrays in an enterprise.	Chapter 5: Installing ISA Server 2000 **Chapter 6: Comparing Enterprise, Array, and Server Policies**
Create an array of proxy servers.	**Chapter 5: Installing ISA Server 2000**
Assign an enterprise policy to an array.	**Chapter 6: Configuring ISA Server Enterprise Policies**

Exam Objectives for MCSE Certification Exam #70-227(continued)

Objective	Chapter: Section
Deploying, Configuring, and Troubleshooting the Client Computer	
Plan the deployment of client computers to use ISA Server services. Considerations include client authentication, client operating system, network topology, cost, complexity, and client function.	Chapter 4: The Need for Planning **Chapter 11: Examining and Configuring ISA Server Clients**
Configure the client computer for secure network address translation (NAT).	**Chapter 11: Examining and Configuring ISA Server Clients**
Install the Firewall client software. Considerations include the cost and complexity of deployment.	**Chapter 11: Examining and Configuring ISA Server Clients**
Troubleshoot autodetection.	**Chapter 11: Examining and Configuring ISA Server Clients** Chapter 13: Examining Troubleshooting Fundamentals
Configure the client computer's Web browser to use ISA Server as an HTTP proxy.	**Chapter 11: Examining and Configuring ISA Server Clients**
Monitoring, Managing, and Analyzing ISA Server Use	
Monitor security and network usage by using logging and alerting.	**Chapter 12: Understanding and Configuring Logging**
Configure intrusion detection.	**Chapter 12: Enabling Intrusion Detection**
Configure an alert to send an e-mail message to an administrator.	**Chapter 12: Configuring ISA Server Responses**
Automate alert configuration.	**Chapter 12: Configuring ISA Server Responses**
Monitor alert status.	**Chapter 12: Configuring ISA Server Responses**
Troubleshoot problems with security and network usage.	**Chapter 12: Understanding and Configuring Logging** Chapter 13: Troubleshooting Common Problems
Detect connections by using Netstat.	**Chapter 13: Testing Your Configuration**
Test the status of external ports by using Telnet or Network Monitor.	**Chapter 13: Testing Your Configuration**
Analyze the performance of ISA Server by using reports. Report types include summary, Web usage, application usage, traffic and utilization, and security.	**Chapter 12: Configuring and Using Reports**
Optimize the performance of ISA Server computer. Considerations include capacity planning, allocation priorities, and trend analysis.	**Chapter 12: (all of the chapter)**

Exam Objectives for MCSE Certification Exam #70-227(continued)

Objective	Chapter: Section
Analyze the performance of ISA Server computer by using Performance Monitor.	**Chapter 12: Monitoring Current ISA Server Activity**
Analyze the performance of ISA Server computer by using reporting and logging.	**Chapter 12: Understanding and Configuring Logging** **Chapter 12: Configuring and Using Reports**
Control the total RAM used by ISA Server for caching.	**Chapter 8: Managing Cache Storage**

B

TRANSPORT LAYER PROTOCOL NUMBERS AND TCP AND UDP WELL-KNOWN PORT ASSIGNMENTS

The following table lists the well-known port numbers 0–1023. Use this list as a reference when choosing the port numbers to allow or deny through your firewall.

Table B-1: Well-known Port Assignments

PORT	PROTOCOL	KEYWORD	DESCRIPTION
0	TCP, UDP		Reserved
1	TCP, UDP	TCPmux	TCP Port Service Multiplexer rfc-1078
2	TCP, UDP	compressnet	Management Utility
3	TCP, UDP	compressnet	Compression Process
4	TCP, UDP	echo	AppleTalk Echo Protocol
5	TCP, UDP	rje	Remote Job Entry
6	UDP	zip	Zone Information Protocol
7	TCP, UDP	echo	Echo
8	TCP, UDP		Unassigned
9	TCP, UDP	discard	Discard; alias=sink null
10	TCP, UDP		Unassigned
11	TCP, UDP	systat	Active Users; alias=users
12	TCP, UDP		Unassigned
13	TCP, UDP	daytime	Daytime
14	TCP, UDP		Unassigned
15	TCP, UDP		Unassigned [was netstat]
16	TCP, UDP		Unassigned
17	TCP, UDP	qotd	Quote of the Day; alias=quote
18	TCP, UDP	msp	Message Send Protocol
19	TCP, UDP	chargen	Character Generator; alias=ttytst source

Table B-1:   Well-known Port Assignments (continued)

PORT	PROTOCOL	KEYWORD	DESCRIPTION
20	TCP, UDP	ftp-data	File Transfer [Default Data]
21	TCP, UDP	ftp	File Transfer [Control], connection dialog
22	TCP, UDP	ssh	Secure Shell Login
23	TCP, UDP	telnet	Telnet
24	TCP, UDP	priv-mail	Any private mail system
25	TCP, UDP	smtp	Simple Mail Transfer; alias=mail
26	TCP, UDP		Unassigned
27	TCP, UDP	nsw-fe	NSW User System FE
28	TCP, UDP		Unassigned
29	TCP, UDP	msg-icp	MSG ICP
30	TCP, UDP		Unassigned
31	TCP, UDP	msg-auth	MSG Authentication
32	TCP, UDP		Unassigned
33	TCP, UDP	dsp	Display Support Protocol
34	TCP, UDP		Unassigned
35	TCP, UDP	priv-print	Any private printer server
36	TCP, UDP		Unassigned
37	TCP, UDP	time	Time; alias=timeserver
38	TCP, UDP	rap	Remote Access Protocol
39	TCP, UDP	rlp	Resource Location Protocol; alias=resource
40	TCP, UDP		Unassigned
41	TCP, UDP	graphics	Graphics
42	TCP, UDP	nameserver	Host Name Server; alias=nameserver
43	TCP, UDP	nicname	Who Is; alias=nicname
44	TCP, UDP	mpm-flags	MPM FLAGS Protocol
45	TCP, UDP	mpm	Message Processing Module [recv]
46	TCP, UDP	mpm-snd	MPM [default send]
47	TCP, UDP	ni-ftp	NI FTP
48	TCP, UDP	auditd	Digital Audit Daemon
49	TCP, UDP	tacacs	Login Host Protocol (TACACS)
50	TCP, UDP	re-mail-ck	Remote Mail Checking Protocol
51	TCP, UDP	la-maint	IMP Logical Address Maintenance
52	TCP, UDP	xns-time	XNS Time Protocol
53	TCP, UDP	domain	Domain Name Server
54	TCP, UDP	xns-ch	XNS Clearinghouse
55	TCP, UDP	isi-gl	ISI Graphics Language

Table B-1: Well-known Port Assignments (continued)

PORT	PROTOCOL	KEYWORD	DESCRIPTION
56	TCP, UDP	xns-auth	XNS Authentication
57	TCP, UDP	priv-term	Any private terminal access
58	TCP, UDP	xns-mail	XNS Mail
59	TCP, UDP	priv-file	Any private file service
60	TCP, UDP		Unassigned
61	TCP, UDP	ni-mail	NI MAIL
62	TCP, UDP	acas	ACA Services
63	TCP, UDP	via-ftp / whois++	VIA Systems-FTP/whois++
64	TCP, UDP	covia	Communications Integrator (CI)
65	TCP, UDP	tacacs-ds	TACACS-Database Service
66	TCP, UDP	sql*net	Oracle SQL*NET
67	TCP, UDP	bootps	DHCP BOOTP Protocol Server
68	TCP, UDP	bootpc	DHCP BOOTP Protocol Client
69	TCP, UDP	tftp	Trivial File Transfer
70	TCP, UDP	gopher	Gopher
71	TCP, UDP	netrjs-1	Remote Job Service
72	TCP, UDP	netrjs-2	Remote Job Service
73	TCP, UDP	netrjs-3	Remote Job Service
74	TCP, UDP	netrjs-4	Remote Job Service
75	UDP	priv-dial	Any private dial-out service
76	TCP, UDP	deos	Distributed External Object Store
77	TCP, UDP	priv-rjs	Any private RJE service
78	TCP, UDP	vetTCP	VetTCP
79	TCP, UDP	finger	Finger
80	TCP, UDP	WWW	World Wide Web HTTP
81	TCP, UDP	hosts2-ns	HOSTS2 Name Server
82	TCP, UDP	xfer	XFER Utility
83	TCP, UDP	mit-ml-dev	MIT ML Device
84	TCP, UDP	ctf	Common Trace Facility
85	TCP, UDP	mit-nil-dev	MIT ML Device
86	TCP, UDP	mfcobol	Micro Focus Cobol
87	TCP, UDP	ttylink	Any private terminal link; alias=ttylink
88	TCP, UDP	kerberos-sec	Kerberos(v5) krb5
89	TCP, UDP	su-mit-tg	SU/MIT Telnet Gateway
90	TCP, UDP	DNSIX	DNSIX Security Attribute Token Map
91	TCP, UDP	mit-dov	MIT Dover Spooler
92	TCP, UDP	npp	Network Printing Protocol

Table B-1: Well-known Port Assignments (continued)

PORT	PROTOCOL	KEYWORD	DESCRIPTION
93	TCP, UDP	dcp	Device Control Protocol
94	TCP, UDP	objcall	Tivoli Object Dispatcher
95	TCP	supdup	BSD supupd(8)
96	TCP, UDP	dixie	DIXIE Protocol Specification
97	TCP, UDP	swift-rvf	Swift Remote Virtual File Protocol
98	TCP	linuxconf	linuxconf
98	UDP	tacnews	TAC News
99	TCP, UDP	metagram	Metagram Relay
100	TCP	newacct	[unauthorized use]
101	TCP, UDP	hostriame	NIC Host Name Server; alias=hostname
102	TCP, UDP	iso-tsap	ISO-TSAP Class 0
103	TCP, UDP	gppitnp	Genesis Point-to-Point Trans Net or X400 ISO E-mail; alias=webster
104	TCP, UDP	acr-nema	ACR-NEMA Digital Imag. & Comm. 300
105	TCP, UDP	csnet-ns	Mailbox Name Nameserver
106	TCP, UDP	3com-tsmux	3COM-TSMUX, Eudora compatible PW changer
107	TCP, UDP	rtelnet	Remote Telnet Service
108	TCP, UDP	snagas	SNA Gateway Access Server
109	TCP, UDP	pop2	Post Office Protocol Ver 2; alias=postoffice
110	TCP, UDP	pop3	Post Office Protocol Ver 3; alias=postoffice
111	TCP, UDP	sunrpc	SUN Remote Procedure Call, rpcbind
112	TCP, UDP	mcidas	McIDAS Data Transmission Protocol
113	TCP, UDP	auth	ident, tap, Authentication Service
114	TCP, UDP	audionews	Audio News Multicast
115	TCP, UDP	sftp	Simple File Transfer Protocol
116	TCP, UDP	ansanotify	ANSA REX Notify
117	TCP, UDP	uucp-path	UUCP Path Service
118	TCP, UDP	sqlserv	SQL Services
119	TCP, UDP	nntp	Network News Transfer Protocol; alias=usenet
120	TCP, UDP	cfdptkt	CFDPTKT
121	TCP, UDP	erpc	Encore Expedited Remote Pro.Call
122	TCP, UDP	smakynet	SMAKYNET
123	TCP, UDP	ntp	Network Time Protocol; alias=ntpd ntp
124	TCP, UDP	ansatrader	ANSA REX Trader
125	TCP, UDP	locus-map	Locus PC-Interface Net Map Server

Table B-1: Well-known Port Assignments (continued)

PORT	PROTOCOL	KEYWORD	DESCRIPTION
126	TCP, UDP	nxedit	NXEdit - Previously: Unisys Unitary Login
127	TCP, UDP	locus-con	Locus PC-Interface Conn Server
128	TCP, UDP	gss-xlicen	GSS X License Verification
129	TCP, UDP	pwdgen	Password Generator Protocol
130	TCP, UDP	cisco-fna	Cisco FNATIVE
131	TCP, UDP	cisco-tna	Cisco TNATIVE
132	TCP, UDP	cisco-sys	Cisco SYSMAINT
133	TCP, UDP	statsrv	Statistics Service
134	TCP, UDP	ingres-net	INGRES-NET Service
135	TCP, UDP	loc-srv / epmap	Location Service / DCE endpoint resolution
136	TCP, UDP	profile	PROFILE Naming System
137	TCP, UDP	netbios-ns	NetBIOS Name Service
138	TCP, UDP	netbios-dgm	NetBIOS Datagram Service
139	TCP, UDP	netbios-ssn	NetBIOS Session Service
140	TCP, UDP	emfis-data	EMFIS Data Service
141	TCP, UDP	emfis-cntl	EMFIS Control Service
142	TCP, UDP	bl-idm	Britton-Lee IDM
143	TCP, UDP	imap2	Internet Message Access Protocol v2
144	TCP, UDP	NeWs	
145	TCP, UDP	uaac	UAAC Protocol
146	TCP, UDP	iso-ip0	ISO-IP0
147	TCP, UDP	iso-ip	ISO-IP
148	TCP, UDP	cronus / jargon	CRONUS-SUPPORT/Jargon
149	TCP, UDP	aed-512	AED 512 Emulation Service
150	TCP, UDP	sql-net	SQL-NET
151	TCP, UDP	hems	HEMS
152	TCP, UDP	bftp	Background File Transfer Program
153	TCP, UDP	sgmp	SGMP; alias=sgmp
154	TCP, UDP	netsc-prod	Netscape
155	TCP, UDP	netsc-dev	Netscape
156	TCP, UDP	sqlsrv	SQL Service
157	TCP, UDP	knet-cmp	KNET/VM Command Message Protocol
158	TCP, UDP	pcmail-srv	PCMail Server; alias=repository
159	TCP, UDP	nss-routing	NSS-Routing
160	TCP, UDP	sginp-traps	SGMP-TRAPS
161	TCP, UDP	sump	SNMP; alias=snmp
162	TCP, UDP	snmptrap	SNMP-trap

Table B-1: Well-known Port Assignments (continued)

PORT	PROTOCOL	KEYWORD	DESCRIPTION
163	TCP, UDP	cmip-man	CMIP TCP Manager
164	TCP, UDP	cmip/smip-agent	CMIP TCP Agent
165	TCP, UDP	xns-courier	Xerox
166	TCP, UDP	s-net	Sirius Systems
167	TCP, UDP	namp	NAMP
168	TCP, UDP	rsvd	RSVD
169	TCP, UDP	send	SEND
170	TCP, UDP	print-srv	Network PostScript
171	TCP, UDP	multiplex	Network Innovations Multiplex
172	TCP, UDP	cl-1	Network Innovations CL/1
173	TCP, UDP	xyplex-mux	Xyplex
174	TCP, UDP	mailq	MAILQ
175	TCP, UDP	vmnet	VMNET
176	TCP, UDP	genrad-mux	GENRAD-MUX
177	TCP, UDP	xdmcp	X Display Manager Control Protocol
178	TCP, UDP	nextstep	NextStep Window Server
179	TCP, UDP	bgp	Border Gateway Protocol
180	TCP, UDP	ris	Intergraph
181	TCP, UDP	unify	Unify
182	TCP, UDP	audit	Unisys Audit SITP
183	TCP, UDP	ocbinder	OCBinder
184	TCP, UDP	ocserver	OCServer
185	TCP, UDP	remote-kis	Remote-KIS
186	TCP, UDP	kis	KIS Protocol
187	TCP, UDP	aci	Application Communication Interface
188	TCP, UDP	mumps	Plus Five's MUMPS
189	TCP, UDP	qft	Queued File Transport
190	TCP, UDP	gacp/cacp	Gateway Access Control Protocol
191	TCP, UDP	prospero	Prospero Directory Service
192	TCP, UDP	osu-nms	OSU Network Monitoring System
193	TCP, UDP	srmp	Spider Remote Monitoring Protocol
194	TCP, UDP	irc	Internet Relay Chat Protocol
195	TCP, UDP	dn6-nlm-aud	DNSIX Network Level Module Audit
196	TCP, UDP	dn6-smm-red	DNSIX Session Mgt Module Audit Redir
197	TCP, UDP	dls	Directory Location Service

Table B-1: Well-known Port Assignments (continued)

PORT	PROTOCOL	KEYWORD	DESCRIPTION
198	TCP, UDP	dls-mon	Directory Location Service Monitor
199	TCP, UDP	smux	SNMP Unix Multiplexer
200	TCP, UDP	src	IBM System Resource Controller
201	TCP, UDP	at-rtmp	AppleTalk Routing Maintenance
202	TCP, UDP	at-nbp	AppleTalk Name Binding
203	TCP, UDP	at-3	AppleTalk Unused
204	TCP, UDP	at-echo	AppleTalk Echo
205	TCP, UDP	at-5	AppleTalk Unused
206	TCP, UDP	at-zis	AppleTalk Zone Information
207	TCP, UDP	at-7	AppleTalk Unused
208	TCP, UDP	at-8	AppleTalk Unused
209	TCP, UDP	tam / qmtp	Trivial Authenticated Mail Protocol/ The Quick Transfer Protocol
210	TCP, UDP	z39.50	wais, ANSI Z39.50
211	TCP, UDP	914c/g	Texas Instruments 914C/G Terminal
212	TCP, UDP	anet	ATEXSSTR
213	TCP, UDP	ipx	IPX
214	TCP, UDP	vmpwscs	VM PWSCS
215	TCP, UDP	softpc	Insignia Solutions
216	TCP, UDP	Atls / CAllic	(Access Technology / Computer Associates) License Server
217	TCP, UDP	dbase	dBASE UNIX
218	TCP, UDP	mpp	Netix Message Posting Protocol
219	TCP, UDP	uarps	Unisys ARPs
220	TCP, UDP	imap3	Interactive Mail Access Protocol v3
221	TCP, UDP	fln-spx	Berkeley rlogind with SPX auth
222	TCP, UDP	rsh-spx	Berkeley rshd. with SPX auth; possible conflict with masqdialer
223	TCP, UDP	cdc	Certificate Distribution Center
224	TCP, UDP	masqdialer	masqdialer
225-241			Reserved
242	TCP, UDP	direct	Direct
243	TCP, UDP	sur-meas	Survey Measurement
244	TCP, UDP	dayna	dayna
245	TCP, UDP	link	LINK
246	TCP, UDP	dsp3270	Display Systems Protocol

Table B-1:   Well-known Port Assignments (continued)

PORT	PROTOCOL	KEYWORD	DESCRIPTION
247	TCP, UDP	subntbcst_tftp	SUBNTBCST_TFTP
248	TCP, UDP	bhfhs	bhfhs
249-255	TCP, UDP		Reserved
256	TCP, UDP	rap	RAP
257	TCP, UDP	set	Secure Electronic Transaction
258	TCP, UDP	yak-chat	Yak Winsock Personal Chat
259	TCP, UDP	escro-gen	Efficient Short Remote Operations
260	TCP, UDP	openport	Openport
261	TCP, UDP	nsiiops	IIOP Name Service TLS/SSL
262	TCP, UDP	arcisdms	Arcisdms
263	TCP, UDP	hdap	HDAP
264	TCP, UDP	bgmp	BGMP
265	TCP, UDP	x-bone-ctl	X-Bone CTL
267	TCP, UDP	td-service	Tobit David Service Layer
268	TCP, UDP	td-replica	Tobit David Replica
269-279			Unassigned
280	TCP, UDP	http-mgmt	http-mgmt
281	TCP, UDP	personal-link	Personal-Link
282	TCP, UDP	cableport-ax	Cable Port A/X
283	TCP, UDP	rescap	rescap
284	TCP, UDP	corerjd	corerjd
285	TCP, UDP		Unassigned
286	TCP, UDP	fxp-1	FXP-1
287	TCP, UDP	k-block	K-Block
288-307			Unassigned
308	TCP, UDP	novastorbackup	Novastor Backup
309	TCP, UDP	entrusttime	EntrustTime
310	TCP, UDP	bhmds	bhmds
311	TCP, UDP	asip-webadmin	AppleShare IP WebAdmin
312	TCP, UDP	vslmp	VSLMP
313	TCP, UDP	magenta-logic	netfusion.co.uk
314	TCP, UDP	opalis-robot	Opalis Robot
315	TCP, UDP	dpsi	DPSI
316	TCP, UDP	decauth	decAuth
317	TCP, UDP	zannet	Zannet

Table B-1:   Well-known Port Assignments (continued)

PORT	PROTOCOL	KEYWORD	DESCRIPTION
318	TCP, UDP	pkix-timestamp	PKIX TimeStamp
319	TCP, UDP	ptp-event	PTP Event
320	TCP, UDP	ptp-general	PTP General
321	TCP, UDP	pip	PIP
322	TCP, UDP	rtsps	RTSPS
323-332			Unassigned
333	TCP, UDP	texar	Texar Security Port
334-343	TCP, UDP		Unassigned
344	TCP, UDP	pdap	Prospero Data Access Protocol
345	TCP, UDP	pawserv	Perf Analysis Workbench
346	TCP, UDP	zserv	Zebra Server
347	TCP, UDP	fatserv	Fatmen Server
348	TCP, UDP	csi-sgwp	Cabletron Management Protocol
349	TCP, UDP	mftp	mftp
350	TCP, UDP	matip-type-a	MATIP Type A
351	TCP, UDP	matip-type-b	MATIP Type B or bhoetty
352	TCP, UDP	dtag-ste-sb	DTAG or bhoedap4
353	TCP, UDP	ndsauth	NDSAUTH
354	TCP, UDP	bh611	bh611
355	TCP, UDP	datex-asn	DATEX-ASN
356	TCP, UDP	cloanto-net-1	Cloanto Net 1
357	TCP, UDP	bhevent	bhevent
358	TCP, UDP	shrinkwrap	Shrinkwrap
359	TCP, UDP	tenebris_nts	Tenebris Network Trace Service
360	TCP, UDP	scoi2odialog	scoi2odialog
361	TCP, UDP	semantix	Semantix
362	TCP, UDP	srssend	SRS Send
363	TCP, UDP	rsvp_tunnel	RSVP Tunnel
364	TCP, UDP	aurora_tunnel	Aurora CMGR
365	TCP, UDP	dtk	Deception Tool Kit (lame www.all.net)
366	TCP, UDP	odmr	ODMR
367	TCP, UDP	mortgageware	MortgageWare
368	TCP, UDP	qbikgdp	QbikGDP
369	TCP, UDP	rpc2portmap	rpc2portmap
370	TCP, UDP	codaauth2	codaauth2

B

Table B-1:   Well-known Port Assignments (continued)

PORT	PROTOCOL	KEYWORD	DESCRIPTION
371	TCP, UDP	clearcase	Clearcase
372	TCP, UDP	ulistserv / ulistproc	UNIX Listserv / ListProcessor
373	TCP, UDP	legent-1	Legent Corporation (now Computer Associates)
374	TCP, UDP	legent-2	Legent Corporation (now Computer Associates)
375	TCP, UDP	hassle	Hassle
376	TCP, UDP	nip	Amiga Envoy Network Inquiry Protocol
377	TCP, UDP	tnETOS	NEC Corporation
378	TCP, UDP	dsETOS	NEC Corporation
379	TCP, UDP	is99c	TIA/EIA/IS-99 modem client
380	TCP, UDP	is99s	TIA/EIA/IS-99 modem server
381	TCP, UDP	hp-collector	HP performance data collector
382	TCP, UDP	hp-managed-node	HP performance data managed node
383	TCP, UDP	hp-alarm-mgr	HP performance data alarm manager
384	TCP, UDP	arns	A Remote Network Server System
385	TCP, UDP	ibm-app	IBM Application
386	TCP, UDP	asa	ASA Message Router Object Def.
387	TCP, UDP	aurp	AppleTalk Update-Based Routing Protocol
388	TCP, UDP	unidata-ldm	Unidata LDM Version 4
389	TCP, UDP	ldap	Lightweight Directory Access Protocol
390	TCP, UDP	uis	UIS
391	TCP, UDP	synotics-relay	SynOptics SNMP Relay Port
392	TCP, UDP	synotics-broker	SynOptics Port Broker Port
393	TCP, UDP	dis	Data Interpretation System
394	TCP, UDP	embl-ndt	EMBL Nucleic Data Transfer
395	TCP, UDP	neTCP	NETscout Control Protocol
396	TCP, UDP	netware-ip	Novell Netware over IP
397	TCP, UDP	mptn	Multi Protocol Trans. Net.
398	TCP, UDP	krypolan	Kryptolan
399	TCP, UDP	iso-tsap-c2	ISO Transport Class 2 Non-Control over TCO
400	TCP, UDP	work-sol	Workstation Solutions
401	TCP, UDP	ups	Uninterruptible Power Supply
402	TCP, UDP	genie	Genie Protocol
403	TCP, UDP	decap	decap

Table B-1: Well-known Port Assignments (continued)

PORT	PROTOCOL	KEYWORD	DESCRIPTION
404	TCP, UDP	nced	Nced
405	TCP, UDP	ncld	Ncld
406	TCP, UDP	imsp	Interactive Mail Support Protocol
407	TCP, UDP	timbuktu	Timbuktu
408	TCP, UDP	prm-sm	Prospero Resource Manager Sys. Man.
409	TCP, UDP	prm-nm	Prospero Resource Manager Node Man.
410	TCP, UDP	decladebug	DECLadebug Remote Debug Protocol
411	TCP, UDP	rmt	Remote MT Protocol
412	TCP, UDP	synoptics-trap	Trap Convention Port
413	TCP, UDP	smsp	SMSP
414	TCP, UDP	infoseek	InfoSeek
415	TCP, UDP	bnet	BNet
416	TCP, UDP	silverplatter	Silverplatter
417	TCP, UDP	onmux	Onmux
418	TCP, UDP	hyper-g	Hyper-G
419	TCP, UDP	ariel1	Ariel
420	TCP, UDP	smpte	SMPTE
421	TCP, UDP	ariel2	Ariel
422	TCP, UDP	ariel3	Ariel
423	TCP, UDP	opc-job-start	IBM Operations Planning and Control Start
424	TCP, UDP	opc-job-track	IBM Operations Planning and Control Track
425	TCP, UDP	icad-el	ICAD
426	TCP, UDP	smartsdp	smartsdp
427	TCP, UDP	svrloc	Server Location
428	TCP, UDP	ocs_cmu	OCS_CMU
429	TCP, UDP	ocs_amu	OCS_AMU
430	TCP, UDP	utmpsd	UTMPSD
431	TCP, UDP	utmpcd	UTMPCD
432	TCP, UDP	iasd	IASD
433	TCP, UDP	nnsp	usenet, Network News Transfer
434	TCP, UDP	mobile-agent	MobileIP-Agent
435	TCP, UDP	mobile-mn	MobileIP-MN
436	TCP, UDP	dna-cml	DNA-CML
437	TCP, UDP	comscm	comscm

Table B-1:   Well-known Port Assignments (continued)

PORT	PROTOCOL	KEYWORD	DESCRIPTION
438	TCP, UDP	dsfgw	dsfgw
439	TCP, UDP	dasp	dasp
440	TCP, UDP	sgcp	sgcp
441	TCP, UDP	decvms-sysmgt	decvms-sysmgt
442	TCP, UDP	cvc_hostd	cvc_hostd
443	TCP, UDP	https	http protocol over TLS/SSL
444	TCP, UDP	snpp	Simple Network Paging Protocol
445	TCP, UDP	microsoft-ds	Microsoft-DS
446	TCP, UDP	ddm-rdb	DDM-RDB
447	TCP, UDP	ddm-dfm	DDM-RFM
448	TCP, UDP	ddm-ssl	aam-byte
449	TCP, UDP	as-servermap	AS Server Mapper
450	TCP, UDP	tserver	TServer
451	TCP, UDP	sfs-smp-net	Cray Network Semaphore server
452	TCP, UDP	sfs-config	Cray SFS config server
453	TCP, UDP	creativeserver	CreativeServer
454	TCP, UDP	contentserver	ContentServer
455	TCP, UDP	creativepartnr	CreativePartnr
456	TCP, UDP	macon-TCP/UDP	macon-TCP/UDP
457	TCP, UDP	scohelp	scohelp
458	TCP, UDP	appleqtc	Apple Quick Time
459	TCP, UDP	ampr-rcmd	ampr-rcmd
460	TCP, UDP	skronk	skronk
461	TCP, UDP	datasurfsrv	DataRampSrv
462	TCP, UDP	datasurfsrvsec	DataRampSrvSec
463	TCP, UDP	alpes	alpes
464	TCP, UDP	kpasswd	kerberos (v5)
465	TCP, UDP	smtps	smtp protocol over TLS/SSL (was ssmtp)
466	TCP, UDP	digital-vrc	digital-vrc
467	TCP, UDP	mylex-mapd	mylex-mapd
468	TCP, UDP	photuris	photuris
469	TCP, UDP	rcp	Radio Control Protocol
470	TCP, UDP	scx-proxy	scx-proxy
471	TCP, UDP	mondex	Mondex
472	TCP, UDP	ljk-login	ljk-login
473	TCP, UDP	hybrid-pop	hybrid-pop

Table B-1:   Well-known Port Assignments (continued)

PORT	PROTOCOL	KEYWORD	DESCRIPTION
474	TCP, UDP	tn-tl-w1	tn-tl-w1
475	TCP, UDP	TCPnethaspsrv	TCPnethaspsrv
476	TCP, UDP	tn-tl-fd1	tn-tl-fd1
477	TCP, UDP	ss7ns	ss7ns
478	TCP, UDP	spsc	spsc
479	TCP, UDP	iafserver	iafserver
480	TCP, UDP	iafdbase	iafdbase
481	TCP, UDP	des/ph	Ph service
482	TCP, UDP	bgs-nsi/xlog	
483	TCP, UDP	ulpnet	ulpnet
484	TCP, UDP	integra-sme	Integra Software Management Environment
485	TCP, UDP	powerburst	Air Soft Power Burst
486	TCP, UDP	sstat/avian	
487	TCP, UDP	saft	saft Simple Asynchronous File Transfer
488	TCP, UDP	gss-http	gss-http
489	TCP, UDP	nest-protocol	nest-protocol
490	TCP, UDP	micom-pfs	micom-pfs
491	TCP, UDP	go-login	go-login
492	TCP, UDP	ticf-1	Transport Independent Convergence for FNA
493	TCP, UDP	ticf-2	Transport Independent Convergence for FNA
494	TCP, UDP	pov-ray	POV-Ray
495	TCP, UDP	intecourier	intecourier
496	TCP, UDP	pim-rp-disc	PIM-RP-DISC
497	TCP, UDP	dantz	dantz
498	TCP, UDP	siam	siam
499	TCP, UDP	iso-ill	ISO ILL Protocol
500	TCP, UDP	isakmp	internet Secuirty Association and Key management protocol
501	TCP, UDP	stmf	STMF
502	TCP, UDP	asa-appl-proto	asa-appl-proto
503	TCP, UDP	intrinsa	Intrinsa
504	TCP, UDP	citadel	citadel
505	TCP, UDP	mailbox-lm	mailbox-lm
506	TCP, UDP	ohimsrv	ohimsrv

B

Table B-1:   Well-known Port Assignments (continued)

PORT	PROTOCOL	KEYWORD	DESCRIPTION
507	TCP, UDP	crs	crs
508	TCP, UDP	xvttp	xvttp
509	TCP, UDP	snare	snare
510	TCP, UDP	fcp	FirstClass Protocol
511	TCP, UDP	passgo	PassGo
512	TCP	print / exec	BSD rexecd, Windows NT Server and Windows NT Workstation version 4.0 can send LPD client print jobs from any available reserved port between 512 and 1023. See also description for ports 721 to 731.
Remote process execution; authentication performed using UNIX loppgin names			
512	UDP	biff	comsat
513	TCP	login	BSD rlogind
513	UDP	who	BSD rwhod
514	TCP	shell	BSD rshd
514	UDP	syslog	BSD syslogd
515	TCP, UDP	printer	Spooler. The print server LP1 service will listen on TCP port 515 for incoming connections.
516	TCP, UDP	videotex	videotex
517	TCP, UDP	talk	Like tenex link, but across computers, BSD talkd
518	TCP, UDP	ntalk	talkd
519	TCP, UDP	utime	Unixtime
520	TCP	efs	Extended file name server
520	UDP	route	Local routing process (on site); uses variant of Xerox NS routing information protocol; alias=router routed
521	TCP, UDP	ripng	ripng
522	TCP, UDP	ulp	User Location Service
523	TCP, UDP	ibm-db2	IBM-DB2
524	TCP, UDP	ncp	NCP
525	TCP, UDP	timed	Timeserver
526	TCP, UDP	tempo	Newdate
527	TCP, UDP	stx	Stock IXChange
528	TCP, UDP	custix	Customer IXChange
529	TCP, UDP	irc-serv	IRC-SERV

Table B-1:   Well-known Port Assignments (continued)

PORT	PROTOCOL	KEYWORD	DESCRIPTION
530	TCP, UDP	courier	RPC
531	TCP	conference	Chat
531	UDP	rvd-control	MIT disk
532	TCP, UDP	netnews	Readnews
533	TCP, UDP	netwall	For emergency broadcasts
534	TCP, UDP	mm-admin	MegaMedia Admin
535	TCP, UDP	iiop	iiop
536	TCP, UDP	opalis-rdv	opalis-rdv
537	TCP, UDP	nmsp	Networked Media Streaming Protocol
538	TCP, UDP	gdomap	gdomap
539	TCP, UDP	apertus-ldp	Apertus Technologies Load Determination
540	TCP, UDP	uucp	Uucpd
541	TCP, UDP	uucp-rlogin	uucp-rlogin
542	TCP, UDP	commerce	commerce
543	TCP, UDP	klogin	kerberos (v4/v5)
544	TCP, UDP	kshell	kerberos (v4/v5), Krcmd; alias=cmd
545	TCP	ekshal	kerberos encryptd remote shell -kfall
545	UDP	appleqtsrvr	Apple Quick Time Server
546	TCP, UDP	dhcpv6-client	DHCPv6 Client
547	TCP, UDP	dhcpv6-server	DHCPv6 Server
548	TCP, UDP	afpoverTCP	AFP over TCP
549	TCP, UDP	ifdp	IDFP
550	TCP, UDP	new-rwho	New-who
551	TCP, UDP	cybercash	cybercash
552	TCP, UDP	deviceshare	deviceshare
553	TCP, UDP	pirp	pirp
554	TCP, UDP	rtsp	Real Time Stream Control Protocol
555	TCP, UDP	dsf	phAse Zero backdoor (Win 9x, NT) as well as dsf
556	TCP, UDP	remotefs	Rfs server; alias=rfs_server rfs, Brunhoff remote filesystem
557	TCP, UDP	openvms-sysipc	openvms-sysipc
558	TCP, UDP	sdnskmp	SDNSKMP
559	TCP, UDP	teedtap	TEEDTAP
560	TCP, UDP	rmonitor	Rmonitord
561	TCP, UDP	monitor	
562	TCP, UDP	chshell	Chcmd

Table B-1:   Well-known Port Assignments (continued)

PORT	PROTOCOL	KEYWORD	DESCRIPTION
563	TCP, UDP	nntps	nntp protocol over TLS/SSL (was snntp)
564	TCP, UDP	9pfs	Plan 9 file service
565	TCP, UDP	whoami	Whoami
566	TCP, UDP	streettalk	streettalk
567	TCP, UDP	banyan-rpc	banyan-rpc
568	TCP, UDP	ms-shuttle	Microsoft Shuttle
569	TCP, UDP	ms-rome	Microsoft Rome
570	TCP, UDP	meter	Demon
571	TCP, UDP	umeter	Udemon
572	TCP, UDP	sonar	sonar
573	TCP, UDP	banyan-vip	banyan-vip
574	TCP, UDP	ftp-agent	FTP Software Agent System
575	TCP, UDP	vemmi	VEMMI
576	TCP, UDP	ipcd	ipcd
577	TCP, UDP	vnas	vnas
578	TCP, UDP	ipdd	ipdd
579	TCP, UDP	decbsrv	decbsrv
580	TCP, UDP	sntp-heartbeat	SNTP HEARTBEAT
581	TCP, UDP	bdp	Bundle Discovery Protocol
582	TCP, UDP	scc-security	SCC Security
583	TCP, UDP	philips-vc	Philips Video-Conferencing
584	TCP, UDP	keyserver	Key Server
585	TCP, UDP	imap4-ssl	IMAP4+SSL (Use of 585 is not recommended, use 993 instead)
586	TCP, UDP	password-chg	Password Change
587	TCP, UDP	submission	Submission
588	TCP, UDP	cal	CAL
589	TCP, UDP	eyelink	EyeLink
590	TCP, UDP	tns-cml	TNS CML
591	TCP, UDP	http-alt	Filemaker - HTTP Alternative
592	TCP, UDP	eudora-set	Eudora Set
593	TCP, UDP	http-rpc-epmap	HTTP RPC Ep Map
594	TCP, UDP	tpip	TPIP
595	TCP, UDP	cab-protocol	CAB Protocol
596	TCP, UDP	smsd	SMSD
597	TCP, UDP	ptcnameservice	PTC Name Service

Table B-1:   Well-known Port Assignments (continued)

PORT	PROTOCOL	KEYWORD	DESCRIPTION
598	TCP, UDP	sco-websrvrmg3	SCO Web Server Manager 3
599	TCP, UDP	acp	Aeolon Core Protocol
600	TCP, UDP	ipcserver	Sun IPC Server
606	TCP, UDP	urm	Cray Unified Resource Manager
607	TCP, UDP	nqs	Nqs
608	TCP, UDP	sift-uft	Sender-Initiated/Unsolicited File Transfer
609	TCP, UDP	npmp-trap	npmp-trap @microsoft.com
610	TCP, UDP	npmp-local	npmp-local @microsoft.com
611	TCP, UDP	npmp-gui	npmp-gui @microsoft.com
612	TCP, UDP	hmmp-ind	HMMP Indication @microsoft.com
613	TCP, UDP	hmmp-op	HMMP Operation @microsoft.com
614	TCP, UDP	sshell	SSLshell @quick.com.au
615	TCP, UDP	sco-inetmgr	Internet Configuration Manager
616	TCP, UDP	sco-sysmgr	SCO System Administration Server
617	TCP, UDP	sco-dtmgr	SCO Desktop Administration Server
618	TCP, UDP	dei-icda	DEI-ICDA @Quetico.tbaytel.net
619	TCP, UDP	digital-evm	Digital EVM
620	TCP, UDP	sco-websrvrmgr	SCO WebServer Manager
621	TCP, UDP	escp-ip	ESCP @pobox.com
622	TCP, UDP	collaborator	Collaborator @opteamasoft.com
623	TCP, UDP	aux_bus_shunt	Aux Bus Shunt @ccm.jf.intel.com
624	TCP, UDP	cryptoadmin	Crypto Admin @cyberus.ca
625	TCP, UDP	dec_dlm	DEC DLM
626	TCP, UDP	asia	ASIA @apple.com
627	TCP, UDP	passgo-tivioli	CKS & TIVIOLI @ckshq.com
628	TCP, UDP	qmqp	Qmail Quick mail Queueing
629	TCP, UDP	3com-amp3	3Com AMP3
630	TCP, UDP	rda	RDA
631	TCP, UDP	ipp	IPP (Internet Printing Protocol)
632	TCP, UDP	bmpp	bmpp
633	TCP, UDP	servstat	Service Status update (Sterling Software)
634	TCP, UDP	ginad	ginad @eis.calstate.edu
635	TCP, UDP	rlzdbase	RLZ DBase @netcom.com
635	UDP	mount	NFS mount Service
636	TCP, UDP	ldaps	ldap protocol over TLS/SSL (was sldap) @xcert.com

Table B-1:   Well-known Port Assignments (continued)

PORT	PROTOCOL	KEYWORD	DESCRIPTION
637	TCP, UDP	lanserver	lanserver @VNET.IBM.COM
638	TCP, UDP	mcns-sec	mcns-sec
639	TCP, UDP	msdp	MSDP
640	TCP, UDP	entrust-sps	entrust-sps
640	UDP	pcnfs	PC-NFS DOS Authentication
641	TCP, UDP	repcmd	repcmd
642	TCP, UDP	esro-emsdp	ESPR-EMSDP V1.3
643	TCP, UDP	sanity	SANity
644	TCP, UDP	dwr	dwr
645	TCP, UDP	pssc	PSSC
646	TCP, UDP	ldp	LDP
647	TCP, UDP	dhcp-failover	DHCP Failover
648	TCP, UDP	rrp	Registry Registrar Protocol (RRP)
649	TCP, UDP	aminet	Aminet
650	TCP, UDP	obex	OBEX
650	UDP	bwnfs	BW-NFS DOS Authentication
651	TCP, UDP	ieee-mms	IEEE MMS
652	TCP, UDP	udlr-dTCP	UDLR_DTCP
653	TCP, UDP	repscmd	RepCmd
654	TCP, UDP	aodv	AODV
655	TCP, UDP	tinc	TINC
656	TCP, UDP	spmp	SPMP
657	TCP, UDP	rmc	RMC
658	TCP, UDP	tenfold	TenFold
659	TCP, UDP	url-rendezous	URL Rendezous
660	TCP, UDP	mac-srvr-admin	MacOS Server Admin
661	TCP, UDP	hap	HAP
662	TCP, UDP	pftp	PFTP
663	TCP, UDP	purenoise	PureNoise
664	TCP, UDP	secure-aux-bus	Secure Aux Bus
665	TCP, UDP	sun-dr	Sun DR
666	TCP, UDP	mdqs	
666	TCP, UDP	doom	Doom Id Software
667	TCP, UDP	disclose	campaign contribution disclosures-SDR Technologies @lambda.com
668	TCP, UDP	mecomm	MeComm @esd1.esd.de
669	TCP, UDP	meregister	MeRegister

Table B-1:   Well-known Port Assignments (continued)

PORT	PROTOCOL	KEYWORD	DESCRIPTION
670	TCP, UDP	vacdsm-sws	VACDSM-SWS
671	TCP, UDP	vacdsm-app	VACDSM-APP
672	TCP, UDP	vpps-qua	VPPS-QUA
673	TCP, UDP	cimplex	CIMPLEX @cesi.com
674	TCP, UDP	acap	ACAP @innosoft.com
675	TCP, UDP	dctp	DCTP @ansa.co.uk
676	TCP, UDP	vpps-via	VPPS Via @cesi.com
677	TCP, UDP	vpp	Virtual Presense Protocol
678	TCP, UDP	ggf-ncp	GNU Generation Foundation NCP
679	TCP, UDP	mrm	MRM
680	TCP, UDP	entrust-aaas	entrust-aas
681	TCP, UDP	entrust-aams	entrust-aams
682	TCP, UDP	xfr	XFR
683	TCP, UDP	corba-iiop	COBRA IIOP
684	TCP, UDP	corbra-iiop-ssl	COBRA IIOP SSL
685	TCP, UDP	mdc-portmapper	MDC Port Mapper
686	TCP, UDP	hcp-wismar	Hardware Control Protocol Wismar
687	TCP, UDP	asipregistry	asipregistry
688	TCP, UDP	realm-rusd	REALM-RUSD
689	TCP, UDP	nmap	NMAP
690	TCP, UDP	vatp	VATP
691	TCP, UDP	msexch-routing	MS Exchange Routing
692	TCP, UDP	hyperwave-isp	Hyperwave-ISP
693	TCP, UDP	connendp	connendp
694	TCP, UDP	ha-cluster	ha-cluster
695	TCP, UDP	ieee-mms-ssl	IEEE-MMS-SSL
696	TCP, UDP	rushd	RUSHD
697-703			Unassigned
704	TCP, UDP	elcsd	Errlog copy/server daemon
705	TCP, UDP	agentx	AgentX @acec.com
706			Unassigned
707	TCP, UDP	borland-dsj	Borland DSJ
708			Unassigned
709	TCP, UDP	entrust-kmsh	Entrust Key Management Service Handler, Nortel DES auth network see 389/TCP
710	TCP, UDP	entrust-ash	Entrust Administration Service Handler @entrust.com

Table B-1:   Well-known Port Assignments (continued)

PORT	PROTOCOL	KEYWORD	DESCRIPTION
711	TCP, UDP	cisco-tdp	Cisco TDP
712-728			Unassigned
729	TCP, UDP	netviewdm1	IBM NetView DM/6000 Server/Client
730	TCP, UDP	netviewdm2	IBM NetView DM/6000 send/TCP
731	TCP, UDP	netviewdm3	IBM NetView DM/6000 receive/TCP
740	TCP, UDP	neTCP (old)	NETscout Control Protocol (old)
741	TCP, UDP	netgw	NetGW
742	TCP, UDP	netrcs	Network based Rev. Cont. Sys.
744	TCP, UDP	flexlm	Flexible License Manager
747	TCP, UDP	fujitsu-dev	Fujitsu Device Control
748	TCP, UDP	ris-cm	Russell Info Sci Calendar Manager
749	TCP, UDP	kerberos-adm	Kerberos admin/changepw (v5)
750	UDP	kerberos-iv	Kerberos authentication (v4); alias=kdc
750	TCP, UDP	rfile	rfile
750	UDP	loadav	
751	TCP, UDP	kerberos-master	Kerberos "kadmin" (v4)
751	TCP, UDP	pump	pump
752	TCP, UDP	qrh	Kerberos password server
753	TCP, UDP	rrh	Kerberos userreg server
754	TCP	krb_prop	Kerberos/v5 server propagation
754	TCP, UDP	tell	Send
758	TCP, UDP	nlogin	
759	TCP, UDP	con	
760	UDP	ns	
760	TCP	krbupdate	kreg, kerberos/4 registration
761	UDP	rxe	
761	TCP	kpasswd	kpwd, Kerberos/4 password
762	TCP, UDP	quotad	
763	TCP, UDP	cycleserv	
764	TCP, UDP	omserv	
765	TCP, UDP	webster	
767	TCP, UDP	phonebook	Phone
769	TCP, UDP	vid	
770	TCP, UDP	cadlock	
771	TCP, UDP	rtip	
772	TCP, UDP	cycleserv2	

Table B-1:   Well-known Port Assignments (continued)

PORT	PROTOCOL	KEYWORD	DESCRIPTION
773	TCP	submit	
773	UDP	notify	
774	TCP	rpasswd	
774	UDP	acmaint_dbd	
775	TCP	entomb	
775	UDP	acmaint_transd	
776	TCP, UDP	wpages	
777	TCP, UDP	multiling-http	Muiltiling HTTP
778-779			Unassigned
780	TCP, UDP	wpgs	
781	TCP, UDP	hp-collector	HP performance data collector
782	TCP, UDP	hp-managed- node	HP performance data managed node
783	TCP, UDP	hp-alarm-mgr	HP performance data alarm manager
786	TCP, UDP	concert	concert
787	TCP, UDP	qsc	QSC
788-799			Unassigned
799	TCP	controlit	
800	TCP, UDP	mdbs_daemon	
801	TCP, UDP	device	
802-809			Unassigned
810	TCP, UDP	fcp-UDP	FCP Datagram
811-827			Unassigned
828	TCP, UDP	itm-mcell-s	itm-mcell-s
829	TCP, UDP	pkix-3-ca-ra	PKIX-3 CA/RA
830-870			Unassigned
871	TCP	supfilesrv	SUP server
872			Unassigned
873	TCP, UDP	rsync	rsync
874-885			Unassigned
886	TCP, UDP	iclcnet-locate	ICL coNETion locate service
887	TCP, UDP	iclcnet_svinfo	ICL coNETion server info
888	TCP, UDP	accessbuilder	AccessBuilder @3com.com
888	TCP	cddbp	CD Database Protocol @moonsoft.com
888	TCP	erlogin	Logon and environment passing
889-899			Unassigned
900	TCP, UDP	omginitialrefs	OMG Initial Refs @eng.sun.com

Table B-1:   Well-known Port Assignments (continued)

PORT	PROTOCOL	KEYWORD	DESCRIPTION
901	TCP, UDP	smpnameres	SMPNAMERES
902	TCP, UDP	ideafarm-chat	IDEAFARM-CHAT
903	TCP, UDP	ideafarm-catch	IDEAFARM-CATCH
904-910			Unassigned
911	TCP, UDP	xact-backup	xact-backup @xactlabs.com
912-988			Unassigned
989	TCP, UDP	ftps-data	FTP protocol, data, over TLS/SSL @consensus.com
990	TCP, UDP	ftps	FTP protocol, control, over TLS/SSL @consensus.com
991	TCP, UDP	nas	Netnews Administration System @fu-berlin.de
992	TCP, UDP	telnets	Telnet protocol over TLS/SSL @consensus.com
993	TCP, UDP	imaps	Imap4 protocol over TLS/SSL @consensus.com
994	TCP, UDP	ircs	irc protocol over TLS/SSL @consensus.com
995	TCP, UDP	pop3s	pop3 protocol over TLS/SSL (was spop3) @microsoft.com
996	TCP, UDP	vsinet	vsinet
996	TCP, UDP	xtreelic	XTREE License Server
997	TCP, UDP	maitrd	
998	TCP	busboy	
998	UDP	puparp	
999	TCP	garcon	
999	UDP	applix ac	Applix ac
999	TCP, UDP	puprouter	
1000	TCP	cadlock	
1000	UDP	ock	
1000-1007			Unassigned
1008	TCP, UDP	ufsd	UFS-aware server
1010	TCP, UDP	surf	surf
1012	UDP	sometimes-rpcl	This is rstatd on an openBSD box
1022-1023	TCP, UDP		Reserved

Glossary

.vpc file — A file generated by the Local VPN wizard, which stores all VPN configuration and is used to configure the remote VPN server.

acknowledgement — Packets sent, typically with TCP-based communication, to acknowledge receipt of data.

active caching — Allows the ISA Server to update cached content before the time to live expires.

Active Directory Service (ADS) — The Windows 2000 implementation of the X.500 database standard. *See* X.500.

Address Resolution Protocol (ARP) — A broadcast-based process used at the Network layer to attain a device's MAC address.

Advanced Research Projects Agency (ARPA) — An agency in the U.S. Department of Defense that created a large area network (LAN) in the 1960s for the free exchange of information between universities and research organizations.

application processes — The programs that use the Application layer in the OSI model.

application-level filters — Developed on a per application basis. Allows for detailed content filtering since the filter can access the incoming or outgoing data stream. ISA Server supports third-party development of application filters.

application-specific elements — Modules, usually written into the base operating system, that perform many common network tasks for communicating between applications. By using these modules, application developers can avoid rewriting large amounts of code, and thus increase application stability.

ARPANET — The precurser to the Internet. The large, wide area network created in the 1960s by the Advanced Research Projects Agency.

array policy — A policy that applies to the single ISA Server arrays throughout the network. These policies typically contain the department-specific restrictions specified by the department management.

Asynchronous Transfer Mode (ATM) — An extremely fast, packet-switched WAN solution that transfers data using fixed packet sizes called cells.

bandwidth priorities — A policy element allowing you to configure priorities from one to 200 to use with bandwidth rules.

baseline — A record of network activity during normal operation.

bits — Data transmitted at the Physical layer.

Bootstrap Protocol (BOOTP) — A method of allowing a diskless workstation to discover its IP address and boot from a network server.

broadcast — Data addressed to all hosts on a given network segment.

broadcast domain — Describes the scope of devices a given broadcast frame can reach on a network segment. All reachable devices are in the same broadcast domain.

Cache Array Routing Protocol (CARP) — The protocol used by ISA Servers array to distribute cached content evenly across array members and ensure content is not duplicated.

capture filters — You can use these filters with the Windows 2000 Network Monitor to screen data captured from the network.

Channel Service Unit/Data Service Unit (CSU/DSU) — A network device, similar to a modem, required to interface with a service provider for T1 and T3 connections. The CSU performs diagnostic functions, and the DSU provides the physical interface.

child domains — Domains below the root domain.

circuit-level filtering — Instead of filtering per port number, filtering applies on a per session basis. This allows applications to open needed ports to communicate without administrators manually opening up needed firewall ports.

classful IP addressing — A network structure where a network administrator uses only standard Class A, B, and C subnet masks to build a network.

classless IP addressing — A network structure where a network administrator applies custom subnet masks to network addresses.

Client Access Licenses (CALs) — A license typically required when accessing a Microsoft server across the network.

client address set — A policy element allowing you to define ranges of IP addresses to represent internal clients.

Committed Information Rate (CIR) — A specified amount of guaranteed bandwidth on a frame relay service.

content groups — A policy element allowing you to group together different MIME types to use when creating site and content rules.

content rules — The rules in an enterprise policy that define what types of content network users can access.

Cyclical Redundancy Check (CRC) — Also called Frame Check Sequence (FCS). A mathematical check at the Data Link layer that allows the receiving device to determine if transmitted data is corrupt.

data-link connection identifiers (DLCIs) — Unique identifiers for virtual circuits in a frame relay WAN. Similar to the MAC address on LANs.

datagrams — Data passing through the Network layer.

default rule — The last item in the bandwidth rule list, the default rule applies to all users and ensures they receive the minimum bandwidth configured in Windows 2000 default scheduling.

Demilitarized Zone (DMZ) — The LAN segment between the external and internal firewall, allowing more lenient security standards for external hosts to access internal Web, SMTP, and FTP servers.

Denial-of-Service attacks — An attack on a network designed to render the network services inoperable by flooding it with useless traffic.

destination set — Defines one or more network devices accessed on the local or remote network.

dial-up entries — Policy elements defined at the array level to configure ISA Server with dial-on-demand capabilities.

discretionary access control list (DACL) — A list of users and groups assigned permissions to an object in the ADS database.

display filters — You can use these filters with the Windows 2000 Network Monitor to filter data displayed in the capture results.

distributed caching — Allows ISA Servers combined in an array to share cached content. Provides both server redundancy and load balancing. Uses the CARP protocol to ensure duplicate items do not cache on multiple servers.

Distributed Computer Object Model (DCOM) — A protocol that enables software components to communicate directly over a Windows network, and is designed for use across multiple network transports, including Internet protocols such as HTTP.

domain controllers — Designated computers in each Windows 2000 domain that manage the ADS database for that domain.

Domain Name System (DNS) — A TCP/IP service that translates user-friendly hostnames to IP addresses.

Dynamic Host Configuration Protocol (DHCP) — A modern implementation of BOOTP allowing for the dynamic allocation of IP addresses.

dynamic network address translation (dynamic NAT) — Allows a one-to-many translation from private IP address ranges to public IP addresses. Dynamic NAT gives network administrators a method of working around the shortage of Internet-valid IP addresses by allowing many internal, private addresses to share one public IP address.

dynamic packet filter — Also called a stateful filter. Opens ports dynamically on the public network interface on a user request to allow public traffic from the requested object to enter the private network. Once session ends, the public port closes.

dynamic packet filtering — A method of packet filtering that allows ISA Server to dynamically open ports to allow for return transmission of requested data.

dynamic port number — The port numbers above 1024 that are available for network application usage.

effective bandwidth — The lowest speed of your network connections. Before you configure bandwidth rules, you must first configure the effective bandwidth so ISA Server can match the lowest-speed connection in your network.

encapsulate — The process of adding a public network header and trailer to an internal network packet, allowing it to cross the Internet in a tunnel.

enterprise policy — A policy that applies to all ISA Servers in the entire corporate network.

enterprise policy behavior — Settings that determine how ISA Server applies enterprise and array policies for the entire network.

Event ID — The Event ID is stored in the Windows 2000 Event Viewer for each recorded event. You can reference this ID on the Microsoft Web site or in ISA Server help files for detailed information about a given problem.

events — Conditions detected by ISA Server during normal operation.

File Transfer Protocol (FTP) — A protocol used typically on the Internet to send and receive files.

firewall — A system designed to prevent unauthorized access to or from a private internal network.

fishnet security — A security strategy that grants everyone access to all resources, and then places restrictions where necessary.

forward caching — Occurs when users on the internal network access the external network and the requested objects are cached.

frame — Data referenced at the Data Link layer between a header and a footer. The frame is the first logical information a receiving computer analyzes.

global catalog — The master database that contains all ADS objects and their properties.

hierarchical caching — Also called *chained caching*. Occurs when ISA Servers use one another in a hierarchical method to cache data. Directs forwarded requests from lower-level cache servers to higher-level cache servers which, if the content is not found, then direct the request to the Internet.

Internet — A collection of local area networks that forms one large, loosely tied, worldwide network of millions of users.

Internet Control Message Protocol (ICMP) — A TCP/IP sub-protocol that handles connection error control and informational messages. Used most commonly with the PING utility.

Internet Protocol (IP) — The method of Network layer logical addressing implemented by the TCP/IP protocol suite.

Internet Protocol Security (IPSec) — A set of protocols currently being developed by the Internet Engineering Task Force (IETF) to allow for secure encryption at the Network layer.

Internet Service Provider (ISP) — A company that provides access to the Internet.

intranet — Private networks that allow users to access internal information within a company or organization. Many intranets tie closely into the Internet, allowing private internal information to be accessed from a public network.

IP Helper-Address — An address that allows routers to propagate certain broadcast frames, such as a DHCP client request, to different network segments.

iron wall security — A security strategy that denies everyone access to all resources, and then grants permission where necessary.

ISA Management console — An MMC snap-in that organizes options for managing every aspect of your ISA Server.

ISA Server arrays — Formed when combining two or more ISA Servers into a collection of machines sharing configuration and cache information.

LAN Emulation (LANE) — ATM technology that allows the Ethernet or Token Ring LAN to treat the ATM network as another LAN subnet.

Lightweight Directory Access Protocol (LDAP) — A universal protocol used to access information from X.500-based directory services.

listener — A configuration that tells the ISA Server external interface how to respond to incoming requests.

live stream splitting — A configuration that allows ISA Server to locally store streamed data for multiple clients, thus minimizing the amount of WAN traffic used for audio or video streaming.

local access rate — The maximum speed allowable from the physical, frame relay connection.

Local Address Table (LAT) — The ISA Server table that identifies an internal network by IP address ranges.

local area network (LAN) — A client-server computer network established in one location, such as an office or building.

Logical Link Control (LLC) — The sub-layer of the Data Link layer that acts as a pointer to an upper Network layer protocol such as IP or IPX.

Media Access Control (MAC) — The sub-layer of the Data Link layer that handles the physical addressing of frames.

Microsoft .NET — Family of Microsoft products, created as a group of applications that allows Windows 2000 to seamlessly integrate into mission-critical Web-based services.

Microsoft Challenge Handshake Authentication Protocol (MS-CHAP) — A Microsoft proprietary implementation of CHAP, a secure user authentication protocol.

Microsoft loopback adapter — A virtual interface designed to emulate a physical network interface card.

Microsoft Management Console (MMC) — Used primarily in Windows 2000 as a tool which houses snap-ins to perform application-specific administrative tasks.

Multicast — A bandwidth-saving method of addressing data to groups of users instead of sending multiple unicast messages.

Multipurpose Internet Mail Extensions (MIME) — A specification defined by the IETF in 1992 which allows users to send character sets other than plain ASCII text (such as GIF or WAV files) across the Internet through e-mail.

negative caching — A feature allowing ISA Server to cache negative Web responses, such as a Web site being unavailable.

Network Address Translation (NAT) — Allows internal networks to use one set of IP Addresses, while another set of IP addresses is used on the external network. NAT then translates between them and hides the internal addresses from ever being seen or used on the external network.

network baseline — The average network usage under normal circumstances. Used when measuring the effect of adding or removing network resources.

Network Control Protocol (NCP) — The first client-to-client protocol developed for the ARPANET.

network firewall — A network system designed to prevent access to or from a network.

network interface card (NIC) — The device that enables a workstation to connect to the network and communicate with other computers.

Open Systems Interconnection (OSI) model — A model designed by the International Standards Organization (ISO) describing how devices communicate across a network. It divides networking architecture into seven layers: Application, Presentation, Session, Transport, Network, Data Link, and Physical.

packet filter — Applied at network firewalls, this filters incoming and outgoing traffic by analyzing IP addresses and port numbers.

packet/datagram — The Protocol Data Unit (PDU) found at the Network layer.

Password Authentication Protocol (PAP) — A basic user authentication protocol where transmission of the username and password occurs in clear text.

Point-to-Point Protocol (PPP) — A Data Link layer method of connecting a computer to the Internet or Virtual Private Network (VPN). The current successor to SLIP.

Policy Elements — The parts of a policy that define the criteria used when deciding to allow or deny a client inbound or outbound access to the LAN or Internet.

port numbers — Used by the Transport layer to tag each data segment with the correct application for which it belongs.

private networking ranges — Describes the group of IP address ranges used on internal LANs; addresses within such ranges are dropped by Internet routers.

Protocol Data Unit (PDU) — Terminology used to describe data as it reaches the various layers of the OSI model. A PDU containing the control information from the Transport layer is called a segment; from the Network layer it is called a packet; from the Data Link layer it is called a frame; and from the Physical layer it is called bits.

protocol definition — A policy element used to define the protocols supported by ISA Server, and the specific protocol configuration.

protocol number — Used by the Network layer to direct data to the correct Transport layer protocol.

protocol rules — The rules in an enterprise policy that define what protocol that network users can use to access an Internet or intranet destination.

Public Switched Telephone Network (PSTN) — The standard telephone network, also called the Plain Old Telephone Service (POTS).

publishing policy — A policy configured on ISA Server to grant secure access to internal servers.

Request for Comments (RFC) — A series of notes about the Internet started in 1969. Anyone can submit an RFC, and, if it gains enough interest, it may become an Internet standard.

reverse caching — Occurs when users on the external network access the internal network and the requested objects are cached.

reverse proxy — A device such as ISA Server that services requests from external users attempting to reach resources on the internal network.

root domain — The first domain created in an ADS tree, typically named after a company Internet domain name.

router — A network device with multiple ports that connects LANs and WANs. Routers are commonly used for remote access.

schedule — A policy element used to define set intervals of time.

scheduled content download — A manual configuration allowing administrators to configure the ISA Server to download specific Web contents on certain time-of-day intervals.

schema — A list of objects and their properties which can be created in the Active Directory.

Secure Network Address Translation (Secure NAT) — A Microsoft modification to NAT which allows for application of ISA Server Policies to incoming and outgoing NAT traffic.

segment — The PDU found at the Transport layer.

Serial Line Internet Protocol (SLIP) — An older data-link method of connecting a computer to the Internet that does not support username/password encryption or DHCP.

server policy — A policy implemented only on stand-alone ISA Server installations.

Simple Mail Transfer Protocol (SMTP) — This is an industry standard e-mail transmission protocol.

Simple Network Management Protocol (SNMP) — A communications protocol used to manage devices on a TCP/IP network.

site rules — The rules in an enterprise policy that define which network users can access a given Internet or intranet destination.

Small Office/Home Office (SOHO) — A computing environment typically for 2–20 users who work at home or in small offices.

socket — Formed by two communicating applications, consisting of an IP address combined with a port number.

source quench — An ICMP-based message that tells the device sending data to slow transmission.

static network address translation (static NAT) — Maps external, public IP addresses to private, internal LAN addresses on a one-to-one basis.

static packet filter — Packet filter configured manually by an administrator, combined with a permit or deny statement to allow or stop incoming or outgoing traffic on specific IP addresses or port numbers.

subnet mask — Used in conjunction with an IP address to determine what portion of the address represents the source and network destinations.

symmetric multiprocessing — A computer architecture that provides fast performance by making multiple processors work together on a single task. Multithreaded applications take the most advantage of multiprocessing since individual tasks in the application can be assigned to different processors.

Synchronous Optical Network (SONET) — A defined standard for connecting fiber optic transmission systems at the physical layer.

TCP three-way handshake — The process TCP-based clients use to exchange sequence and acknowledgement numbers before establishing a reliable session.

TCP/IP client — Any network device that has a valid TCP/IP address.

TCP/IP port numbers — Used by TCP and UDP to pass information to the correct upper-layer application.

TCP/IP protocol suite — A suite of protocols allowing for network connectivity. Most commonly used when connecting to the Internet.

Time to Live (TTL) — The amount of idle time content remains in the cache before deleted.

Transmission Control Protocol (TCP) — A reliable, Transport layer protocol allowing two clients to exchange streams of data with guaranteed delivery.

trust relationships — Logical links that tie together Windows 2000 domains and allow rights assignments between domains.

tunneling — Sending private data across a public network backbone, such as the Internet, and disguising it to look like public network traffic.

unicast — A data frame addressed to one individual network device.

User Datagram Protocol (UDP) — Provides a fast, "best-effort" delivery system for IP-based packets. Typically used for broadcasts.

Variable Length Subnet Masking (VLSM) — A strategy that uses two different subnet masks in an organization, such as one in California and one for the rest of the sites.

virtual circuits (VCs) — Paths defined through the frame relay cloud that act like a physical connection between two end devices.

Virtual Private Network (VPN) — Allows private internal network communication across a public network backbone.

Web caching — Also referred to as passive caching. This is the typical form of caching supported on most proxy servers. As a user accesses Web content, the ISA Server retrieves the requested data for the user and caches it, allowing the next user accessing the data within the TTL to retrieve the content locally.

Web Proxy Auto Discovery (WPAD) — An entry in the DNS or DHCP server that directs Firewall and Web Proxy clients to ISA Server for automatic configuration information.

well-known port numbers — The port numbers below 1024 that are reserved for specific network applications.

wide area network (WAN) — This is typically two or more Local Area Networks (LANs) connected across a relatively large geographic area.

Windows Internet Name Service (WINS) — A system that maps NetBIOS names to IP addresses.

Windows Sockets (SOCKS) — A platform independent protocol for handling TCP traffic through a proxy server. Individual application design must support the SOCKS protocol to use it when communicating.

World Wide Web Consortium (W3C) — An agency founded in 1994 that develops standards for the World Wide Web. W3C was founded by Tim Berners-Lee, the creator of the Web.

X.25 — The first packet-switching network technology developed. Predecessor to frame-relay.

X.500 — The ISO standard for the structure of global network directories.

zone of authority — The scope of hostnames assigned to a given DNS server to manage.

Index

Microsoft Certification Exam Objectives
#70-227: Installing, Configuring, and Administering Microsoft Internet Security and Acceleration (ISA) Server 2000, Enterprise Edition

Continued from front inside cover

Monitoring, Managing, and Analyzing ISA Server Use	Chapters
Monitor security and network usage by using logging and alerting	12
Configure intrusion detection	12
Configure an alert to send an e-mail message to an administrator	12
Automate alert configuration	12
Monitor alert status	12
Troubleshoot problems with security and network usage	12, 13
Detect connections by using Netstat	13
Test the status of external ports by using Telnet or Network Monitor	13
Analyze the performance of ISA Server by using reports. Report types include summary, Web usage, application usage, traffic and utilization, and security.	12
Optimize the performance of the ISA Server computer. Considerations include capacity planning, allocation priorities, and trend analysis.	12
Analyze the performance of the ISA Server computer by using Performance Monitor	12
Analyze the performance of the ISA Server computer by using reporting and logging	12
Control the total RAM used by ISA Server for caching	8